A word fitly spoken
is like apples of gold in
settings of silver.

PROVERBS 25:11

APPLES OF GOLD
IN SETTINGS OF
SILVER

Stories of Dinner as a Work of Art

CAROLIN C. YOUNG

SIMON & SCHUSTER

New York London Toronto Sydney Singapore

SIMON & SCHUSTER
Rockefeller Center
1230 Avenue of the Americas
New York, NY 10020

For information regarding special discounts for bulk purchases,
please contact Simon & Schuster Special Sales at
1-800-456-6798
or business@simonandschuster.com

Designed by Jeanette Olender
Manufactured in the United States of America

1   3   5   7   9   10   8   6   4   2

Library of Congress Cataloging-in-Publication Data
Young, Carolin C.
Apples of gold in settings of silver : stories of dinner as a work of art /
Carolin C. Young.
p.   cm.
Includes bibliographical references and index.
1. Dinners and dining—History.   I. Title.
TX737 .Y68   2002
394.1—dc21   2002026808
ISBN 0-7432-2202-4

Frontispiece: *The Last Supper,* 1495–1498, by Leonardo da Vinci, fresco.

IN MEMORY OF KATHARINE WASHBURN

Contents

Acknowledgments

My profound thanks go out to my editor, Denise Roy, and Simon & Schuster, for their patience and enthusiasm, as well as to my agent, William Clark, for understanding my work so completely and finding it a good home. The enormous generosity that has been extended to me by members of the culinary history community, the art world, family, friends, and sometimes even strangers throughout the writing of this book has truly stunned me. I am extremely grateful to Vincent Plescia and the Sotheby's Institute of Art, New York, for giving me an opportunity to deliver extracts of this book as lectures and re-create the dinners, with the help of Cathy Kaufman. Their continued enthusiasm and assistance profoundly exceed the scope of my talks. I am equally grateful to Deborah Lambert, and Christie's Education, London, who not only gave me a foundation of knowledge upon which this book is dependent, but who have been kind enough to act as my advisors. In this same capacity, I am indebted to Julia Abramson, Kirk Ambrose, Ken Albala, Christopher Brooke, Ivan Day, Lisa Jacobs, and Paul Micio, who have all gone beyond the call of duty in looking at my work and offering suggestions. Professors Carole Kaske, John Clark, and Clement Salaman were kind enough to not only allow me to borrow from their translations, but also to contribute suggestions that have improved my use of them.

My debt to Cathy Kaufman and Barbara Ketcham Wheaton, not only for their knowledge and suggestions but for their immense support, runs deep. Without Cathy's culinary proficiency, historical knowledge, and tireless support in the kitchen, I could not have created the banquets for my dining history series at

Sotheby's. I feel privileged to be a part of the culinary history world, whose membership has an immense generosity of spirit. I must especially thank, as fellow foodies and friends who have contributed to making this possible, Alexandra Leaf, Andy Smith, Cara de Silva, Harlan Walker, Tom Jaine, Lynne Rossetto Kasper, Gillian Riley, Jane Levi, and the Oxford Symposium on Food and Cookery.

Patrice de Vogüé at Vaux-le-Vicomte, Eric Barbaret-Giraudin at the Château de Valençay, Tamara Préaud at the Archive de la Manufacture, Sèvres, Norah Gillow at the William Morris Gallery, Linda Roth at the Wadsworth Atheneum, Dr. Tobias Natter at the Belvedere, Galerie Welz, Salzburg, the Dresden Porzellansammlung, and not least among these my friend and mentor Sue Reed, at the Museum of Fine Arts, Boston, have all provided enormous assistance that has immensely enriched my research.

The Bibliothèque nationale de France, the Schlesinger Library, the Houghton Library, the Harvard Fine Arts Library, the Biblioteca Berenson, the Biblioteca Marciana, the Boston Public Library, the New York Public Library, the Bibliothèque municipale de Dijon, the Bibliothèque Mazarine, the Guildhall Library, and the British Library have all been exceptionally kind in extending their facilities to me.

To family and friends who have stood by me through everything from the sublime to the ridiculous, and especially for the latter, I thank you. In addition to my parents, Linda and John Young, and my brother, Jonathan Young, I would be remiss not to mention the assistance of John Bennett, Viviane Mikhalkov, Rosemary and John Matthews, Peter and Leslie Fairbank, Meg Fairbank, Laura Zoldak, Sondra Reid, Kelly Galligan, Guy Lesser, Liesl Schillinger, Anthony Palliser and Diane Lawyer, Edward Munves Jr. and James Robinson, Inc., Luigi Attardi, Desmond O'Grady, Jérôme Letellier, Todd Merrill, Grace Kaynor, Philip Reeser, Tim Bogardus, Charlie Scheips, Jacquie Turner, Ilse and Carl Whisner, Sandy Lopes, Jared Goss, Terence Riley, Lucas Schoormans, Michael Morris, Todd Black, David Carpenter, Faith Zuckerman, Catherine Bennett, Dodi Wexler, Faith Pleasanton, Letitia Roberts, Vincent Lacava, Carne Ross, and Karole Vail, who have all offered help and encouragement along the way.

And pomp, and feast, and revelry,
With mask and antique pagentry;
Such sights as youthful poets dream . . .

MILTON, *L'Allegro*

Introduction

Richard Wagner (1813–1883) composed operas of epic length in attempts to create the ultimate *Gesamtkunstwerk* (total work of art), which he defined as a masterpiece fusing the myriad arts together in a single work summing up the whole of human existence. More than a century after Wagner's death, artists of every discipline still struggle to reach this elusive goal. However, Wagner's towering ambitions have long been fulfilled at extraordinary feasts that archaeologists have shown existed even before the inventions of opera, art, or written language. At its most sophisticated, dinner is the ultimate *Gesamtkunstwerk,* which sates all five senses because the table is where we, as human beings, enact the theater of our lives.

Marsilio Ficino (1433–1499), who founded the Florentine Neoplatonic Academy at the core of Western civilization, believed, "[O]nly the meal embraces all parts of man . . . for . . . it restores the limbs, renews the humors, revives the mind and sustains and sharpens reason" *("De sufficientia . . .").* Ficino understood that to dine is not merely to eat. The second is a discrete act that fulfills our biological needs; the first is more ethereal, swirling with those same intangible qualities that distinguish our humanity.

The British epicure Thomas Walker (1784–1836) defined the art of dining as "aristology," a term he based upon the Greek word *ariston,* meaning "dinner." By extension, he called students of this field "aristologists." *Apples of Gold in Settings of Silver* is an aristological history of Western Europe, from the medieval period to the years just prior to World War II, told through the stories of twelve emblematic meals. The food served at these occasions impressed those who attended them. But taste is just one of the five human senses. Music, décor, perfumes, and etiquette are equally intrinsic to the experience of a feast. The art of dining is not just the apple; it is apples of gold in settings of silver.

Fashioned after a book of hours, this text is a calendar of the reasons we dine. The motivations to make a meal noteworthy have changed little in the course of human history, although menus and manners have varied enormously. Ficino gathered his fellow Neoplatonists to banquet, just as friends renew their ties over supper today.

The soul of any good dinner party resides in the personalities around the table. The French philosopher Michel Eyquem de Montaigne (1533–1592) advised, "One should not so much consider what one eats as with whom one eats. . . . There is no dish so sweet to me, and no sauce so appetizing as those derived from the company." As the stories in this book demonstrate, neither well-polished silver nor perfectly matched porcelain is necessary to raise dinner to an art form. But rather, this is achieved when the intellects, emotions, and spirits of its celebrants are nourished.

At one time or another, each of us has partaken of a meal so spectacular that we desire a souvenir of the occasion: place cards or recipes, sheet music or centerpieces. But the juice that spurts and then oozes from a roast carved by candlelight cannot be preserved. We may never replicate the taste of such foods as they were eaten generations ago, just as the original colors of centuries' old paintings have been obscured over time. Even the most basic ingredients—the size of eggs, the strains of wheat, the breeds of animals—have evolved and changed. Historical reconstruction, particularly of the ephemeral experience of dining, invites error. The meals recounted in this text are based upon contemporary descriptions and evidence rounded out with reference to materials such as period cookbooks, objects, and etiquette manuals. Like theater, "[t]he best in this kind are but shadows; and the worst no worse, if imagination amend them," as Shakespeare wrote. It is my hope that any inaccuracies inadvertently contained in this book will not obscure the richness of the twelve aristological treasures contained herein.

No image embodies dinner as a work of art more than Leonardo da Vinci's *Last Supper*. This crumbling and heavily restored fresco at Santa Maria delle Grazie in Milan has been so infinitely reproduced, imitated, and bastardized that it has become virtually synonymous with the actual biblical event. As Magritte's pipe reminds us, the painting is not a dinner at all, but a depiction of one. It is not just an image of dining, however, but also an image to dine with, emblazoned as it was upon the wall of a monastic refectory. Johann Wolfgang von Goethe (1749–1832), who viewed the fresco in 1788 before Napoleon's troops damaged its already fragile condition, described it *in situ:*

Opposite to the entrance, at the bottom, on the narrow side of the room, stood the Prior's table; on both sides of it, along the walls, the tables of the monks, raised, like the Prior's, a step above the ground: and now, when the stranger that might enter the room, turned himself about, he saw, on the fourth wall, over the door, not very high, a fourth table, painted, at which Christ and his Disciples were seated, as if they formed part of the company. It must, at the hour of the meal, have been an interesting sight, to view the tables of the Prior and Christ, thus facing each other, as two counterparts, and the monks at their board, enclosed between them. For this reason, it was consonant with the judgment of the painter to take the tables of the monks as models; and there is no doubt, that the table-cloth, with its pleated folds, its stripes and figures, and even the knots, at the corners, was borrowed from the laundry of the convent. Dishes, plates, cups, and other utensils, were, probably, likewise copied from those, which the monks made use of.

There was, consequently, no idea of imitating some ancient and uncertain costume. It would have been unsuitable, in the extreme, in this place, to lay the holy company on couches: on the contrary, it was to be assimilated to those present. Christ was to celebrate his last supper among the Dominicans, at Milan.

Leonardo's painting simultaneously illustrates the sacred distribution of the Eucharist and the human poignancy of a man gathered with his friends for a final supper, even as it bears witness to the meals of the brothers of Santa Maria delle Grazie assembled before it. The single image eloquently captures Ficino's words of the previous generation, timelessly declaring, "[O]nly the meal embraces all parts of man."

Apples of Gold in Settings of Silver

Chapter One

Dining with God

Peter the Venerable and the Monks at Cluny, Burgundy, A.D. 1132

O taste and see that the Lord is good.

Psalm 34:8

ETER THE VENERABLE (1092/4–1156),
wielding the lizard-crested crosier of his office, led 1,212 monks and 200 priors into
the newly completed church of the monastery of Cluny. As abbot of this most
powerful order, answerable only to the Pope, he had convoked the general chapter
of Cluniac monks from more than a thousand satellite priories and abbeys—
stretching from Italy, Germany, and England to as far as the edges of the Orient—
for this stirring occasion in the year 1132. Together, they marched in a single
procession, chanting in unison as they went.

Never, since the abbey's foundation in 909/910, had such an elaborate celebration, with so many participants, been staged. The new church, dubbed Cluny III
by twentieth-century archaeologist Kenneth J. Conant, was consecrated with an
unprecedented swelling of pride. Construction on the colossal structure, which

3

embodied the order's ripe flowering after nearly two centuries of tending by sage and devout abbots, had begun on 25 October 1088, under the guidance of Saint Hugh (abbot 1049–1109). Although the choir had been used since 1120, and Pope Innocent II had dedicated the sanctuary in 1130, building continued into 1132 before it was ostensibly complete. Situated in southern Burgundy, in the valley of the Grosne, west of the mountains of Mâconnais, it was the largest church in all of Christendom, with a nave 187 meters (614 feet) long and a cupola estimated to have crossed its great transept at a height of 40 meters (131 feet). Soaring octagonal bell towers, visible through the surrounding hills, proclaimed Cluniac ascendancy. Inside the sanctuary, a profusion of florid, almost Gothic carvings of biblical stories and saints entwined within native grapevines enlivened the Romanesque solemnity of massive stone walls and arches.

Life within the abbey unfurled as gracefully as the curling tendrils of her ornamental sculptures. Cluniac monks followed the Rule of Saint Benedict of Nursia (ca. 480–547), as revised by Saint Benedict of Aniane (d. 821), which ritualized every aspect of monastic life, from the hours and order of worship, to the proper way to sleep (in an open row of beds with a candle burning) and personal comportment (walk with bowed head). By the time the first stone of Cluny III was laid, the order had richly embellished Saint Benedict's basic tenets to develop its own intricate culture. The chanting of psalms, originally recited on a single note without inflection, became marked by dramatic passages of ascending and descending movement. So too, the daily rituals spiraled in complexity, which were meticulously recorded in a series of Customaries.

Feast days were the most spectacular Cluniac occasions. From its inception, the

Christian faith, with Jesus' blessing of the bread and the wine, itself an act overlaid upon the ancient ritual meal of the Jewish seder, at its core, feasted to mark important anniversaries in the ecclesiastical calendar. A "feast day" might include extra or special foods, such as the pound of special flat cakes Cluniac monks received on their five most important holidays. However, dating from the early Church, fasting, to honor God with the piety of self-denial, was equally a feast-day practice. A diversion from the usual menu was only one of the elements employed at an ecclesiastical feast; appropriate sermons, readings, and music also added to these celebrations.

Figure 1.3
A river from the Four Rivers of Paradise capital from Cluny III, first quarter of the twelfth century.

Figure 1.2 *(facing page)*
Four Rivers of Paradise capital from Cluny III, first quarter of the twelfth century.

Nowhere in Christendom were feasts more elegant than at Cluny, renowned for richly embroidered vestments, the glorious singing of antiphons, and the joyful ringing of bells. Colorful banners waved through its processions. Magnificent liturgical plate gleamed in its sanctuary. Sometimes, elaborate liturgical dramas brought the story of Christ's Passion to life as a *tableau vivant* in the choir. Most awe-inspiring of all, the great jewel-encrusted Corona of Cluny, suspended from the ceiling of the church like a hanging crown, and ceremonially lit with candles reflecting "the flame of crescents from all the facets of her stones," impressed observers as one of the great wonders of the age. Cluniac feasts grew so numerous and complicated that they were broken into six hierarchical classes, each celebrated with commensurate splendor. However, at Cluny, even the days on which no saint was honored abounded with ornate ceremony.

In the musical flow of Cluniac observance, dinner was a rest. For seven hours each day they chanted psalms because the Bible entreated, "Seven times a day I do praise thee because of thy righteous judgments" (Psalm 119:164). Aside from a small breakfast of bread, cheese, and sometimes eggs taken shortly after matins, for most of the year, the monks ate but once daily. Yet this break from the rigorous schedule of chanting, praying, and readings was itself a form of worship, as ritualized as the performance of daily offices.

A monk's adherence to the vow of poverty was shown by the austerity of his diet. Although the sick and elderly in the infirmary were permitted meat, under no other circumstances were the brethren allowed to eat the flesh of "four-footed animals." Abstinence from meat constituted a devotional sacrifice. Saint Benedict, known to be kind but firm, recommended that each table be offered two cooked dishes, "on account of individual infirmities, so that he who for some reason cannot eat of the one may take his meal on the other." A third dish of fresh fruits or vegetables was permitted, when these were in season. The abbot had the power to adapt or alter Saint Benedict's basic recommendations, but the Rule instructed that the good monk should be addicted neither to wine, nor to eating. To take too much pleasure in the food one ate was gluttony, one of the seven deadly sins. The Customaries of Ulrich record that under Abbot Hugh monks at Cluny were served a plate of broad beans and a plate of vegetables, accompanied on Monday, Wednesday, and Friday by cheese and two eggs and on the other days by either five eggs or fish. Fish, one of the earliest and most universal symbols for Christ, predating the cross as a sign of the baptized on ancient sarcophagi, and whose letters, in Greek, form the initials of the words Jesus/Christ/of God/the Son/Savior, was the centerpiece of the monastic table; eggs and cheese offered variety.

The Cluniac diet, like its art, elegantly mingled Benedictine beliefs with the rich offerings of the Burgundian soil. More than a pound weight of bread, baked from local grain, formed the staple of the monastic diet, but it simultaneously evoked both the sacred wafer of the Eucharist, and the Mystic Mill, symbolizing Christ, into which Moses poured the grain of the Old Testament, which Paul received as the flour of the New Testament. Wine from Cluny's lush vineyards was carefully measured out into flasks, so that each monk received the same amount. In the Church, wine was the blood of Christ; for the monks at Cluny, it was also the soul of their native region. Burgundy had already been exporting wine in bar-

FIGURE 1.4
Monk harvesting wheat,
manuscript illumination,
Cirey Bible of Cîteaux,
A.D. IIII.

rels to Rome for at least two centuries when Saint Martin of Tours (ca. 316–397) converted the pagans of France to Christianity. The local viticulturists soon adopted him as their patron saint and paid their taxes to the monastery on his feast day, which Cluniacs celebrated with especial import.

Cluny's cooks introduced playful flourishes to the frugal Benedictine menu with mustard and vinegar, whose acidity was deemed suitably ascetic. Long before the start of the Crusades in 1096, Cluny, with its trade ties with Spain, also had access to more exotic tastes such as ginger, pepper, and cinnamon, officially valued for their restorative properties. Such herbs as chervil, grown for medicinal purposes, lent a burst of local freshness to the daily fare. Sweet honey, cheesecakes, and *crispellae,* fritters made from flour and herbs cooked in oil, were pleasurable treats. Cherries and apples, from the surrounding orchards, graced the Cluniac table, despite the latter's association with Adam's fall from grace.

Even the hours of the meal reflected both the liturgical and agricultural seasons; Saint Benedict ordained, "From holy Easter until Pentecost let the brethren take dinner at the sixth hour and supper in the evening. From Pentecost throughout the summer, unless the monks have work in the fields or the excessive heat of the summer, let them fast on Wednesdays and Fridays, until the ninth hour, on other days let them dine at the sixth hour. . . . From the Ides of September until the beginning of Lent let them always take their dinner at the ninth hour." And so in winter, after the service of None, amidst the fading light of late afternoon, the monks processed single-file past the cloister to the refectory.

Wearing the black robes and cowls of the Cluniac Order, the brethren took their places at benches on either side of rectangular tables. The first form of excommunication for disobedience was revocation of the privilege of dining in the refectory. Offending monks were fed separately, after others had finished. Exclusion, rather than hunger, was the punishment. Community lay at the heart of the Rule, which originated from the premise that monks who lived together, sharing possessions and beliefs, and submitting to the rule of an abbot, remained strong in their devotion.

The abbot, symbolically representing Christ, sat at a "high table" on a dais, to signify his elevated status. Because he was also secular lord over his followers, a magnificent salt cellar stood before him, as at the table of a nobleman. The Rule implored, "Let the Abbot's table always be filled with guests." As Saint Benedict ordained, a separate kitchen prepared a menu befitting the dignity of the abbot and his guests, who, over the course of Cluny's illustrious history, included dukes, kings, emperors, and popes.

Although, with the exception of the abbot, the Rule forbade "distinction of persons at the monastery," by the eleventh century, Cluny was the most aristocratic of abbeys, whose residents were broken into a strict hierarchy. Only professed monks were permitted to dine in the refectory. The lowly *conversi* (monks who entered the monastery as adults), novices, and those too weak or old to adhere to the strictures of the monastic diet were banned from the premises. Oblate children, given to the monastery by their families in infancy, could enter but had to stand, not sit, throughout the meal.

When the monks were assembled at their tables, the abbot might have been presented with an exquisite bronze *aquamanile,* an object often made in the form of a lion or a dragon. This ewer held the water with which the abbot would ceremoniously wash his hands. (In spite of their fancy vestments, Cluny's brethren were criticized by generations of abbots for their lack of hygiene. Although monks were shaved on fourteen feast days per year, five *essui mains* for hand washing were not installed in the cloister until the abbacy of Bertrand de Colombier [1296–1308], who also decreed that the monks wash their faces and hands daily and bathe before Christmas and Easter.) After the hand washing, a prayer acknowledged God as the provider of the food that sustained them.

Pristine white linens, the primary decoration to the medieval table, must have been supremely elegant, perhaps even imported from Damascus. However, even in this rarified abbey, table settings were sparse before the introduction of the dinner plate and fork in Europe. Thick slices of stale bread, known as trenchers, were piled at each place to sop up juices. Fingers served as the primary means to convey food to mouth; spoons, if needed, were shared, even at noble estates. Among the few possessions permitted monks, a cup and a multipurpose knife, worn during every waking hour, could be carried into the refectory for personal use.

Not a word was uttered during the meal, in observance of the vow of silence. Saint Benedict believed that this regulation, especially enforced in the refectory, prevented idle chatter that led to sinful words. The discipline required to maintain this promise manifested obedience and humility, and created an atmosphere of meditative contemplation. By the time of Saint Hugh's abbacy, the vow's importance had been amplified within Cluny's unique culture. An early biography of Saint Odo (abbot 927–942) recorded that one group of monks, who refused to speak even when tortured by their Viking kidnapper, miraculously escaped when God struck down their captor.

To avert the temptation to converse, the Rule specified that everything be passed from one monk to the next. Should a necessity to communicate arise, Saint Benedict commanded this be done "in some audible sign other than speech." The Cluniacs developed their own complex language of hand signals. Berno (abbot 909–927), first abbot of Cluny, began a rudimentary system of gestures, which Saint Odo developed more fully. By the last quarter of the eleventh century, the monks Ulrich and Bernard had compiled a list of the signs in the Customaries, roughly a third of which concerned the meal.

"Because it is customary for bread to be round," the sign for bread was formed by making a circle with the thumb and forefinger and its two adjacent digits. For another variety of bread, "cooked in water and which is better than the bread served on most days," after making the generic signal, the monk placed the palm of one hand over the other, "as if oiling and wetting." By contrast, following the bread sign with a cross over the middle of the palm specified *torta,* "because bread of this type is generally divided into quarters." "A wave of the hand like a fish in water" signified all fish, while further signs distinguished between trout, pike, salmon, eel, lamprey, and cuttlefish. To call for a low, saucerlike beaker for drinking, Cluniacs would "bend three fingers considerably and hold them upwards." Precious glass drinking vessels could be signaled for by adding to the previous gesture "two fingers around the eyes, to signify the splendor of the glass to the eye."

Throughout the meal, a designated reader cried out Holy Scripture to nourish the soul even as the body was fed. Saint Augustine (354–430) heard the voice of the Almighty say from on high: "I am the food of grown men; grow and thou shalt feed upon Me; nor shalt thou convert Me, like the food of thy flesh, into thee, but thou shalt be converted into me." Readers served for a week's time, rotating duties each Sunday. After the Communion Mass, the assembled brethren prayed that the incoming reader would be free from a spirit of pride. In response, the reader intoned three times, "O Lord, open my lips, and my mouth shall declare Your praise."

After the monks had eaten, the almoner supervised the collection of their trenchers, complete with drippings and juices, for distribution as charity to the poor. Though the same practice took place in secular manors, the monastery considered feeding the hungry one of its primary occupations. By the late eleventh century, Ulrich the monk claimed that seventeen thousand poor were fed at Cluny each year, although this figure was probably hyperbole.

The gifts God provided at table were not to be wasted; even this philosophy found ritual expression in Cluny's refectory. Custom dictated that monks meticulously pick up and eat any crumbs left scattered on the table. On his deathbed, one monk had a vision of the devil testifying against him before God because he had let his crumbs fall. Saint Odo, second abbot of Cluny, known for his pious adherence to the Rule, was visited by a miracle as a young monk. Realizing that he had forgotten to pick up his crumbs, he gathered them hastily in his hand and confessed his sin to the abbot. When he opened his palm, the crumbs had turned into pearls.

The horrors that befell those who broke from Saint Benedict's Rule or Cluny's Customaries appeared luridly vivid in the holy days of Cluny's sainted abbots. Saint Odo believed that food would stick in the mouths of monks who ate animal flesh and they would die a terrible death. However, even before the construction of Cluny III was complete, accusations that these sacred practices were being abandoned circulated everywhere. There were claims that monks at some of the outlying dependencies were dining on meat. Widespread reports cited idle chatter and even laughter in refectories throughout the Cluniac realm, although the Rule explicitly forbade such behaviors. Worst of all, in 1122, Pons de Melgueil (abbot 1109–1122), spiritual father of the entire order, had been forced to flee in disgrace to the Holy Land because of his intemperate love of display and ostentation. The beauty of Cluny's church, the feasts, the rituals, the vestments, the music—it was all a tribute to God. But these inherently sensuous achievements required Odo's and Hugh's purity of heart and strict discipline to maintain their soul.

Even before Pons fled, the rival Cistercian Order (founded 1088) rebelled against Cluny's ornamental worship by offering a new, austere form of Benedictine devotion. The Cistercians' most vociferous spokesperson, Saint Bernard de Clairvaux (1090–1153), scathingly criticized Cluny as decadent. Puritanical in spirit, he declared their grand feasts, replete with numerous courses and inventive sauces, more appropriate for royalty than monks and thought the Corona a vain and un-necessary extravagance.

When Pons's successor died after only a few months in office, a conference of the Cluniac leadership unanimously elected Peter of Montboissier, later called Peter the Venerable, ninth abbot of Cluny with the hope that he would render the spirit of their order as shining as their Corona. Peter agreed with Bernard that laxity had infected his abbey. He, however, found the flowery quality of Cluniac worship spiritually uplifting. In response to Bernard's critique of Cluny's feasts, Peter retorted, "The Cistercians have two meals on Sunday to honor our Lord—we have them on other days not only in honor of our Lord, but his Saints." Nevertheless, he knew that in order to restore Cluny's status as a beacon of civilization, he needed to undertake a thorough revision from within. As a man who promoted a spirit of understanding, writing treatises on Judaism, and sponsoring a translation of the Koran, Peter hoped he could institute his reforms with charity and kindness.

His job was not easy. When, in 1125, Peter was called away to Cluniac houses in the Aquitaine, Pons, with the help of rebels lurking within the abbey walls, and outside in the town, mounted a ferocious campaign to retake the monastery, collapsing one of the high vaults of the still unfinished nave of Cluny III. Peter quashed the rebellion with assistance from his own, loyal followers.

Although Peter had defended Cluniac monasticism in his correspondence with Bernard, he quickly realized that the widespread abuses in his order warranted more severe censure. In a circular letter distributed throughout the Cluniac houses, Peter decried the growing laxity of their repasts:

Pork boiled or baked, fat heifers, rabbits and hares, geese chosen from out of the whole tribe of their fellows, hens and every quadruped and fowl that man has ever domesticated, cover the tables of the holy monks. And now even these pall, and we turn to strange regal delicacies. The forests must be drawn; we need our huntsmen. Fowlers must trap for us pheasants, partridges and turtledoves, lest the servants of God die of hunger. Is this how we follow the Rule?

Peter was careful to add, "Let no one say these changes were not made without good cause by our fathers. I myself argue in this way when writing of other matters to the abbot of Clairvaux, but for eating fleshmeat no excuse will serve."

Throughout his career, Peter the Venerable upheld Saint Benedict's tenet that profound fellowship is created around the dinner table. Before becoming abbot of Cluny, when Peter was prior of Vézelay, he had offered a sermon on the sacred meal of Saint Anthony and Saint Paul the Hermit, the founders of monasticism. According to Saint Jerome's biography of Paul, when the saint was leading an ascetic life in the Egyptian desert, divine providence sent every day a bird with bread to sustain him. When Anthony visited the hermit, the portion miraculously doubled. Peter called their meal a "transmission of the bread of eternal life" and preached it was a metaphor for the enriching bonds of monastic community. The scene was also carved into two of the capitals of Vézelay's elegiac nave for the monks to behold.

FIGURE 1.5
The Meal of Saint Anthony and Saint Paul the Hermit capital from Vézelay, first quarter of the twelfth century.

It was not, however, until Cluny III was ready for consecration that Peter had occasion to demonstrate his order's finest blend of aesthetic flourish and austerity with a triumphant celebration designed to lead by example. By convoking the monks from his far-flung dependencies for this historic event, Peter hoped that the beauty of the architecture might rekindle the purity of Cluniac monasticism practiced when the church's construction had begun under the enlightened abbacy of Saint Hugh. When the 1,212 monks and 200 priors had assembled in the sanctuary, Peter issued a series of reforms, insisting upon a unity of practice among all Cluniacs. Though no specific text survives, it is known that the bulk of his decrees concerned the rituals surrounding the monks' daily meal.

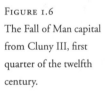

DINING WITH GOD

With the members of his order before him in the elegiac sanctuary, Peter the Venerable implored the brethren to observe their vows more rigorously. He reminded them of the importance of strict adherence to Saint Benedict's most fundamental tenets, as well as the more florid rituals sacred at Cluny. If Cluny lost her mealtime discipline, her influence and reputation would soon follow.

Peter the Venerable's 1132 sermon was only one part of an ongoing campaign to root out decadence within the flock. Fifteen years later he issued a second series of statutes, which survive as testimony to his heartfelt belief that the manner in which his monks ate and lived manifested their faith as much as their hours of chanting.

In the 1147 statutes, Peter decreed that absolutely no flesh meat was permitted except to weak and sick brethren. He reimposed the firm silence maintained during meals and added, "[I]t would be a disgrace for Cluny, which had reformed the entire monastic community, to be faulty in this matter." The single-meal regime set forth in the Rule was being ignored even as each sitting included increasing numbers of complex dishes. Peter reasserted its observation from September to the beginning of

FIGURE 1.6
The Fall of Man capital from Cluny III, first quarter of the twelfth century.

Lent, except for certain feasts and the Christmas season. Bread and wine were being saved for future use within the monastery. Peter declared that "all the leftovers from the tables in the refectory and the infirmary should without any exception be given in alms." There would be no half measures to charity while Cluny was under his watch. So too, the oblate children, who had been made to stand in Cluny's refectory, were thenceforth to sit as equals with the professed monks.

Saint Benedict had specified, "[L]et no one be exempted from kitchen service except by reason of sickness or occupation of some important work. For this service brings increase of reward and of charity." However, by Peter's era, lay servants, called *famuli,* performed the majority of these functions for the complex society dwelling within the mother abbey. Peter banned them from serving in the refectory for both spiritual and practical concerns; he believed it "more respectable for the *conversi* than for secular *famuli* to live with the monks"; yet he also wanted to prevent the *famuli* from stealing leftovers.

The majority of Peter the Venerable's statutes merely sought to bring all Cluniacs back into the observance of their fundamental Benedictine vows. Others, however, addressed the more subtle issue of balancing the call for asceticism with Cluny's decidedly artistic culture. The rival Cistercians denigrated Cluny's fondness for expensive, luxurious, even voluptuous spices. Moderate in nature, Peter the Venerable had no wish to destroy the elegance of Cluniac life; this was the abbey's pride. (Antonin Carême [1783–1833], who later brought *haute cuisine* to its highest pinnacle, attributed the refinement of French cooking to the inventiveness and subtlety required by fast-day strictures. The epicurean debt to monks, inventors of myriad cheeses, liqueurs, and confitures, cannot be underestimated.) However, sensuous pleasure had to be curbed. Peter banned the previously permissible use of lard for frying or other forms of cooking on Fridays. As early as Saint Hugh's day, Cluny had enjoyed "the drink which is flavored with honey and wormwood." After Bernard pointedly declared, "What are we to say of the practice that some monasteries are said to observe by custom, of taking their wine in the *frater* on great feasts mixed with honey and flavored by spices?" Peter the Venerable ruled, "[N]o spice of honey is to be used in wine."

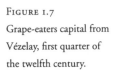
Peter complained that "many feasts have been recently introduced not for the love of the saints themselves, but for the sake of recreation, so, the fast of the Rule has been all but abolished to make room for solid food." He therefore reduced the number of feasts for which the fast could be dispensed with and decreed that only a holiday of the highest rank could override the standard Sunday liturgy. By his orders, the great Corona of Cluny was thenceforth lit only for the very highest-ranking feasts. Peter explained, "[E]ven the most splendid spectacles pall if seen too often."

Although Peter the Venerable differed from Bernard, the Cistercian, in his defi-

FIGURE 1.7
Grape-eaters capital from
Vézelay, first quarter of
the twelfth century.

nition of what constituted a suitably Benedictine meal, the two developed a warm, lifelong friendship and mutual respect. It was, in fact, Bernard who first added "the Venerable" to Peter's name—an acknowledgment of the devout wisdom and sincerity with which the Cluniac abbot acted upon his faith. Peter strove to ensure that as his flock ate their daily bread from native grain and drank the lush Burgundy wine, they dined with the vision of their Savior always before them. In so doing, he hoped their silent meals might ring out to God as loudly as the psalms they sang over and over again:

> Sing unto the Lord with thanksgiving;
>   sing praise upon the harp unto our God:
> Who covereth the heaven with clouds,
>   who prepareth rain for the earth,
>   who maketh grass to grow upon the mountains.
> He giveth to the beast his food,
>   and to the young ravens which cry.

(Psalm 147:7–9)

Chapter Two

Friendship

MARSILIO FICINO AND
THE NEOPLATONISTS,
VILLA CAREGGI, FLORENCE,
7 NOVEMBER 1468

Only the meal embraces all parts of man . . . for . . . it restores the limbs, renews the humors, revives the mind, refreshes the senses and sustains and sharpens reason.

Marsilio Ficino, *"De sufficientia . . ."*

On 7 November 1468, a revolution that fueled the embers of the burgeoning Renaissance was staged at the Medici Villa Careggi without the aid of cannons, or guns, or even fireworks. Instead, a small group of like-minded humanists, who called themselves the Neoplatonic Academy, gathered peacefully in the hills outside Florence to honor Plato with a banquet and an evening of high-minded discussion, in imitation of the ancient symposiums. The repast was modest but exquisite, as were the wines; even the conversation passed gently, blending with the sound of the lyre that drifted out through the garden. The dinner was as perfectly balanced as a painting by Raphael.

Marsilio Ficino, the leader of these Florentine philosophers, immortalized the evening in *De amore*. In the preface to this fictionalized account of the events he records:

Plato died at the age of eighty-one at a banquet on 7 November, his birthday. This banquet, which commemorated both his birthday and the anniversary of his death, was renewed every year by all the first followers of Plato down to the time of Plotinus and Porphyry. But for twelve hundred years after Porphyry, these solemn feasts ceased to be celebrated, until in our own time Lorenzo de' Medici, wishing to restore the Platonic Symposium, appointed Francesco Bandini as master of the feast *(architrichlinum)* who, to celebrate that 7 November, received at Careggi in a truly royal manner, nine Platonic guests . . . so that . . . we completed the number of the muses.

Among the many Medici properties, Careggi was particularly beloved by the family. Lorenzo "the Magnificent" (1449–1492) attended its grape harvests from boyhood and went there in retreat, as did his father, Piero "the Gouty" (1416–1469) and grandfather, Cosimo "the Elder" (1389–1464). Lorenzo's great-grandfather, Giovanni di Bicci de' Medici (1360–1429), founder of the family's banking fortune, purchased the villa in 1417. Cosimo later appointed his favored architect, Michelozzo Michelozzi to transform the fourteenth-century fortified stronghold, complete with a crenellated gallery, into an idyllic haven for meditation and reflection. The villa's renovation was acclaimed for mirroring its owner's elegant simplicity; clean white walls with cool gray moldings imposed an atmosphere of restful clarity. The sixteenth-century painter and art historian Giorgio Vasari later attributed to Michelozzo the fountain bubbling in the garden amidst Cosimo's phenomenal collection of ancient statuary.

Humanists heeded such ancient writers as Seneca, Varro, and Martial, who taught that mental repose was the reward of rural retreat. Leon Battista Alberti advocated the advantages of a villa for intellectual, spiritual, and physical health in his *Ten Books on Architecture* (completed 1452, published 1485). Marsilio Ficino advised in *Three Books on Life* (1489) that houses should be "high and far away from heavy and cloudy air." The Medici villa at Careggi, built on the hillside of Monterivecchi with a view over the vineyards and down into the city, offered an ideal setting for Ficino's philosophical feast.

Cosimo the Elder had installed Ficino in a small estate near his villa at Careggi in 1462, with a commission to translate the works of Plato and to tutor his grandsons, Lorenzo and Giuliano (1453–1478). Cosimo had long mentored Ficino, the gifted son of his personal physician Diotifeci Ficino (1402–1479). With his love of philosophy and talent for ancient Greek, young Ficino promised to fulfill his patron's desire to found a Neoplatonic academy in Florence, a wish born decades earlier, at the 1439 ecumenical conference Cosimo hosted with the lofty aim of reconciling the Eastern and Western churches. Though unsuccessful in its purported goal, the event brought Cosimo into contact with an eighty-three-year-old philosopher named Georgius Gemistus Plethon, who had founded a Neoplatonic academy at Mistra in the Peloponnesus. Their conversations inspired Cosimo's aspiration for Florence to have a similar school. Ficino's banquet in celebration of Plato, almost thirty years later, and four years after Cosimo's death, realized this long-awaited dream.

The host of this momentous feast, Lorenzo de' Medici, was just nineteen years old when his erudite guests arrived at Careggi. Though he had not yet inherited the villa outright, the health of his father Piero had deteriorated past the point of his hosting such an ambitious event.

Although young, Lorenzo was well equipped to perform the duties of host and participate in heady conversation. He had made his first state visit at age five and a half, dressed up in French style to pay homage to John of Anjou. Before his sixth birthday, he began to study Latin and Italian texts in the extensive family library under the tutelage of the finest minds in Florence.

Ficino thanked Lorenzo for providing the Neoplatonist banquet when he published *De amore*, nevertheless, his patron appears nowhere in it. This discrepancy has not been explained, yet members of the untitled Medici banking family, although powerful, differed from medieval aristocrats, in that they habitually welcomed poets, artists, and philosophers to their table as equals. In later years, Lorenzo lingered over dinners with Ficino and Michelangelo Buonarroti, whom he moved to Careggi when the artist was fifteen. Vasari recorded that Michelangelo "always ate at Lorenzo's table with the sons of the family and other distinguished and noble persons who lived with that lord, and Lorenzo always treated him with respect."

At the banquet Lorenzo appointed, in his stead, the distinguished priest and diplomat Francesco Bandini (ca. 1440–1489) as master of the feast *(architrichlinum)*. Ficino dedicated his *Life of Plato* to Bandini and considered him one of his closest personal friends. Ficino's father was present, as was Antonio Agli (1400–1477). A scholarly cleric (bishop of Fiesole, tutor of Pope Paul II, and author of *On the Immortality of the Soul*), Agli wrote extensively on friendship and love, the subjects under discussion that night. Also in attendance were the renowned poet Cristoforo Landino (1424–1492), who also wrote commentaries on Horace and Virgil, the rhetorician Bernardo Nuzzi, and Tomaso Benci (1427–1470), a merchant who dabbled in bawdy theatrical verse. Completing the guest list were two of Ficino's students—Cristoforo and Carolo Marsuppini (sons of the poet Carolo)—and his beloved friend, the noble statesman, diplomat, and scholar Giovanni Cavalcanti (ca. 1444–1509).

The list of invitees perfectly reflected Ficino's thoughts on ideal dining. In *"De sufficientia . . . ,"* a treatise on banqueting written as a letter to Bernardo Bembo, the philosopher reaffirmed the rule set down by the ancient Roman writer Varro—and practiced at Careggi—that the guests should be "neither fewer than the three Graces, nor more than the nine Muses." "Moreover," he continued, "it is quite clear what kind of people the participants should be: they should be graced by the Graces, gifted by the Muses, and men of letters."

The divergent minds invited to Careggi were bound in an intricate web of friendships. In 1456, Ficino dedicated his *Declarationes platonicae disciplinae* to Landino, who, in turn, dedicated one of his own poems to Nuzzi, a distinguished classicist who was appointed Secretary to the Republic of Florence in 1486. Landino taught both Lorenzo de' Medici and Cavalcanti, who tutored the Marsuppini brothers. Ficino later dedicated *De amore* to Cavalcanti for enriching his understanding of what it means to be a friend.

Friendship is a union wrought between free individuals. Just as the Neoplatonists defined themselves as such, they valued nurtured relationships of kindred spirits over those forced upon them by ties of blood. To Ficino, friends were "those who strive for virtue with equal zeal, and who help one another to cultivate their souls." Cavalcanti's poetry reprised the theme. Strengthening such bonds was the Neoplatonists' highest goal, and the inspiration for their feast. Plato taught them that earthly love, between friends and sexual partners, mirrored higher, divine Love. Contemplation of the former was a means of approaching the latter.

Although Plato's philosophy had deeply homosexual overtones, Ficino, who took priestly vows in 1473, advocated celibacy for intellectual as well as spiritual advancement. His *Three Books on Life* included a section titled, "The Special Enemies of Scholars Are Five: Phlegm, Black Bile, Sexual Intercourse, Gluttony, and Sleeping in the Morning." Women had no place at Ficino's table; the Neoplatonic Academy was a confraternity of men.

FIGURE 2.1
The Last Supper,
ca. 1445–1450, by Andrea
del Castagno, fresco.

We imagine them sitting with the solemnity of the Disciples in Andrea del Castagno's *Last Supper* (1445–1450) at Sant'Apollonia, Florence, as Lorenzo's servants approached with a ewer of fragrant water, a matching basin, and a generous towel for hand washing. Ficino shared Plato's disdain for flamboyant dress. He cited the example of Plato, noting that, "at a feast, Dionysius had ordered everyone to dance dressed in purple. Aristippus promptly danced but Plato declined, saying that women's things did not become a philosopher." Ficino's biographer, Giovanni Corsi, described his subject as having "a mild and pleasant aspect. His complexion was ruddy; his hair was golden and curly and stood up on his forehead." Like Socrates, Ficino lacked the physical beauty of a young Apollo and joked about his short stature and hesitant speech. The Neoplatonists were not without a sense of humor or fun, despite the earnest intent of their banquet. "For," to Ficino's thinking, "enjoyment is the seasoning of things: it is the food of love, the kindling of genius, the nourishment of will, and the strength of memory."

Ficino, who synthesized ancient philosophy with Christianity in his quest to understand man's true nature, advocated the pursuit of happiness, a revolutionary break from medieval theology. In his opinion, the savor of such earthly delectations as a tasty comfit or a sip of clear wine brought one closer to God. Ficino's friend and fellow humanist Bartolomeo Sacchi, called Platina (1421–1481), completed his seminal text and cookbook, *De honesta voluptate et valetudine* (On Right Pleasure and Good Health), three years before the gathering of the Neoplatonists at Careggi. As Platina's book's title implies, he also allied enjoyment with the promotion of physical and spiritual well-being. Although Cosimo and Lorenzo de' Medici had patronized his scholarship, Platina knew that other powerful figures of the era, who believed corporeal delight begat sin, would censure his explicit advocacy of pleasure. Platina's text begins with a defense of his theory:

> I know well enough that the spiteful will speak out vehemently that I ought not to have written about pleasure for the best and most continent of men, but let those voluptuaries who pretend to be Stoics (who make judgements with upraised eyebrows, not about human experience but only about the sound of words) say what evil well-considered pleasure has in it, for the term is neutral, neither good nor bad, as is health. Far be it from Platina to write to the holiest of men about the pleasure which the intemperate and libidinous derive from self-indulgence and a variety of foods and from the titillations of

sexual interests. I speak about that pleasure which derives from continence in food and those things which human nature seeks.

Platina's words echo the speech of Pausanias in Plato's *Symposium:* "We had a choice between eating, drinking, singing, or having a conversation. Now, in itself none of these is better than any other: how it comes out depends entirely on how it is performed." However, Platina's fears of repercussions were not unfounded; in February 1468 the Pope arrested him, along with several other members of the Roman Academy. Epicureanism, carrying the suggestion of pagan immorality, was thought to have been among the charges, which were never aired in full. Platina was imprisoned and tortured in Castel Sant'Angelo not long before Ficino and the Florentine Neoplatonists feasted at Careggi under the blissful protection of a tolerant patron.

Did they sit out on the colonnaded loggia to look over the trees and let the air loosen their spirits? Ficino considered "the frequent viewing of shining water and of green or red color, the haunting of gardens and groves" advantageous to long life. Sensibly, however, he warned philosophers to avoid chills. Perhaps, by 7 November, the Neoplatonists preferred to partake of the view from the *saletta.* That sweeping vista over Careggi's gardens is captured in Piero del Pollaiuolo's *Annunciation* (ca. 1470), which now hangs at the Gemäldegalerie, Dahlem, Berlin. The painting also details the room's marble-lined walls and floor, whose rich, mottled colors rival those depicted in Castagno's *Last Supper.*

The feast might instead have been served in the large hall, the main room of the *piano nobile,* at the head of the barrel-vaulted staircase leading up from the atrium. An enormous fireplace and hooded chimneypiece of cool, gray stone, carved with the Medici coat of arms, delicate candelabra-style arabesques, and the date "1465," dominated this space. Michelozzo retained its straightforward timbered ceiling, with a *palcho* of exposed joints, adding a tiled floor, glistening with colorful geometric patterns. Small glass panes, each with an *occhio* (eye) in its center that refracted the view of the surrounding hills, were pieced together in frames to create large windows. Interior walls would typically have been lined with Flemish verdure tapestries, whose foliate designs created the illusion of a garden.

Although common in the ancient world, permanent dining rooms were not part of the medieval or Renaissance domestic interior. Thus, the Neoplatonic banquet might have been held in any number of rooms, according to whim. Trestle tables covered in layers of fine linen were portable, as was seating. The most elegant Florentine examples were walnut benches, delicately patterned with ivory and other rare inlays, and Roman-inspired, X-form, "savonarola" chairs, fitted with upholstered cushions. Although the Neoplatonists self-consciously imitated the ancients in many arenas of life, their cultural borrowing did not extend to the practice of reclining during meals. If we are permitted to imagine the banqueters' position at table, just as Ficino idealized their conversation in his retelling of the event, let them sit at a round table. In Plato's universe, nothing embodies perfection more than the pure geometry of a circle. Such tables did exist in fifteenth-century Florence, where freedom from the hierarchy of the rectangle would surely have befitted the republic's most enlightened humanists.

Tiered credenzas (sideboards), stacked with as much impressive plate as the host could afford, were as essential at a proper banquet as the table itself. Certainly, such display manifested the wealth and status of the family who owned such treasures. Ficino abhorred extravagant and ostentatious feasts, yet, with his special strain of humanism, steeped in magic and astrology, he believed that silver, from Venus, and gold, from the sun, possessed intrinsic spiritual properties whereby the magnificent power of the sun and the mysterious allure of the moon might be transferred to those who gazed upon these precious metals. Further, held Ficino, "infusing gold or silver, especially red-hot, and their leaves, in drinks or even in soup is likely to be helpful, and also to drink and consume food in a gold or silver vessel."

According to *De amore,* Cavalcanti told them, "Beauty is the light that attracts the human spirit. The beauty of the body is nothing else but the light which manifests itself in the charms of lines and colors, just as the beauty of the soul is just the splendor born of the harmony of doctrine and morals." Platina believed that attractively decorating the room and the table where one dines promotes the enjoyment of a meal and, in turn, health. He advised:

> [I]n autumn, let the ripe grapes, pears and apples hang from the ceiling. Napkins should be white and the tablecloths spotless, because, if they were otherwise, they would arouse squeamishness and take away the desire to eat. Let a servant scrub the knives and sharpen their edges so that diners will not be delayed by dullness of iron. The rest of the dishes should be scrubbed clean, whether they are earthen or silver, for this meticulous care arouses even a sluggish appetite.

Sophisticated Italian diners were no longer content to eat off of bread trenchers, even with wood or pewter liners. Precious serving platters had graced wealthy tables since the early glories of Rome. However, the most elegant Renaissance households began to offer individual dinner plates of silver, or even gold. For a country evening of philosophizing, simpler ware was more appropriate. Maiolica (tin-glazed earthenware) boldly colored with golden yellow, manganese purple-brown,

and green, accenting the overall blue on white, was becoming a fashionable Florentine table accessory. According to Eleonora della Rovere, writing in the sixteenth century, these rustic wares, which had become quite opulent by her generation, were *"una cosa da villa"* (a villa thing).

Ficino believed "the universal soul and body, as well as each living being, conform to musical proportion." Song exemplified music's highest state because "po-

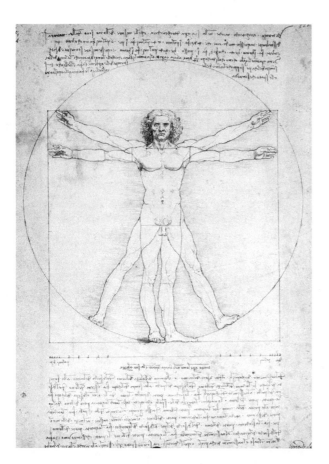

etry does what is also proper to divine harmony. It expresses with fire the most profound and, as a poet would say, prophetic meanings, in the numbers of voice and movement. Thus not only does it delight the ear but brings to the mind the finest nourishment, most like the food of the gods; and so seems to come very close to God." Ficino was himself noted for his talent on the lyre. He held in high esteem those who shared his affinity for this ancient art; those who refused a lyre at banquet he deemed ill-educated. Indeed, depictions of fifteenth-century Florentine banquets abound with musicians playing the lyre or the lute as the guests enjoy the pleasures of the table. According to Greek mythology, Mercury invented the lyre and gave it as a gift to Apollo, whose attribute it is. When Lorenzo de' Medici (a musician and composer in his own right) recommended Leonardo da Vinci to the Sforza court in Milan, he recalled Apollo's attribute by commissioning the artist to craft for the duke's family a silver lyre, symbolizing the harmonious alliance between the two families.

Music promoted good health because, Ficino explained, "sound and song easily arouse the fantasy, affect the heart, and reach the inmost recesses of the mind; they still, and also set in motion, the humors and the limbs of the body." The Neoplatonists believed in the indissolubility of body, mind, and spirit: "[S]ince the patron of music and discoverer of medicine are one and the same god, it is hardly surprising that both arts are often practiced by the same man. In addition, the soul and body are in harmony with each other by a natural proportion, as are the parts of the soul and the parts of the body. Indeed, the harmonious cycles of fevers and humors and the movements of the pulse itself also seem to imitate this harmony."

As Ficino and his friends feasted in Plato's honor, they aspired to improve every part of their being. Achieving this goal lay, in part, with the simultaneous nourishment of all five senses. Fragrance especially promoted this end. We can imagine them surrounded by an impressive brass perfume burner, such as the one Lorenzo had at his villa Poggio a Caiano. For a cold evening, Ficino recommended warming scents such as cinnamon, citron, orange, cloves, mint, lemon balm, saffron, aloe wood, amber, and musk . . . but above all, the bouquet of a nice wine.

FIGURE 2.3 Drawing of the ideal man according to Vitruvius's first-century treatise, *De Architectura*, called Vitruvian Man, ca. 1492, by Leonardo da Vinci, pen and ink on paper.

A generation before Leonardo da Vinci created his Vitruvian Man of mathematically perfect proportions, the Neoplatonists, who influenced him, composed their menu to correct imbalances within their own minds and bodies. Ficino believed that the correct diet consumed in the proper circumstances could prolong life expectancy: "Plutarch reports that many people who were otherwise physically infirm have attained a long life just by taking care of themselves."

The humoral medical theory favored by the ancient Greeks and, in turn, their Renaissance disciples, was promulgated by Plato's most famous student, Aristotle, and expanded by the physician Galen in the second century A.D. Platina offered a Renaissance interpretation: "This body by which we are all sustained and live is composed, it is agreed, of four humors, for it has in it blood, red bile, which we call choler, black bile, which we call melancholy, and phlegm, which is called *pituita* in Latin." These humors were each ascribed a combination of hot, cold, wet, and dry qualities, which correspond to the four basic elements: blood/air (warm and wet), choler/fire (warm and dry), melancholy/earth (cold and dry), phlegm/water (cold and wet). Well-being was the equilibrium of these qualities; illness, the result of an imbalance. If the body was dominated by a particular hu-

FIGURE 2.4
Fol. ii from *De vita libri tres,* 1489, by Marsilio Ficino.

mor, it was believed that equilibrium could be restored by eating foods with the opposite quality. Platina advised a varied menu "so that each may acquire what is agreeable, flavorful, and nutritious. To my mind, no one eats what fills him with distaste, or harms, or pains, or kills."

These theories recalled the wisdom of Chinese scholars, among the earliest documented aspirants of inner harmony. The Taoist classification system, whereby cold and hot, earth and heaven, female and male—all the elements of the universe, including all foods—are designated yin or yang, was in place by the Chou dynasty (1122–256 B.C.). During the Western Han dynasty (202 B.C.–A.D. 9), each of the five elements (metal, wood, water, fire, and earth) was paired with a corresponding flavor (bitter, sour, hot, salty, and sweet) whose relative properties dictated the organization of menus.

The Neoplatonists must have taken great care at the Villa Careggi to heed Ficino's warning that "frequent agitation of the mind greatly dries up the brain." He took his cue from Plato's *Theaetetus,* in which the scholar found intelligent people prone to excitability and melancholy. "My author Plato in the Phaedrus seems to approve this," Ficino noted, "saying that without madness one knocks on the doors of poetry in vain." Yet, he counseled intellectuals against courting insanity. To avoid melancholy, the mind had to be kept from becoming too cold and dry by partaking of moist foods and physical exercise. Phlegm and black bile, which suffocated the intelligence and unsettled judgment, were considered equally pernicious to scholars.

Those who wished to promote health were forced to abstain from many popular foods. According to Terrence Scully, a fifteenth-century Neapolitan recipe collection provides the earliest known Italian instructions for cooking eggplant, which had long since reached the region through trade with the Arabs. The instructions for this simple dish appeal to the modern palate. After the peeled and quartered eggplants are boiled in salt water for no longer than "two *Our Father*'s," they are lightly fried with oregano, ground garlic, pepper, saffron, salt, verjuice, and vinegar and served with mild spices. Ficino, however, explicitly warned that eggplant contributed to "that most awful kind of black bile."

Health-seeking intellectuals were also to avoid heavy wines and any dark, burnt, roasted, fried, hard, dry, or stale food. Ficino categorically denounced vegetables as dangerous for scholars and particularly warned against the ill effects of broad beans, lentils, cabbage, radishes, garlic, onion, leeks, and carrots. Beef, old cheese, and foods pickled in brine were also highly suspect. This rough fare was suitable for peasants, not philosophers. Ficino's presentation of humoral dietary theory reveals a poetic sensibility. The scholarly spirit must guard against "everything that is black; anger, fear, pity, sorrow, idleness, solitude, and whatever offends the sight, smell and hearing, and most of all, darkness."

Ficino considered milky foods advantageously moist, especially cheese and sweet almonds. He also advocated cooked fruits and gourds, game birds, poultry, sucklings, and eggs. An overabundance of moisture, however, introduced the danger of slime and putrefaction— a particular risk with milk, fish, mushrooms, meat, and vegetables, "which are too soft."

A median balance in flavors was ideal. This "taste halfway between sour and sweet," might occur in nature (as with the pomegranate) or by the artistry of the cook.

Renaissance preoccupation with divine proportion extended into a hierarchy of the food chain. According to Ficino's system, pork was most appropriate for "bodies which are pig-like, as are those of rustics and hardy men"; small birds were a refined luxury, "suitable only to the stomach which has no tolerance at all for denser foods." Scholars were best able to digest a "moderate sort of meat . . . as that of barnyard cocks, capons, peacocks, pheasants, partridges, perhaps even of young doves, especially if domesticated. Such also are roebucks and bull-calves, yearling wethers and likewise wild boars. Nor do I reject the suckling kid and fresh cheese."

Spice, increasingly available, for a price, after the fall of Constantinople in 1453, was not considered a frivolous luxury, but a healthful medicine. Ficino declared cinnamon, mace, and nutmeg beneficial in almost any meal, as were melon seeds, cucumbers, and washed pine nuts. Saffron, like the golden rays of the sun, had the power to warm foods considered to be cold. Sandal, now prized solely for its aromatic properties, was, then, valued as a medicinal spice, which, in powdered form, could turn any dish a fiery red or yellow capable of heating the blood of those who consumed it.

Despite the complexity of Ficino's recommendations and subsequent advances in science, some of his advice remains sound today. Long before the circulatory system was understood, Ficino correctly advised that olive oil was beneficial for the blood, the proper care of which was requisite for longevity. He understood the benefits of fresh food, while his mystical, poetical sense believed the beauties of the climate that produced it could be digested together with its nutrients: "[Y]ou should select animals, green vegetables, fruits, field-produce, and wines from regions that are high and fragrant, as we have said, kept clear by temperate winds, warmed by the pleasant rays of the sun."

Any chef to the Neoplatonists would have needed a thorough knowledge of these medical theories as much as a talent for cooking. Platina advised hiring an experienced cook free from "all filth and dirt." His ideal was "the man from New Como," the mysterious Maestro Martino, from whose *Libro de arte coquinaria* the effusive Platina, who was not a cook, had plagiarized a large portion of his recipes. His compliments were meager compensation under the circumstances. However, Martino de Rossi had copied long portions of his own text from an even earlier recipe collection. Platina took as much from Pliny's *Natural History* and the Roman cookbook writer Apicius as he did from Martino. Originality mattered little in the arena of dietary theory, where knowledge was valued above all.

The quest for understanding pervaded humanist thought. Leonardo sought to penetrate the psychological interior of the soul; Michelangelo sculpted the rippling nuances of the human form. This new appreciation for the individual extended to the table. Diners not only selected foods that most suited their unique humoral requirements; some also differentiated themselves by taking their food from the communal platter by means of a personal fork. The Florentines were among the first in Europe to use the utensil; Lorenzo de' Medici had eighteen in his inventory. The instrument had existed as a cooking tool in the ancient world; Homer described five-pronged forks that were used to roast the meat of the ritually slaughtered heifer on the altar flame; delicate two-tined forks whose use is unclear survive in rare numbers from the Early Roman Empire; but reclining diners did not eat with a fork. A Byzantine princess, who married the Doge of Venice around the year 1060, is the first on record to use a dinner fork in Europe. The two-tined gold fork she used to protect her fingers, like her insistence that eunuchs gather the morning dew for her bath, was perceived as a sign of overly precious, vain, and immoral behavior. The Church damned her and rejoiced that God had answered its prayers when she dropped dead not long afterward. Perhaps for the same reason, Venice's famed courtesans adopted the habit. However, by the fifteenth century, wealthy Florentines began commissioning exquisite two-tined dinner forks with precious handles of cast-and-chased silver or gold, carved ivory, rock crystal, and coral, often set with precious gems. Such objects were highly prized personal tools, carried as an eccentric accessory rather than offered uniformly to those at table. The fork physically separated its user from the food and others; its decoration distinguished the taste and inclinations of the person who carried it. The fork was the mark of an individual.

Wine helped ply the soul into flight. In spite of Ficino's earnest philosophizing, Corsi noted that "he did select the most excellent wines, for he was rather disposed toward wine, yet he never went away from parties drunk or fuddled, though often more cheerful." Platina was adamant that "[d]inner and lunch without drink is not only considered unpleasant but also unhealthful." Ficino suggested that to combat the evils of nausea and gluttony "[n]othing . . . is better against this pest than wine which is light, clear, pleasant, fragrant—the best adapted to generate the spirits clearer than any others." He preferred "red rather than white, with a taste, as it were, a little bitter; and it will be best, unless heat or sweating precludes it, if unmixed and drunk a little at a time." In an era long before the introduction of the cork, he advised, "Wine, whether it be white or red, should be . . . the kind that needs tempering with water, unless perchance you find a wine which is both light and durable, which is very rare."

Ficino believed that "wine especially refreshes the spirit," which "is defined by doctors as a vapor of blood—pure, subtle, hot, and clear." Nevertheless, the humanists at Careggi were careful to guard against rampant drunkenness. Ficino warned, "[J]ust as the use of wine helps the spirits and the intelligence, so the abuse harms them." In a world that idealized balance, drinking and eating within one's limits was essential. Ficino advised, "[I]f wine is excessive or too hot and strong, it will fill the head with humors and very bad fumes. I pass over the fact that drunkenness makes men insane." Similarly, he cited Galen on the dangers of consuming too much food, warning that "the mind that is choked up with fat and blood cannot perceive anything heavenly."

Ficino recommended that "[d]ishes which are more liquid should certainly be consumed before harder ones. But when the food has been consumed, coriander is appropriate, quince seasoned with sugar, pomegranates, sour pears, medlars, dried peaches, and similar things." These sweet delicacies were believed to aid in digestion. Glistening sugar, imported primarily by the Venetians, but also by the Genoese and the Spanish, sold in loaves graded by purity, and sometimes coated with lead to whiten it further, was considered the most magical, health-promoting elixir of all.

After the body had been nourished, the intellect could not be neglected. Ficino instructed, "In feeding the mind we ought to imitate gluttons and the covetous, who always fix their attention on what is still left." In a letter to the Aristotelian philosopher Francesco Tebaldi, Ficino noted that the Peripatetic philosophers "discussed the soul after a banquet as if they thought that the body should be refreshed before the soul could be brought into being. For my part, although I created the little soul of this letter before dining, I nevertheless agree with them about the order of creation." At Plato's birthday celebration, Ficino and his fellow Neoplatonists, honored their ideological forerunners. Although Ficino recommended that difficult thinking be avoided for two or three hours after dining, by his account: "After the meal, Bernardo Nuzzi took Plato's book, titled *The Symposium,* and read all the speeches that were delivered at the banquet. When he had finished, he asked the other guests to each interpret one of them. Everyone agreed."

In ancient Greece, a symposium was the ritualized wine drinking and discussion that followed on the heels of a banquet. Plato's *Symposium,* written sometime after 385 B.C., recalls the poet Agathon's celebration of his first victory in a dramatic contest in Athens in 416 B.C., retold through the voice of Apollodorus some years later. Nine guests, including Plato's teacher Socrates, recline in the dining room. After feasting, the guests drink a libation to the god and sing a hymn. The guests agree to imbibe sparingly because they are hungover from the previous evening's festivities. So too, they dispense with the flute girl and decide instead to spend their evening in conversation. The master of the cup asks each one to define the nature of Love. The speeches praise *erōs*—passionate love or intense attachment or desire, usually sexual, as well as the god *Erōs,* who personified these states.

Ficino's *De amore,* based on the actual dinner that the Neoplatonists shared at Careggi, is a discussion of Plato's *Symposium* which, like the work that inspired it, puts forth its philosophy by recounting the after-dinner speeches. Both writers gloss over the details of the banquet that precedes the discussion, yet both are careful to establish its existence as a necessary precursor. Love was the topic discussed at both events; gathering to share food and ideas was the means of promoting it.

When Nuzzi finished reading the *Symposium,* Cavalcanti commenced the Neoplatonist response with an analysis of Plato's first speech, that of Phaedrus who defined Love as "the most ancient of the gods, the most honored, and the most powerful in helping men gain virtue and blessedness, whether they are alive or have passed away." Cavalcanti thanked his fellow Neoplatonists for assigning him to comment on a man whose disposition inspired universal admiration, and whose physical beauty moved Socrates to chant the Divine Mysteries to him on the banks of the Ilissus. After defining Beauty as "harmony and balance, which we look for in the voice, the body, and the spirit," Cavalcanti concluded that the diners had proved their membership within the Platonist family "because nothing interests us which is not festive, joyous, celestial and divine."

Ficino wrote that the bishop, Antonio Agli, assigned to discuss Pausanias's passionate defense of homosexual love, and his father, the physician, asked to comment upon the speech of the doctor Eryximachus, were obliged to leave early, "one to assure the health of a soul—the other, a body." Whether or not this was really true, in *De amore,* Cavalcanti spoke in their places. When Cavalcanti finished his discourse, Cristoforo Landino explained the speech given by Aristophanes, to whom Plato gave one of the most poetic explanations of why human beings spend their lifetimes seeking love. Split in half by the gods as a punishment, each person is incomplete without finding its missing partner. Then, Carolo Marsuppini, "treasured child of the Muses," summarized the discourse of Agathon by calling Love the "happiest of gods, the most beautiful, youthful and delicate." He was followed by Tomaso Benci, "loyal imitator of Socrates," who, Ficino recorded, "began to comment, with a good heart and smiling lips, upon the propositions of his master." Finally, it came time for Cristoforo Marsuppini, whom Ficino described as the most cultivated member of the group, to discuss the speech of Socrates' beautiful lover and pupil, Alcibiades, who arrives drunk after Agathon's other guests have spoken.

Through analysis of Plato's texts, Ficino and his comrades unleashed their own ideas. The flow of these thoughts led them to give birth in the soul, which, in Plato's *Symposium,* Socrates defines as the noblest objective of love. Ficino later wrote, "If we did not allow Man himself, that is the soul, to perish from hunger while we feed the body, the dogs, and the birds, then each man would live content and plenished; just as now no one is content." The feast of the Neoplatonists at Careggi was an attempt to rectify this imbalance.

We cannot imagine that Ficino allowed their conversation to continue too late, since he warned scholars not "to stay awake too often for much of the night, especially after dinner, with the result that you are forced to sleep even after sunrise." Nevertheless, this extended discussion after the plates had been cleared from the table could not be rushed. As an overriding recommendation for a successful banquet, Ficino advised, "everything should be seasoned with the salt of genius and illumined by the rays of mind and manners, so that, as was said about the dinner of Plato and Xenocrates, the fragrance of our meal [*convivium*] may spread further and be sweeter the next day." The ideas ignited within the warm camaraderie of the Platonic feast at Careggi quite literally gave birth to Ficino's *De amore*. Ficino dedicated it to Cavalcanti, not only for his lead in the discourse that night, but also for suggesting the book when Ficino was inflicted by a "bitterness of spirit." Ficino credited this friend with helping him discover the true meaning and power of Love, of which his previous knowledge had been merely studied, rather than experienced.

The import of this feast extended far beyond the text directly inspired by it. This banquet accomplished what Ficino had set out to do: it reestablished the celebration of Plato's birthday as a living tradition of the Neoplatonic Academy in Florence. Art historians Ernst Gombrich and Erwin Panofsky, among others, have argued that Sandro Botticelli painted his famous *Primavera* as a visual interpretation of Ficino's philosophy. The 1468 dinner was followed by subsequent celebrations of Plato, which furthered the spread of his teachings. Ficino reminisced to Jacopo Bracciolini (1441–1478) about one such occasion, held "at princely expense" at Francesco Bandini's:

> I was among the company when you, Bindaccio Ricasoli, our Giovanni Cavalcanti and many other members of the Academy sat down to the feast. Of the many things we discussed at that gathering, I often reflect especially on the conclusion we reached before the feast, about the nature of the soul. I will gladly remind you of it now, for nothing befits a man more than a discourse on the soul. Thus the Delphic injunction "Know thyself" is fulfilled and we examine everything else, whether above or below the soul, with deeper insight. . . .

We all agreed that the reasonable soul is set on a horizon, that is the line dividing the eternal and the temporal, because it has a nature midway between the two.

Ficino's follower, Pico della Mirandola, argued that through free will, the individual could form himself into an angelic being. Indeed, at the time of Ficino's death in 1499, the ideals of harmony and balance approached elegiac sublimity with the heroism of Michelangelo, the compositional perfection of Raphael, and the piercing humanity of Leonardo. The overflowing abundance of masterpieces created at that one moment are the physical remains of a generation of individuals who conceived of themselves in a revolutionary yet timeless way. The Neoplatonist feast at Careggi was a masterpiece in the art of living; it was a moment of perfect harmony.

Celestial perfection flourished for just one brief, earthly moment. As art ascended to its most lyrical, violence and danger continued to pervade the tumultuous, backstabbing world of fifteenth-century Florence that created it. In 1478, as Lorenzo de' Medici and his younger brother Giuliano left Sunday Mass, they were attacked by a group led by Francesco Pazzi and Bernardo Bandini. Lorenzo struggled and broke loose from two murderous priests, managing to take refuge within the crowds stunned to see such sacrilege. Giuliano, however, succumbed to fatal stab wounds. Popular opinion rose against the conspirators and their protector, Pope Sixtus IV. The crowds slaughtered the treacherous priests and overran the Pazzi palace, eager to hunt down and destroy every member of the family as well as any suspected collaborators. In the ensuing investigations, Jacopo Bracciolini, with whom Ficino had so fondly discussed the soul, was hanged as a conspirator.

The violence, chaos, and rupture underlying Florentine life made Ficino's message, and the serene example of the 1468 banquet, especially resonant. Ficino himself only narrowly escaped excommunication and imprisonment for the radical mix of astrology and pagan philosophy evident in his *Three Books on Life,* but managed to live out his days peacefully in harmonic concord with his espoused beliefs.

Long after Ficino's death, the spirit of his banquet lived on. In the next century, the painter Andrea del Sarto and eleven of his colleagues formed the *Compagnia del paiuolo* (company of the cooking pot), a dinner club of gourmandizing artists. For each meeting, one guest was elected to bring a dish "prepared with some beautiful invention." When it was del Sarto's turn, he brought "an octagonal temple similar to the baptistry of Florence but raised upon a mosaic pattern made with several patterns" composed entirely of edibles: sausage columns with capitals of Parmesan cheese, cornices of sugar, and, in the center, a choir desk formed from veal and lasagne, with musical notes of peppercorns, surrounded by a choir of rare game birds. Behind the dazzle of such aesthetic marvels lay inclusive intentions; every member of the group brought a dish, which was passed and shared so that "every man partook of everything."

The same spirit of camaraderie later brought the Impressionists, including Renoir, Pissarro, Sisley, and Monet to the restaurant of their friend, the collector, novelist, and pastry chef Eugène Murer, for Wednesday night dinners. And, so too, whenever friends and colleagues gather together of an evening, sharing laughter, goodwill, and wine, letting their ideas mingle and mix and blend together like a slowly simmered stew, human imagination is transformed and friendship strengthened, as the body is nourished. Ficino believed that "[i]ndividual men, formed by one idea in the same image, are one man. It is for this reason, I think, that of all the virtues, wise men only named one after himself: that is, humanity, which loves and cares for all men as though they were brothers, born in a long succession of one father." As Agathon, the host of Plato's *Symposium* expressed it, "Love fills us with togetherness and drains all of our divisiveness away. Love calls gatherings like these together. In feasts, in dances, and in ceremonies, he gives us the lead."

Chapter Three

Fête Champêtre

A FEAST OF THE GODS
WITH TITIAN, SANSOVINO,
AND THE DIVINE ARETINO,
VENICE, 1 AUGUST 1540

Oh what a feast, how spectacular,
How beautiful the lagoon looks
When everything is silent
When the moon is high up on the sky.

Anonymous, Venetian song

*M*ARBLE WALLS APPEARED TO SLITHER
in the heat as piercing light melted the palazzi of Venice into her canals. Silken courtesans perched themselves on Persian carpets draped out of trefoil-shaped windows that framed each like a Madonna in a devotional altarpiece to watch the resplendently dressed Doge, the senate, and a vast array of dignitaries, officers, and ecclesiastics pass in ceremonial procession while decorated gondolas crowded the canals. It was *ferrare agosto,* 1 August 1540, a holiday Venetians celebrated with the vigorous luxuriance that Veronese nostalgically recalled in such jubilant paintings as *The Feast in the House of Levi* and *The Marriage at Cana.*

In the ecclesiastical calendar, the occasion inaugurated the extended celebrations leading up to the Feast of the Assumption on 15 August, commemorating the Virgin Mary's rise into heaven. Titian (ca. 1487/90–1576), born Tiziano Vecellio, dramatically captured the event in the high altarpiece at Santa Maria Gloriosa dei Frari, where a bevy of chubby, pink-fleshed cherubs majestically lift the Madonna up on a cloud and carry her into the golden light of heaven and the divine embrace. Its almost indulgent riot of color—yellows melding into gold in a great sphere and the sensuous scumbling of red melting over pink on Mary's generous, billowing dress—hint at the joyous pleasure with which Venetians approached even the most pious of holidays. In Venice, official Catholic dogma was bent to glorify the republic as artfully as the untamed lagoon had been groomed into a man-made wonder of palazzo-lined canals. As the Serenissima's power began to wane in the decades after the discovery of the New World and the rounding of the Cape of Good Hope, her official pomp and dazzle grew showier, almost as a battle cry against the encroaching decay. As John Ruskin eloquently wrote, "[T]he dying city, magnificent in her dissipation, and graceful in her follies, obtained wider worship in her decrepitude than in her youth." In such an atmosphere, *ferrare agosto* meant nothing more than an opportunity to venerate the Serene Republic herself.

Amidst the whirl of that summer day in 1540, with its myriad processions of churchmen and aristocrats, three of the city's most defining personalities—Pietro Aretino (1492–1556), Jacopo Tatti called Sansovino (1486–1570), and Titian—were nowhere to be found. Aretino, whom the poet Ludovico Ariosto dubbed "the divine Pietro Aretino, [S]courge of Princes" for the daggerlike stabs of his pen, exploited the power of the nascent publishing industry with the calculated shrewdness of a modern-day pop star; his famously depraved personality far exceeded any of his literary achievements. Sansovino, *protomaestro* (chief architect and superintendent of buildings) to the Venetian Republic, envisioned the modern face of the city with his designs for the colossal Libreria Sansoviniana and the buildings to finish Piazza San Marco, as well as numerous churches, *scuole,* and palazzi. Titian, the sublime painter whose unsurpassed handling of color rendered his works the republic's most sought after commodity, possessed the most soft-spoken manner and monumental talent of the three. Together, they formed a powerful cultural triumvirate. But on the night of *ferrare agosto* they escaped the crowds and official pomp to enjoy a pastoral feast of their own.

Such conspicuous and urbane personages would have had their pick of the choicest spots from which to watch the holiday proceedings. They might have gone to Sansovino's extensive rooms on the third floor of the Procuratie Vecchie, directly overlooking Piazza San Marco, where he sometimes invited guests to view such spectacles as the Maundy Thursday running of the bulls. Sansovino was known as a generous host, one to whom Giorgio Vasari ascribed a fondness for excesses of all kind.

Or instead, this worldly trio might have feasted at Aretino's small yet princely palazzo on the Grand Canal, with a view of the Rialto Bridge and the German traders' warehouses frescoed by Titian. Innumerable dinner parties unfolded beneath the palazzo's spectacular glass dome. Aretino's gorgeously liveried servants danced attendance. The Scourge complained, "So many gentlemen break in on me continually with visits that my stairs are worn with their feet like the pavement of the Capital with the wheels of triumphal cars." They came from France, Germany, Spain, even Turkey and India, he claimed. Guests were so plentiful that Aretino's house resembled an inn; on one occasion strangers wandered in, requested a salad, wine, and much else, and offended the servant when they later asked for the bill. In addition to this constant stream of visitors, Aretino housed a personal harem of some of Venice's most beautiful courtesans, sometimes up to twelve at a time, along with their illegitimate children and a variety of pretty young lads (officially engaged as "secretaries"), who together proudly called themselves the "Aretine."

Is it any wonder that with a household swimming in people and intrigue, Aretino opted in favor of a lyrical picnic in Titian's garden? "What a heartfelt pleasure it is to get away from everyone in a gondola," he noted.

From 1531, Titian lived at Nos. 5179–83 Cannaregio, across from the Rio dei Gesuiti. He shared the extensive apartment on the upper floors with his students, his sons Orazio and Pomponio, his daughter Lavinia, and his sister Orsa, who kept house for him after his wife Cecilia's death. The apartment was large, with a spacious hall and reception room fitted with generous windows to let in light. By this date the noble artist also rented the ground floor as a storage area, the mezzanine, and a separate building, probably used as a studio. However, the highlight of his property was its extensive garden with a sublime view of the Lagoon of Venice and the islands of Murano and San Michele.

The lagoon was more than a mere backdrop of surface decoration; it was the soul of Venice. The crescent of the lagoon, formed from three rivers—the Sile, the Piave, and the Brenta—flowing down from the Dolomites and dipping out into the expanse of the Adriatic, had given the Serene Republic her unrivaled ascendancy in trade and her safety since the sack of Constantinople in 1204. While cities in the rest of Europe built fortresslike castles to protect themselves against the vagaries of war and nature, Venice opened an expanse of glass windows onto the canals. The mystical bond between the city and the lagoon was honored each year on Ascension Day, when the Doge performed the ceremonial marriage of Venice to the Sea, tossing a gold wedding band into the canal as a symbol of their sacred bond. So too, for the celebration of *ferrare agosto* in 1540, the supreme painter of landscapes gave place of honor to the lagoon herself.

Who better to call forth the beauties of the land and sea than the great master? To see the lagoon through Titian's eyes was not least among the pleasures offered on that summer's night. The artist's like-minded friends were by no means indifferent to such a treat. Once, when Aretino, feeling ill, was forced to dine alone, he recorded for Titian his delight in watching the light dancing over rippling waters, imploring, "Nature, mistress of all masters! How miraculous is her brush, how wonderful is her pencil! I know that your pencil, my Titian, is the rival of Nature, and you her most beloved son: so I cried out three times Titian, Titian, Titian, where art thou?" Happily, on the present occasion Aretino had been invited to enjoy both the company of his gifted friend and his enchanting garden.

"Titian transforms nature into art," wrote the Scourge, and indeed, that was exactly what the artist did on 1 August 1540. More than three hundred years before Manet's *Déjeuner sur l'herbe,* the gods of Venice gathered in Titian's verdant garden at the edge of the city for a feast taken *en plein air.* For these libertine deities, a garden party was just innocent, lighthearted escape. Yet, their unfettered, almost pagan celebration of the splendor of the natural world was as riotously sensuous as the rolling hills and golden skies that Titian painted. The Florentine grammarian Francesco Priscianese, in attendance that night, described it as a "Bacchanalian feast" in a letter published as an addendum to his 1540 *Della lingua romana.* To his classical, philosophical taste, this evening of inebriated laughter and carefree indulgence seemed comparable only to the frenzied orgies of the carousing Bacchus, god of wine and fertility; the party was Titian's *Bacchanal of the Andrians* (color plate IV) sprung into life.

This painting, now in the Prado in Madrid, swirls with frolicsome figures who dance, play music, eat, and drink heartily alongside a river flowing with red wine. The subject comes from the third-century *Imagines* by Philostratus, which, as part of a fantasy tour of an ancient picture collection, describes a work depicting the merrymaking on the Greek island of Andros:

> The stream of wine which flows on the island of Andros and the Andrians made drunk by the river are the subject of this picture. . . . If you think it is water it is not a large river but if you think it is made of wine then it is large, and of a truth, divine. . . . Such things, as I apprehend it, do the Andrians, crowned with ivy and sage, sing to their women and children. Some of them dance on the one and some on the other shore, and others recline on the ground.

Priscianese could not for the life of him figure what *ferrare agosto* was intended to celebrate, or how it could possibly be considered Christian. A fact, he wrote, they debated heartily that night. In actuality, the holiday merely replaced the ancient festival of *Feriae Augustae,* whose pagan soul continued to ooze out from beneath the thin ecclesiastical veneer laid over it. Though the Church of San Pietro in Vinculus at Rome had, since its earliest years, held the Festival of the Chains of Saint Peter on the Calends of August, *ferrare agosto* remained obscure outside of revelrous Venice. In spite of his reproachful tone of shock in the face of it, the priggish Florentine seemed, nevertheless, to enjoy himself thoroughly.

The guests arrived while the sun still shone brightly, illuminating every corner of Titian's idyll, and the lagoon beyond. Priscianese, accompanied by Jacopo Nardi, author of a somewhat rambling history of Florence, recorded that the charm and beauties of the garden elicited "singular pleasure and a note of admiration from all of us."

The sheer force of personality generated by the triumvirate could not have been a more striking contrast to the gentle repose of the view. Handsome Sansovino, pale with a red beard, was always exquisitely groomed, with a noticeable taste for excess and bawdy talk of women. The adventuring goldsmith Benvenuto Cellini, one of the greatest braggarts of all time, had been stunned by the immodest self-praise Sansovino granted himself even as he denigrated the genius of Michelangelo. If he overwhelmed Cellini, Sansovino paled in comparison with Aretino, whom Priscianese could only characterize as "a new miracle of nature."

Although the occasion was a relaxed picnic, we cannot imagine that the Scourge of Princes dressed in anything less than regal resplendence, dripping with jewels and brightly colored silk. Titian's portrait of the man, painted five years after this event, and now at the Palatine Gallery, Florence, depicts his immense body, as expansive as his personality, cloaked in luscious cut velvets and gold chains. Aretino adored making a glittering impression on any occasion and sported ludicrously showy finery. More than any other possession, he treasured the massive gold chain that François I of France (r. 1515–1547) sent him (after repeated demands by the recipient). Numerous vermilion-enameled pendants shaped like poisoned tongues dangled from its thick links, each inscribed "LINGUA EIUS LOQUETUR MEDACIUM" (His tongue uttereth great lies); he wore it with pride and devilish amusement.

Aretino gloried in his fame and his riches, for he had struggled up from the very bottom of society. His father had been a mere cobbler; his unsurpassed wit and erudition were almost entirely self-taught. He had endured ignominious years employed in a seemingly endless assortment of humble occupations—mule driver, tax collector, pimp, hangman's mate, and finally lackey—before catapulting himself to fame in 1516, when he wrote a cruelly hilarious Last Will and Testament for the Pope's ridiculously cosseted pet elephant Hanno (whose death was commemorated in a gigantic portrait commissioned from Raphael).

Titian, whom Vasari described as a "gentleman of distinguished family and most courteous ways and manners," mitigated the introduction of the prim Florentines to his flamboyant friends. This painter of emperors and kings enjoyed his pleasures as much as Aretino and Sansovino, but he always behaved with the utmost discretion. With such self-evident genius, universally recognized in his generation, and his noble upbringing, Titian had no need either to brag or to insult others. Rather, he strove to put those less-gifted persons around him at ease. Nardi and Priscianese were charmed. The grammarian described his host as "a person really fitted to season by his courtesies any distinguished entertainment."

The greetings dispensed with, Priscianese recalled that "before the tables were set out, because the sun, in spite of the shade, still made its heat much felt, we spent the time in looking at the lively figures in the excellent pictures, of which the house was full." Aretino, to be sure, found the dog days of summer "very trying on the person and the patience." He argued: "There are those who like the season on account of the abundance of its fruits, lauding the cherries, the figs, the fishes and the eggs; as if the truffles and the olives of winter were not worth more than all those things. . . . If it were not that the memory of watermelons, those pimps of the palate, assailed you, which is the only thing that makes their summer temple desirable, you would flee the heat as knaves do the cold." The unbearable warmth of the August day quelled any desire to eat. Instead, they whet their appetite with their host's scrumptious pictures. Perhaps they looked at the *Pardo Venus,* painted that year and now at the Louvre, a lyrical reverie in which the nude goddess of beauty lies sleeping beneath a tree surrounded by magical Pan-like creatures and Cupid with his arrow, with a view onto the water and mountains beyond.

To the contemporary eye, Titian's landscapes, with their carefully composed blue mountains and framing coulisses of trees, appear extremely artificial. Titian painted a fantasy of nature: dreamlike forests and fields inhabited by handsome shepherds, nubile nymphs, and mythic beasts. So too, his garden picnic was an artfully constructed fête champêtre, an enchantingly orchestrated celebration of Mother Nature aided by human touch. Certainly, it would be hard to imagine such worldly men squatting on the ground and nibbling nuts like squirrels. To Aretino's princely taste, it was not enough merely to sit and converse in the shadow of a beech tree, because "in such a place a thousand harlot appetites attack one. In such a case there is a call for the song of birds, the murmur of waters, the sighing of zephyrs, the freshness of a lawn and similar conceits."

Aretino, with all his suavity, was not exempt from pastoral fantasy. In 1528 he wrote to his friend Simon Bianco, "What a gentle world belongs (instead) to those who humble themselves to the honesty of nature, observe the modesty of its orders with tempered sobriety and, by not ruining the privileges of docility with the vanity of pride, are satisfied to care for themselves, suffering not that animals should usurp such an honor!" What rapture to dine "with the appetite of a fisherman" on a salad and sausages roasted over the fire, in the company of a cat and one's shadow; to leisurely shop for provisions from a small village market (hearts and livers, calf's head for a stew, a bit of fish, a few eggs, young capons or hens on Easter and the solemn feasts, a goose on All Saints' Day); to buy radishes, mixed wild greens wrapped in a handkerchief, the summer plums, figs, grapes, and a huge and heavy melon; and then, after carrying it all home, to go at the melon "with nose and knife almost at once" and, after eating a couple of sweet, juicy slices, to "down a shot of wine of such flavor as penetrates to the very bone."

48

Was Aretino genuine in his desire to forgo the luxuries of his Venetian palazzo? Of course not. The same pastoral yearning would later fuel the eighteenth-century philosophy of Jean-Jacques Rousseau and even cause Marie-Antoinette to dress up as a milkmaid and to declare: "[P]eople think it easy to play the queen—they are wrong. The constraints are endless, it seems to be natural is a crime." Aretino would have sympathized with her complaint. She, in turn, would have approved of the lavish artifice which Titian's household undertook to transport his friends into a living embodiment of the mythical land of Arcadia, the garden paradise of the god Pan, inhabited by shepherds and shepherdesses, nymphs and satyrs.

The Greek poet Theocritus gave Arcadia its first literary form; a theme later reprised in the Italian Renaissance by Pietro Bembo, whose portrait Titian painted, and other poets at the court of Caterina Cornaro in Asolo. Jacopo Sannazaro's *Arcadia,* published in the 1490s, captured the magical scene Titian's guests beheld as, at last, they sat down to supper:

FIGURE 3.1
Kitchen for the Country,
1570, engraving from
Bartolomeo Scappi,
Opera.

> It was the hour when sunset had embroidered all the West with a thousand variety of clouds; some violet, some darkly blue and a certain crimson; others between yellow and black, and a few so burning with fire of backward-beaten rays that they seemed as though of polished and finest gold.

Kenneth Clark's classic, *Landscape into Art,* traces the emergence of European landscape painting, like pastoral poetry, to man's taming of the natural world. So, it was the nurturing environs of the Serene Republic, safely ensconced in the lagoon, which gave birth to Giovanni Bellini and his *Feast of the Gods* (color plate III), and in the same resplendent setting that his student, Titian, held an actual feast on a summer night. The elegant picnic, like the genre of landscape, grew popular as nature proved more soothing than dangerous.

Titian himself heavily reworked *Feast of the Gods,* left unfinished when Bellini died in 1516, to hang with three of his own bacchanalia, including the *Bacchanal of the Andrians,* in the *studiolo* of the *camerini d'alabastro* (alabaster chambers) belonging to Duke Alfonso I d'Este (1476–1534) of Ferrara. It was especially there at

49

FIGURE 3.2
Design for a fork and two
spoons, Italy, late sixteenth
century, pen and brown
ink, brush and brown wash
over traces of black chalk
and charcoal on off-white
laid paper.

the Este court, rather than Venice, where Titian observed that a banquet might
honor Mother Earth as artfully as his sublime landscapes.

As Titian painted his Dionysian rites, Alfonso's *scalco* (chief steward) Cristoforo
di Messisbugo staged them in the castle's gardens, as recorded in his posthumous
Banchetti, composizioni di vivande e apparecchio generale (1549). During the frequent trips he made to Ferrara, while completing the commission from 1518 to
1524, the painter would have had ample opportunity to observe these festivities. In
1524, if not on other occasions, it is known that nobly born Messisbugo personally
escorted the artist from Venice. One incredible picnic described in *Banchetti,* given
on 20 May 1529 by Ippolito II Cardinal d'Este of Ferrara for his brother Ercole II,
began with a farce and a concert. Dancers and musicians then accompanied fifty-
four distinguished guests to the head table. Foliate festoons and trophies were
strung overhead. A stacked credenza stood at one side, lending décor and facilitat-
ing service; entertainers performed in a leafy thicket on the other. Salads of herbs
garnished with festively cut lemons, of spinach, and of anchovies; dishes of pignoli
nuts; and small plates of sturgeon fritters had been laid out on the table, amidst
scattered flowers and miniature emblems of the Este arms. Sugar sculptures of
Venus, Bacchus, and Cupid marked the occasion as a glorious bacchanal. The
party sat down to eat at ten o'clock in the evening and finished consuming eighteen courses of eight dishes each at five o'clock in the morning.

Titian's picnic, although it shared the boisterous spirit of the Este family bacchanals, would not have been as supremely showy as that of his princely patron.
While the visitors toured the studio, Titian's staff set the banqueting table in the
shade of some cypress trees. It is not inconceivable that they did so in accordance
with the 1526 pamphlet by Eustachio Celebrino da Udine. The text, the first in
Italian devoted to the serving of the meal, provided advice for the courtly office of
the *scalco,* a professional position typical within Italian noble houses from the medieval period, but not known elsewhere in Europe. Titian's household was considerably smaller than such an establishment would have been; his sister supervised
the servants and his children. However, the noble painter was renowned for his elegance. For a "sumptuous banquet" Celebrino advised laying wooden boards over

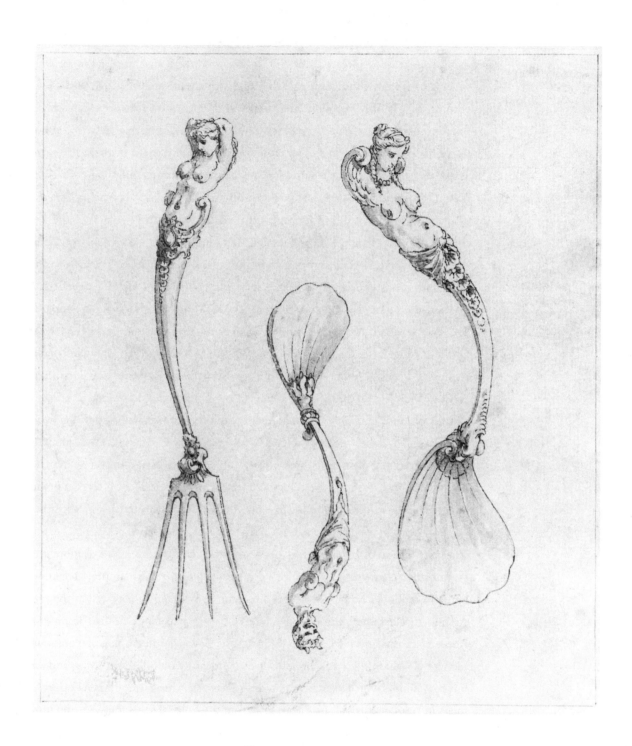

tripod legs to form a table, which should be draped with three layers of fine damask. A plate, a piece of bread, a cracker *(biscotello)*, and a cake *(pignochato)* covered by a napkin should sit at each place, with a knife and fork at the side. (According to Claudio Benporat, the dinner fork makes its first appearance as a proper utensil in this Venetian publication. Around this same date, Martin Luther purportedly said, "God protect me from forks.") Even for the *al fresco* meal, a great sideboard (credenza) would be set up outside, to display dazzling plate as well as provide a convenient space for tempting offerings of the first course, symmetrically arranged in readiness for the servants to transfer to the table after the antipasti. We can imagine Titian's guests, seated on luxuriant X-form chairs, gazing out at the islands beyond the lagoon, while bold silver candelabra, heavily interlaced with bands of ornamental strapwork, lit the festivities as the sky grew dark.

Priscianese described the supper as "no less beautiful and arranged than copious and well provided. Besides the most delicate viands and precious wines there were all those pleasures and amusements that are suited to the season, the guests, and the feast." Priscianese's lavish praise of his host's largesse indicates that Titian put on quite a show with three, if not four, courses, composed of numerous bowls and platters of food. Unlike Messisbugo, who had a Mannerist predilection for overwhelming rare delicacies with spice and garnish, Titian preferred food, like art, that discreetly highlighted nature's inherent splendor without completely disguising it. On a visit to Aretino in October 1532 the painter decided to forgo a grand banquet being held in his honor to enjoy the simpler pleasure of some thrushes "boiled with a bit of dried beef, two leaves of laurel and a pinch of pepper." It was a straightforward dish that these two enjoyed as much, Aretino wrote, as more pretentious diners craved heavily spiced ortolans, pheasants, and lamprey. For these nature worshippers, the pastoral was an aesthetic for the palate as well as the eye. Aretino mocked the gluttonous banquets of the papal court he had known in Rome, with their decided preference for exotic flavors and complex preparations. He wrote, "My mind, I am sure, if it had the means would feed on real grandeur, but my mouth, which exercises some little sway over my taste, finds its nourishment in rustic victuals. If it is a sin to devour a whole salad, along with an entire onion, then I am branded, for I find in them a sharpness of flavor which those kitchen-falcons who flock about the table of Leo never enjoyed."

What more perfect way to celebrate nature than the artfully composed salad. Aretino considered salads the gastronomic equivalent of a landscape, each a delicately exquisite composition of discrete elements. Aretino's letter to Girolamo Sarra of 4 November 1537, an elegy to the glories of salad, is as eloquent as a Titian in paying homage to the beauties of Mother Earth. He lauded those gifted at judiciously mixing the sourness of some herbs with the sweetness of others—especially praising the perfection of wild radicchio, mixed with a bit of calamint—to achieve a balance, neither bitter nor sharp. Enraptured by the scent and beauty of flowers scattered amidst the delicate leaves, he declared in a frenzy of adoration:

Certainly, I am amazed that poets don't wager their pants in order to sing the virtues of salad. And monks and nuns are wrong not to praise it, because the former steal hours away from prayer in order to spend them in cleansing it from little stones, and the latter, almost like nursemaids unto it, spend all their time washing and caring for it. I think that its inventor must have been Florentine, nor can it be otherwise since the setting of tables, their decoration with roses, the washing of glassware, the little plums in the dip-dishes, the dressing of chopped liver, the making of flour bread-cakes and the serving of fruit after meals all came from Florence. Its little brains, its thirsting ones, its humble hard-workers, with all their subtlety and foresight, have grasped all the points by which cuisine can tempt even those who are inappetent.

We can imagine that after the guests washed their hands in perfumed water strewn with flower petals, Titian's servants laid a variety of salads on the table. These might have been accompanied by tarts, figs, and melons—as an August meal in Messisbugo's *Banchetti* had commenced—or even a bit of fresh cheese perfumed with rosewater and sugar, candied ginger and nuts, as Celebrino recommended. Aretino concurred with Nero that "antipasti are of the gods."

A first course typically comprised light dishes, served cold or at room temperature, as well as soups; then followed roasts and stews nestled in pasta. Vegetables and pastas, often sprinkled with sugar, nutmeg, and a grating of Parmesan, might be served throughout the meal.

The markets of Venice offered great quantities of local and imported produce. Aretino delighted in watching the tumult and bustle from his well-placed window: a score of sailing boats moored together, each piled high with fresh melons, sniffed, weighed, and counted by mere housewives gleaming in silk and gold and jewels. What the markets could not provide, Titian and Aretino assiduously garnered through their own wide network of connections. The painter's family sent him wild roosters from his native Cadore, whose delicate breasts he sometimes "while dining and drawing" shared with his companion. Once, he gave Aretino two succulent wild chickens, which his roguish friend "took the liberty of presenting to myself, being commissioned by him to present them in his name to a great lord." Titian obviously intended these rich gifts to garner favor with a potential client, but his devilish counterpart was never one to subvert his own desires.

Aretino shamelessly commandeered whatever tasty treats his friends and colleagues had at their disposal. After thanking his publisher, Francesco Marcolini, for sending the freshest pickings from his gardens—orange flowers pickled in herbs, cherries, strawberries, cucumbers, figs, musk-pears, melons, plums, grapes, and fish—he demanded, "But where are the artichokes which you have for so long sent to my table? And where the gourds which I have eaten, fried in the platter, before I would have sworn they were in bloom? Of beans I do not speak, except to remind you in case you have forgotten." Correggio and Roccabianca gifted Aretino with fishes; others sent pears, olives, quails, and thrushes, which he liked to be "cooked in two turns of the skillet, sandwiched with lettuce and sausages in careless fashion." In the autumn he received mushrooms, which he ate "boiled with two slices of bread and fried in oil," not to mention innumerable barrels of red and white wine. He never hoarded these delicacies, but rushed to invite his friends and even servants to enjoy his treasures. Dining in good company doubled the pleasure.

The triumvirate scoffed at the accepted practice of choosing foods according to their cold, hot, wet, and dry properties to counterbalance the humors. They preferred to eat what was fresh, tasty, and simple even though an overabundance of melons, fresh fruits, and vegetables in the diet was considered unhealthful. Their wantonness in this regard must have shocked Priscianese and Nardi, the logical, earnest Florentines. Vasari later noted with censorious awe that Sansovino's stomach was "so strong that he was not worried about anything, and made no distinction between good and harmful food; and in summer he lived almost solely on fruit, very often eating up to three cucumbers at a time, and half a lemon, in his extreme old age." Though numerous courts wished to engage Sansovino as royal architect, according to Vasari, he declined them all because "he was not intending to exchange his condition of life in a republic for that of an absolute prince." Neither would he submit the sensuous pleasures of his appetite to the uptight dietary strictures of his time. These Venetian divinities ate as Titian painted, their palates awash with the color of nature's bounty.

Titian's feast was not an occasion to worry fussily about whether one was feeling slightly melancholic or more sanguine. Nor, in spite of Aretino's pastoral yearning, was it an Arcadian idyll. Imbued with the abandon of the early worshippers of Bacchus, the triumvirate could not help but honor that deity. As Priscianese noted, Titian's precious wine flowed freely that evening, in fitting tribute to the god. Perhaps, on such a hot summer's night, plentiful bottles of red, white, and sweet Malvasia wine, especially beloved in Venice, sat chilling in great coolers of luxurious ice and water, as Celebrino suggested and as seen in Tintoretto's *Last Supper* at San Giorgio Maggiore. Robust drinking was, after all, the essence of bacchanalian rites. They sought the swooning libertinism of Titian's *Bacchanal of the Andrians* with its mystical river of wine, reaching beyond the rational, the logical, and the sensible, by imbibing the grapes fermented from the fruits of the earth into this potent elixir.

The triumvirate knew that to be divine *(divino)* in some way meant being "of wine" *(di vino)*. As Luba Freedman points out, Aretino playfully connected the two on more than one occasion. In a 1545 letter to Michelangelo, he wrote that while the colossal genius was *"divino,"* he, the Scourge, was not of water. Thanking Girolamo Agnello for a gift of wine, Aretino finished by stating, "There is nothing else to say except that, with all due respect to my immortality, I would become of wine *(di vino)* as well as divine *(divino)* if you would visit me at least once a year with such a pressing."

This elixir of truth and gift of the gods held the power to unleash the frenzy of the passions, reaching beneath polite civility to the soul of humanity as well as man's lurking bestiality. Wine was to be enjoyed but respected. In Aretino's play, *The Philosopher,* the learned man's lackey is transfixed by a conversation he overheard which instructed:

> [W]ine should be poured out on musical principles. We should hold out the goblet at a certain distance from our chests and watch the liquor glittering, twinkling and fizzing, delighting in the pearls it produces, quite big at first then growing tinier and tinier till they disappear. He went on to say that we ought to drink from a perfectly full cup, taking care not to spill a drop, because by absorbing all that rich juice in two successive sips of the parted lips, wrinkling the nose and raising the eyebrows to signalize the solemnity of the occasion, till half of a large beaker has been drunk—a small one not enabling us to perform such miracles—our palate is refreshed, our gums revived by the liquid and our teeth cleansed, while the tongue as it explores the little lake of wine, which must not be swallowed at a draught, obtains the same satisfaction as the teeth, the gums and palate. Finally, when the mind instructs the legs, the body the mouth, the mouth the thirst, and the thirst the state of confusion arising from the desire to drink the whole glass up, the throat and gullet work together to guarantee wisdom. Whereby the belly, the lungs, the liver, the spleen and the bowels, thus activated, rise to float upon a sea of bliss. In this condition the senses render the face of the drinker rubicund, hot, cheerful, proud, bright, calm and vigorous. Such favors lend strength to the tongue, sparkle to the eyes, revival to the breath, enlargement to the veins, animation to the pulse, expansion to the skin and reinforcement to the nerves.

Such Proustian observation, to the very drop clinging to the edge of the tongue and slowly wending its way through the body, evinces the depth of respect that these Venetians rendered the offering of Bacchus. They did not abandon themselves recklessly, but stopped to observe and smell and slowly savor the clarity and "biting" taste of the wine they favored.

They drank from magically translucent glass that only the Serene Republic knew how to produce. More elegant than the brim-filled beakers of the tavern were *cristallo* tazzas, made from soda-glass as clear as the precious mineral they were named after, with stems as elongated as Parmigianino's Madonna's neck, and wide, flat bowls that gave each guest his own pond from which to sip. They were produced on the island of Murano, the tree-lined focal point past the line of the horizon that Titian and his guests watched as the sun sank over the lagoon and they continued to drink into the night. Since at least the thirteenth century, the island had produced glass from the silica obtained from the crushed pebbles of the river Ticino, soda from the ash of plants, red lead, and calcium. Almost a century before Titian's picnic, Angelo Barovier (d. 1460) revolutionized the industry when he discovered that the addition of "Piedmont manganese" produced a glass clearer than anything but rock crystal itself. Even the sophisticated blowers of ancient Rome had made nothing comparable. As Titian and his guests drank from these exquisite vessels, the workers who made them labored as virtual prisoners on the island across the lagoon. To leave the Republic of Venice with the secret of making *cristallo* was a capital offense, and those who tried were hunted down and killed. Venetians had already lost too many monopolies, but this, for the moment, they still kept.

Titian's guests gazed at the island of Murano as they drank, but it was not the glass blowers to whom their thoughts drifted in the haze of the wine. Priscianese wrote: "This part of the sea, as soon as the sun went down, swarmed with gondolas, adorned with beautiful women, and resounded with the varied harmony and music of voices and instruments, which till midnight accompanied our delightful supper." As in Titian's *Bacchanal of the Andrians,* where there was wine, there were women and song. Music and dance were intrinsic to the celebration of bacchic ritual in ancient times, and the drunken god was usually depicted with a female devotee, the bacchante, swirling with abandonment as she beat a tambourine, while others played pipes and danced.

A sheet of paper inscribed with a single line of music and the words "Qui boyt et ne reboyt, il ne scet boyre soit" (He who drinks and does not drink again, does not know what drinking is) lies in the foreground of the *Bacchanal of the Andrians.* Edward Lowinsky argues that the composition was written by Adriaan Willaert (circa 1490–1562) and is a *canon per tonos,* in that the music, for four voices to be read up or down, backward or forward, is intended to rise or fall by a whole tone with each repetition. The form was so uncommon that it was not used again for another hundred years. While Titian painted his bacchanals and Messisbugo created them in the castle gardens, Willaert, a Flemish composer trained in Paris, was also in the service of Alfonso d'Este. But in December 1527 the composer assumed the position of Maestro di Cappella at the Basilica San Marco in Venice, where he remained for the rest of his life. In addition to his ecclesiastical works, he himself wrote popular madrigals, chansons, and rustic villanellas that might have been heard wafting over the waters that night.

The floating courtesans alternated their voices in harmonic combinations, some chords echoing across the water, others swallowed by the waves, as they proffered their siren song to Titian's guests. These Venetian charmers were famous throughout Europe for their beauty and brazen resplendence. When Montaigne visited the city in 1580 he was "exceedingly struck, as much so as by anything else, with the style in which some hundred and fifty or so of the principal courtesans live; their houses are kept up, and themselves maintained and dressed quite as magnificently as though they were all princesses, and yet they have nothing to live upon but what they make themselves by their profession. Some of them are kept by Venetian noblemen in the most open and public manner, there being no sort of attempt made to conceal the connection." Aretino and Sansovino knew them all familiarly and delighted in flirting with them in the most joyously libertine manner. To Titian's embarrassment, the Florentines got to experience Venice's famous dissipation firsthand.

FIGURE 3.3
Tazza *a fili e retorti,*
ca. 1500–1550, glass,
Venice or *façon de
Venise.*

Despite all of the merrymaking, Titian's servants performed their duties with the utmost civility. Their conservative master kept his household strictly disciplined. He was extremely critical of Aretino's lackadaisical behavior in this regard, for this shameless blackmailer continually let himself be robbed and cheated by his help. To Titian's scolding, Aretino replied, "The fact that my staff take advantage of me doesn't make me angry but happy. . . . I, who am feared rather than loved by the great ones of the earth, am glad that my grooms and kitchen maids do not respect me. For that situation prevents me from getting a swelled head." Titian thought this sheer madness and permitted no such shenanigans in his own home. Orderliness in the service permitted the revelers to enjoy themselves without the annoyance of emptied bottles or dirtied plates. Without interrupting the guests, the servants would have silently removed everything from the table and taken off the top cloth before setting out the *frutta*. Then, if they conformed to Celebrino's instructions, they would have offered perfumed water and clean towels for a second hand washing. Dessert, on display at the sideboard, probably fresh and candied fruits, a few sweets, and nuts, would then be transferred to the table. Perhaps they brought a compote of melons, marinated and stewed in good vinegar, flavored with cinnamon, ginger, cloves, and a touch of verjuice and white wine, as suggested by an anonymous Venetian recipe of 1530. As they laid out the dessert, the servants courteously delivered a letter to Priscianese, from his friend Ridolfi, describing another garden banquet at which dinner was followed by a serious discussion of literature, which praised Latin over the Tuscan language. The earnest Florentine grammarian insisted on reading it aloud.

He later wrote a reply to his friend to describe his own experience at Titian's, glossing over what must have happened next. Priscianese glowingly reported: "Aretino attacked your opinion in the most brilliant and delightful fashion, and I should like to have in ink on paper his discourse." Was he really so delighted by Aretino's scathing response? If the Scourge of Princes made the Holy Roman Emperor Charles V (r. 1519–1556) and Francis I tremble, he could gobble up a prissy, sycophantic little grammarian in one predatory bite. Priscianese admitted that the Venetian divinities were "a little annoyed at the incivility not to mention spite" of

Ridolfi who "thrust the bitterness of grammatical argument into the pleasures of dining and conviviality." Philosophizing after dinner might be *de rigueur* with the Florentines; but in Venice, serious discussion after a delightful meal was considered rude.

Priscianese had made a serious misstep. Aretino must have licked his lips at the delicious prospect of viciously tearing apart this maladroit intruder. In the frenzied orgies of ancient bacchic celebrations, a bull or goat, representing the god of fertility, was wildly ripped to pieces and eaten raw. Aretino, apparently, had to be restrained, so his wild carnage was merely verbal. After a good meal and much wine, and with an audience of courtesans on hand to watch, Priscianese's error offered Aretino a release from the constraints of civil behavior.

Aretino had no use for pretentious courtly manners or standing on ceremony. When Baldassare Castiglione circulated the manuscript of *Il libro del cortegiano* (The Book of the Courtier) prior to its publication in 1528, Aretino quickly released his satirical response to it: *La cortegiana* (The Courtesan). Castiglione's text situates itself in a discussion held after a banquet, modeled on the refined court at Urbino. The diners conclude that the self-conscious pursuit of *grazia* (gracefulness) and *sprezzatura* (seeming effortlessness) are the most essential virtues necessary to the perfect gentleman. Aretino's character Maestro Andrea voiced the Scourge's cynical retort: "The principal thing which a Courtier must know is how to blaspheme; he must be a gambler, invidious, a whore-chaser, a heretic, an adulterer, a slanderer, an ingrate, ignorant and asinine; he must know how to cheat, how to play the nymph, and he must be at once active and patient." Aretino, the son of a cobbler, proudly built his fame on an ability to unpretentiously state what he really thought (unless, of course, he was paid to change his opinion).

Priscianese made a double blunder, for the letter that he so rudely attempted to thrust upon the defenseless diners, extolled the virtues of the Latin tongue over vernacular Italian. Aretino's humble beginnings precluded him from studying ancient languages. Rather than insecurely worrying about this educational deficiency, he bragged about it, declaring himself a modernist. With his haughty bravura, Aretino scoffed at the humanist scholars with their heads buried in ancient texts of Greek and Latin. Certainly, his lack of formal education never stopped him; he published his first volume of poetry at the age of eighteen. The six volumes of his correspondence, which he issued between 1537 and 1556, were the first letters published in Italian. Just as Sansovino ate what he pleased and sneered at the teaching of Galen, Aretino let loose his invective against the entire litany of classical teaching without feeling the slightest compulsion to keep the full force of his cruel wit to himself. We can imagine him delivering to Priscianese the words that he wrote:

> I am a free man. I do not need to copy Petrarch or Boccaccio. My genius is enough. Let others worry themselves about style and so cease to be themselves. Without a master, without a model, without a guide, without artifice I go to work and win my living, my well-being, and my fame. What do I need more? With a goose quill and a few sheets of paper I amuse myself with the universe. They say I am the son of a courtesan. I may be so; but I have the soul of a king. I live free, I enjoy myself, and I call myself happy.

Luckily, Aretino did like to enjoy himself, and after giving himself the pleasure of speaking his mind, he turned his attention to more titillating matters than the stuffy Florentines. Priscianese took his beating in good stride; as a classicist he understood that mere mortals risk everything when they dare to sit at the table of the gods. He survived the experience, which made him a hero, and told his tale for the world to hear, declaring: "All passed in delight and gallantry." And thus the Venetians continued their revelry, nibbling fruit, sipping wine, laughing, and enjoying the company of indulgent beauties into the early hours of the morning and, indeed, for many years to follow.

Despite (or because of) their complete disregard of the laws of humoral dietary theory, all three of these pleasure-loving characters lived extremely long lives. Aretino spoke for them all when he declared, "To those who assert that in following sensual appetite we hasten death I reply that a man prolongs his life precisely in proportion to the extent that he satisfies his desires. And it is I who say that, not

Plato." He was the first to die, keeling over in his chair while laughing at a smutty joke at a tavern, quite literally going out at the height of the party. Sansovino lived to be eighty-four, eating his cucumbers and talking about the ladies until the very end, while Titian, whose birth date remains obscure, reached the age of eighty-six by conservative estimates and more than a hundred by other accounts, painting and feasting in celebration of nature.

Chapter Four

Cementing a Bond

THE WEDDING BANQUET
OF MARIA DE' MEDICI
AND HENRI IV, FLORENCE,
5 OCTOBER 1600

O happy Nymph, to unite your greatness with France
And accept the yoke of love of a valorous king,
What lazy demon can keep you so long in Florence
On the Tuscan strand, far from your new destiny?
Come, fulfil the desires of our Mars, who goes forth to meet you.
O, what a company of Gods and Goddesses awaits you.
The strong sea winds will soon appear on the wave,
Already the Mists return to prolong our night.
May the Hymeneal Wedding Bark advance and not delay the feast:
The lovers do both burn with a natural flame,
Between war and peace may all France now sing,
O Hymen, Hymen, O Hymen of Love.

> Nicolas Rapin, "To the Queen," Song for the wedding
> of Maria de' Medici to Henri IV of France

ON 5 MAY 1600, CHARLES DE NEUFVILLE, Marquis d'Alincourt, arrived at the Palace of Fontainebleau on the outskirts of Paris. Without pause, he presented to his Sovereign, Henri IV, King of France (r. 1589–1610) and Navarre, important news from Florence: on 25 April the marriage contract joining the King to the Princess Maria de' Medici (1573–1642) had been officially signed at the Palazzo Pitti by her uncle and ward, Ferdinando I de' Medici (1549–1609), Grand Duke of Tuscany. A Te Deum was chanted at the palace and in the Church of the Annunciation, after which Maria dined publicly as Queen of France, seated on a dais above her illustrious uncle as a mark of her new rank. The Duke of Bracciano presented the water with which she washed her hands and the French ambassador, Nicolas Brûlart, Marquis de Sillery, proferred the towel with which she wiped them. The King was officially betrothed.

D'Alincourt handed Henri a portrait of his fiancée framed by a border of diamond brilliants. Although not classically beautiful, Maria was young and attractive. Her eyes flashed with proud intelligence, her hair was as golden as her dowry rich, and her alabaster skin glowed like Chinese porcelain. Such a bride should have been sufficiently alluring to pique the interest of a middle-aged king.

Henri, however, could not have been more indifferent to the news. He was preoccupied with his mistress, Henriette d'Entragues, whose favors had cost him one hundred thousand crowns (before gifts) and a written promise that he would make her queen if she gave birth to a son within a year. She already presided over his court as if she wore the crown. His subjects had hardly recovered from Henri's threat to marry his previous mistress, the glamorous Gabrielle d'Estrées, whose children he had legitimized. Only Gabrielle's untimely death during childbirth in April 1599 had stopped him (rumors of poison persisted). A mere three weeks later, several of the King's courtiers, hoping to distract him from his gloomy mourning, had arranged his introduction to Henriette.

Gabrielle's death prompted the King's first wife, Marguerite de Valois, to finally agree to their divorce, after years of withholding her consent (that he would so quickly dangle her crown before an equally unsuitable contender was not immediately apparent). The union between the Huguenot King of Navarre and a Princess of France had proved disastrous from the start. Their wedding on 18 August 1572 had been a glorious occasion, bringing Catholics and Protestants together for a double ceremony in front of Notre Dame, but the extended celebrations that followed had climaxed in the Saint Bartholomew's Day massacre of 24 August, a brutal rampage that left thousands of Huguenots dead. Henri survived only by abjuring Protestantism. His gorgeous bride had bravely defended him, but his mother-in-law, Catherine de' Medici (1519–1589), had been chief among the conspirators who had plotted to squelch the Protestants. Henri can perhaps be forgiven for his failure to greet the prospect of marrying Catherine's cousin, however distantly related, with anything more than mild indifference.

Henri IV inherited the French throne when Henri III (r. 1574–1589), the last of the Valois kings, was assassinated in 1589. Henri III had named his Bourbon cousin heir presumptive after his youngest brother died in 1584. In spite of this, the staunch Catholics of the Holy League refused to recognize Henri IV as King of France because he had reconverted to Protestantism immediately upon his return to Navarre after the massacre. The new monarch had to do battle and, finally, abjure his faith yet again, before he made his royal entrance to the capital and was crowned at Chartres in 1594. "Paris is well worth a Mass," he purportedly said.

After all the tumult, the King's Chief Minister and Chamberlain (and d'Alincourt's father), Maximilien de Béthune (1560–1641), Marquis de Rosny, later first Duc de Sully, was eager to secure a bride for Henri who could ensure the stability of the realm by producing a legitimate heir. In Sully's view, an alliance with Maria offered several advantages. The young lady's uncle, eager to forge a rapprochement with the French after generations of Spanish influence in Florence, had underwritten and aided Henri's struggle for the throne. More recently, the Grand Duke, who had been a cardinal until he inherited the duchy from his brother (Maria's father) Francesco I (1541–1587), had used his influence over the Florentine Pope, Clement VIII, to help procure Henri's divorce.

FIGURE 4.1
Study for the Medici arms combined with those of the French royal family, 1600, by Ludovico Cigoli, charcoal on paper.

Henri initially dismissed the match; the Medicis were not many generations from being mere bankers. Emperor Charles V had only created the Duchy of Tuscany in 1529 for the illegitimate son of Pope Clement VII. Clement had worked hard to rebuild the family's position, which had plummeted after Lorenzo the Magnificent's son, Piero, cowardly opened the gates of Florence to French troops in 1494. It was Clement who had negotiated Catherine's marriage to the second son of François I. However, not until Maria's grandfather, Cosimo I de' Medici (1519–1574), from the Popolano branch of the family, took power in 1537 did the Medicis live and rule on a par with the sovereigns of Europe. His first act as Duke was to exile the Councilors of Florence, who had accorded him the title; in 1559, he completed his campaign to create a unified state of Tuscany; a decade later his territories had been elevated to the status of a grand duchy.

Sully pointed out to the King that Maria's mother had been Joanna of Austria, sister to the Holy Roman Emperor Maximilien II (r. 1564–1576). Moreover, Catherine de' Medici's tenure as Queen and Regent, though despotic, had established a precedent for an alliance between the Medicis and the French royal family.

When the King fell headlong into his affair with the ambitious Henriette, Sully forced the issue. The People, Sully argued to his Sovereign, wanted a queen and an heir worthy of their King. Sully did not miscalculate Henri's concern for "the Will of the People." He genuinely loved his subjects, and as he was remembered for the slogan "a chicken in every pot every Sunday," he held their affection in return. For their sake, Henri agreed that his minister could negotiate for Maria's hand. However, after the contract was finalized and announced, jealous Henriette banned discussion of the impending nuptials from her presence, and since she was always with the King, he soon put the matter almost completely out of his mind.

By contrast, in Florence, preparation for the royal wedding escalated into a flurry of activity from the moment the betrothal was announced. The occasion would transform a second Medici into the Queen of France. Henri II (r. 1547–1559) had only been the second son of François I when he married Catherine de' Medici. Maria's impending wedding to the reigning monarch of France, only forty-one years after her grandfather's promotion to Grand Duke, marked the apogee of Medicean ascendance. The ceremonies to forge this irrevocable knot needed to manifest every ounce of royal splendor, which the binding ties of matrimony, joining the Medicis to the House of Bourbon, showered upon them all; magnificence was the order of the day.

On 10 May 1600, Ferdinando entrusted the planning for the festivities to Giulio de' Nobili and Ridolfo Altoviti, who had supervised the Grand Duke's own wedding in 1589. Donato dell' Antella and Cavalier Raffaello de' Medici were also appointed to assist in this most honorable task. Ferdinando informed his Deputies

FIGURE 4.2
Device for Lifting Any Large Cauldron onto the Fire, 1570, engraving from Bartolomeo Scappi, *Opera.*

that he hoped the ceremonies might happen before summer; there was not a moment to waste.

Four days later, the committee sent the Grand Duke a detailed reply, complete with recommendations for housing the onslaught of distinguished foreigners and renting a sufficient supply of wooden tables, backed stools, and wine chests. The keeper of the *guardaroba* (the closet) inventoried kitchen and service equipment. Hay, feed, and stalls for all the extra horses were organized. The Chief Steward submitted lists of necessary provisions for the feast and suggested confectionery for the Grand Duke's review. Within this short interval, the Deputies had devised

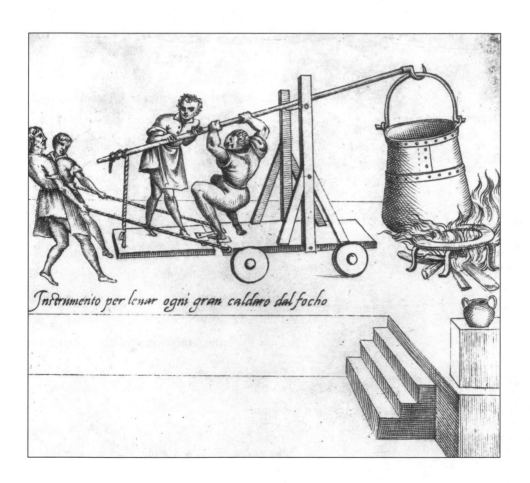

Instrumento per levar ogni gran caldaro dal focho

a seating scheme for the overflow of guests expected for the banquet, suggesting extra apartments in the palace suitable to hold tables for the husbands of the court ladies and younger courtiers, expected to help serve the banquet. (They recommended limiting the table for the husbands to ten to twelve of those closest to the court, as a greater number would cost a lot for little gratitude or reward.)

The Deputies also posed numerous questions that required the Duke's personal attention. In order to make the *guardaroba* and the credenza look regally impressive, but still have enough silver and plate to serve the meal, they would need at least a thousand extra maiolica dishes. Did the Duke perchance have a stash of them at one of his houses? Could extra kitchen equipment be borrowed from his villa at Poggio? How many people did the Duke want to accompany Maria on the voyage to Marseilles? Sufficient food and supplies would have to be ordered. Perhaps, they wondered, the Duke would agree that it might be a good idea to have a separate galley just to carry these items and the servants, so that the sight of washing and preparation would not offend the noble passengers?

A mere four days after receiving their instructions, Ferdinando's Wedding Deputies had the situation well in hand. Tuscany might be only a grand duchy to France's kingdom, but these Florentines had no doubts that they were more culturally sophisticated. Only days after D'Alincourt had reached Fontainebleau with Maria's portrait, the scheme for seating and decorating the banquet was approved and service items were delivered to the goldsmiths on the Ponte Vecchio for replating and polishing.

By no means can the Florentines be given credit for inventing the practice of cementing a marriage with a banquet, or even for being the first to dazzle with the extravagance of such festivities. The earliest surviving text devoted solely to the description of a feast describes the wedding banquet of Caranus held in Macedonia about 275 B.C. At this astonishing event, the guests were presented with gifts of silver cups, gold circlets, and hampers of plaited ivory with which to carry away their loot. Great platters of bronze, silver, and gold, piled high with every imaginable delicacy including "proper Erymanthian boars, spitted on silver spears . . . served to each on square dishes with gold rims," appeared in succession as the finest wines of the ancient world were liberally poured out and "women acrobats, naked, who breathed fire and did somersaults over swords" entertained the guests.

Caranus's feast set a very high standard for what constitutes a lavish wedding. Nevertheless, the Florentines believed themselves capable of rivaling even this grandeur. By Maria's day, Florence was well versed in the practice of hosting world-class nuptials. In 1565, Cosimo I had pushed Giorgio Vasari to finish his famous corridor, linking the Uffizi to the Palazzo Pitti, in a mere five months and had had the courtyard of the Palazzo Vecchio completely restored for the December marriage of Maria's parents. When Francesco subsequently married his true love, Bianca Cappello, in 1579, he outdid these previous festivities. In 1586, Francesco commissioned Bernardo Buontalenti (1536–1608) to build the spectacular Teatro Mediceo in the Uffizi and to design sets and costumes for the performances held there for the nuptials of his half sister Virginia and Cesare d'Este. Three years later, Buontalenti also created the spectacles for Ferdinando's wedding to Christine of Lorraine, for which Emilio de' Cavalieri, Cristofano Malvezzi, and Luca Marenzio composed the proto-operatic musical extravaganza *La Pellegrina*.

FIGURE 4.3 *(facing page)*
Principal Kitchen, 1570, engraving from Bartolomeo Scappi, *Opera.*

FIGURE 4.4
Cool Area for Working with Milk, 1570, engraving from Bartolomeo Scappi, *Opera.*

71

These nuptial celebrations established that a grand Medici wedding would reach a soaring crescendo in a great banquet that followed the church ceremony and gradually diminish over several days of continued festivities. The family name was glorified in every aspect of these proceedings, in accordance to a system of "appropriate allegories" defined at the time of Joanna of Austria's 1565 arrival in Florence. Precedence made it easier for Maria's wedding to be planned in haste.

The French, however, with apathetic Henri at the helm, prevaricated about the date. The spring wedding was postponed. The King cited the conflict with Charles Emmanuel I, Duke of Savoy (1562–1630), over the territory of Saluzzo, which had disintegrated into full-fledged war. Henri himself led the triumphant invasion into Savoy; his marriage would have to wait. The Florentines were left hanging for months, as one excuse followed another. Finally, in September, when he could not, in good faith, delay any further, the wedding was scheduled for 5 October. The King, however, informed the Grand Duke that he was too busy to attend, and dispatched the Duke de Bellegarde, Grand Equerry of France, to stand as a proxy in his stead.

The fact that the groom would not be in attendance seemed a small matter, amidst the excitement of preparing for a royal wedding. The Grand Duke was not overly concerned that his niece's betrothed did not make time to marry her in person. Reigning monarchs often declined to leave their sovereignty, even to get married. The Duke's own wedding to Christine of Lorraine had been performed at Blois without him before the bride journeyed on to Florence. He duly fêted her arrival, and the marriage was happy and close. His mother, Eleonora da Toledo, daughter of the Viceroy of Naples, married Cosimo I by proxy in March 1539 and was treasured by her husband as long as she lived. However, the extended delay of Maria's wedding further complicated its logistical challenges. With the French at war, extra security was needed to protect the groom's noble entourage. The change in season also meant that the menu had to be entirely reworked, and a different list of provisions gathered, within a few short weeks.

As the date of the ceremony drew near, Florence declared a veritable state of emergency. The Wedding Deputies issued a proclamation on 9 September: all poultry, game birds, eggs, and such supplies as the committee deemed necessary for the banquet were banned from sale at the public market. Maria's marriage brought honor to all of Tuscany; every citizen was expected to do his part. Numerous civilians and aristocrats had already been recruited to assist in the pageantry; even the outlying cities offered the services of their ablest young men. Arezzo, for example, sent twenty-one men capable of serving as stewards or at table, twenty-three suitable to work in the kitchen, with the service of the wine, or at the credenza, and another twelve less talented, but able, bodies to assist wherever necessary. On 23 September, another public proclamation was issued, this time asking that all Florentines show suitable respect toward the foreign guests (or, more to the point, toward the Grand Duke in front of the guests).

That very day, the Duke de Bellegarde arrived with forty splendidly dressed French nobles, whose solemn duty was to bring honor to their King through their chivalrous behavior and impressive appearance. Antonio de' Medici and an entourage of Florentine cavaliers met them in Livorno and escorted them

FIGURE 4.5 *(facing page) Outdoor Space for Washing Dishes,* 1570, engraving from Bartolomeo Scappi, *Opera.*

FIGURE 4.6 *Spit-roasting Device with Three Levels,* 1570, engraving from Bartolomeo Scappi, *Opera.*

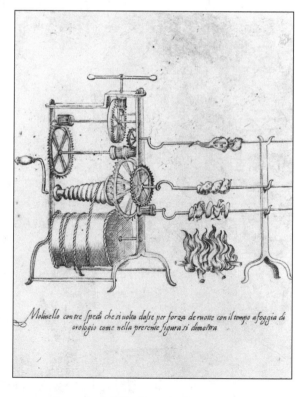

73

directly to the Grand Duke, to whom Henri's representative delivered gifts and letters. A week later, the Marquis de Sillery and the Duke of Mantua with his wife, Maria's sister, arrived in Florence. Niccolò Molino, the Venetian ambassador, soon followed.

On the eve of the wedding, the anticipation reached a feverish pitch as crowds lined the streets to watch the arrival of Cardinal Pietro Aldobrandini. This nephew and legate of the Pope, descended from one of Florence's most distinguished families, was met in person by the Grand Duke at the Porta Romana and escorted into the city by a German guard and two hundred gentlemen carrying the Medici arms. Ecclesiastical and secular officials led the procession; they were followed by Florence's handsomest noble pages wearing white with gold sashes, pearl collars, and velvet caps. The pages supported a white canopy, embroidered with gold, and dangling with pendants bearing the arms of the Cardinal, the Pope, and the Grand Duke, over the Cardinal's head as he rode on a magnificent horse. More than five hundred citizens and foreign guests marched in shimmering silks and velvets of red, purple, gold, and black. Sixteen prelates and fifty distinguished Florentine gentlemen, brandishing halberds, took up the rear, as the group proceeded to the great Duomo of Florence, where the Cardinal dismounted for a brief Te Deum.

When the Cardinal had finished, the entourage escorted him on to the ducal palace, where a regal supper awaited. This was the seventeenth-century equivalent of a rehearsal dinner, with all the players of the next day's ceremonies in attendance: the Grand Duke, the Dukes of Mantua and Bracciano, the Princes Juan and Antonio de' Medici, and the Duke de Bellegarde as proxy for the groom. The banquet officially honored the Cardinal, but all eyes focused on Maria, the fleshly symbol of the union between Tuscany and France. At the end of the meal, the Cardinal solemnly announced the complete satisfaction of the Sovereign-Pontiff at the union upon which he was about to pronounce his blessing. Maria replied, it was said, with grace and dignity.

The next day, an even greater crowd assembled to observe the ceremonial procession from the Palazzo Pitti to the Duomo. Members of the bourse and high-standing Florentines took the lead; they were followed by 120 of the Grand Duke's men wearing gold livery. An enormous gold cross was carried down the route. Then, the Grand Duke and the Cardinal appeared under fringed parasols. Distinguished foreign guests and younger family members preceded the bride's regally red carriage, carrying the Grand Duchess, her young son Cosimo, and the Duchesses of Bracciano and Mantua, along with Maria. An estimated sixty to eighty of Florence's most distinguished ladies followed, walking hand in hand; 247 young virgins dressed in white trimmed with silver marched at the rear.

The cathedral was arrayed as luxuriantly as the members of the bridal procession. Lights burned through the aisles and the transept, flooded the cupola, and hung from great crowns suspended in front of the high altar, just as at previous Medici weddings. A raised dais covered in red cloth had been erected in the *cornu evangelisti* with a gold-covered chair for the Cardinal so that, as the authority of God, he might sit above all others. Maria stood on the Cardinal's left, with her family on a platform behind her, opposite the most illustrious guests. Two full choirs, under the direction of Marco da Gagliano, filled the nave with music as the bride, in a white dress densely embroidered with gold, and encrusted with the incredible jewels of her dowry, was escorted to the Papal Legate by two monsignors. At this solemn moment, her uncle, also in white and gold, with several enormous diamonds in his plumed cap, stepped in to play the part of the absent King, bearing the marriage contract and the Papal Letter and Bull as symbols of his authority. Ferdinando proudly placed on Maria's finger the enormous ring that the groom had sent with the Duke de Bellegarde, and received the marriage blessing in Henri's place.

The groom could be dispensed with, but without a feast the wedding would have been incomplete. The allegorical banquet, held in the Salone dei Cinquecento of the Palazzo Vecchio, was the summit of the spectacles that had hitherto taken place. From its completion in 1511, this enormous hall, which dominates the *piano nobile* of the palazzo, became the central hub of Florentine power. When Cosimo I raised Tuscany into a grand duchy, both the scale and the décor of the room were amplified to assert that the name "Medici" be thenceforth synonymous with, and inseparable from, the Tuscan state. Under Vasari's supervision, its ceiling was heightened by more than twenty-six feet and its expansive walls covered with more than forty paintings recounting Cosimo's conquests of the Tuscan territories and the glorious history of the Medici family. The four largest canvases, on the northern and southern walls, commemorate Cosimo's elevation, while Ferdinando is lauded on the eastern and western sides. While the guests assembled to partake in the living theater of Maria's historic wedding banquet, every angle of the room offered a reminder of the illustrious events that made this moment possible.

Officially, Don Giovanni de' Medici was in charge of the banquet decorations, but the exuberant grottoes and mechanical inventions that greeted the guests that evening revealed the touch of Bernardo Buontalenti, who had masterminded previous Medici spectacles, from Cosimo I's funeral to Ferdinando's wedding. He was a true Renaissance man who, indeed, lived up to the promise of his name. In addition to the Teatro Mediceo, his numerous architectural projects included the designs of the Baldacchino of San Lorenzo, the Tribune of the Uffizi, the villa of Pratolino, and much of the Boboli Garden. He designed sets and costumes for theatrical spectacles, but had also engineered cannon and other military items for the Duke of Alba. In Florence, he was called Bernardo delle Girandelle for the extraordinary fireworks that he invented. The witnesses to Maria's wedding feast attest that he did not disappoint.

At the southern end of the room, a credenza, shaped like an enormous fleur-de-lis, spanned the generous breadth between the two windows and stretched nearly thirty *braccia* (arm lengths) high (close to 70 feet). Much of it was formed in *pietre dure,* semiprecious stones, such as agate, chalcedony, jasper, and lapis lazuli as well as pieces of colorful marble that were polished and cut into intricate mosaics at the workshop Ferdinando had founded in 1588. An enormous *baldacchino,* an honorific canopy of state, soaring almost to the ceiling, emphasized this display of the rarest objects in the Duke's extraordinary collections. Such overt exhibitions of wealth typically included massive silver and gold platters, Chinese porcelain, rock crystal, and shell cups in jewel-studded mounts—the stranger and more exotic, the better. Ferdinando's holdings offered many such wonders to choose from. Cosimo had amassed four hundred pieces of costly Chinese porcelain, revered for

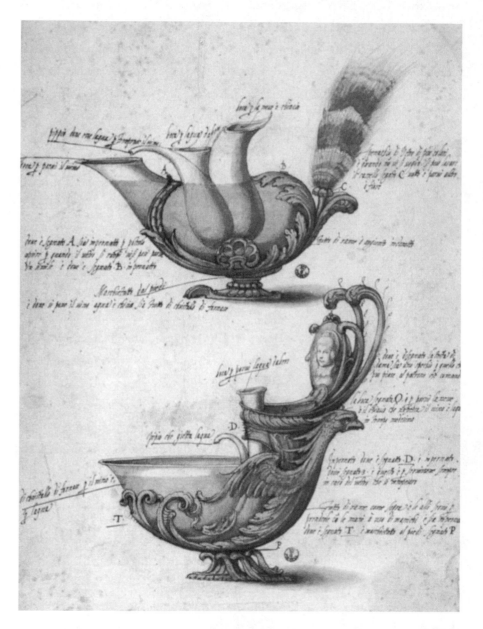

FIGURE 4.7
Vase designs for the wedding of Maria de' Medici, 1599, by Jacopo Ligozzi, watercolor and ink on paper.

its impermeable white body, the secret formula for which Europeans had failed to discover. But Maria's father, known as "Francesco of the Laboratory" had made Florence into a center for producing other staggeringly innovative objects. He had founded a glassworks manufacture in 1566, under the direction of an escaped Venetian glassblower, that replicated Murano *cristallo*. Even more magically, Francesco's Medici Porcelain Manufacture, under Buontalenti's direction,

came close to reproducing the ethereal translucence of true porcelain. Made from white clay from Vicenza, mixed with powdered rock crystal, white sand, calcined lead, and tin, and fired to a temperature of 1100° C, a single piece of blue-and-white Medici porcelain, even when its shape slightly melted in the kiln, was a precious gift for royalty. A credenza crammed full of such marvels announced that Florence was not just imitating the height of aristocratic splendor, it was setting a new standard.

The center of the room was dominated by two fantastic grottoes, sprouting an abundance of trees and foliage. Silvered statuary—*Apollo and Mnemosine* and *Hymen and Lucinda*—stood at either side of these, along with six gilded statues of the virtues raised on pedestals. Each base was decorated with an episode from classical mythology illustrating its virtue in bas-relief. In spite of Henri's absence, the Florentines made him symbolically present by choosing male examples to personify each of these. Buontalenti was a theater designer quite experienced in the art of illusion. Vincenzo de' Rossi's marble statues of the labors of Hercules reinforced the image of Henri as the Greek hero reborn as a French king.

The focal point of the entire scheme was the Queen's Table, placed at the northern end of the room in a great niche bordered by gilded pilasters that supported an enormous canopy opposite the towering credenza. The table's crisp, white linen cloth from Rheims provided a snowy background for a miniature replica of a winter hunt scene, which densely covered its surface. Confectionery trees and shrubbery, bulls, horses, rabbits, deer, and even a rhinoceros and an elephant, scurried from hunters. The sides of the table had been studded with jewels, and the dinner napkins folded into astounding shapes.

In addition, Giambologna had been commissioned to create classically inspired sugar sculptures in the Hercules theme. Although Christopher Columbus had expanded the sugar supply by introducing cane plants to the Caribbean in 1493, it was still a precious commodity, stored in locked silver boxes, and for courtly banquets, an artistic medium that warranted handling by the most gifted talents. On this occasion, however, unbeknownst to the Grand Duke, Giambologna had his talented assistant Pietro Tacca execute these ephemeral masterpieces, many of which were subsequently cast in bronze; editions of *Nessus and Deianira,* first seen in sugar at Maria's feast, are now in the collections of the Louvre, the Frick, and the Hermitage.

Candles and torches in silver-and-gilt candelabra burned throughout the room, their light reflecting off jewels, mirrors, and glistening sugar. Other torches were hidden to cast the credenza, the grottoes, and especially the Queen's Table into theatrical relief, as on the set of a grandiose opera, an artistic form invented in Florence only three years before Maria's wedding. The banquet was a living drama, a self-conscious performance to solemnize the irrevocable union between bride and groom, between two families, and between two political states, whose diva, the Queen, always held center stage. The entire feast was designed to be experienced from her perspective: the arrangement of the décor, the serving of the meal, and the entertainment; and yet it was she who was the primary object on display.

She sat facing the crowd with the Duchess of Mantua, the Grand Duchess, and the Duchess of Bracciano to her right, and the Papal Legate, the Grand Duke, and ten-year-old Prince Cosimo to her left. Two large oil paintings by Jacopo da Em-

FIGURE 4.8
Flask with the arms of Philip II of Spain, ca. 1581, produced by the Medici Porcelain Manufacture, soft-paste porcelain and silver.

poli—one, a re-creation of Catherine's wedding; the other, Maria's envisioned in advance—framed the table to remind the guests that they were watching history in the making. Every guest in the room, whether seated at one of the tables staffed by twenty-five teams of servants (each led by a captain and wearing a different color) or merely standing in the gallery, was called upon to be a witness. The spectacle of watching Maria dine with the privileges and honors of a queen made the transformation of her status a reality. Henri sat in effigy before her, cast in an enormous equestrian statue of sugar. (Maria later commissioned Tacca to produce the full-scale bronze version that was to stand at the Pont Neuf from the time of her

FIGURE 4.9 (a)

regency until the French Revolution.) Maria's marriage to a man she had never met was made real and legitimate in the eyes of the world by this public feast. Yet, at every turn the festivities, determined wholly by her uncle and his retinue, simultaneously underlined his magnificence as the Grand Duke.

As the ladies took their seats, the figure of a recumbent lion, placed in front of Maria, rose suddenly on two paws to reveal a large fleur-de-lis on his breast and two eagles on his side. Buontalenti's awe-inspiring mechanical wonder, as noted in the official memoirs of the event, paid homage to an effect Leonardo da Vinci had created on behalf of Florence as a gift for François I.

The royal meal began with a selection of thirty cold dishes carried by the servants from the credenza, where they had been on display. These ranged from standard fare—salads assembled in basins, halved plums, beans, and stuffed *tortigliogni*—to delicacies like fig-stuffed jellies and a variety of stewed game birds. Theatrical rarities that matched the baroque superfluity of the décor were favored overall. Tradition was honored with peacocks served in their plumage, pastry fortresses stuffed with game birds, and liver-filled tarts in the form of unicorns. The New World delicacy, turkey, was presented in pastry cases shaped like hydras, alongside other tarts in the manner of cranes, boars, and dragons. Slices of prosciutto were formed into roosters crowing before castles of salami. Lamprey were flooded with cream sauce, and needlefish in Spanish bread were garnished with coats-of-arms and figural designs. Since the majority of those present merely watched the proceedings, the menu emphasized visual appeal.

FIGURE 4.9
(a) & (b) *The Manner of Serving a Grand Banquet,* 1570, engraving from Bartolomeo Scappi, *Opera.*

The first hot service from the kitchen comprised a modest eighteen dishes. Roasted game birds were featured—ortolans, quails, pigeons, turkeys, and pheasants—as well as stewed boneless capons covered with ravioli. Warm tarts, pastas, and sliced blancmange accompanied these, along with spicy veal breasts stuffed *alla moresca,* for an exotic touch, and rabbit painstakingly larded *alla francese,* as a tribute to Henri.

Entertainment, during both this and the subsequent course of further roasts and pies, came in the form of flamboyant carving and service, a skill for which the Italians were renowned. Nineteen years earlier, Vincenzo Cervio, carver to Cardinal Farnese, published *Il trinciante* (The Carver). Cervio explained that although German and French royalty often employed carvers of noble birth, these men merely inserted the carving fork into a plated bird or a piece of meat. By contrast, Italian carvers, ideally of good family, but sometimes, like Cervio himself, of humble origin, performed with the bravura of Caranus's naked fire-breathing acrobats. In the full presence of host and guests, the carver skewered birds, entire

81

roasts, or even fruits, on forks wielded high into the air and then, with a knife held aloft in the opposite hand, sliced with swift precision so that the pieces fell elegantly onto the plate. Some of the more daredevil Roman carvers would tackle three or four birds in one go, a fashion that Cervio denounced. However, he practiced the trick of carving with two knives held in one hand, while the other steadied the uplifted fork. The ideal carver was as handsome and graceful as his hand was steady. His tools, often bearing jewel-studded or ivory-inlaid handles, were equally elegant.

Cervio grudgingly acknowledged that in the hierarchy of table service the *scalco* (steward) and the *coppiero* (cupbearer) performed duties of prestige and importance equal to that of the carver. As a tribute to the Queen's royal status, the Duke of Bracciano held the honor of serving her, while her uncle, Don Giovanni de' Medici, acted as the cupbearer. Everyone present at this wedding banquet, from the lowliest kitchen scullion to Maria, the Grand Duke, and the foreign guests, was called upon to execute a prescribed role with seemingly effortless grace. Instructional manuals, made newly possible by the intertwined phenomena of an exploding publishing industry and increased literacy, offered advice for cooks and guests alike. The giant among culinary texts, both in sheer size and in importance, was Bartolomeo Scappi's *Opera dell'arte del cucinare,* published in 1570. Scappi, who was Pope Pius V's "private chef," included more than a thousand recipes in his text, along with numerous banquet descriptions; exhaustive diagrams of equipment, from spit roasters to pasta cutters; and instruction on the proper arrangement of kitchens and the correct manner to serve a meal. Stefano Guazzo's *La civil conversazione* of 1575, the standard etiquette, was soon to be replaced by Ottaviano Rabasco's *Il convito overo* of 1615. Rabasco's text advises hosts to organize their banquets suitably in advance, so that when guests arrive, they may seem relaxed, welcoming, and attentive. For their part, guests are to appear engaged and complimentary, without, if possible, betraying any urge to get away.

The success of any dinner depends as much upon interaction between hosts and guests as on its menu. However, the pressure at a wedding banquet for two newly linked families to overlook differences in taste and tradition exceeds that of

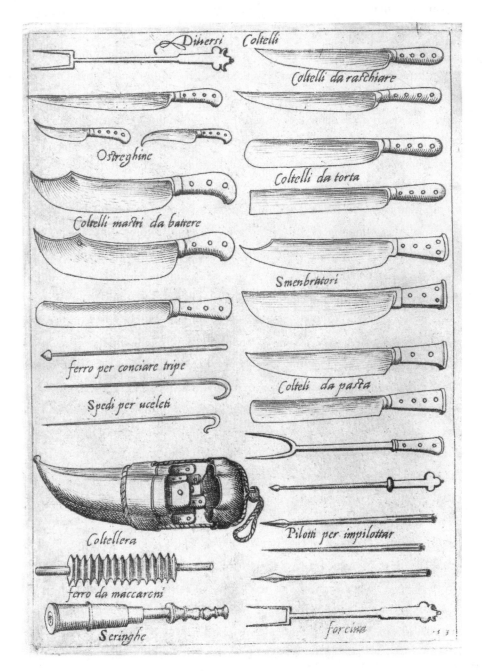

Diuersi   Coltelli

Coltelli da raschiare

Ostreghine

Coltelli da torta

Coltelli maestri da batrere

Smenbratori

ferro per conciare tripe

Coltelli da pasta

Spedi per uceleti

Coltellera

Pilotti per impilottar

ferro da maccaroni

Seringhe   forcina

FIGURE 4.10
Types of Knives, 1570, en-
graving from Bartolomeo
Scappi, *Opera*.

a casual evening among friends. The bride, more than anyone else present, bears the stress of unifying the divergent personalities brought together in her honor. Maria's wedding was no exception. Although given no voice in choosing the decorations, the menu, or even her mate, as the banquet's honoree and, by the prestige of her marriage, the highest-ranking person in the room, she had to lead the way. It was her job to impress the French and the Papal Legate in order to bring honor to her family, who had engineered her elevation.

She must have been relieved when, after the third course of truffle tartlets, fritters, and cakes and pastries decorated with the arms of the King and Queen, the torches that had been focused upon her throughout the banquet finally dimmed. A tremendous rumbling of drums brought the room to attention, and all eyes turned toward the grottoes. As if by magic, torches blazed to light Buontalenti's fanciful pastoral creations. Trees, plants, and statues disappeared by means of hidden mechanisms. Billowing clouds suddenly appeared over both grottoes, from which bejeweled chariots gently descended. One, drawn by peacocks majestically fanning their feathers, carried Vittoria Archilei, the most famous Roman singer of the era, dressed as Juno, queen of the sky. She held her scepter aloft for all to see. The second, pulled forward by a unicorn, held another cantatrice, dressed as Minerva, with helmet, armor, and shield. Juno, protector of marriage and childbirth, the powerful consort to Jupiter, and Minerva, Jupiter's daughter, goddess of wisdom, warrior for peace, and champion of the arts, both serenaded Maria, each asserting the supremacy of her own virtues. The singers alternated their melodious blessing of the French queen with music by Emilio de' Cavalieri, who had created a sensation with *La Pellegrina* at Ferdinando's wedding, and a text by Giovanni Battista Guarini, famous for his 1590 *Pastor fido.* The mock competition that was the theme of the entertainment was resolved when a colorful rainbow rose up between the two singers and over the new Queen of France as a symbol of unity. All who watched hoped that Maria would bring both wisdom and fertility to France and that this marriage would initiate a time of peace.

As the singing goddesses ascended back into the heavens, the lights were restored, along with Maria's place within them. The *frutta* was served as a digestive end-course. It included not only jellied quinces and both fresh and candied fruits but also olives, fish in wine, eggs, and artichokes. These light refreshments allowed banqueters a respite from the almost suffocating opulence that had been heaped upon their senses. The banquet was approaching its natural conclusion. These delicacies graduated the descent from the enveloping magic of the jewel-encrusted hall to the mundane reality of everyday life that awaited outside.

Yet, fantasy needed a grand finale. To the stupefaction of the spectators who clamored for glimpses of the Queen, her table began to rotate. In its first revolution, the surface was transformed into a plane of decorated mirrors. The audience feasted their eyes on the sight of Maria, surrounded by her reflection, suspended between the painting of Catherine's nuptials on one side, and her own wedding on the other. Maria, who had begun the day as a Medici, was now the Queen of France for all to behold.

In an instant, the table revolved again, the mirror replaced by a delicate miniature garden, complete with scampering animals and songbirds. Transfixed, witnesses craned their necks in the gallery as they nibbled on tidbits from buffets. The thrilling surprise of Buontalenti's mechanical table produced a final surge of adrenaline. Then, when the flash of excitement passed, the guests were gently released from the banquet with the lingering image of this restful, pastoral scene.

The festivities continued for several more days, as Florence prepared to send Maria to France. The day after the wedding, *Euridice,* the first surviving European opera, premiered in the Sala Bianca of the Palazzo Pitti before select members of Ferdinando's entourage. Written by Jacopo Peri and Ottavio Rinuccini, who had invented opera three years earlier, the story adapted classical mythology to allow Orpheus and Eurydice to live happily ever after, an ending deemed more auspicious than the original for this occasion. The next day, Riccardo Romolo, patriarch of the wealthy Riccardi family, invited the wedding entourage for a tournament and festive ball, followed by a tour of the collections at his Villa da Valfonda. As a final send-off for the bride, the revolutionary opera *Il rapimento di Cefalo* was performed in Buontalenti's Teatro Mediceo. Although the work was ostensibly written by Gabriello Chiabrera, with music by Giulio Chiabrera, the entire artistic community of Florence, and even Francesco's illustrious guest Niccolò Molino, contributed to the creation of this dazzling spectacle. However, the real opera was Maria's marriage, a mythological fiction as artificially scripted as the rewritten ending of *Euridice*. The sets, costumes, and choreography of Maria's wedding very probably exceeded anything ever produced for the theater; the role she was henceforth to play most certainly did.

On 13 October, Maria began the journey to her new home. An astonishing ship, seventy feet long, encrusted in gilding and precious inlays of diamonds and gems, carried the bride from Livorno to Marseilles. Six further galleys from the Grand Duke and five from the Pope carried her extensive entourage of family members and servants. Despite the opulence, the journey was long and uncomfortable as they weathered stormy seas. The captain suggested they turn back; but Maria insisted they press on.

At last, on 3 November, Maria safely landed in Marseilles. As King of France, Henri ensured that Maria's official arrival in France would be as regal as her departure from Florence. A huge retinue of dukes, cardinals, and princes had been dispatched to greet her. Banquets to rival those of Florence, official tours, and glittering receptions welcomed the new Queen. Crowds lined the streets, applauding and tossing flowers at her carriage. Henri, however, stayed away.

Maria reached Lyon on 3 December, nearly two months after her wedding. Although Henri had asked to be informed when his bride approached the city, somehow her arrival preceded his; she received the regal welcome, the Te Deum, and the nuptial rejoicing alone. Later that afternoon, the King's messenger announced to Maria that her husband would arrive on the morrow. As she took her supper in the semiprivacy of her rooms to rest before the long-awaited meeting, there was a sudden straightening of the guards as a man casually entered the room in military undress. Maria's chancellor whisperingly identified him as the King. Henri had tried to steal an undetected glimpse of his bride. Offended by this disrespect, Maria regally pretended not to notice, so he slunk away as wordlessly as he entered. When Henri knocked loudly on her door that night, she received him with perfect equanimity. A new ceremony was staged on 18 December 1600, again conducted by Cardinal Aldobrandini, at which the groom was finally present, and another round of banqueting and celebrations followed. But as soon as he could, Henri hurried to Paris to rejoin Henriette, leaving his bride to make her way alone. When Maria finally reached the capital, there was no royal welcome, no great banquet, or ceremony, or fireworks to greet her; the household had even forgotten to prepare her rooms in the Louvre.

As sometimes happens, the marriage was as wretchedly unhappy as the wedding banquet had been magnificent. Maria's husband shamelessly paraded his mistress before her or, at best, simply ignored her. However, the nuptial festivities in Florence had made Maria Queen of France. Out of a premonition, on 13 May 1610, the Queen had herself ceremonially crowned at Saint-Denis. One day later Henri was assassinated. Having waited so patiently and played her role so uncomplainingly, Maria clenched the power of her regency tightly, as had her cousin Catherine before her. Three years after reaching his majority, Louis XIII (r. 1610–1643) had to exile his mother in order to rule on his own. To reestablish her reputation, Maria commissioned Peter Paul Rubens to reinvent the fiction of her wedding in the enormous propagandistic series of paintings known as the Maria de' Medici cycle (color plate VI), now at the Louvre. The glittering gown, the jewels, Minerva, and the promise of the rainbow first seen at her wedding banquet reappeared in the paintings, as Maria, depicted as the goddess Juno, meets her Jupiter. In the end, the illusory spectacle of the groomless wedding feast, not the marriage, defined reality.

Chapter Five

Taking Office

THE CORONATION
OF CHARLES I, LONDON,
2 FEBRUARY 1626

Not all the water in the rough rude sea
Can wash the balm from an anointed king . . .

Shakespeare, *Richard II,* act 3, scene 2

ON 25 MARCH 1625, JAMES I, KING OF
England (r. 1603–1625), and VI of Scotland (r. 1567–1625) died; his son, Charles
Stuart (r. 1625–1649), was proclaimed King of England, Scotland, and Ireland
amidst trumpeting fanfare and rolling drums: God save the King! To celebrate this
announcement, the Crown distributed luxuriant edibles throughout the realm;
Worcester, for example, received claret and sack, figs, sugar, cakes, and other costly
delicacies. Though popular goodwill was purchased, genuine optimism greeted
the occasion.

No English monarch has ever believed more sincerely in the Divine Right of
Kings than Charles I; he assumed his new position with the utmost solemnity. Yet,
in spite of his auspicious ascension, no English sovereign's government has ever
gone more violently astray than that of poor Charles, who was forced into flight

by the members of his Parliament, was the catalyst of a bloody civil war, and was eventually tried and beheaded.

How could he go so far wrong? The story surrounding the events of the English Civil War and the precipitous power struggle between King and Parliament is complex. Charles, however, committed a grave and singular error in failing to garner the favor of his people. His mistake was glaringly evident from the start.

Since William the Conqueror's Coronation on Christmas Day 1066, English monarchs have traditionally been crowned at Westminster Abbey. After the conqueror's son William Rufus (r. 1087–1100) erected the expansive walls of the Great Hall of Westminster Palace, this secular room became the site of the ritual dinner that followed the ecclesiastical ceremony. The two events were symbiotically linked together by the majestic procession that led from one space into the other and back again. They were, in fact, two aspects, one sacred, one worldly, of the same ceremony whereby a new and exalted status was granted to the honoree both in God's eyes and in those of the people. A fifteenth-century manuscript illumination depicts the Coronation of Henry I (r. 1100–1135) with the Crowning and the Feast as dual images within the same frame.

On 2 February 1626, Charles became the sacredly anointed King of England. But, while God may have recognized him as such, Charles neglected the ritual of his people, most notably, that of the Coronation Feast that had traditionally been held in Westminster Hall since that room was built.

In truth, the King's decision to forgo this ancient rite stemmed from his anxiety, as a fervently devout High Anglican, to conclude the Christian ceremony of Coronation as quickly as possible. He sacrificed the secular, almost pagan, celebration of the Feast in order to see this happen. Although Charles had inherited the crown de facto at the time of his father's death, until the sacrament of Coronation transpired, kingship was merely a job and not a divinely sanctioned state of being. The rituals of Crowning and Anointing, which were performed in the Old Testament to legitimize kings such as Saul and David, mystically transformed the person upon whom they were enacted into a holy appointee of God. The ceremony of Anointing a king resembles that performed for a bishop. Charles might not have been inherently against the tradition of the Coronation Feast, but his genuinely religious bent overlooked the banquet's value as a ceremony of equal importance.

When James I died, Charles was too preoccupied with other matters to arrange for the Coronation. Foreign policy was dicey; Charles's brother-in-law, Frederick V, Elector of Palatine (r. 1610–1620, King of Bohemia 1619–1620), had dragged him into what would come to be known as the Thirty Years' War. Funds were lacking, and the military sorely unprepared. However, domestic matters within Charles's household weighed most heavily upon the King. On 7 May 1625, he staged for his late father the most ornate funeral that England had ever seen. A day earlier, he had married fourteen-year-old Henrietta Maria, sister of Louis XIII, by proxy. A second wedding was staged at Canterbury Cathedral one month later. Then, most distressingly, after a hot, dry summer the plague broke out in London. The pestilence was so serious that Parliament had to be temporarily relocated to Oxford. When Charles returned to London with his new bride, the triumphant procession planned for her welcome had to be canceled owing to the threat of disease.

Fall slipped into winter; the numbers of the sick and dying began to abate, but Christmas came and went without a Coronation. The King declared two national days of thanksgiving, 29 January and 19 February, to celebrate the passing of the plague. Finally, on 1 January 1626, he issued a "Notice of the Committee of Bishops," to announce his appointments to the honorable task of planning the manner of the Coronation Service. William Laud (1573–1645), Bishop of Saint David's, Scotland, was chief among them.

The ceremony used to crown an English monarch changed little through the centuries. Its essential features had been codified by at least 973, with the Crowning of King Edgar (r. 959–975) at Bath, when Westminster Abbey was still only a small monastery on the "Isle of Thorns." The ritual grew more complex, but from Henry IV (r. 1399–1413) to Elizabeth I (r. 1558–1603) it followed the *Liber Regalis,* a fourteenth-century manuscript setting out the Order of Service, probably for the 1382 Coronation of Anne of Bohemia (1366–1394), the wife of Richard II (r. 1377–1399). The 1603 service anointing James I was performed in English, as all subse-

quent Coronations have been, but it merely translated the Latin of the old ceremony. There was no reason, Charles thought, why the ceremony could not be organized and performed posthaste.

On 17 January 1626 Charles issued a proclamation "to declare His Maiesties
pleasure touching His Royall Coronation, and the Solemnitie thereof":

> Whereas Wee have resolved, by the favour and blessing of GOD, to celebrate
> the Solemnitie of Our Owne Royall Coronation, together also with the Coro-
> nation of Our most dearely beloved Consort the Queene, upon the second
> day of February next, being Candlemas day, at our Palace of Westminster: . . .

Charles commanded that his beloved subjects meet him at Westminster Palace
on the afternoons of 26, 27, and 28 January to plan the proceedings of the Coronation. Normally, the duties of the Lord Great Chamberlain, who continues to control Westminster Hall to this day, included the preparation of the Palace for the
Feast. So too, the other appointees must have expected to render the time-honored
services of the banquet as well as the religious ceremony. Certainly, William, Earl
of Pembroke, appointed by Charles to this prestigious office, had other distinguished responsibilities to fulfill. In the procession from the Palace to the Abbey,
he carried Saint Edmund's Crown, marching directly in front of the Archbishop of
Canterbury and the King; it was Pembroke who later disrobed his Sovereign for
the sacred ritual of the Anointing.

Charles gave little indication that events would not proceed as usual, although
he did postpone the Procession from the Tower of London to Westminster Palace,
traditionally held on the eve of the Coronation. In the same proclamation, Charles
announced:

> We have thought fit by reason that the late great and grievous Infection of the
> Plague in Our Sayd Citie, hath for the most part left the same unfurnished,
> both of Materials, and of able and experienced workemen, which are necessar-
> ily to bee imployed in an Action of so great State, as is Our proceeding from

By the King.

¶ A Proclamation to declare His Maiesties pleasure
touching His Royall Coronation, and the
Solemnitie thereof.

Hereas Wee haue resolued, by the fauour and blessing of G O D, to celebrate the Solemnitie of Our owne Royall Coronation, together also with the Coronation of Our most dearely beloued Consort the Queene, vpon the second day of Februarie next, being Candlemas day, at our Palace of Westminster: And soralmuch as by the ancient Customes and Usages of this Realme, as also in regard of diuers Tenures of sundry Manors, Lands, & other Hereditaments, many of Our louing Subiects doe claime, and are bound to doe and performe diuers seuerall Seruices on the said day, and at the time of Our Coronation, as in times precedent their Ancestors, and those from whom they claime, haue done and performed at the Coronations of Our famous Progenitors and Predecessors, Kings and Queenes of this Realme: We therefore, out of Our Princely care for the preseruation of the lawfull Rights and Inheritances of Our louing Subiects whom it may concerne, haue thought fit to giue notice of, and publish Our Resolution herein, and doe hereby giue notice of, and publish the same accordingly.

And Wee doe hereby further signifie, That by Our Commission vnder Our great Seale of ENGLAND, We shall appoint and authorize Our right trustie and right welbeloued Counsellors, Sir Thomas Couentrie Knight, Lord Keeper of Our great Seale of England, and Iames Lord Ley, Our high Treasurer of England, Our right trustie and right welbeloued Cousins and Counsellors, Edward Earle of Worcester, Keeper of Our priuie Seale, Thomas Earle of Arundell and Surrey, Earle Marshall of England, and William Earle of Pembrooke, Lord Chamberlaine of Our Household, Our right trustie and right welbeloued Cousin, Edward Earle of Dorset, and Our trustie and

FIGURE 5.1

Charles I, King of England, *A Proclamation to declare His Maiesties pleasure touching His Royall Coronation, and the Solemnitie thereof,* 1625 (i.e., 1626).

Our Tower of London through Our said Cities to put offe and deferre Our said proceeding, untill the first day of May next . . .

The stately Coronation Procession dated from no later than the 1377 Crowning of ten-year-old Richard II. Triumphal arches, allegorical figures, and even a specially erected mock castle had greeted him along the way. Each of the castle's four turrets held a maiden of the King's age, who sprinkled gilded leaves and imitation florins. He stopped so they might proffer him wine in a golden cup, whereupon a gilded angel bent down to offer him a crown. Subsequent monarchs aspired to exceed, or at least equal, the splendor of Richard's three-hour parade through the streets of London. While Charles, in deference to his citizens, would eventually enact the Procession, the delay, which rendered the event an afterthought, could hardly have pleased his subjects. His decision to postpone the parade appears predicated on a shortage of workmen rather than fears for the safety of public health. Similar concerns may have influenced his cancellation of the Feast, but he made no note of this. Indeed, the bishops at work preparing his Coronation Book, assumed it would take place.

In the end, the bishops were forced to contend with quite a number of surprising irregularities. The first of these they had known about since Charles had placed Bishop Laud on the committee organizing the ceremony. Charles substituted Laud for the Dean of Westminster, who by ancient custom instructed the Monarch on matters of the Coronation, prepared the Sanctuary, and assisted in the Anointing. To this day, in return for these services, the Dean is entitled to everything brought into the church for the occasion: bells, thrones, carpets, as well as "an hundred manchets [loaves], the third part of a tun of Wine, and Fish . . . for the Dean and Chapter's Repast on the Coronation Day." Laud filled this time-honored role for no reason other than that the standing Dean, Dr. John Williams, Bishop of Lincoln, was out of favor, and Laud, through his friendship with the King's sycophantic advisor, the popularly hated George Villiers (1592–1628), First Duke of Buckingham, was preferred by the King. This blatant favoritism hinted at difficulties that would arise when Laud, appointed Bishop of London in 1628, became one of the King's closest advisors. At the time of the Coronation, however, Charles's alteration of royal and ecclesiastical precedent was swallowed because the Dean submitted a formal relinquishment of his duties.

What the Bishops did not count on was that Charles's arrogant wife would refuse the King's desire that she be anointed and crowned by a Protestant bishop at his Coronation. Encouraged by her French attendants, the adolescent Queen declined to have anything whatsoever to do with the Anglican ceremony, or even to attend. Certainly, Henrietta Maria's very public absence on this important occasion may have caused Charles to waver on the great banquet. Exasperated, that summer he would send her attendants back across the Channel, in defiance of their marriage contract. Three years later the couple's relationship blossomed into deeply devoted love. Charles forgave, but others never forgot, that the willful, popish Queen had sneered at the Anglican Coronation.

The King's ill luck persisted. During the cleaning of the ceremonial Regalia, one of the wings of the Rod with the Dove, symbolizing virtue and equity, broke off. Charles demanded that the original be repaired. Adamant in his belief that the Coronation was divine, he feared that any deviation from sacred tradition might nullify his appointment by God. Secretly, a new wing was substituted without the King's knowledge. Later, people remarked that his intuition had proven trustworthy, but, at the time, everyone was grateful that the deception calmed his raging temper.

Since the Coronation Procession was not to occur, Charles broke further from precedent and chose instead to stay in his habitual quarters at Whitehall, rather than in Westminster Palace, on the eve of the ceremony. For his part, Laud did not neglect his duties as acting Dean of Westminster. He entreated the Monarch to spend some time in contemplation and delivered the customary red silk shirt, with holes strategically slit to facilitate the Anointing.

On the appointed morning, the peers of England, the newly created Knights of Bath, nobles, and ecclesiastics began to assemble inside Westminster Hall for the procession that would lead from the Palace to the Church. The events leading up to the service seemed indistinguishable from those of any prior Coronation. A reassuring sense of the unchanging stability and continuum of the English monarchy was imparted by the ancient architecture. King William II had erected the original walls of Westminster Hall, 290 feet long and 68 feet wide. (The Hall is one of the largest rooms of its type ever built.) At the end of the fourteenth century, Richard II had had his mason-architect Henry Yevele replace the original roof, held up by two rows of pillars, with a soaring wooden hammer-beam version, designed by Hugh Herland, to span the vast space without any supports. The focal point remains the west wall, dominated by a spectacular gothic stained-glass window, illuminating the Great Seal of England surrounded by rows of crests and heraldic devices rendered in jewel-like vermilion, blue, and yellow against a background of clear glass. As if in preparation for the feast, the King's Table and Chair of State stood on a platform, ominously called a scaffold.

The King came by water from Whitehall, intending to land at the steps of Sir Robert Cotton, who held a copy of the Gospels purported to have belonged to King Athelstan (r. 925–939), and upon which "for divers hundred yeares together the King of England had solemnlie taken ther coronation oath." The barge, however, "bawked those stepps," and it was only with the aid of neighboring boats that Charles managed to land at all. In spite of these difficulties, John Bradshaw, Windsor Herald, recorded that the King arrived at Westminster at approximately nine o'clock.

Once dressed in his Robes of State, Charles mounted the scaffold and took his prescribed place. Then, in solemn procession, the Archbishop of Canterbury, with Laud and other bishops, followed by church officers, and the Westminster choristers, reverently brought the ancient Regalia to the King, who handed them in turn to the Duke of Buckingham, who placed them on the table.

The spectacle of Buckingham threatened to overshadow this dignified rite. Members of the noble retinue were unnerved as they watched this opportunist, who had risen from ignominious beginnings to become one of James's indulged favorites, handling the Royal Regalia. How could sober, modest Charles be taken in by this rascal as his father had? No one hinted that there was any romantic connection between them, as people had with James, but they were not happy to see him at the King's side on this sacred occasion. The players in this grand pantomime, nevertheless, remained deferential toward their Sovereign. Those who had refused the order of knighthood had thereby forfeited their right to attend. This, too, was not spoken about.

There were murmurs, however, about Charles's incredible choice of garment for the day. The King, usually so tasteful and elegant,

> on that day was cloathed in *White,* contrary to the Custom of his Predecessors, who were on that day clad in *Purple.* And this, he did not out of necessity, for any want of Purple Velvet, enough to make a suite, (for he had many yards of it in his outward Garment) but at his choice only, to declare that Virgin Purity with which he came to be espoused unto his Kingdom. . . .

Polite though they might be in the presence of His Majesty, the courtiers disapproved of Charles's decision to introduce new symbolism into the ceremony. The sanctity of Coronation depended upon honoring ancient tradition; innovation had no place. Later, they said he looked like a victim.

At ten o'clock the enormous procession set forth from Westminster Hall to the nearby Abbey, while crowds of spectators lined the Palace Yard to watch. Regally blue cloth marked the route. Marshals cleared the path and were followed by trumpeters to announce the approach of the royal entourage: aldermen, judges, fifty-eight Knights of Bath marching two abreast "in their order," Privy Councillors, Gentlemen of the Chapel and Prebends of Westminster, "all in copes and singing all the way." Heralds marked the approach of the Barons in their Parliament robes "all bareheaded with swords at their side," the Bishops in scarlet gowns, pairs of Viscounts "in their Creation robes of velvet with caps and coronets in their hands," and the Earls, similarly attired. Two Esquires of Honor, representing the dukedoms of Normandy and Guyen, preceded the Regalia itself: the Spurs, the Swords, the Rod, the Crown, and the Orb of Rule, carried by the most distinguished members of the nobility, who were interspersed by other dignitaries, including the Mayor of London with his Mace, and the Lord Great Chamberlain of

England. Finally the Bishop of London, with the Regale (the chalice of sapphire and gold), and Laud, holding the Patima (the cover of the chalice), walked before the King, marching bareheaded under the Royal Canopy carried by the Barons of the Cinque Ports. The Bishops of Durham and Bath walked at his sides, trainbearers and guards following behind. The majestic pageantry of the procession conformed to the custom established at the Crowning of Richard I (r. 1189–1199).

After the royal parade had assembled in the church, George Abbot, Archbishop of Canterbury, presented the bareheaded King to the four sides of the room in the Recognition by the People: the House of Commons seated to the north and south, the nobility and the clergy at the west and east. He asked, "Sirs,

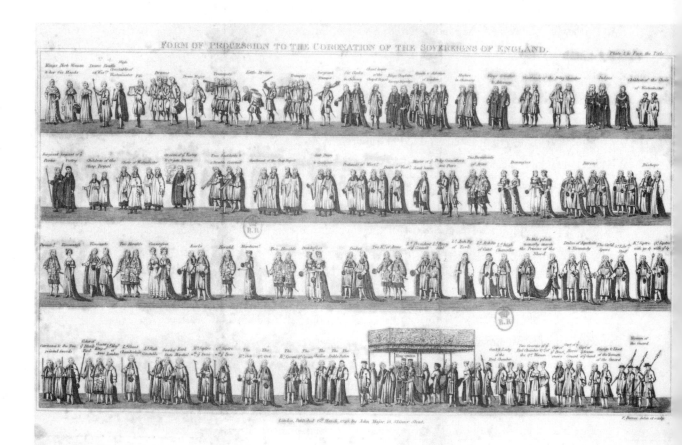

FORM OF PROCESSION TO THE CORONATION OF THE SOVEREIGNS OF ENGLAND.

Here I present unto you King Charles the Rightfull Inheritour of the Crown of this Realme. Wherefore all you, that come this day to doe your homage and service and bounden duty; be ye willing to do the same?" Laud noted that the Archbishop accidentally took Charles north, south, east, and west instead of east, south, west, and north. Worse than that, the question was met with a long, dead silence until Lord Arundel led the witnesses in the requisite reply, "God save King Charles!"

The Constable and the Earl Marshall placed the customary gold bar upon the altar, after which the Bishop of Carlisle preached a sermon intended to inspire. Unfortunately, he chose Revelation 2:10, "Be thou faithful unto death, and I will give thee a crown of life." His text, people later recalled, seemed more appropriate for a funeral than a Coronation.

With the Archbishop prompting, Charles swore the Oath, which bound him to grant and keep the laws and customs of England. When Laud was tried for treason in 1644, he was accused of adding the phrase "to the King's Prerogative" and omitting the phrase "which the People have chosen" to the Oath. Although it was later proved that Charles had sworn exactly the same words as his father, the accusation illustrates how literally the people interpreted the Oath's promise.

Then, like every Christian King in England since the ceremony Offa, King of Mercia, performed for his son, Ecgfrith, in 787, Charles was anointed with the Holy Oil; it was dispensed into the ancient silver Anointing Spoon, used since the Coronation of King John (r. 1199–1216). Laud recorded, however, that Charles chose not to wear the traditional red silk shirt with the slits; the King deemed it unnecessary, since his father, likewise, had declined this awkward costume.

The King retired to Saint Edward's Chapel to put on the sleeveless *Colobium Sindonis,* similar to a bishop's rochet, and the gold-clothed Close Pall (long coat), lined with crimson silk, the ceremonial robes that connoted his appointment. The loathsome Buckingham fulfilled the honor of carrying the Spurs from the altar, after which the Archbishop presented the Sovereign's Sword. Charles was then invested with the Armill, a kind of stole, and the Royal Mantle. The archbishop blessed Saint Edmund's Crown and placed it upon the Monarch's head. The Ring,

FIGURE 5.2

Form of Procession to the Coronation of the Sovereigns of England, 1820, engraving from Richard Thompson, *A Faithful Account of the Processions and Ceremonies of the Kings and Queens of England.*

"the ensign of kingly dignity," was placed on the fourth finger of Charles's right hand, whereupon the Scepter, the Rod of the Kingdoms, the Rod of Virtue, and the Orb of Rule were reverentially blessed and handed to the King. When Charles had received the Regalia, the Dukes, Marquesses, and Earls, who had carried their coronets into the service, placed them upon their own heads.

In the midst of these proceedings the tremor of an earthquake was felt; the service continued, but in this superstitious age, the joyous refrains of the choristers could not drown out a sense of foreboding. Nevertheless, they proceeded.

Charles was escorted to a red-carpeted platform at the high altar and seated on the Coronation Chair, used at nearly every English Coronation since Edward I commissioned it to enclose the sacred Scottish Stone of Scone in 1296 (the stone was returned to Scotland in 1996).

At this juncture, the peers of the realm traditionally knelt down and swore homage to their King. According to the Archbishop of Canterbury, to simplify this process (James had sold so many peerages that they were now quite numerous), the Duke of Buckingham "did swear all the Nobility besides to be Homagers to his Majestie at his Majesties knees. Then as many Earls and Barons as could conveniently stand about on the Throne did lay their hands on the Crown on his Majesties head, protesting to spend their bloods to maintain it to him and his lawful Heirs."

Next came the service of the King's Communion, his offerings to the altar, accompanied by the elegiac singing of the Westminster choristers, and a final round of prayer. After six hours of ceremony, interspersed with anthems and music, no one in Christendom could say that Charles was not the King of England before God.

The Coronation Book prepared by Laud and the committee of bishops ordained that Charles should then retire to disrobe in Saint Edmund's Chapel, setting Saint Edmund's Crown upon the altar, whereupon the Archbishop would place another crown, made for this day, upon Charles's head. When he had changed, the Regalia would be handed back to him: "The King so crowned taking into his hands the Sceptor & ye Rod (after the Traine is set in order before him) goeth from St. Edward's Altar and so up to ye Stage; and so through the midst of ye Quire and the Body of the Church out at ye West dore returneth to the Palace in the same he came."

The recessional to Westminster Hall, symbolically completing the circle as the participants returned transformed, should have been the cue for the celebration of the Feast. After a short rest in the Inner Court of Wards, the new Monarch would sit at his canopied table, wearing his Crown and carrying his Orb and Scepter, as the festivities began.

Beforehand, the Sergeant and Gentlemen of the Ewry and the Officers of the Pantry, answerable to the Lord Great Chamberlain, would have decorated the Hall with tapestries and hangings on its unpainted walls and great buffets stacked with royal plate. An audience would observe from specially erected galleries. Other galleries would hold trumpeters and musicians who offered a regal fanfare, while the peers and lords of England, headed up by the Barons of the Cinque Ports, crowded long rows of tables that afforded a sidelong view of the Monarch. These participants were served their dinner during the King's recess.

The Gentlemen of the Ewry would ceremonially lay the Cloth on the Royal Table; the Officers of the Pantry set the King's Salt. When two Esquires of the Body took their places on small footstools at either side of the Royal Chair, the audience knew the Monarch would soon reappear.

When the newly crowned King was seated and his robes arranged by the pages, with the ancient ceremony of Bringing up the First Course, the meal began. The ritual retained its distinctly medieval character right up until the last time it was performed, at the Coronation Feast for George IV (r. 1820–1830). The Servers approached the Dresser of the Kitchen, whereupon the Sergeant of the Silver Scullery demanded a dish of meat, wiped it from underneath, and tasted it. Three mounted horsemen—the Earl Marshall, the Lord High Steward, and the Lord High Constable—would ride abreast up the length of the Hall. Then, the King's dishes were paraded up to his table to the accompaniment of the State Trumpeters and thunderous applause from the crowd. Gentlemen carried in the numerous hot dishes; then came Pensioners, two by two, the Sewer and his assistant, the Carver,

FIGURE 5.3

A Ground Plott of Westminster Hall shewing the Position and Dimensions of the severall Tables, Seats, etc., 1687, engraving from Francis Sanford, *The History of the Coronation of . . . James II.*

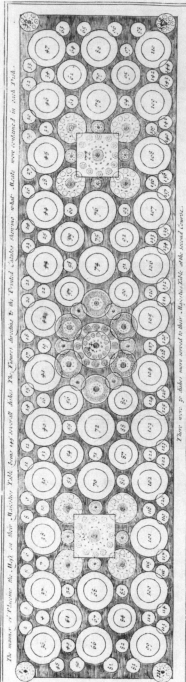

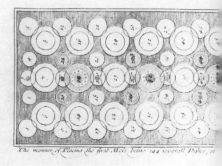

The manner of Placing the first Mess being 144 severall Dishes, at

A Ground Plott of WESTMINSTER HALL,
Cupboards, Galleries &c.

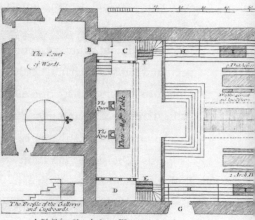

The Profile of the Galleries and Cupboards.

A. The Passage from the Court of Requests into the Court of Wards.
B. The Passage out of the Court of Wards into Westminster Hall.
C. The Box where Prince George and the Princess Anne of Denmark sate. Over which was a Gallery for ye Kings Heralds and Pursts of Arms.
D. A Large Box, and over it a Gallery, in both which sate Ambassadors, Forreign Ministers, and Strangers of Quality.
E. The Kings Cupboard.   F. The Queens Cupboard.

The manner of placing One Mess, being 144 severall Dishes at 6 up

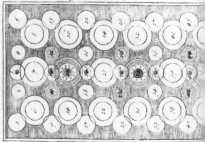

102

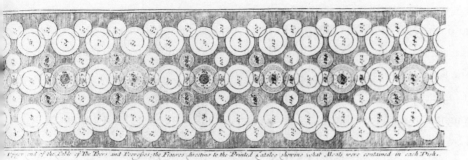

Upper end of the Table of the Peers and Peeresses; the Figures directing to the Printed Catalogue shewing what Meats were contained in each Dish.

shewing the Position and Dimensions of the severall Tables, Seats,

on the day of their Majesties Coronation. 23. Apr. 1685.

A scale of Feet, according to 20 Feet in an Inch.

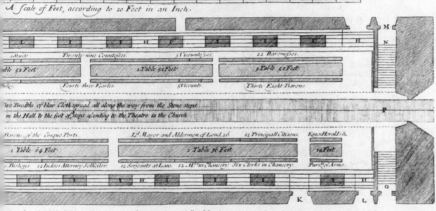

			M
Twenty nine Countesses.	3 Viscountesses.	22 Baronesses.	N
1 Table 52 Feet	2 Table 52 Feet	3 Table 52 Feet	
Fourty three Earles.	3 Viscounts	Thirty Eight Barons	

Two Breadths of blew Cloth spread all along the way from the Stone steps
in the Hall to the foot of Steps ascending to the Theatre in the Church

Barons of the Cinque Ports.	Ld. Mayor and Aldermen of Lond. 26.	12 Principall Citizens	Kings Herald &c.	P
1 Table 64 Feet	2 Table 76 Feet		14 Feet	
Bishops	12 Judges Attorney Solicitor	12 Serieants at Law.	12 Mrs in Chancery Six Clerks in Chancery	Pursu. at Arms.	O

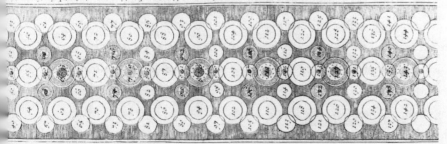

M. The Entrance into the Chequer Court where Sweetmeats &c were deposited

N. The Stone Steps leading up to the Court of Exchequer over which was a
Gallery for Spectators.

O. The Stone Steps leading up to severall Offices belonging to the Exchequer
over which was a Gallery for Spectators.

P. A Portico erected at the Great North dore leading into the New Palace
yard Over which was a Gallery for the Trumpetts and Kettle Drums.

Upper end of the Table of the Bishops, Judges, and Barons of the Cinque Ports: The figures directing to the Printed Catalogue, shewing what meats were contained in each Dish.

the Lord of the Manor of Addington, and two Clerks of the Kitchen at the rear. When, at last, the Clerks reached the Royal Table, they solemnly placed each dish before the King.

Next came the Service of the Ewry, performed by the Lord Great Chamberlain, who brought a large gilded ewer and basin to the Monarch. The Royal Cup-Bearer assisted by pouring water on the Sovereign's head, and the Lord of the Manor of Heydon proffered a towel. The Bishop of London would say Grace before the meal began in earnest. At the end of the course, the Lord of the Manor of Addington presented the "dillegrout," or "mess of potage," a customary dish of gruel offered by the clan for so many generations that its meaning had been forgotten. The Royal Cupbearer then poured the King his first cup of wine, after which others in the room were free to drink.

When the Remains of the First Course were removed as ceremoniously as they had been delivered, the three mounted officers had to back their horses down the length of the Hall in reverse to remain facing His Majesty. (Horace Walpole noted that when Lord Talbot was Lord Stewart to George III [r. 1760–1820], "he piqued himself on backing his horse down the Hall and not turning its rump towards the King, but he had taken such pains to dress it to that duty that it entered backwards; and at its retreat the spectators clapped.")

With dramatic bravura, the King's Champion then charged into the room fully clad in armor on a handsome mount, flanked by the Earl Marshall and the Lord High Constable in their state robes and coronets on either side of him. The Challenge of the Champion was the theatrical high point of the Coronation Feast. The Champion rode through the crowd, while from the other end of the Hall, a Herald proclaimed that the Champion would meet in combat "any person, of what degree soever, high or low, shall deny or gainsay our sovereign lord . . . to be right heir to the imperial crown of this realm . . . or that he ought not to enjoy the same; here is the Champion . . . being ready in person to combat with him." As these loyal words were recited, the Champion dropped a glove in readiness to meet anyone that might dare to decry the lawful King. The Herald then returned the glove to the Champion. The entire procedure was repeated twice more, as the

Champion approached the Monarch, until he stood before the Royal Table. At Elizabeth I's Coronation, Sir Edward Dimmocke acted out this ritual, after which the Queen, enacting her part with equal aplomb, raised up "a cup of gold full of wine, dranke to him thereof, and sent it to him for his fee together with the cover." With a deep bow, the Champion then took his leave. Tradition holds that the cus-

FIGURE 5.4
The Manner of the Champion Performing the Challenge, 1687, engraving from Francis Sanford, *The History of the Coronation of . . . James II.*

tom originated when Sir John Dymoke, Lord of the Manor of Scrivelsby in the reign of Richard II, arrived at the west door of the Abbey after the Coronation had finished and was summarily told to offer his services at the Feast. The coverless cups collected by the generations of Dymokes who fulfilled this service suggest that in the excitement the cover often got left behind.

The performance of the Largess and the Proclamation of the King's Style followed as the three Provincial Kings-at-Arms, wearing their crowns, and trailed by the College of Heralds, went to the lower end of the Hall, bowed, and advanced toward the Royal Table. They repeated their reverence in the places where the Champion had dropped his glove. From the top of the stairs the Garter King-at-Arms cried "Largess" three times. The Monarch recognized this by offering a favor. Then, the Style, or title, of the new Sovereign was proclaimed; at Elizabeth I's Feast they called out three times: "Of the most high and mightye Princesses our dread Sovereigne Lady Elizabeth, by the Grace of God, Queen of England, France, and Irelande, defender of the trewe auncient and Catholic [i.e., Christian] faithe, most worthy Empress from the Orcade Isles to the Mountaynes Pyrenes," first in English, then in French, and finally in Latin. After this honorific pageantry, the Second Course would be served with commensurate solemnity.

From the Coronation of Richard I, feasting the newly created King entailed massive expenditure on food, as much as on pageantry. When Edward I (r. 1272–1307) returned from the Holy Land for his Westminster Coronation, 380 cattle, 430 sheep, 450 pigs, 18 wild boars, 278 flitches of bacon, and nearly 20,000 capons and fowls made their way through the Royal Kitchens and into the Hall for the magnificent dinner. For the Crowning of Henry VI (r. 1422–1461 and 1470–1471), the menu included gilded grouse, the head of a panther crowned with ostrich feathers, and haunches of venison, including one appropriately inscribed "Te Deum laudamus." Paid for by the royal coffers, such free-flowing wine (sometimes, as at Richard II's Feast, an enormous wine fountain was even erected in the Palace Yard) and abundant delicacies, which even the spectators could demolish once the King had eaten his fill, acted as gifts to the attendees. As a rule, it is much harder for one's enemies to speak unkind words if their mouths are full.

Offering and receiving the sustenance of food and drink linked the King and his People. After the Second Course, it was customary for the Lord of the Manor of Nether Bilsington in Kent to present the Monarch with three carved maple cups. The Mayor and Eight Burgesses of the City of Oxford then presented the King with a gilt cup of wine. The King, in turn, would give the maple cups to the Mayor of Oxford, whereupon the Lord of the Manor of Leiston, responsible for producing wafers for the King's Table, offered a dish of them to the Sovereign. Fi-

nally, the Lord Mayor of London, accompanied by twelve Civic Fathers, would approach the King with a gold cup of wine.

The Coronation Feast traditionally concluded with a repetition of the Service of the Ewry and a final blessing. As the Monarch prepared to retire, one of the peers would stand and propose the health of the Sovereign with "three times three," at which everyone in the room rose to his feet for nine rounds of cheers. It was then the turn of the Lord Chancellor to declare, "We drink the health of a subject three times three; we should have drunk that of His Majesty nine times nine," which initiated a new round of toasts. This hearty, enthusiastic finale, no

doubt aided by the glow of the wine, would be capped off when the King, standing, would thank his peers for drinking his health and reciprocate by toasting
them and his people.

Although the words and actions were entirely scripted, repeated from one
monarch to the next with little variation, the scene must have been overwhelming
to witness, particularly in a generation where kingship was powerfully vital. Speaking the ancient words aloud, performing the timeless rituals, sharing in the celebratory consumption of food, which mystically changes form within the human
body to sustain life—the Coronation Feast transformed a man or woman into a
Monarch through human ceremony, just as the sacred service of Coronation
bound the Sovereign to God within the tenets of his faith.

The bishops who prepared Charles's Coronation Book in accordance with the
Liber Regalis expected the Feast would take place. However, it never transpired.
Laud added a margin note near the instructions for the King's procession back to
the Hall: "But because thear was no Dinner: These [the Regalia] were delivered to
ye Bishop of S. Davids [Deputy Dean of Westminster] for solemnitie upon ye
stage of Westminster Hall." The parade circled back to the Palace and into an anti-
climactic void. The site of the ancient feast was used as a dressing room, whereupon the newly crowned King of England, according to the account of John
Bradshaw, Windsor Herald, left off his regal trappings and headed straight back to
Whitehall without any further ado.

Charles, so scrupulous about royal precedent and prerogative, should have
known better; somehow he didn't. Certainly, he should have understood the value
of banqueting as theatrical propaganda, which manifested the political reality of
his reign and cloaked it in laudatory imagery. The banquet played an essential role
in Stuart court life, as it had for the Tudors before them, although in these centuries the term was not synonymous with "feast," but connoted an elegant end-
course, replete with sugary treats, frothy syllabubs, and entertaining diversions. It
was usually held in a separate space with luxurious furnishings and candlelight.
Henry VIII built at Greenwich one of the most sumptuous banqueting houses; its
silk floor coverings were embroidered with gold lilies.

During James I's reign, the riotous Tudor banquet entertainments of jugglers, jesters, and acrobats evolved into the polished theatrical form of the court masque. The playwright Ben Jonson and the architect and designer Inigo Jones set the tone with their extravagant collaborations, performed by actors as well as members of the court. Jones built the stone-clad Banqueting House at Whitehall, which replaced an earlier Elizabethan example, to provide a setting tailored to the needs of these cultivated evenings. Charles performed in his first masque at the age of ten, staged in celebration of his elder brother's Ceremony of Investiture on 5 June 1610.

Charles's reign saw the blossoming of both banquet and masque into mature art forms. He established "the King's Musick," which included recorders, flutes, oboes and sackbuts, viols, and twenty-four "lutes and voices," in addition to trumpets, drums, and pipes. He later commissioned Peter Paul Rubens to paint the interior of Whitehall's Banqueting House in a series of images extolling the virtues of his father's government. However, when these glorious paintings were finally installed, the damaging effects of the torches used at performances were deemed too dangerous, so the space could not be used for its intended purpose. The refinement of the Caroline court became increasingly distended from reality.

In *The Accomplisht Cook* (1660), Robert May nostalgically recalled "the Noblesses Hospitalities did reach to" in Charles's golden age. To re-create that era's "Triumphs and Trophies of Cookery," he instructs readers to make an edible display with a miniature pastry ship, complete with flags, streamers, guns, a cannon, a stag shot with an arrow, and a castle with drawbridges and turrets decorated with gilded bay leaves. Pies colored with saffron and gilt are brought with these to the banquet table. The ladies then pull the arrow out of the stag, which will release claret, hidden in a blown egg, like blood from a wound. A battle ensues; the ship and the castle fire at one another. To lessen the stink of the gunpowder, the ladies toss eggshells filled with sweet water. When the lids are removed from the pies, frogs leap out of one, with the intention to "make the Ladies to skip and sreek"; live birds alight from the other, their motion extinguishing the candles. The effect, May promises, "will cause much delight and pleasure to the whole company."

The festivities of the banquet, as well as its descendant, the masque, drew their inspiration from "sotletes," edible sculptures, sometimes combined with entertainment, presented as the crescendo to a medieval feast, of which the tradition-bound Coronation Feast was a staid holdover. For the 1443 installation of John Stafford as Archbishop of Canterbury, the feast included an eleven-dish "subtletie" representing the bishop with his crosier and radiating golden beams, kneeling before Saint Andrew. The Stuart masque retained the overtly propagandistic symbolism of these misnamed intermezzo-centerpieces, but performed within the cloistered shelter of the court, served only to falsely seduce its insulated participants with flattery.

Although Charles avoided Westminster Hall, with its inherently public atmosphere, in the end, Westminster Hall found Charles. For one infamous week in January 1649 the King stood trial in this historic room as "a tyrant, traitor and murderer . . . and public enemy." On 27 January 1649 his subjects dared to sentence Charles I, King of England, with treason. Three days later, he was led onto a platform in front of the boarded-up Banqueting House at Whitehall, where his most sophisticated masques had been staged. A single stroke of the ax severed the King's head, which was then raised high before the assembled crowd. Many rushed forward to mop their handkerchiefs with the royal blood. If Charles had arrogantly dismissed legitimization from his people, seeking only God's approbation of his kingship, at the very end he perhaps understood that the theater of regal pageantry meant more than elegant diversion. He specially requested a second shirt to shield him from the cold of that bleak winter morning. The only monarch in British history to be executed by his people, Charles did not want their last glimpse to be of a shivering coward.

Charles's tragic end was not a direct result of his failure to hold a Coronation Feast, though its cancellation was symptomatic of his fatal missteps. When his son, Charles II (r. 1660–1685), was restored to the throne in 1660, a Westminster Coronation was among his first priorities upon his return to London. His father's Coronation Book was scrupulously examined to reinvent the ceremony with all its former splendor, and the Regalia, melted down during the Commonwealth, re-created. The son, however, did not err in the ways of his father. "Good times Charlie" was a man of the people, a beloved rascal with seventeen mistresses, including the popular actress Nell Gwynne. This was a king who would never dream of spending six hours in church without a party to follow.

A generation after Charles I's Coronation, it had been forgotten, and it seemed inconceivable, that there had been no Feast. Francis Sanford's *History of the Coronation of James II* (1687) meticulously recorded the preparations undertaken by Charles II's advisors, but noted "as to the Coronation dinner of Charles the First, they could give no Answer, all the Books and Records of the Counting-House being lost in the Late War." So they looked back further, to reestablish the ritual feast that embodied the unchanging stability of the monarchy after such tumultuous years. Even after the Coronation Ceremony itself was altered on the accession of William of Orange and Mary (r. 1689–1702, Mary d. 1694) to ensure that no Catholic would ever again sit on the English throne, the Feast stayed intact.

By the time George IV held the last traditional Coronation Feast in 1821, amidst extraordinary expense and opulence, the event had become more of a circus than a sacred ritual of the populace. Sandwiches, Savoy cakes, ginger beer, and other refreshments were sold by Messrs. Waud and Perry to viewers in the stands of the Palace Yard watching the King's Herb Woman and her maids, dressed in white, strewing flowers before the great procession. Even Sir Walter Scott was "somewhat disappointed" when he witnessed the ancient Challenge of the Champion firsthand. Nevertheless, although Queen Victoria (r. 1837–1901), like William IV (r. 1830–1837) before her, decided to forgo the antiquated ceremony, a family dinner was held at Buckingham Palace. The occasion allowed them to commemorate and relive the events of what had become, in the Queen's eyes, "a pretty ceremony." She recorded that they stayed in the dining room, late into the evening, after which she went "out on Mamma's balcony looking at the fireworks in Green Park, which were quite beautiful." In almost every time and place, kings, chieftains, popes, mayors, and virtually anyone stepping into an important office have formalized their change of status with a feast. All except for Charles, and look what happened to him.

Chapter Six

Showing Off

Nicolas Fouquet Impresses the King, Château de Vaux-le-Vicomte, France, 17 August 1661

Vaux will never be more beautiful than it was that evening.

Jean de La Fontaine, letter to Maucroix, 22 August 1661

*F*IVE YEARS OF COLOSSAL BUILDING, planting, and sculpting and three frantic weeks of polishing, rehearsing, baking, and decorating came to a halt; Vaux-le-Vicomte was as ready as it would ever be. The violins were tuned and the tables were laid. Only the kitchens deep beneath the building continued to swirl with activity: simmering, sautéing, chopping, and roasting. From the lowliest groom to the host, all else took their places in the courtyard, where the thick scent of orange blossom topiaries stifled the hot, still air.

At precisely 6 P.M. on 17 August 1661, the gilded carriage carrying Louis XIV (r. 1643–1715), King of France, his brother Philippe, Duke d'Orléans (1640–1701), known as Monsieur, and three of his favorite ladies arrived at the gates of the château. His mother, Anne d'Autriche (1601–1666), followed in her own carriage;

then came the litter of Madame, the glamorous Henriette d'Angleterre. Powdered and primped, the entire court, accompanied by servants and footmen, had set out three hours earlier from the Palace of Fontainebleau: Princes of the Blood, nobles, ministers, the Musketeers led by Charles de Batz-Castelmore d'Artagnan (ca. 1620–1673), courtiers, intellectuals, and artists, including the novelist Mademoiselle Madeleine de Scudéry (1607–1701) and the poet Jean de La Fontaine (1621–1695). The Abbé de Choisy (1644–1724) estimated that six thousand people attended the party, although the actual numbers were probably less. Only the pregnant queen—Marie-Thérèse (1638–1683)—and Jean-Baptiste Colbert (1619–1683) declined the invitation to Vaux.

Guarded by massive carved satyr heads on tapering columns, Vaux-le-Vicomte's stately entrance, like a salty *amuse-gueule,* whet the appetite for the banquet to come. The open bars of its wrought-iron gate decorously revealed, rather than protected, the château looming ahead, a mass of shimmering stone rising up from a glassy moat. Unlike the elongated proportions previously favored in France, the building was a powerful geometric composition of robust squares, full ovals, and voluptuously swollen curves. Built from 1656 to 1661, Vaux-le-Vicomte was the first and most brilliant collaboration of the architect Louis Le Vau (1612–1670), the landscape gardener André Le Nôtre (1613–1700), and the interior painter and designer Charles Le Brun (1619–1690). Inspired by the great Palladian villas, it was the first seamlessly coordinated garden, interior, and exterior design in France and initiated a new style in French architecture. A powerfully unified symbolism, derived from classical mythology, apotheosized its owner inside and out, from the top of its enormous domed cupola to the carpets lying on the floor. Two side wings rippled forward from Vaux's central block to showcase its grandiose entrance: thick, rusticated columns, supporting a monumental pediment, surmounted by reclining figures of Apollo and Rhea, representing heaven and earth. Vaux-le-Vicomte was, indeed, a house fit for the gods, if not a king; but Louis, for all his cavernous palaces, owned nothing comparable. The building embodied its owner's motto, "Quo non ascendet" (What heights will he not reach).

Nicolas Fouquet (1615–1680), who possessed and created this vast estate, was, however, neither royalty, nor even a grand aristocrat. He ranked among the "nobility of the Robe," a powerful new class of civil servants, and had risen meteorically through the rungs of government to be appointed Superintendent of Finance to the King of France in 1653. Fouquet had learned to stay close to the powerful cardinals who controlled France's weakened crown. He began his career as a seventeen-year-old protégé of Richelieu. Later, devious, pleasure-loving Mazarin had

FIGURE 6.1
Portrait of Nicolas
Fouquet, ca. 1650,
engraving.

taught him how to skim enormous sums from the state bankroll, groomed his taste for fine living, and turned his eye to Italy. Fouquet flourished during the political instability known as the Fronde (1648–1653), the peasant rebellions in the wake of the Thirty Years' War, and the campaign by factions of aristocrats to topple the monarchy. He lent money to the government and became a hero in the hour of need, repaying himself lavishly for his trouble.

But Fouquet's interest in money derived from the pleasures it afforded him and the passions it let him indulge. He was the greatest patron of the arts of his generation, lavishing his riches on poets and playwrights, from the aging master Pierre Corneille to the rising talent La Fontaine. He collected rare books on an extraordinary scale; his library was the envy of Paris. The artist Nicolas Poussin, at the French Academy in Rome, chose large shipments of paintings, sculptures, and antiquities to adorn Fouquet's Italianate estate. Profoundly intellectual and subtle, Fouquet counted some of the finest minds of his generation as his closest friends—not least among them, Marie-Rabutin-Chantal, Marquise de Sévigné (1626–1696). Yet, he was also an inveterate schemer, engaged in risky ventures with the Dutch and in the Americas. Fouquet maintained a private army and a fortified island, called Belle-Isle, off the coast of Normandy, tempering his bellicosity with the delicate companionship of exquisite ladies and rare treasures. His bearing recalled that of an ancient Persian despot—opulent, sensual, and ruthless.

Vaux-le-Vicomte encapsulated Fouquet's immense paradoxes, the complex, intertwined rawness and elegant ornamentation emblematic of the baroque style—and of his person. To furnish his beloved obsession, his defining creation, he founded a factory nearby at Le Maincy, where nearly three hundred craftsmen, including nineteen Flemish tapestry weavers, worked solely to fill Vaux-le-Vicomte with custom-designed furniture, including a monumental tapestry cycle of Alexander the Great. The essence of Vaux's magic, however, lay in its lyrically human proportions, which kept its rich surfaces from becoming garish or overpowering. Its human scale reflected the soul of a man whose greatest pleasure was to read late into the night with the silk curtains of his bed drawn around him.

In the spring of 1661 Mazarin died, and Louis was ready to assert the full force of his kingship. As a fourteen-year-old ward of the cardinal, Louis had been terrified when marauding throngs invaded his bedroom. In response Louis declared his majority, and peace was restored. In practice, however, he still ruled from beneath his advisor's shadow. The incident, and the threat of the regicidal aristocrats who encouraged it, left the young King with a lifelong fear of treachery and an urgent desire to rule powerfully and single-handedly. When Mazarin died, the King demanded that he personally oversee and sign every edict, every order being executed by his ministers. Suddenly, Fouquet's actions were scrutinized and the sources of his vast wealth queried. Fouquet's cold-blooded rival, Colbert, whose emblem was a snake, bent the King's ear against him.

Vaux-le-Vicomte had caused questions even before 1661. The King had been invited to visit the château the previous year, so it was no secret. However, Fouquet had tried to conceal the extent of his undertaking. Colbert had been caught spying on the construction, thwarting Fouquet's efforts to maintain discretion. Despite orders to hide workmen from unwanted visitors from the nearby Palace of Fontainebleau, rumors of nine hundred craftsmen and laborers flew swiftly through court circles; the actual numbers were probably even higher. It was impossible to hide the razing of three entire villages, the digging of canals, the unprecedented scale of construction.

Fouquet weathered the storm and begged the King's forgiveness for his greed and deception. Spring turned into summer, and he enjoyed the King's indulgence; Louis was happy, and so the court was happy. He reigned free from the overweening influence of Mazarin; his bride was expecting an heir to the throne; and he was hopelessly in love with Louise de la Vallière (1644–1710), a seventeen-year-old lady-in-waiting to his sister-in-law, Madame. The King's amorous mood made it an especially glittering social season by all accounts.

But then Fouquet made a false step. Was it merely flattery, or did it cross the line into flirtation? He tried to ingratiate himself with Mademoiselle de la Vallière. The gossips whispered that Fouquet sent his best friend, Madame Du Plessis-Bellière, as an emissary to offer Louise twenty thousand pistoles. Some claimed that the finance minister, in this era in which such gifts were not unusual, sought only to gain her well-placed favor. Others more sinisterly implied that Fouquet brazenly intended to seduce his Sovereign's mistress. The young lady supposedly replied that twenty million would not induce her to make such a faux pas.

The King was furious. Fouquet desperately needed to regain Louis's favor. So he took the ultimate risk and invited the King, together with the entire court, to come to Vaux-le-Vicomte for an extravagant evening feast. It would be a party that boldly declared that France had ingested the most sophisticated elements of Italian culture, had digested them, and now spewed forth a majestic art of her own; a feast to rival the most voluptuous banquets of Persian despots of the fourth century B.C. that had dazzled Alexander the Great with Oriental spices and luxuriant splendor. Louis accepted the invitation with alacrity. A date was set for three weeks hence.

Fouquet's expectations for this dinner were staggering; his life, literally, depended on it. He aspired to a perfection described in the 1674 cookbook authored by L.S.R. and titled *L'Art de bien traiter:*

[I]t is . . . the exquisite choice of meats and dishes, the delicacy of their seasoning, the politeness and correctness in serving them, the quantity appropriate
to the number of guests, and the general arrangement of things that is essential
in contributing to the goodness and ornament of a meal where the mouth and
the eyes find equal charm in an ingenious diversity that satisfies all the senses.

Fouquet's chief maître d'hôtel, François Vatel (d. 1671), universally renowned
for his talent and resourcefulness, was the most capable talent to oblige. The minister fielded frequent requests for Vatel's services from no less than the King and
the Princes of the Blood. No mere servant, Vatel was a highly paid executive, as
well as a trusted friend, who supervised the construction at Vaux; it was he who
had warned Fouquet of Colbert's snooping. He managed huge sums of money,
designed menus, and coordinated the extensive staff of the *cuisine,* the *office,* and
even the stables. The responsibilities of maintaining Vaux-le-Vicomte, as well as
Fouquet's other households, were so extensive that Vatel had other maîtres d'hôtel
to assist him in these herculean duties. Yet, he had earned his reputation for the
meticulous care with which he reviewed every minute detail.

Vatel asked Fouquet's resident designers to push forward on the unfinished
château with all possible haste. The Alexander the Great tapestries, among numerous other objects, were still years from completion, so furnishings, tapestries, silver, and provisions had to be gathered from Fouquet's other residences, borrowed,
or rented. Vatel collaborated with Fouquet's secretary, the poet Paul Pellisson-
Fontanier (1624–1693), who supervised Fouquet's arts patronage, to organize the
entertainment. Le Brun designed the elaborate decorations; and the ingenious
Italian Giacomo Torelli (1608–1678), known as Il Gran Stregone (the Great Wizard), planned fireworks and special effects. Preparation for any situation was crucial, for attendance at these royal occasions was impossible to predict.

From his basement office, near the extensive kitchens under his care (among
the first in France built directly under the main edifice of a château), Vatel supervised the manifold banquet preparations. In the *cuisine,* larders and storerooms
burst with provisions. Bouillons simmered in great vats; birds roasted on rotating

Habit de Cuisinier

spits; charcoal ovens and cooking ranges blazed. In the *office,* confectionery and pastries suffocated its clean, cool rooms with the rich smells of freshly baked sugar and butter; wines, linens, silver, and plate were inventoried in the storerooms; fruits and salads were candied and pickled and decorously garnished; and dough rose in the bakery.

As Fouquet's team of artists, cooks, and servants strove toward triumphal perfection, Colbert insidiously plotted his rival's demise. He spied on the preparations, twisting and exaggerating every detail to alienate the King further from Fouquet. For three straight weeks, Vaux-le-Vicomte frantically labored, Colbert laid his plans, and the court gossiped in anticipation. Fouquet obsessively reviewed the peparations, despite a raging fever. Suddenly, the day arrived, and exactly on schedule the serpentine line of carriages was heard, and then seen, making its way along the dusty road to the château.

The gates were opened, the trumpets were sounded, and the intricate ballet of courtly ceremony began. The Royal Carriage proceeded down the central path of the entry courtyard and stopped at a second gate for the occupants to descend while the horses were led away to the stables. The King stepped forth and played to the crowd. Twenty-three, dashingly handsome, and deeply cunning, Louis XIV radiated a hypnotic charm over commoners, courtiers, and ladies alike. The man who embodied "L'État, c'est moi" had arrived. He was as soaringly ambitious and mesmerizingly charismatic as Alexander the Great himself. La Fontaine noted that "the Nymphs of Vaux always had their eyes on the King; his health and good looks ravished them all."

Nicolas Fouquet, the sensuous aesthete possessed of a refinement his King could never acquire, descended the steps of his palace with the ease of a lifelong statesman to welcome his Sovereign and guest. His sumptuous attire, piercing eyes, and confident stance hid the fever and fatigue raging through his body. His pose held the unflinching assurance of forty-six years of personal success. His wife, Marie-Madeleine de Castille, a coldly dignified beauty, followed a few steps behind. Le Brun had recently immortalized her in an allegory of conjugal fidelity; she did, indeed, remain loyal to the very end.

An uncertain pause ensued as all present thrilled to behold the meeting of host and guest, subject and king. Beneath title and etiquette, an older man, oozing sophistication, wit, and incomparable elegance stood before a younger man haughtily determined not to be outdone. Earlier that morning Louis had threatened to arrest Fouquet at the dinner. His mother, Anne d'Autriche, had pleaded against such a brazen act. Even a king was not exempt from the bounds of politesse. The story had flown through the court. Mme. Du Plessis-Bellière sent a warning to Fouquet, but his face betrayed no fear. He bowed deeply and kissed the King's hand; Mme. Fouquet curtsied. The moment passed smoothly, and the King was escorted inside for a brief rest. A discreet shiver of relief and disappointment rippled through the onlookers. Their host would not himself be dinner, at least not that night.

As the last of the carriages trickled in, Louis declared himself ready. The trumpets sounded again, and the evening commenced in earnest. La Fontaine tells us it began with a walk in the garden. The King and his mother were presented with upholstered and fringed carriages designed to navigate the narrow garden paths. The rest of the court hobbled behind in their high heels. Like an ant colony, they fell automatically into formation for this "casual" evening stroll.

As they walked beyond the imposing bulk of the château, the sweeping vista of Le Nôtre's exuberant masterpiece of terraces, parterres, and fountains opened up to them. As far as the eye could see, the landscape had been transformed into complexly ordered rhythms of water, grass, and sculpture accented by scrolling hedges and flower beds. Stone pathways and manicured lawns were groomed into exacting geometric patterns. Beds of exotic anemones and tuberoses splashed color onto the parterres. Rows of fantastically costly tulips revealed Fouquet's deep trade ties with the new Dutch Republic. Deep-green shrubs had been trimmed into cones, spheres, and swirling arabesques that punctuated the flat lawns. Huge trees—elms, limes, sweet chestnuts, cherries, and laurels—had been transplanted full-grown to form a perimeter border, an Arcadian frame for the pristine terraces within. As Claude Lorrain painted idealized classical landscapes in Rome, Le Nôtre built one at Vaux. Rational man had conquered unruly nature to flatten, irrigate, prune, and sculpt it into art. This was the first true *jardin à la française.*

Fouquet led his guests straight down the central walkway, pausing as unexpected views and surprising wonders revealed themselves. Gravity-defying fountains abounded in every direction, each a tour de force of engineering and unique artistry; one, in the form of a crown; another, as tall as the King; others, spilling into pools and falling into tiered rows of shells. Water trickled down cascading levels, spurted from the mouths of cupids, and formed entire walls. Mlle. de Scudéry, whose novel *Clélie* described Vaux's garden in loving detail, wrote, "[N]othing is more pleasant than to hear the murmurs of all these Jets of water, whose equality of delightful harmony is very apt to produce an agreeable amusement" (as Pellison's lover she had gotten an advance look at them). La Fontaine remarked that the courtiers did not know which was the most wondrous.

Richly carved sculptures, including twenty-four designed by Poussin, were positioned along the pathways. Louis and his courtiers found themselves among "various spirits of the flowers and fruits of the earth, male and female figures with the whole human bust," as well as gods and nymphs "holding flowers, fruit and a cornucopia to their breasts, as marks of a fertile and delightful villa." They continued past a low, round pool with a fountain shooting a stream high into the air and moved on to a shimmering mirror of flat, still water. Further still, they passed an entire wall of dancing fountains in front of a marble grotto. Languid river gods reclined beneath a green slope beyond. As the guests walked toward it, the terrace dropped down abruptly with a great thunder of rushing water. A long, narrow canal graced by a statue of Neptune and three horses in its center came into view.

Painted gondolas rowed them across the canal to the grotto, and they climbed up to the tip of the sloping plain. A large statue of Hercules resting from his labors and a pair of ancient pyramids intended for the site could not be installed in time for the banquet. But here, from the highest point in the garden, the guests turned to survey the ordered perspectives of the garden and the majestic domed palace directly before them. La Fontaine delighted in the courtiers' colorful silks, ribbons, and feathers that dotted the paths.

The King and court returned for a tour of the château, a logically organized double row of rooms, saturated in color, stucco, fringe, and pattern. Innovative

FIGURE 6.3
View and Perspective of the Garden of Vaux-le-Vicomte, 1660, by Israël Silvestre, engraving.

cove ceilings *à l'italienne* allegorically glorified Fouquet in paint. In the *Salon d'Hercule* the Greek hero ascended to the heavens in a chariot of gold above red silk walls and a checkerboard marble floor. In the *Chambre des Muses,* a study in blue, the sun god Apollo, embodying music and poetry, shared the ceiling with Clio, the muse of history; Clio's sisters decorated the surrounding walls amidst painted cupids and garlands. The gossips swore they spotted a portrait of Mademoiselle de la Vallière among them. Louis, as always, noticed everything.

Imposing cabinets-on-stands, of deeply carved ebony and tortoiseshell, were

topped by large blue-and-white garniture sets imported from China, alternating convex and concave vessels made of the porcelain that Europe could not yet produce. Tables and chairs were as bold, masculine, and geometric in their proportions as the architecture that contained them, yet sensuous in their materials of colored marble, carved and gilded wood, tassels, feathers, and silk. The protruding chimneypiece of the traditional French château had been eliminated to purify the geometry of each room. Luxurious paned-glass windows offered decorous views of the expansive gardens. Vaux contained one of France's first permanent dining rooms, equipped with a built-in buffet adorned with painted fruits and garlands, as well as a sumptuous stucco-and-gilded bedroom for the King, created in the ambitious hope that Louis would deign to stay.

They came to Vaux's most glorious space, the *Grand Salon,* an enormous oval room whose dimensions extended up the full height of the building to a great dome that appeared to be supported by hulking terms with baskets of fruit and

garlands on their heads. Three arches opened directly onto the garden so that Le Nôtre's carefully constructed views became the room's central decoration. Le Brun had intended to bring together the decorative symbolism of the entire building on the room's ceiling with an apotheosis of Fouquet, rising up to the heavens as a new star, "plac'd in the midst of the Heavens . . . illuminated . . . by the command of the sun." The painting was never completed. Instead, the King and courtiers probably gasped at a *collation* arranged *en ambigu.* This new fashion offered a mixture of savory and sweet delicacies arranged into sculptural forms to delight the eye while tempting the palate. A *collation* held seven years later at Versailles included edible mountains whose caverns were filled with cold meats; marzipan palaces; and lawns of green mousse topped by orange topiaries entirely covered with candied fruit. Topiaries "in full fruit and blossom" stood in large pots on the floor and in small vases perched upon buffets. Thick, sweeping garlands of aromatic flowers, strung on tasseled silver cords, hung in swags over doorways and windows, across buffets, and along the sides of every table.

At a time when Nicolas Bonnefons had lyrically celebrated every known variety of fruit and vegetable in *Les Délices de la campagne* and still-life paintings were at the height of fashion, Fouquet employed the most gifted gardener of his generation, Jean de La Quintinie (1624–1688), who knew the secrets of cultivating rare fruits and vegetables out of season. The *office* arranged them with ravishing artifice. The pyramids that Fouquet had intended for his garden would have appeared as towering pyramids of fresh, dried, and candied fruits, confections, and flowers. This was the original era of "vertical food," a fashion for table presentation that continued well into the next century. Doorways stretched higher to accommodate these elaborate creations, some even frozen into place with special iron ice molds.

FIGURE 6.4
Party Given in the Small Park at Versailles, 1668, by Jean Le Pautre, engraving from André Félibien, *Relation de la feste de Versailles.*

We can imagine tiered buffet tables, covered in white damask, loaded with massive silver platters, Chinese porcelains, gilded perfume urns, and crystal ewers full of colorful Italian liqueurs, as similar events offered. Other buffets would stand ready for service, with piles of extra plates, intricately folded napkins, stemware, and massive ewers of perfumed water next to basins for hand washing; beneath, enormous silver wine cisterns, with gadrooned oval sides and imposing lion's head handles, chilled wine in iced water.

As if by magic, thousands of costly white wax candles now flickered through the house and the gardens. Light danced over diamond necklaces, crystal carafes, Venetian wall mirrors, silver plates, and silk-covered walls as the daylight dwindled. Branching *girandoles* of beaded Venetian glass blazed atop massive gilded and carved *guéridons* arranged with rhythmic precision. Chandeliers hung from the ceilings, and mirror-backed sconces with bulbous crystal drops adorned the walls. Every window, overmantel, and balustrade defied the setting sun with a row of pristinely spaced candles. As La Fontaine described it, "the Heavens were jealous." It was man's triumph over the sun and the hours.

Fouquet escorted the King to his seat, probably at the center of the *Grand Salon,* symbolically, as well as architecturally, the most important position in the building. Louis dined alone in his palaces, as French Kings had done since Charlemagne, but on festive occasions such as this, he asked a few favored ladies to surround him, "with no regard to rank." Sometimes, his brother Monsieur joined him, but the only other man who ever dined at table with Louis XIV was Molière; breaking bread with a subject would have been far too intimate an act. Additional tables for ambassadors and important guests probably radiated into the garden, while outlying buffets served the remaining courtiers, who would have felt privileged to stand in a semicircle at the edge of the room. Royal watching was never more popular than in Louis's day, but the show of pomp and ceremony was never more spectacular.

Another fanfare of trumpets would announce the arrival of the Royal Dish-Bearers, kitchen officers, and staff, in colorfully liveried uniforms and carrying an immense number of covered platters and dishes. When the King dined at the house of a commoner, dishes had to be passed from the house servants to the King's noble staff, who placed them at the Royal Table under the protection of a Swiss guard; the reverse took place when the platters were cleared. Although Vaux's kitchens and the *Grand Salon* were within the same building, and Vatel had added a pair of staircases to improve efficiency, the food had quite a distance to travel. To preserve heat, cookbooks sometimes recommended preparing important dishes in silver bowls, which then came directly to the table; silver food-warmers also helped. Luckily, hot food was not a taste of the period.

First-course dishes would be placed on the table in symmetrical patterns that echoed Le Nôtre's garden *broderies*. Earlier French banquets, such as the 1453 Feast of the Pheasant held by the Duke of Burgundy, had offered guests an overwhelming abundance of exotic dishes such as roasted peacock presented in its feathers. Platters, however, were placed on the table haphazardly. Banquet planners of Vatel's generation described the old method as *service en confusion* and replaced this with the new *service à la française,* which remained in style until the mid-nineteenth century. In the age of Descartes, elegance was synonymous with geometric perfection.

Fouquet's previous banquets had been praised for "sauces beyond compare, tarts of *fines herbes,* ragoûts in pastry, cakes, biscuits, and pâtés and superb chilled wines." At Vaux that evening, La Fontaine thought "the delicacy and choiceness of the dishes served were outstanding; but the graciousness with which the Superintendent and his wife did the honors of their house was even more so." Little is known about the actual menu; an anonymous account described five or six courses including pheasants, ortolans, quails, and partridges, all expensive game birds, as well as newly fashionable bisques, ragouts, numerous "delicacies" and great quantities of wine. Three courses, composed of numerous dishes, would have been considered generous at the time.

Typically, grand French suppers of the period began with numerous *potages,* meaning not just soup but any dish cooked in a pot. Pierre de Lune's *Le Cuisinier* of 1656 recommended deboned turkey, chicken with chicory, stuffed quail, and mushrooms with capon for summer. These would be surrounded by *entrées* such as hashes of mushrooms and artichokes, fricassées, boiled or stewed meats, and savory pigeon tarts, two per *potage.* Plates of delicate *hors d'oeuvres* formed a border placed "outside of the work." The anonymous 1662 *L'Escole parfaite des officiers de bouche* suggests pâtés, foie gras, sausages, figs, raspberries, radishes, and hot venison pastry. As at a modern buffet, guests were not expected to eat everything on offer. A host's goal was to impress and to demonstrate that every taste had been catered to.

None of these tempting delicacies could be sampled until royal protocol had been dispensed with. The chaplain had to say a benediction before the ritual hand washing. Louis was presented with a moistened linen towel carried to him in a pair of golden plates. Then, in carefully choreographed synchronicity, the Carvers would have stepped forward to perform their duties, with linen towels folded over their left shoulders, dissecting each dish with dramatic flair. The most fashionable Parisian carving of the era was in the Italian style, with birds flamboyantly held and sliced in midair. *L'Escole parfaite des officiers de bouche* offers instructional diagrams.

The Royal Taster, a position reserved for the noblest subjects, next stepped forward to sample a morsel of each dish prepared for the King. The act was ceremonial, but it hinted at the antagonism that lay beneath the refined surface of the evening.

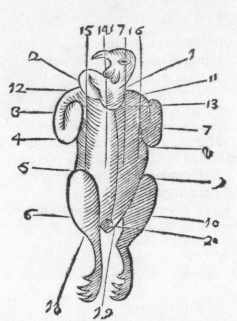

Twenty-four violins played in the garden, the florid melodies wafting through the scented air. Jean-Baptiste Lully (1632–1687), the most renowned composer of the day, had been commissioned to write music for the banquet. Italian by birth, though raised in Paris, Lully breathed new life into the stately forms of court music. According to André Félibien (1619–1695), "Lully found the secret of satisfying and charming the world" and in his music "there was nothing that did not perfectly express the passions or ravish the spirit of the listener." He had been named Superintendent of Music to the King only one month earlier, in honor of the charming pieces he had composed for a royal party at Fontainebleau. It is even possible that the twenty-four violins heard at Vaux that night were played by the famous "Twenty-four Violins of the King," the ancestor of the modern orchestra. Music melded with the murmuring fountains to complete the spectrum of sensual pleasures.

At last, Louis began to eat and the others were free to follow. His appetite for food was as gargantuan as his desires for women, power, and glory. At one sitting alone, he was said to have consumed four *potages,* an entire pheasant, a partridge, a large plate of salad, minced mutton in garlic sauce, two generous slices of ham, and a plate of pastries, as well as fruit and sweets. He also liked his food to be twice as spiced as that of his subjects. Louis thought forks were unmanly and ate with his hands, a knife, and sometimes a spoon. It was as if his royal blood gave him the metabolism of a Nietzschean *Übermensch,* always bigger, bolder, stronger.

Fouquet, by contrast, ate in the newest and most elegant style. In an age that considered *propreté,* meaning "correctness," "cleanliness," and "one's own," to be the highest virtue, he owned one of the first complete sets of flatware known in France, with vermeil forks, knives, and spoons for twenty-four. This rare extravagance not only allowed him to appear gracious toward others but also kept others' fingers, not just his own, out of the food. Fouquet would have been completely at ease with the complexities of the new etiquette, which dictated that confitures were served with a fork and dragées with a spoon, while salt should be taken from the end of a knife.

The Greek chorus of gossips watched and listened intently to the King. Louis was renowned for tossing out questions or, even more playfully, food, as he flirted mischievously with the ladies. While at Vaux, the courtiers searched for hints of his reaction to the overwhelming luxury in which his finance minister had ensconced him. They later claimed that on that famous evening Louis, in wide-eyed amazement, complimented Fouquet on the massive sugar caster that had been placed to his right. Fouquet was said to have replied that it was made of solid gold, and the King heard to mutter that the Louvre had nothing comparable. So too, stories of five hundred dozen plates of solid gold seen at Vaux that night have reached through the centuries, repeated by writers from Alexandre Dumas to Anatole France. In fact, Paul Micio has proved that the sugar caster was silver gilt, as were seventy-five of Fouquet's plates, while others were silver, and probably faience or Chinese export porcelain. Many service items were probably rented. These fictions contain the truth that Louis was both amazed by and jealous of the unrivaled richness before him.

The bounteous courses at such affairs moved with swift efficiency; the last guest

FIGURE 6.6
*Diagrams for Carving
Pears,* 1662, engraving from
*L'Escole parfaite des officiers
de bouche.*

at each table would hardly be served when the great parade of removing and re-placing the dishes began. This was done in careful geometric order, no more than four at a time, while a second set of servants stepped in to set down the new plat-ters. The baroque aesthetic could not permit the sight of a naked table. For a sec-ond course, L.S.R. recommended serving twenty to thirty roasts—a mixture of rare game, lamb, and beef for grand occasions; perhaps a beef *en tremblant,* as ro-bustly movemented as a Rubens; an entire lamb surrounded by pigeons and quails; or lightly salted partridge with a warm venison tart. The Carvers might add newly invented sauces made with rich bouillon, bouquet garni, and roux to finish each serving. Smaller roasts surrounded the central platters alongside colorful, aro-matic salads sculpted by the *sommelier* into pyramids and colorfully adorned with aromatic herbs and flowers. Perhaps the Royal Table even featured *salade couron-née,* shaped into a crown and garnished with oranges, lemons, red pomegranate seeds, and chopped fresh herbs, with orange flower water and sugar as accompani-ments. A second service of more delicate roasts and rare birds stuffed with force-meat—perhaps the ortolans and pheasants mentioned at Vaux by the anonymous guest—might follow. Then came the *entremets,* rare delicacies such as truffles, pi-geon wings, pigs' ears, meat pastries, asparagus, and artichokes, possibly followed by a large ham or venison served with *blancmanger,* creams, savory tarts, and jel-lied meats. Iced wines—perhaps Reims, Chablis, and Tonnerres, as well as the newly fashionable Champagne (still, not sparkling)—would have been offered from the buffet, but only after the King had called for his first drink.

The darling of the season was the fresh green pea served simply with English butter. Audiger had created a frenzy at the court when he brought it back from Italy and presented it to Louis XIV in January 1660. The fresh pea was a whiff of the coming Rococo taste for light pastoral charms, for the artificial ease of the painter Jean-Antoine Watteau's *fêtes galantes.* For the next thirty years, Parisians bankrupted themselves to serve it. Always a trendsetter, Fouquet would have wanted to be the first to get his talented gardener to grow them for his table.

The charming novelties of dessert are designed, as L.S.R. explained, "to bait the appetite and spark thirst." During the final course, "the spirit revives, the wittiest words are spoken, the most agreeable topics debated. . . . [I]t is then that the funniest stories are told. . . . [A]s they say, between the pear and the cheese, a thousand pleasantries are invented to pass the time and entertain good company, which provide the greatest charm in life." Sophisticated Parisians of the era served resplendent fruits: pears, figs, apricots, cherries, plums, and slightly lascivious melons appeared fresh, candied, in syrups, or peeled and carefully rewrapped in their skins. Grapes artfully cascaded from footed baskets as if hanging from the vine. Sugared fruits glistened alongside decorated petits fours, tarts, confections, lusciously melting cheeses, perfumed tongues, and hams. Royal marzipans were painted in reds, greens, and yellows as rich as those covering Vaux's walls. Butter-rich pastries and cakes were modeled into flowers, hearts, ovals, lozenges, and birds. Guests breathlessly stopped to witness the dexterous transport of towering pyramids of fruit to the table. Madame de Sévigné recorded that the feat was not always successful. However, on that August night, ice would have been the most magical of all effects and tastes, beautifully shimmering and flouting the season in iced cheeses, creams, fruits, and wines. In 1581, Michel de Montaigne had been astonished to have ice mixed with his wine on a hot summer night in Florence; not quite a century later Vaux-le-Vicomte had its own exterior ice vault and Fouquet's "superb chilled wines" elicited poetic praise.

They did not linger too long before Fouquet invited his King and the assembled guests into the garden. Fouquet led them down to the *allée des sapins,* the fir-tree path, beneath a *grille d'eau,* an enormous wall of fountains, which acted as the backdrop for a stage embellished with thick foliage, towering arcades of columns, sculpted satyrs, garlands, and topiaries designed by Le Brun and Torelli. Hundreds of torches set through Vaux's gardens created an ethereal glow in stark contrast to the blackness of the surrounding woods. Molière strolled onstage in street clothes and feigned surprise at finding the King and audience before him. A rock transformed itself into a shell, and the glamorous actress Béjart emerged like Aphrodite, amid twenty jets of spraying water. She recited a syrupy prologue by Pellisson, a glowing tribute to both host and King, and called forth a fleet of dancing nymphs, dryads, fauns, and satyrs from behind the lantern-draped trees. It was the premiere of *Les Fâcheux,* the world's first comedy-ballet. The debut of Molière's *École des maris* had been well received by an audience at Vaux in July; Fouquet would accept nothing less than a premiere. With only fifteen days to write, rehearse, and orga-

nize the whole production, Molière decided to intersperse each act of this new play with ballet. The choreographer Pierre Beauchamp wrote the music, and Lully contributed an additional piece. This light comedy recounted an aristocrat's continuing misadventures with chatty simpletons, flatterers, and provincial fools. La Fontaine wrote of Signor Torelli's special effects, "[W]e saw rocks open and Terms move, and many a figure turn on its pedestal." The audience, including the King himself, was uproariously delighted. Louis had the piece replayed at Fontainebleau just a few weeks later. It remained a court favorite until the French Revolution and was enacted 106 times within Molière's lifetime.

As the play ended, a cascade of fireworks rose up over Fouquet's Grand Canal. Courtiers turned from the stage to applaud Torelli's exploding carnival of colors, swirling patterns, fleurs-de-lis, and monograms. Fire melded with water, in sparkling showers exploding from bubbling fountains. As one side of the garden darkened, another burst into light. At last, the din quieted, until the trickling of the fountains could be heard once more. The evening appeared to have reached its conclusion, so Louis and his entourage turned back toward the house. Then, as they reached the center alley, Torelli unleashed his last and grandest spectacle, an even more intricate pattern of fireworks that soared above the great dome of the château. The building itself had been packed closely with lanterns along its cornices and windows so that it, too, seemed to be on fire. It was Vaux-le-Vicomte's and Fouquet's most glorious moment.

Back at the château, the *office* had outdone its dessert in a last *collation* of sculpted and festively garnished savories and sweets. One courtier described enjoying "every sort of the most rare and beautiful fruit, while the violins of Lully were heard one last time." L.S.R. wrote that "the beauty of a meal is infinitely greater in the evening, by torchlight, than during the day, and one even eats better, for when business affairs have been put at a slight distance, and when the number of intrusions have diminished, one is naturally destined to discover the sweeter pleasures of life." His lyrical descriptions of garden *collations* have led some to conclude that he may have been the chef at Vaux that very night, although no evidence supports this. His timeless words, however, capture the delight and fascination of the event.

FIGURE 6.8
The Arrival of the Four Seasons, 1664, by Israël Silvestre, engraving from André Félibien, *Les Plaisirs de l'Isle enchantée.*

As a grandiloquent gesture, Fouquet, it was said, offered the entirety of Vaux-le-Vicomte to his King with an elegant wave of the hand. It was a flickering moment of glory, but it could not save him. As Paul Morand wrote: At 6 P.M. Fouquet was the King of France; at 2 A.M. he was nothing. Louis gave the signal that he was ready to leave; the King's Bedroom would not be used. He had had enough of these festivities, which seemed to mock him. Playing the gracious guest had exhausted him, so the royal entourage began the three-hour journey back to Fontainebleau in the wee hours of the morning. Visions of the house, the fountains, the dinner, Apollo, and Hercules must have flooded Louis's mind as his carriage bumped along darkened roads. He had seen the seductive power that Fouquet's dinner had held over the court. Its beauty and sheer extravagance staggered him. The Duke de Saint-Simon later described Louis as a man with a "distaste for all merit, intelligence, education, and, most of all, for all independence of character and sentiment in others." He did not take kindly to being outdone by a subject. Fouquet had been too successful; he had made the King jealous. In Louis's eyes the beauties of the evening at Vaux were, as the Abbé de Choisy noted, the ultimate proof of Fouquet's dissipation. Choisy believed that it was Louis, already determined to squelch his powerful finance minister, who had first suggested the dinner.

The enchanted spell that had surrounded Vaux was broken. The courtiers had departed and the candles were extinguished. Fear descended now that the adrenaline had been spent. Nervously, Fouquet asked his friend Gourville what the court was saying. Gourville replied, "One group thinks that you will be declared First Minister; the others, that they will form a great cabal to destroy you."

In the city of Nantes, three weeks after the dinner, on 5 September 1661, the King summoned fever-wracked Fouquet to an audience. Louis smiled knowingly at his minister, but the meeting was uneventful. Fouquet left without incident, but as his carriage reached the nearby church, d'Artagnan signaled him to stop and arrested him. He was charged with treason and embezzlement from the French treasury. All those guests, the flatterers whose favor he had tried to purchase, abandoned him. Only the poets, a smattering of the ladies, and Vatel, who was forced into exile, remained loyal.

But even with Fouquet vanquished, images of his glittering party haunted Louis's mind. Although the King lacked the eye of an aesthete, he had seen the power contained within the multisensory extravaganza at Vaux-le-Vicomte. Within the year, he commissioned Le Brun to create the famed Galerie d'Apollon at the Louvre. The next year Louis XIV adopted Apollo as his official symbol, and the Sun King was born. Le Brun, Le Vau, and Le Nôtre were summoned to create Versailles as Louis's regal version of Fouquet's self-apotheosizing château, only bigger, grander, and overwhelmingly magnificent. The water-spouting putti of Versailles were first seen at Vaux, but while Fouquet had a fountain as tall as the King, Louis had one that was twenty times higher. Fouquet's factory at Le Maincy became the royal workshops at Gobelins, and the tapestries in production for Vaux-le-Vicomte were hung on the walls of Versailles with the King's monogram in

135

place of Fouquet's. Jean de la Quintinie, Fouquet's kitchen gardener, was transferred to Versailles, where he created the famed *potager du Roi*. The terms designed by Poussin were physically transplanted from Vaux to Versailles along with 1,250 standing trees and shrubs, including the orange topiaries, which were placed in the famed Orangerie designed by Le Vau. Even Vaux's shrub trimmer, Antoine Turmel, was put to work at the Palace. The King seized much of Fouquet's incomparable art, furnishings, and books, while Colbert purchased items put up at auction for the royal collections. Louis was clearly obsessed.

On 5 May 1664 Louis inaugurated the gardens of Versailles with seven days of banquets, theater, music, games, and fireworks known as "Les Plaisirs de l'isle enchantée" (The Pleasures of the Enchanted Isle), coordinated as a giant publicity tool to emphasize the power and generosity of the King. As with the Palace and its gardens, the festivities took their inspiration from Vaux-le-Vicomte, but sought to exceed its grandeur. The multi-day entertainments were based upon a story by Ariosto in which brave Roger and his knights are held captive on a pleasure-filled island by an evil sorceress. A fanfare of trumpets and drums called forth the opening parade of liveried courtiers, in fiery silks, plumes, and ribbons. Louis XIV, shimmering in diamonds and silver lamé, sitting astride a horse whose harness sparkled with silver, gold, and gems, made a dramatic entrance as brave Roger. A giant figure of Apollo followed in a gilded chariot, as members of the court enacted the roles of the drama. A glorious *collation* was served in the garden by attendants dressed as the four seasons, nymphs, and fauns. Spring arrived on a Spanish horse, summer on an elephant, autumn rode a camel, and winter, a bear. Forty-eight valets dressed in costumes to evoke each season balanced large baskets of fruit, confitures, and delicacies on their heads. Like the dinner at Vaux-le-Vicomte, the "Pleasures of the Enchanted Isle" were designed to showcase the fountains and grottoes of the garden. Every space was heavily decorated with topiaries, floral garlands, temporary colonnaded buffets, and magical lights. André Félibien estimated that more than four thousand white wax candles burned each evening. The guests were once again serenaded by Lully's melodies, entertained by Molière's theater, and dazzled by stupendous fireworks. The grand finale on the very last night was, in fact, a reprisal of *Les Fâcheux,* although it had absolutely nothing to do with the Ariosto story.

Fouquet's famous trial did not begin until November 1664, six months after the inaugural banquets for Versailles. In the intervening years the courtiers had softened and forgiven him; after all, few among them were innocent of Fouquet's crime. He defended himself eloquently at the trial. In the end, thirteen judges voted for banishment, nine for death. But Louis was not content with the thought of such a clever, powerful rival living abroad. The sentence was increased to life imprisonment at Pignerol. Fouquet died there in 1680, as the spectacular festivities of Versailles carried on.

It is hard to know why a man so shrewd held an event whose extravagant beauties became the ultimate proof of his corruption. Did Fouquet think that the young King could be impressed or distracted by mere frivolity and entertainment? Impressing one's superiors is always a reckless game. The opulent banquets offered by the Persian despots inspired Alexander the Great to entertain more luxuriantly in Macedonia, but he conquered his hosts all the same. Perhaps, knowing he was doomed, Fouquet saluted fate with an homage to Apicius. When the famed first-century Roman cookbook author and gourmand could no longer afford to keep a table luxurious enough for his taste he spent the remainder of his fortune on one great banquet at which he committed suicide. As La Fontaine noted, Fouquet's party proved that the French "owed nothing to Rome." Although La Fontaine never finished his poem to commemorate the evening, "Le Songe de Vaux," the dreamlike memory of that evening lives on.

Chapter Seven

Insatiable Gluttony

Count Heinrich von Brühl Dines Alone, Dresden, Mid-Eighteenth Century

Did you not know, then, that today Lucullus dines
with Lucullus?

Plutarch, "Lucullus"

*G*LUTTONY. IN THE CATHOLIC CHURCH IT
is one of the seven deadly sins. The ancient Chinese considered it a crime capable
of felling entire dynasties. The Roman historian Suetonius believed that the Emperor Vitellius (r. 69) would have bankrupted Rome with his ravenous feasting if
he had not been violently murdered within the first year of his reign. Certainly, he
made a considerable dent in the fortune of his friends, from whom he demanded
banquets of mind-boggling expense, attending several on a single day. Vitellius's
appetite was so insatiable that he snatched the sacred flesh off the fire at sacrificial
feasts. He is but one of the countless decadent gluttons still popularly blamed for
the fall of the Roman Empire. They were not all emperors; perhaps the most famous of all was Lucullus (ca. 110–56 B.C.), a general and governor more renowned
for his extravagant table than any military victory.

139

Serious preoccupation with gluttony as a frightening and tangible evil peaked in the Middle Ages. The flesh-despising, darkly apocalyptic medieval mind imagined the glutton burning forever alongside murderers, rapists, and extortionists. Never again would this sin be so luridly captivating. But once the idea of hell reached its creative zenith with Dante's *Inferno,* fascination with gluttony began to wane. Without a sufficiently hair-raising vision of eternal damnation in the afterlife, it is hard to conjure up much enthusiasm for denying the pleasures of this one. The word "gluttony" feels antiquated, evoking images of obese seignorial lords gnawing greedily on fistfuls of roast. While contemporary Western culture shares the medieval obsession with fat, certainly more than our counterparts in any intervening era, rarely is the term "glutton" bandied about in more than a metaphoric sense. That, however, is where we go wrong. We condemn the fat man, but not the glutton, and confuse the social transgression of being overweight with a crime that is older and more universally acknowledged than human history can record.

How does the glutton reveal himself? The jumbled confusion between the epicure and the glutton began with the earliest followers of Epicurus (ca. 341–270 B.C.) himself. The Greek philosopher espoused the idea that pleasure is the supreme good and its pursuit the highest goal in life. By defining "pleasure" as tranquility of mind and the absence of pain, he mitigated the unfettered hedonism his philosophy might otherwise imply. That some among his followers chose to ignore this subtlety in order to rationalize a life abandoned to self-gratification led to centuries of negative associations with Epicureanism. The glutton can be a sly bird indeed. What of the Dorian Grays of the world whose bodies never reveal the sins they have transgressed?

Heinrich Graf von Brühl (1700–1763) was just such a man. He lived in the Age of Reason, or Enlightenment, and also a time of aristocratic indulgence, when educated circles considered it ludicrously superstitious, and worse, bad form, to seriously accuse someone of gluttony. It was a time in which the English Dr. Johnson defined the epicure as "a man wholly given to luxury." The epithet conveyed a mild censure of self-indulgence, yet fell far short of a condemnation of the soul.

Count Brühl, however, inhabited the much less prudish city of Dresden, where luxuriance reigned. Saxony would not permit the grumpy, mocking satire of a Hogarth to dampen the state machine of merrymaking; it was the perfect place for a glutton to mask himself as a gentleman of consummate taste.

The Elector Friedrich August I (r. 1694–1733), August II, King of Poland (r. 1696–1733), set the jolly tone of the city. His nickname, Augustus the Strong, did not refer to his military brilliance or fortitude (he had to be replaced in his stint as commander of the Imperial Army against the Turks and later suffered defeat against Charles XII in the Great Northern War) but to his seemingly inexhaustible capacity for women and drink. He finally died in Warsaw after a particularly raucous binge with General Grumkov (the general died several weeks later from the aftereffects of this same event). But while he lived, the court rejoiced in a continual round of hunting parties, balls, and banquets. The exuberant dome of the Frauenkirche, known as the "Stone Bell," epitomized the city's baroque glory. Though the Frauenkirche's architecture was widely admired, the capital sprouted gilded pleasure palaces, more than churches, at an astonishing rate. The architect Matthäus Daniel Pöppelmann and the sculptor Balthasar Permoser built the most sumptuous of these, the Zwinger, an undulating, high baroque temple to entertaining in the grand French style. The *Taschenbergpalais,* playfully Turkish in inspiration, was added nearby, and another in a "Dutch" style. Augustus installed the Pillnitz in the Grosser Garten park, with a *Wasserpalais* (water palace) and *Bergpalais* (hillside palace) in chinoiserie style, reached by gondola for summer amusements. These sophisticated playhouses offered escape from the strain of court formality. Under Augustus, there was a continual demand for new and increasingly elaborate diversion.

The Elector quested for ever more beautiful and enchanting mistresses; however, his overriding passion was porcelain. The pride of Saxon achievement was true hard-paste porcelain, the magical substance whose secret had eluded European understanding for centuries, produced locally by the Elector's own manufactory, Meissen. Johann Friedrich Böttger (1682–1719), a renegade alchemist captured and held prisoner by Augustus, discovered the basic formula in 1708; a year later he managed to produce his first specimen of glazed white porcelain, and in 1710 a factory was opened not far from the capital. Böttger learned that the addition of petuntse (feldspathic clay) to kaolin (white china clay) produced a translucent body, impervious to liquids, when fired at extremely high temperatures (1,250–1,350 degrees Celsius). The factory employed the most talented craftsmen to invent boisterous colors, vigorous shapes, and fancifully exotic designs to appeal to the highest taste of the period. Augustus the Strong was dazzled; the new wares were an aesthetic and scientific triumph for Saxony, which added glamour to his collections as well as his parties. He commissioned numerous dinner services and thousands of sculptures, the bigger the better, which he showcased at his Japanese Palace.

For all his licentiousness, Augustus's attempts to satiate his robust desires should not be confused with the pure selfishness of a glutton. Nothing pleased the Elector more than sharing the things he loved. When Augustus built a breathtaking new opera house (opera was his other consuming interest), he offered free admission every night to the fifteen hundred to two thousand attendees. He opened the art gallery of the Zwinger and two wings containing his personal library to the public so that they might partake of his treasures. Fun was his goal, which required mirthful companions and laughter. He kept a retinue of dwarves and clowns continually at his service. The primary duty of his courtiers was to assume a tone of light frivolity, wear a cheerful smile, and perpetuate the merry-go-round atmosphere. Life in the Dresden court was like a giant porcelain-encrusted music box, preciously twirling around and around.

This was the environment in which Heinrich von Brühl learned the ways of the frolicking capital; and Dresden was the enchanting city that his insatiable gluttony almost single-handedly destroyed, centuries before the devastating air raids in the final months of World War II. When the Seven Years' War ended in 1763, tales of the Count's unbridled dissipation found their way into print. In no uncertain terms, the philologist and alchemist Johann Christoph Adelung (1732–1806) declared: "The distressed condition of the Electorate of Saxony is occasioned not more by war and invasion, and by the general depravity of the inhabitants, than by the iniquity of a few.—In wealth and power count Brühl is comparably the greatest man in Saxony."

Brühl's life began far more modestly. Heinrich was the youngest of four sons whose father was an impoverished member of the petty nobility in Thuringia. Without a fortune to secure his future, young Brühl was placed in the service of Princess Elizabeth of Weissenfelser Hof as a page in 1713. Augustus the Strong encountered Brühl in the Princess's service and found him attractive, attentive, and intelligent. In April 1719 the Count joined the Dresden court in the ignominious role of a page. In this capacity, Brühl witnessed the flurry of building and preparations for the October wedding of Augustus's son, Crown Prince Friedrich August (1696–1763; from 1733, Friedrich August II, Elector of Saxony; and from 1735, King Augustus III of Poland) to the Archduchess Maria Josepha, daughter of the Habsburg Emperor. But at that date, who could have foretold that this charming, modest servant harbored an ambition so unquenchable that he would destroy them all? Perhaps only those who noticed that even then, beneath his smiling, fresh-faced expression, he kept to himself, greedily plotting how he might get more than his fair share of the pie. . . .

Brühl's enemy, Adelung, said, when first he met the Count, at the height of Brühl's power, "I was more charm'd with him than any person I ever knew in the whole world; nothing came from him but *Your intirely devoted and humble servant; You may command me in any thing:* These were his very words and frequently repeated." Brühl disarmed his inferiors in a flood of courteous niceties such that they were overcome, thus impressing his superiors and squelching the jealousy of his peers. No one ever saw him behave with less than perfect poise. Nevertheless, Adelung "found that the flood of politeness with which he continued to deluge me, were no more than so many mechanical motions, to which his body had been long habituated, without his soul having any meaning in them." Handsome and rosy-cheeked as a youth, somewhat portly in middle age, but no more so than the average eighteenth-century gentleman, Brühl did not look the part of the grotesque medieval glutton, wiping his greasy mouth on his sleeve.

As Augustus the Strong and his jovial court drank and ate with carefree revelry,

Brühl craftily schemed, waiting for his opportunity. Eight years passed before Brühl was appointed a Gentleman of the Elector's Bedchamber, an honor, but not an exclusive one. He was careful to please Augustus with his humility and attentions, biding his time, observing everything as he climbed through the ranks of the Bedchamber to become a Groom of the Stool.

Brühl noticed that Pauli, who was Secretary to the Cabinet, responsible for writing all of the Elector's correspondence and President of the College of War, was an inveterate tippler. Brühl was not alone in remarking Pauli's drunkenness; Adelung claimed that the King himself said that it was only in the morning that he had Pauli. His habit was "not of that kind of social inebriation very common among the ministers and secretaries of Vienna, by a brisk circulation of glasses at dinner, and never carried to the total extinction of reason. No, Pauli's drunkenness was so beastly that it unfitted him for any kind of business." One afternoon he plummeted to his death after an especially reckless binge, and Brühl volunteered his own services to Augustus. It was never proven, but the rumor persisted that the ambitious young count, with a Cheshire cat smile, had personally poured the wine that Pauli had appreciatively imbibed.

On 30 March 1730, Brühl was promoted to Chamberlain of the King's Wardrobe. Just two months later came Brühl's chance to impress the court in organizing the enormous festivities for the military exercises at Zeithain, held 30 May to 29 June. Thirty thousand men performed in the event, which forty-seven members of the royal house attended together with an entourage of courtiers, pages, and attendants for hunting, opera, and feasts. Brühl efficiently delegated the logistical tasks and enjoyed, for the first time, the role of overseeing his guests. Count Wackerbarth organized with tactful diplomacy the complicated military parades. Pöppelmann built and decorated the gorgeous temporary pavilions. Pieces from the first porcelain dinner service ever produced at Meissen, the Yellow Lion Service, painted with fantastic chinoiserie designs, probably made their debut at the lavish banquets for this event. Dresden's most talented confectioners created an enormous cake, containing one thousand kilograms of flour, one hundred kilograms of butter, and thirty-six hundred eggs, among other ingredients. It was so massive that the bakers needed the assistance of horses to lift the dough into and out of the oven. The festivities went splendidly, and Brühl, who contributed relatively little, proudly took credit for it all. The Prussian King Friedrich Wilhelm I (r. 1713–1740) was so impressed by Saxon hospitality that he awarded to Brühl alone Prussia's highest honor, the Order of the Eagle. His son, the Crown Prince, later known as Frederick the Great (r. 1740–1786), was the first to congratulate the Count. Brühl had succeeded in making a formidable name for himself.

Just one year later, Brühl was promoted to the multiple titles of Director of Internal Affairs, Inspector of Metalworks, and Supervisor of State Property and Mines, and was assigned work in the Secret Service. The appointments came one after another to the Elector's favorite. In 1732 he became the First Lord of the Bedchamber, the following year, Secretary of the Treasury and a minister on the Royal Council. These honors were accompanied by the financial remuneration one would expect. In 1731 he bought Count Römer's property in Herzberg for thirty thousand taler, an incredible sum, especially from a man famous for his stinginess despite his imperial taste. His household became increasingly magnificent, lined with silk wall coverings and filled with rare porcelain. But he had no real friends with whom to share his treasures, only allies and paid spies delivering secret messages: Count Hennicke, who served as a lackey, and Count Wackerbarth, who mentored him through the labyrinth of court politics. What Brühl had coveted, he now hoarded; he had adopted Augustus's taste, but not his spirit.

In spite of what Brühl had achieved, when the Elector died, his prospects under Augustus II were uncertain, at best. As Crown Prince, the new Elector had relied almost exclusively upon the council of Alexander Joseph Fürst von Sulkowski (1695–1762). August II had distrusted his father's reliance upon Brühl, seeing the minister as an insidious opportunist. Nevertheless, the Elector had a problem: Sulkowski was Catholic and therefore barred from holding a government post in Saxony. Augustus the Strong had converted to Catholicism in order to claim the Polish crown, but Saxony had remained firmly Lutheran. Brühl delicately pointed out the impossibility of Sulkowski's serving as Minister, and graciously volunteered to resign from his post as First Lord of the Bedchamber so that his rival might have it. He deferentially refrained from asking anything in return, thereby being perceived as a selfless hero. In gratitude, the new Elector appointed him First Commissioner of the Treasury. From that moment forward, Augustus II would not hear a word spoken against his cunning minister and even Brühl's rival, Sulkowski, became a supporter.

For a time, Sulkowski and Brühl ruled together with the help of Brühl's lackey Hennicke, still being paid by the Count to divulge secrets and plot on Brühl's behalf. Power was shared, but the balance was loaded. Augustus II took little interest in matters of state, letting his advisors make the decisions while he hunted for pictures for his extraordinary collection and attended the opera. Paintings by Titian, Canaletto, and Bellotto made their way into the royal collection. Formal ties were made to secure Johann Sebastian Bach, working as the municipal music director in nearby Leipzig, as Royal Saxon Court Composer in 1736.

A few people complained; a satirical medal struck in Holland, bearing the inscription, "Es sind unserer drey / Twey Pagen und ein Laquay" (Though now so mighty, in us three / Two Pages and a Skip you see), was circulated on the sly. However, those who criticized the ministers began to vanish with increasing frequency, imprisoned or quietly murdered by Brühl's secret agents.

In 300 B.C., Archestratus described a particularly succulent fish on the island of Rhodes (probably a sturgeon or dogfish) and advised, "And even if you risk your life, and they refuse to sell it to you, seize it. . . . Afterwards, put up with whatever is fated to you." When the yearning to obtain a desirable flavor incites theft, gourmandizing has execrably devolved into gluttony. The glutton's appetite often beguiles him into performing unspeakable acts to fulfill his aching hunger; this is the essence of what makes the sin so disturbing.

As a masked glutton, Brühl shared nothing if he could help it, least of all power and money, from whence all other things flowed. Slowly and stealthily, he took his rival unaware. First, he promised the Queen's confessor, Father Guarini, that he would look out for Catholic interests in Saxony. The priest turned Maria Josepha against Sulkowski; she complained to her husband about his loyal aide until he succumbed to the poisonous words. In 1738 Sulkowski was barred from court and stripped of all his appointments except his rank as general.

Now, no one could stand in Brühl's way. From that moment on, he took the titles of First Minister (Prime Minister from 1746), Minister of the Royal Council, Chief of the Courts and the Civil Service, Administrator of State, Secretary of the Treasury, Overseer of the Library and State Collections, and General of the Army. The Elector, who did not share his father's interest in porcelain, also made Brühl the director of the Meissen factory. Although Augustus II revoked his own royal entitlement to the company's wares, asking that the company continue work on his father's unfinished sculptures only when more profitable projects were not at hand, he granted Brühl the unprecedented privilege of commissioning whatever pieces he might want.

Needless to say, Brühl did not hesitate to avail himself of the opportunity. Among numerous other items, he ordered a staggering dinner service, composed

FIGURE 7.1
Diamond-shaped tray from the Swan Service, 1740, model by Johann Friedrich Eberlein, produced by Meissen, hard-paste porcelain.

of more than twenty-two hundred individual pieces, known as the Swan Service. Roasted swan, served rewrapped in its snowy plumage, often appeared as the breathtaking pièce de résistance of medieval feasts; at Brühl's table, the bird's milky whiteness graced the glazed surface of every plate. By this date, many of Saxony's wealthiest households had adopted the fashion for porcelain tableware set by Augustus the Strong, but never had such a variety of masterful forms and designs been assembled together in one set. There were platters, trays with handles, bowls of every size, shell-shaped side dishes, sauceboats, cruets, sugar casters, footed salts, spice boxes with gilt-bronze mounts to hinge the covers, and great, domed dish covers to keep food warm. Serving spoons and dessert spoons were modeled entirely in porcelain, as were the delicate handles of dessert knives. Tall coffeepots and matching milk pitchers, chocolate cups with covers and teacups with saucers offered elegant service for these newly popular beverages. Delicate *Wermutbecher,* like miniature tankards, were made to hold vermouth. Footed cake stands, candy dishes, and confectionery boxes allowed a meal to end as ornately as it began, while porcelain candelabrum and candlesticks lit the table, and decorative vases held real or artificial flowers.

FIGURE 7.2
Nymph Galatea tureen
from the Swan Service,
1740, model by Johann
Joachim Kändler,
produced by Meissen.

As director of Meissen, Brühl controlled the order and speed with which commissions at the manufactory were completed. He had previously been made a supervisor to the factory in 1733, and his plans for the service first date to 1736. Even though he placed his own order at the top of the list, the Swan Service took four years to complete. Johann Joachim Kändler (1706–1775) supervised the project with the assistance of Johann Friedrich Eberlein (1693/6–1749); both had originally been trained as sculptors. Kändler quickly made a name for himself with the colossal porcelain sculptures of exotic birds and animals he created for Augustus the Strong's Japanese Palace and became chief modeler at the factory in 1733. He was fascinated with porcelain as an intrinsically beautiful substance, ethereally white and luminescent from within, that could be modeled into the exuberant forms of high baroque sculpture.

The revolutionary dinner service created for Count Brühl pays homage to the undulating waves of the sea, which inspired it. Seashells, dolphins, maritime motifs,

and, most frequently, swans swim across the pieces with the swirling movement made fashionable by the French silversmith Juste-Aurèle Meissonnier, whose work the modelers knew from engravings. An enormous soup tureen, more than half a meter tall, carries the figure of the mythical sea nymph Galatea and a sweet-faced putto, encircled by a dramatic billowing drape on its domed cover. Another, almost as high, bears the goddess Venus in a seashell chariot. Smaller tureens hold leaping dolphins and gliding swans, putti and nymphs. An enormous scallop-rimmed monteith for chilling wine has mermaid handles that stand as pertly upright as Viking figureheads. Even the most mundane dinner plate became a sculptural work of art, rendered in three dimensions, with the motif of the swan delicately modeled in relief and a gentle curvature to the rim. Whereas earlier Meissen services utilized porcelain as a flat surface for spidery, chinoiserie designs, rendered in saturated blues and reds, the Swan Service uses color as a highlight to showcase the dazzling brilliance of the white clay.

Brühl also commissioned elaborate centerpieces overflowing with the riotous spirit of the German baroque as it cascaded into the superfluity of the rococo. The Swan Service included an enormous porcelain table fountain, spouting water from the mouths of dolphins into shell-shaped basins with a hulking figure of Neptune on the top. Tritons and nymphs holding confectionery dishes aloft were to be placed symmetrically around it. However, Brühl's gargantuan appetite for porcelain was far from sated. In 1737 he ordered another example, decorated with chinoiserie figures and birds sitting on blooming branches that could hold cruets for vinegar, olive oil, and mustard on the upper level. Still, his orders continued, for additional centerpieces as well as epergnes with Chinese figures and cruets at the sides. In 1748, Sir Charles Hansbury-Williams, the British envoy to Saxony, wrote to Henry Fox to describe an event of the previous year:

I was once at a dinner where we sat down at one table two hundred and six people (twas at Count Brühl's) when the Dessert was set on, I thought it was the most wonderful thing I ever beheld. I fancied myself either in a Garden or at an Opera. But I could not imagine that I was at Dinner. In the middle of the Table was a fountain of the Piazza Navona at Rome, at least eight foot high, which ran all the while with Rose-water, and its said that Piece alone cost six thousand Dollars (Taler). I verily believe that Count Brühl has above thirty thousand Pounds worth of China in his house.

Indeed, he was so impressed with Count Brühl's dessert centerpiece that he ordered a number of Meissen pieces on behalf of Lady Caroline Fox. Like Lucullus's numerous dining rooms, each corresponding to a particular level of expenditure and season, Brühl's ever-expanding collection of porcelain was adaptable to any occasion.

In addition to all of his other wares, Brühl collected a large number of porcelain figurines with which to decorate the table: miniature churches, palaces, farmhouses, barns, dovecotes, stables, and even a man riding a mule. Kändler envisioned the dessert table set like an abundantly decorated garden, with an open-air gazebo in the middle, surrounded by cottages, trelliswork, orange trees, flowerpots, and statuary, all created in porcelain. Such ornamental figurines sat in combination with elaborate sugar, caramel, and marzipan designs by Brühl's master confectioner, Lachapelle. A 1753 inventory of the Count's possessions included confectionery gods, mythological and allegorical figures, putti, animals, theater characters, ranking officials, tradesmen, musicians, and pastoral groups with elegant women dressed in the height of contemporary fashion, as well as peasants sporting their regional costume. The man who ruled Saxony had replicated his universe on his dessert table.

Brühl did not invent the dessert-table fashion for interspersing porcelain figurines with glistening sugar sculptures upon parterres of colored sugar "sand." In 1738, Brühl's rival, Sulkowski, ordered a 653-piece dinner and coffee service that included a 64-piece *Confect-Aufsatzstück* (dessert centerpiece), with 160 figurines and 48 small floral bouquets. Two years earlier Sulkowski had purchased an enormous Meissen dinner service, featuring Kändler's first modeled designs, including a massive soup tureen with silver mounts. From that time forward, Kändler had raced to fill the popular demand for these wares. New porcelain factories cropped up across

Europe: Vienna, 1719; the French soft-paste factory at Vincennes, 1738; Capodi-monte in Naples, 1743; Chelsea, in England, 1744. All of these and the numerous German concerns that rose up over the subsequent decade imitated Meissen in creating these table figures.

Brühl tapped Kändler's genius at the height of his powers. Never would the vitality and crisp vigor of this modeler's figures be surpassed. However, the Count's desire for porcelain could not be assuaged. Where Sulkowski had one imposing centerpiece, Brühl had at least three. Following the example of Augustus the Strong, he ordered a gigantic porcelain glockenspiel and a great porcelain wine barrel.

The Count did nothing by half measures. His extraordinary collection needed a suitable home to contain it and a feast worthy to be consumed in it. In 1735, he had acquired a substantial property in Friedrichstadt; then, as Director of the King's Estates and Buildings, he availed himself of the finest architects, craftsmen, and designers available. In 1740 he bought a palace on Augustusstrasse overlooking the Elbe, with a *Festsaal* for entertaining 87.5 meters (287 feet) long. He had 877 paintings in his gallery and a freestanding library of 62,000 volumes. Simultaneously, he acquired numerous estates in the outskirts of Dresden and in Poland, as well as the sumptuous Schloss Knöffel that served as a stopping-off place between the two capitals. He eventually accumulated more property than any of the landed gentry in Saxony. He underwrote numerous manufactories and craftsmen to supply these properties with everything from textiles and parquet floors to soap. The Count's accumulations recalled Lucullus's renown for his many lavish estates with vast gardens, baths, and palaces filled with rare sculptures and paintings. When criticized for making a house pleasant for summer, but uninhabitable in winter, Lucullus smiled and answered, "You think me, then, less provident than cranes and storks, not to change my home with the season."

Just as Lucullus kept so many hundreds of costly purple robes that he forgot what he owned, Brühl's wardrobe was considered one of the great wonders of Dresden. He purportedly had "no less than three or four hundred suits of rich cloaths, with boots and shoes in proportion: He has collected all the finest cloths, velvets, and silks of all manufactures, besides lace and embroideries. He calls for his books of patterns, which are all numbered, and chuses that which pleases his fancy for the day."

Nowhere was Brühl's extravagance greater than at his dinner table, where, in his velvets and jewels, he lorded over his miniature porcelain universe, as a great parade of the choicest delicacies in Europe was served with all the pompous ceremony of a royal banquet. A small army of servants labored to create these elaborate meals. Adelung claimed:

> Count Brühl's family, officers and servants included, did not amount to less than 200 persons; he had 12 chamberlains, 12 pages, equerries, stewards, clerks of the kitchen, and yeomen of the cellar: with all the train of various denominations found in the most splendid court; in the kitchen are head cooks, 12 inferior, with scullions to the number of about 30; to the cellar and confectionery belong very near a much like number; and as for the servants in livery they exceed a hundred.

He further observed that in all the years he spent in Dresden:

> never less than 30 dishes of meat were served up to count Brühl's table, and that with such waste, that servants easily found the means to smuggle very costly things out of the house; the standard of a private treat was 50 dishes, and every publick entertainment at least consisted of 80 or 100; since that time I have been at the court of kings where the stated number of dishes for the royal table was only 12, and when the sovereign dined in publick it did not exceed 24 or 30.

By comparison, the 1739 edition of Amaranthes' *Frauenzimmer-Lexicon,* an alphabetized reference book for Saxon housewives, whose entries ranged from biographies of famous women in history to instructions on cooking and cleaning, suggested menus and diagrams for setting the table with six, eight, fourteen, twenty, but never more than thirty dishes at maximum. The diagrams provide sophisticated table designs, including a flamboyant table in the shape of a gigantic swirling "S." Written for a bourgeois rather than aristocratic audience, the book offers advice for creating simplified versions of French courtly menus, commencing with large tureens of *potages* surrounded by numerous smaller dishes. However, even the most aristocratic French table settings, culminating with the wildly exuberant table plans suggested by Joseph Gilliers in *Le Cannameliste français* of 1751, or the grand menus of Menon's *Les Soupers de la Cour* of 1755, never approached the everyday splendor of Brühl's table.

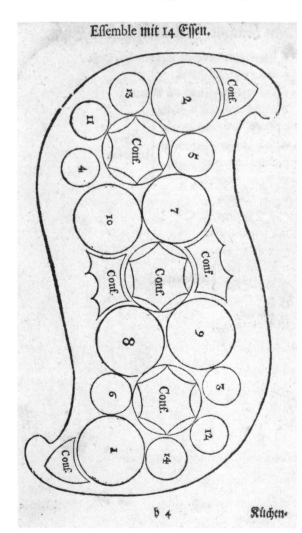

Essemble mit 14 Essen.

b 4   Küchen.

It could be argued that such magnificence was requisite for the important entertaining Brühl, as Chief Minister, had to undertake on behalf of the state. Indeed, the Count frequently hosted such official occasions. When Augustus's daughter became engaged to the Dauphin of France, Brühl held a party for three hundred guests on 11 January 1747. His astounding porcelain grotto and table fountain, surrounded by numerous other pieces from his collection, created an astounding dessert table in the picture gallery. There were other grand banquets held to forward diplomatic and political objectives; in 1746, one hundred and sixty guests came to dinner in honor of the Bavarian Elector. Every Saturday he held a lavish reception, and ministers often visited on other evenings, especially after Augustus retired for bed.

Yet, ultimately, Count Brühl's lifestyle far exceeded the luxury appropriate to his official duties. His excess went far beyond the bounds of generous hospitality because his motivations were wholly selfish. No one expected Brühl to entertain in less

FIGURE 7.3 *(facing page)*
Table-setting diagram,
1715, from Amaranthes,
Nutzbares . . .
Frauenzimmer-Lexicon.

FIGURE 7.4
Plan and decorations for a
table, 1751, from Joseph
Gilliers, *Le Cannameliste*
français.

than august style or to be insufficiently compensated for his exalted position. Nor was Brühl by any means the only scoundrel in Dresden, or for that matter, in Europe. A previous director at Meissen, Count Heinrich Karl von Hoym, had been caught selling unmarked pieces on his own account in Paris. Even Adelung was forced to admit that Sulkowski had skimmed millions from the treasury in his short stint in office; yet, he found that "compared with Count Brühl, he must appear a minister of great probity and disinterestedness." Brühl's shameless acquisitiveness was surely offensive. As Adelung pointed out, Brühl's "gallery of pictures is incomparably more magnificent than the king's and an hundred and fifty six ells long, which is eighteen more than that of Versailles." Such inordinate consumption, exceeding that of his own sovereign and even the King of France, could not be deemed a necessity of his position.

Brühl published a pamphlet to justify his extravagance, stating that it was "advantageous to Saxony; as encouraging trade, imploying artificers, and causing circulation of money." However, Adelung noted that aside from the huge quantities of porcelain, which Brühl received free of charge (his capacious orders therefore draining, rather than replenishing, the resources of the factory),

> the traders of Saxony are little beholden to count Brühl's dissipations; his shoes come from Paris, 100 pair at once, and his wigs by the dozen; and even his tarts used to be sent by post from the same city, *that mother of abominations of the earth.* Dresden and Leipsic make very good chocolate, but that for his excellency must come from Rome or Vienna; in short, I scarce saw any thing in his house which was either the product or manufacture of Saxony.

The French philosopher Montesquieu disparagingly observed, "The Germans eat and drink practically anything with pleasure. Their main object is to swallow instead of taste." However, the *Frauenzimmer-Lexicon* makes it clear that even Saxons of modest means in the reign of Augustus II had an enormous concern for taste, especially for things French. While the copious recipes include local favorites such as *Schweinefleisch mit Sauerkraut* (pork with sauerkraut) and *Hirschwildpret mit Wacholderbeeren und Zwiebeln* (wild venison with juniper berries and onions), simple treats such as *Lachs grillé en Cais* (salmon grilled en papillote, with a dab of butter and vinegar); medieval holdovers, like *Pfau in einer Pastete* (peacock in a pastry shell); and Eastern dishes like *Karpfen mit einer Polnischen Schwarzen Brühe* (carp with a Polish black sauce of wine, vinegar, eggs, ginger, pepper, cloves, onion, and raisins); the book instructs readers in how to cook delicacies in the height of the newest Parisian style. There are definitions of cooking terms such as *à la braise, à la daube, bouillon* (and even instructions on how to make bouillon cubes), *jus,* and *coulis,* and recipes for such French classics as *Roberts Brühe* (that is, *sauce à la Robert*), *boeuf à la mode,* and *potage à la reine.* And just as the Parisians did, the Germans had assimilated their favorite Italianate dishes, as, for example, with *Hüner mit Italianischen Nudeln und Parmesan-Käse* (chicken with Italian noodles and Parmesan cheese).

The same year that the 1739 edition of Amaranthes' encyclopedic text was published saw a German translation of Massialot's *Le cuisinier roïal et bourgeois.* In fact, from the end of the Thirty Years' War, numerous German editions providing instruction for French cooking appeared in rapid succession, such as *Der frantzösische Confitirer* (1655), *Der frantzösische Becker* (1665), and *Parisische Küchenmeister* (1667). The supremacy of French cuisine was spreading throughout Europe. Nor was Brühl, with his *confiturier* Lachapelle, alone in wanting not just the French style, but authentic preparation by a native chef. The most famous French cookbook of the period was written by a chef working in England and the Hague, Vincent La Chapelle (perhaps a relation of the Count's confectioner) who published the English *The Modern Cook* in 1733, two years before it ever appeared in French.

Nevertheless, as parcels of tarts arrived from Paris and chocolates from Rome and Vienna, Brühl's justification of his vast expenditure as a boon to Saxon trade rang hollow. Like Archestratus, who, according to Athenaeus, "in his love for pleasures, traveled over every land and sea with precision, in a desire, as it seems to me, to review with care the things of the belly," Brühl, in his insistence on dining upon the rarest and most exotic delicacies, knew no bounds. At bottom, the Saxon Count's interest in making an impression extended only as far as the resplendently attired man whose image greeted him as he looked into the mirror-lined walls of his palace.

Lucullus was far more honest in his selfishness. Plutarch records that when several visiting Greeks declined to join Lucullus daily for the lavish feasts he offered because they were ashamed to have him incur such expense on their behalf, Lucullus smilingly replied, "Some of this, indeed my Greek friends, is for your sakes, but more for that of Lucullus." Once, when his servant brought him a single course for dinner, and a rather meager one at that, he reproved his steward, who confessed

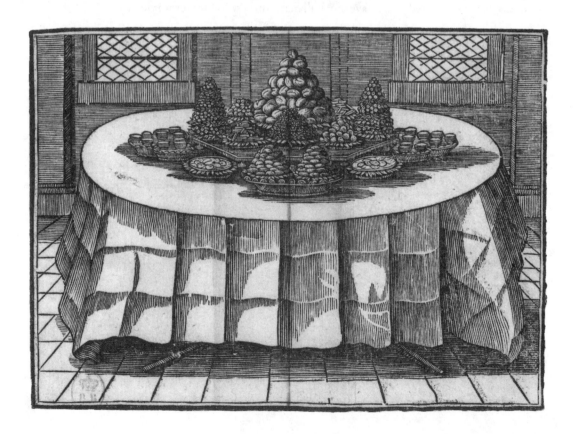

that he thought one course sufficient in the absence of company. "Did you not know, then," he replied, "that today Lucullus dines with Lucullus?" His words ring out through the centuries as the glutton's motto.

Dining alone offers its own enticements: a chance to savor a favorite treat without interruption, to slowly contemplate its succulent flavor, to pause at the beauty of one's surroundings and ingest deeply in the repose of needing neither to speak or to listen. For Lucullus, every meal offered an opportunity to transform the act of feeding his body into the art of dining. The solitude, for a man who hosted and attended so many parties, must have been refreshing. His taste for fancy living, while decadent, resembled the vivacious joviality of Augustus the Strong more than that of a pernicious glutton like Brühl. Like the Elector, Lucullus opened his vast library to all Greeks, liberally gave away his clothing and his choicest delicacies, and wholeheartedly enjoyed the company of his friends.

Brühl, by contrast, was always alone, even when he surrounded himself with company. Having a paid lackey as a friend hardly counts. His relationships with other people, even his wife and children, revolved around how they could help him hoard more money, porcelain, and rare delicacies. Whenever he could, he would steal himself secretively away. His house was filled with hidden passageways so that he could slip in and out without notice. His spies would alert him to any unexpected arrivals, and the angel-faced glutton would instantly transform his expression into one of deep piety or meditation. But did Brühl really enjoy himself?

In the 1930s, after more than a century of gentlemen's dining societies glorifying the gourmand, A.J.A. Symons wrote:

> The epicure is not a man who thinks of, and lives for, his belly alone; he is not
> a sensualist for whom dinner is merely an elaborate prelude to sexual passion;
> he is not a hedonist who sees life as a succession of pleasurable sensations to be
> obtained by hook, crook, or levitation; he is not a table-bore who rams his one
> subject down your throat; he is not a pride-starved victim of insufficiency

FIGURE 7.5
Dessert table, 1692, engraving from François Massialot, *Nouvelle Instruction.*

159

striving to assert a false superiority by making undue fuss over wine and food. He is simply "one who cultivates a refined taste for the pleasures of the table."

But the glutton, whose appetite is insatiable, never finds satisfaction in a fleeting taste of perfection or sits back after dining in blissful contentment. There is no joy in his unending quest for more, and certainly no generosity.

Brühl lived as lavishly as he could imagine. He never hesitated to order up whatever he desired. However, he hated to pay up his accounts. There were stories of tradesmen lining his hallways, hoping to collect bills that had been sitting for weeks, even years. He happily sold secrets to the Viennese and reduced the army to cover his own debts. Surely, Augustus II must be held complicit in these events. He allowed Brühl to control the information he received and do as he pleased without restraint. His philosophy as Elector translates as "Ignorance is bliss." He enjoyed the lack of responsibility, and his picture collection was a triumph; in 1754 he acquired Raphael's coveted *Sistine Madonna*.

Augustus II may not have seen the detriment of Brühl's despotic rule on the state of Saxony, but Frederick the Great did. The Prussian King, who had been the first to congratulate the ambitious chamberlain at the Zeithain exercises so many years before, realized that the Prime Minister's selfishness left Saxony vulnerable to invasion. In December 1745, he invaded Dresden, whose common citizens greeted the Prussian troops as liberators. This should have been a wake-up call to Augustus, but it was not.

On 29 August 1756 the Prussian troops marched into Saxony yet again; by 9 September they reached Dresden, vanquishing its population, burning and pounding its defensive artillery, and pummeling the city center. The jewel of central Europe was crushed into sand and engulfed in flames. Seven years of war followed; in the end Saxony was merely a pawn to be traded between the Austrians, the Prussians, and the Russians. When peace was restored in 1763, it took sixty years for Dresden to recover its former population.

Count Brühl did not live to see his country helpless before her conquerors. Was he engulfed by the flames of destruction or killed in the horrors of war? On the eve of the Prussian invasion, he and Augustus II escaped to Warsaw, where his grand lifestyle continued unabated. He returned unscathed as peace seemed imminent and quietly died of asthma in his silken bed, with his vast collections around him. Perhaps he burns in a medieval hell, after all. Without question, he fulfilled the dire predictions of the ancient Chinese: Augustus II and his son died just before Brühl, Augustus's grandson lost Poland, and Saxony never again flourished. The glutton should never be confused with the epicure.

Chapter Eight

Seduction

Casanova's
"Souper Intime," Venice,
November 1753

I become ardent; but she needs only a single kiss to calm me, and two words: *"After supper."*

Casanova, *The History of My Life,* vol. 4, chap. 3

I T WAS A CHILLY NOVEMBER EVENING IN Venice; the year, 1753. Cupid's arrow seemed to have hit all of Europe; Tiepolo covered Venetian ceilings with voluptuous scenes of swirling sensuality, while Boucher decorated French walls with fleshly lovers and putti who exalted romance. This was the century of *Dangerous Liaisons,* in which seduction was pursued as both a sport and a religion; privacy was the ultimate luxury. France's celebrated chefs and gourmands even invented a new type of meal. The *souper intime* (intimate supper) featured delicate aphrodisiacs set forth in jewel-like rooms. The servants were kept far away.

Food and seduction have been inextricably linked since Eve first tempted Adam with the fruit of paradise; in the twentieth century, M.F.K. Fisher wrote, "Our three basic needs, for food, for security, and for love, are so mixed and mingled that we cannot straightly think of one without the other." No one, however, has ever interwoven the pleasures of the flesh more artfully than Giovanni Giacomo Casanova, Chevalier de Seingalt (1725–1798). In the generation between Bach and Mozart, Casanova was the maestro of adding a delicate trill to the music of life itself. His amorous escapades are so legendary that his name has become a proper noun. The real man was a consummate seducer, adventurer, gambler, and bon vivant who knew how to extract every ounce of delight the world had to offer; an exquisite dish or a fine wine thrilled him as much as a beautiful woman; to enjoy all three together was sheer heaven.

In the preface of his twelve-volume autobiography, *The History of My Life,* Casanova declared, "Cultivating whatever gave pleasure to my senses was always the chief business of my life; I have never found any occupation more important. Feeling that I was born for the sex opposite to mine, I have always loved it and done all that I could to make myself loved by it. I have also been extravagantly fond of good food and irresistibly drawn by anything which could excite curiosity." His favorites included "highly seasoned dishes: macaroni prepared by a good Neapolitan cook, *olla podrida,* good sticky salt cod from Newfoundland, high game on the very edge, and cheeses whose perfection is reached when the little creatures which inhabit them become visible. As for women, I have always found that the one I was in love with smelled good, and the more copious her sweat, the sweeter I found it." Dinner provided the melody to the dance of his love affairs, giving them a cadence and rhythm from which he could unleash his magnetic charms, while allowing him to indulge his Epicurean tastes. When the words "after supper" fell upon his finely tuned ears they swelled into a symphony of expectant sensuality; he did not hesitate but rang for dinner at once.

At the time of this adventure, Casanova had spent more than two years in Paris. He had taken refuge there in 1750, after his debauched lifestyle and illicit experiments with black magic forced him to flee his native Venice. Paris seduced him with *le haut goût* (the high taste); he adored everything from her culture to her cuisine, later choosing to write his memoirs in French because he considered the language more universal than his own.

Le Souper fin

A.P.D.R.

FIGURE 8.1
Le Souper fin, 1781,
by Jean-Michel Moreau
("le Jeune"), engraving
from *Le Monument
du Costume.*

If the glittering court in France was the sun radiating over European culture, Venice was the silvery moon. This was the city of shimmering palazzi captured by Canaletto and Guardi; the interior world painted by Pietro Longhi; a decadent playground of gambling houses and *carnivale,* whose denizens hid behind masks for months at a time. One eighteenth-century visitor, Lady Mary Wortley Montagu, observed that "these disguises occasion an abundance of love adventures, and there is something more intriguing in the amours of Venice than in those of other cities."

Casanova, in 1753, was a man of twenty-eight, at the height of his seductive powers. In his youth, he had at first considered an ecclesiastical career, taking minor orders in 1741, and even attending seminary. Although expelled for his licentious adventures, he went on to work for a bishop and a cardinal.

Later, he had worked as a violinist for the San Samuele Theater in Venice, playing music to accompany charming domestic dramas by Carlo Goldoni. Light-hearted, theatrical antics were the preferred entertainment of his age; the Italian commedia dell'arte played to packed houses from Paris to Saint Petersburg. Porcelain figurines of Harlequin, Columbine, and the entire cast of commedia characters ornamented fashionable dessert tables, complementing the real-life amours unfolding around them. Despite this, Casanova considered his own job in the theater humiliating; the world would be his stage. The child of commedia actors, Casanova was not a born aristocrat: Is it any wonder that he surpassed his social betters in the artifice of rococo love?

In the spring of 1753, Casanova returned to Venice, where he immediately plunged into an all-consuming affair with the beautiful C. C. (Caterina Capretta); he even asked for permission to marry her. In response, C. C.'s father (probably quite wisely) whisked his daughter into a convent on the island of Murano, demanding four years of fidelity from the young adventurer before any further talk of marriage. Casanova tried diligently to fulfill this promise. For months, he assiduously attended the convent mass so that C. C. could see him from behind the screen that separated the nuns and boarders from the congregation. Yet, as he himself put it, "with a nature like mine how could I possibly remain satisfied without positive love?" He became depressed, listless, and altogether ready for a new adventure. It found him in the form of a most extraordinary invitation to dinner.

On All Saints' Day, 1753, Casanova was again among the congregation. As he left the church, a letter mysteriously fell at his feet. An old woman he thought from the convent scurried away. He picked up the thick, creamy envelope and caressed it, desperate to break its gold-speckled wax seal. Not until he was safely ensconced in his gondola did he open it and begin reading: "A nun, who has seen you every feast day for the past two months and a half in the church of her convent wishes you to make her acquaintance."

First, she offered to appoint a lady, unknown to him, to escort him to the visiting room of the convent so that he could observe her without any obligation to be introduced or to reveal his identity. More daringly, she invited him to meet her alone, any evening he wished, at a private apartment in Murano; he could stay and dine with her or leave after fifteen minutes. Her third, and most outrageous proposition, was to meet him for supper in the city of Venice, anywhere he wanted; she asked only that he meet her "alone, without a servant, masked, and holding a lantern."

"A *casino* at Murano!" Casanova declared. "The possibility of going to Venice to sup with a young man! It was all very surprising." The nun later told him that "slipping away is not considered possible. . . . You may be sure that I am the only one [who can perform this miracle], and that gold is the powerful god who performs it." Casanova's professed shock somewhat exaggerated the rarity of such an occurrence. By the beginning of the eighteenth century, Joseph Addison had noted that "the nuns of Venice are famous for the liberties they allow themselves. They have an opera within their own walls, and, if they are not much misrepresented, often go out of their bounds to meet their admirers." Casanova's contemporary, Rousseau, had once gotten himself smuggled into Pio Ospedale della Pietà, Venice's famed convent-orphanage for foundling girls, to share a dinner with the young ladies to whom Antonio Vivaldi taught music. Rousseau, however, was never invited to dine out with them (perhaps he had not sufficiently tried; he thought them unattractive, although charming). But for a nun to send an anonymous proposition to dine with an unknown man exceeded even Venetian standards of acceptable depravity.

"Making such a request was sheer madness," Casanova wrote, "yet I found a dignity in it, which forced me to respect her." The velvety feel of the paper hinted at soft, tender flesh. Her beautifully turned French phrases did not go unnoticed by such a Francophile as Casanova; nor did her tone, which evinced both a highly attuned aesthetic sensibility and a flamboyant taste for danger to rival his own. The invitation beguiled him; the occasion provided a seemingly innocuous and innocent excuse to bring them together (as would-be seducers continue to say, "It's only dinner, after all, and everyone has to eat"). And yet, what other activity, except for sexual intercourse itself, is as intimate, as voluptuously sensuous, and as engagingly tactile as a shared meal? Why else would so many conservative cultures, such as those of Arabs and Orthodox Jews, ban seating the sexes together at tables outside of the family setting? This eighteenth-century nun knew that dinner makes a perfect first date.

Casanova, the epicure of all of life's pleasures, lost none of the implied nuances of the meal she proposed: "She was a vestal. I was to taste a forbidden fruit, and who does not know that, from Eve down to our own days, it is the fruit which has always appeared most delicious." Every nerve in his self-indulgent body tingled at the idea of supping with this feisty ecclesiastic, for she herself was the feast he longed for. (He had a decided preference for nuns and convent girls throughout his life.) "What a depraved taste!" he proclaimed of himself in the preface to his autobiography. "How disgraceful to admit it and not blush for it! This sort of criticism makes me laugh. It is precisely by virtue of my coarse tastes, I have the temerity to believe, that I am happier than other men, since I am convinced that my tastes make me capable of more pleasure." After the long months of separation from C. C., how could Casanova possibly resist such an appetizing proposal?

He suspected, or rather hoped, that the letter came from the nun who was teaching his darling C. C. to speak French, a woman whom C. C. had described as "handsome, rich, gallant, and generous." This, however, was merely conjecture; after all, what if she was old and ugly? Or what if it was a trick or some kind of ma-licious joke? He did not delay in responding but opted to proceed cautiously, and so began with her first offer and agreed to meet her in the nuns' parlor.

The introduction transpired exactly as promised; a countess, unknown to Casanova, escorted him, masked, for a glimpse of the cloistered temptress. He tells us that the nun's name was quite famous, but refers to her only by the two initials "M. M." To this day scholars continue to debate her true identity; all that is certain is that the lady in question was no penitent Mary Magdalene. And, far from being old and ugly, she was "about twenty-two or twenty-three . . . a perfect beauty, tall, so white of complexion as to verge on pallor, with an air of nobility and decision but at the same time of reserve and shyness, large blue eyes; a sweet, smiling face, beautiful lips damp with dew." Her elbow and forearm he compared to the finest carving of Praxiteles. Casanova was instantly smitten, although not one word passed between them.

"Despite all this," Casanova claimed, "I did not regret having refused the two meetings over a supper, which the divine beauty had offered me. Sure that I would possess her in a few days, I enjoyed the pleasure of paying her the tribute of desiring her." He could almost taste her, but he implicitly understood that when desire is too easily gratified, it loses its allure. He believed that "[w]e bear hunger in order to savor culinary concoctions better; we put off the pleasure of love in order to make it more intense; and we defer a vengeance in order to make it more deadly."

His calculations proved a bit overconfident. On his next attempt to call on her, he was kept waiting for hours before being brusquely sent away by the attendant, who had bungled the instructions of her mistress. Miscommunications, bruised egos, and hurt feelings prolonged their separation. Weeks passed before he finally saw her again. Their whispered conversation, their first exchange, was devoted to the logistics of their long-awaited supper.

Casanova had "decided that she must have an acknowledged lover, whose pleasure it was to make her happy by satisfying her caprices." How else could she possibly escape her cloister to meet him for supper? It was all so deliciously in want of unraveling; his curiosity and his appetite had both been piqued. When he made discreet inquiries of his friend, the Countess Coronini, about this libertine nun, she retorted, "What is incomprehensible, is the caprice that she took suddenly to become a nun, being handsome, rich, free, well-educated, full of will, and to my knowledge a Free-thinker. She took the veil without any reason, physical or moral; it was sheer caprice." This sentiment was a motif of the period: *capriccio* (caprice) was a favored form of genre painting, especially in Venice, where Canaletto and Guardi exalted in combining real architectural views into fantasy landscapes; as well as the musical term for a kind of light, lively fugue performed "according to the fancy of the performer." *Capriccio* also revealed itself on the dinner table and in the bedroom. It was the spirit that inspired Casanova and M. M.'s *souper intime.*

M. M., however, was offended when Casanova asked her if her lover "forgives you your amorous caprices." She did not deny his existence, but she disliked the implication that her interest in Casanova was merely frivolous. M. M. retorted, "What do you mean by 'caprices'? A year ago he obtained possession of me, and before him I had never belonged to a man; you are the first who inspired me with a fancy." Indulging her sensual desires was a serious business. Their supper, the liaison she envisioned, was to be an exquisitely orchestrated masterpiece created from her sophisticated taste and imagination; she would plunge them into a sea of aesthetic titillation, as luscious as a bowl of plums by Chardin. Casanova, realizing he had met his match, or even a mentor, left in awe of her audacious, high-minded pursuit of pleasure.

At two hours after sunset, he set out to meet her, masked and alone. A single candle helped him navigate the labyrinthine canals of the city and out to the island of Murano. Casanova, who had only narrowly escaped the brutal censure of the Venetian authorities, was well aware that his meeting with M. M. presented the gravest danger to them both. Risk heightened the thrill of his anticipation, adding a brisk rush of adrenaline to the November chill.

He arrived at the green doorway of her *casino,* and effortlessly slipped her key into the lock. He passed through the anteroom to the salon, where she had instructed him to unmask and read by the fire until she arrived. It was, as she had foretold, an enchanting love nest, charmingly lit by "candles in girandoles in front of mirrors and by four other candelabra on a table on which there were some books."

The eighteenth-century Venetian *casino* was a luxurious pied-à-terre used for private gambling parties or illicit meetings with the city's famed courtesans, a suite of delicate rooms especially designed for extravagant, yet intimate, debauchery. It was the Venetian equivalent to the French *petits appartements* designed as ideal settings for a *souper intime*. Not long after this supper with M. M., Casanova rented the most extravagant example he could find:

> The casino had five rooms, furnished in exquisite taste. It contained nothing that was not made for the sake of love, good food, and every kind of pleasure. Meals were served through a blind window, which was set back into the wall and filled by a revolving dumb-waiter which closed it completely. The masters and servants could not see one another. The room was decorated with mirrors, chandeliers, and a magnificent pier glass above a white marble fireplace; and the tiles with small squares of painted Chinese porcelain, all attracting interest by their representations of amorous couples in a state of nature, whose voluptuous attitudes fired the imagination. Some small armchairs matched the sofas, which were placed to the left and to the right. Another room was octagonal and walled with mirrors, with floor and ceiling the same; the counterposed mirrors reflected the same objects from innumerable points of view.

This was the age of the rococo, whose name came from the decorative motif of the *rocaille,* riotously scalloped shells and S-shaped curves, which covered every conceivable surface in gilded languor. The style was an unabashed celebration of femininity, abundantly replete with cupids and pastel flowers. Portable without the aid of servants, luxury furniture achieved a new lightness and informality, sacrificing nothing in the quality of materials. By the mid-eighteenth-century the most important piece was the *commode.* A chest of drawers, its name also means "commodious" or "comfortable," and the undulating *bombé* of its shape seemed to echo a woman's body.

At M. M.'s *casino,* the furnishings were decidedly French, produced by lead-ing craftsmen who exhibited a graceful restraint when executing rococo objects, which became garish and overbearing in lesser hands. Casanova admired "the small pictures which decorated the room," which, "were so well painted that the figures seemed to be alive." The best Gallic artisans applied meticulous attention to the finish of jewel-like ormolu mounts, respected the handsome veneers to which these decorations were adhered, and catered to the human body in the gen-tle curvature of chairs that cradled their occupants more comfortably than any produced before or since. Indeed, Casanova described the sofa at M. M.'s *casino* as "commodious," and ideally suited to receive the unexpected fall of a swooning lover.

Casanova did not have long to inspect his surroundings. She was waiting for him, "dressed in secular clothes of the utmost elegance." Her attire exuded the feminine sophistication of Madame de Pompadour herself: pale rustling silks, lace ruffles, wide ribbons, glittering jewels, and an elegant chignon. Casanova had begged her to dress for the evening in her nun's habit. M. M. preferred to play the role of an aristocratic courtesan. Now that he stood before her, he was not disap-pointed in the least. He fell to his knees, like Lancelot paying homage before Guinevere, to show her his "boundless gratitude" by "constantly kissing her beau-tiful hands." Alone with her at last, his patience evaporated.

M. M. would not be swayed by her suitor's ardor. "Ah, those charming re-fusals!" Casanova remembered wistfully. For two hours he groped and pleaded while she rebuked him with firm but gentle words mouthed between stolen kisses. As the nineteenth-century American essayist, novelist, and agriculturalist Donald Grant Mitchell wrote, "Coquetry whets the appetite; flirtation depraves it."

At last, M. M. pleaded hunger. She proposed an impromptu supper, which, in reality, had been as meticulously planned as any formal banquet. Gifted players at *souper intime* cultivated this fiction, essential to the spirit of romance.

She rang the dinner bell to summon a well-dressed serving woman, "neither young nor old and whose appearance betokened respectability." M. M. had warned Casanova in advance: "There will be people there; for we will have to be served; but no one will speak to you and you need speak to no one." The *souper intime* required a minimum of peering eyes and gossiping tongues (doubly true in the case of a nun). Technical innovations, such as the dumbwaiter Casanova described at his rented *casino,* helped eliminate the need for intrusion. Thomas Jefferson famously exported the invention to the United States after encountering it in France, installing in Monticello dumbwaiters to carry wine from the cellar directly to the dining room. On this occasion, however, Casanova and M. M. depended upon the old-fashioned loyalty of a servant, who was trusted to carry her knowledge of their illicit rendezvous to her grave.

Despite this pressure, the serving woman betrayed neither the slightest curiosity nor any hint of nervousness. She brought the meal in to them where they were, laid a table for two, and then set up a second table for service. Casanova reveled in noticing such details; supping intimately at an inn he approvingly observed "everything was new—linen, plates, glasses, knives, spoons, and everything very clean." Though he did not mention forks at that dinner, from boyhood he carried with him always a silver fork and spoon, gifts from his grandmother. At his student boarding house in Padova, the proprietress cruelly confiscated these precious utensils and forced him to eat with a vulgar wooden spoon. Nothing, however, was amiss at M. M.'s ravishing, yet unprepossessing, table.

The presentation must have been informally utilitarian, yet drippingly sensuous. A damask cloth might have been flirtatiously knotted at its ends when draped over a small table for two, as seen in such images as Jean-Michel Moreau's engraving *Le Souper fin* (page 165). Hourglass handles and shell-encrusted patterns worthy of Venus may have graced the flatware at each place. It was an era when even simple silver serving spoons, spice boxes, and candlesticks twisted suggestively.

Were there perhaps a few small arrangements of flowers? If so, they would have been delicate, low bouquets that never barricaded one lover's view of the other or obstructed the reach of a hand across the table. Imitation flowers were preferred to fresh-cut blossoms in this culture besotted with staged artifice. Porcelain blooms were the choicest, but there were also wax and paper versions. For his part, however, Casanova raved about the aphrodisiac effect imparted by the fragrance of fresh tuberoses. M. M. might instead have perfumed the room with incense or potpourri in Chinese celadon porcelain with French gilt-bronze mounts, the pinnacle of fashion. How could two sentient individuals have resisted the primal powers of scent?

The serving woman fetched their supper, placing the dishes on "silver boxes filled with hot water which kept the food always hot." Chafing dishes have existed since the ancient world; Seneca noted that "daintiness gave birth to this useful invention in order that no viand should be chilled and that everything should be hot enough to please the most pampered palate." M. M.'s silver boxes performed the same function, keeping their meal warm, ready, and available, in case they got distracted.

The servant stayed just long enough to plate their food, before shutting the door behind her. Casanova claimed the meal was served on Sèvres porcelain, precious wares produced by the French royal manufacturer. This incredible statement continues to be dismissed as an instance of Casanova's predilection for exaggeration and bragging, or his occasionally confused memory. In November 1753, the Sèvres factory was still known as Vincennes, after the city where it had been founded in 1738. It would not move to Sèvres until 1756. The mistress of Louis XV (r. 1715–1774), Madame de Pompadour, enchanted by the wares, persuaded the King to grant the company the official title "Manufacture Royale de Porcelaine" in 1753. The most glamorous pieces wore boldly saturated ground colors, such as *bleu celeste,* a rich turquoise that was the rage of 1752, and shimmered with the factory's famous gilding, a tastefully

Figure III

Feast of the Gods, 1514–1529,
by Giovanni Bellini and
Titian, oil on canvas.

FIGURE IV
Bacchanal of the Andrians,
1523/4, by Titian, oil
on canvas.

FIGURE VII

Château de Vaux-le-
Vicomte, Maincy, France,
built 1656–1661, designed by
Louis Le Vau, André Le
Nôtre, and Charles Le Brun.

FIGURE VIII
Detail of the dining room,
Château de Vaux-le-
Vicomte, Maincy, France,
interior painting by
Charles Le Brun.

Figure IX
Plate from the Swan
Service, 1737, model by
Johann Joachim Kändler,
produced by Meissen,
hard-paste porcelain, with
enamel and gilding.

Figure X
(facing page)
Detail of *Les Rémois*
(The Inhabitants of Reims),
ca. 1710, by Nicolas
Lancret, oil on canvas.

FIGURE XI
*The Marriage Banquet
of Napoleon I and
Marie-Louise given in the
Palace of the Tuileries,
2 April 1810,* 1812,
by Francesco Casanova,
oil on canvas.

FIGURE XII
The Woodpecker, 1885,
designed by William
Morris and woven at
Morris & Co.,
Merton Abbey, high
warp tapestry.

FIGURE XIII
(facing page)
At the Sideboard, 1903,
by Carl Moll, oil
on canvas.

FIGURE XIV
Autumnal Cannibalism,
1936, by Salvador Dalí,
oil on canvas.

muted gold applied in thick pools along borders or tooled into intricate patterns. Could Casanova and M. M. have even nibbled off a plainer set of Vincennes, decorated with a light sprinkling of scattered flowers on the flat white of the soft-paste body? The demand Madame de Pompadour created for Vincennes outpaced its production to such a degree that only those within her personal circle, or receiving a royal gift, were able to acquire even the simplest piece. The porcelain was so closely associated with its illustrious patroness that the mere mention of it sufficed to conjure an image of her dainty, rosy-cheeked visage and her silken dresses covered in ruffles and bows.

The luxury of M. M.'s dishes impressed Casanova so deeply that he recorded this detail in the memoirs he wrote four decades later. The quality of the porcelain hinted at the mysterious identity of M. M.'s powerful lover, the man who could sneak a nun out of a convent and possess this lavish *casino*. Casanova volunteered to reveal his own identity, if only M. M. would name his rival for her affections. She refused him as coyly as she had rebuffed his amorous advances, telling him, "[W]e must leave it to time to satisfy our curiosity."

Their supper consisted of eight "made dishes," enough variety to charm and enliven their appetites, but not so much as to overwhelm them. The *souper intime* was a meal with Watteau's elegant breeziness and Rousseau's naturalistic simplicity; a bloated, leaden belly does nothing to stimulate erotic desire, so the generation of whimsical caprice extended their taste for lightness from the graceful foliate tendrils of their *boiseries* to the food on their plates. *Les dons de Comus*, a French cookbook of 1739, summarized this aesthetic in its opening sentence: "Cooking—like all of the other arts invented for need or for pleasure, was per-

FIGURE 8.2 *(facing page) Fleuriste artificiel,* 1763–1777, engraving with diagram for making artificial flowers by Lucott and Defehrt, from *Encyclopédie: Recueil des planches.*

FIGURE 8.3 *The Grape Eaters (Mangeurs de raisins),* ca. 1752, produced by Vincennes after a design by François Boucher, soft-paste porcelain, veneered wood, metal.

fected by the genius of man and has become more delicate to the measure that they have become more polite." Casanova was of the same mind; at another *souper* he explained, "[T]he dishes were exquisite because nothing was elaborate. Game, roast, delicious fish, and excellent cheeses. I spent an hour and a half eating, drinking and talking."

The eight dishes composed an octave of flavors. On a subsequent occasion, Casanova likewise asked his chef to prepare no more than eight dishes, to be served two at a time. In 1755, Père Polycarpe Poncelet articulated the similarity between gastronomy and music, which Casanova and M. M. had understood instinctively. In his introduction to *Chimie du goût et de l'odorat*, a manual for making liqueurs and perfumes, Poncelet argued that:

> Flavors consist in stronger and weaker vibrations of salts that act upon the sense of taste, just as sounds consist in stronger and weaker vibrations of air that act upon the sense of hearing; there can, therefore, be a Music for the tongue and for the palate, just as there is one for the ears; it is very probable that the flavors to excite different sensations in the soul, have, like the corpus of sounds, their generative pitches: dominants, majors, minors, bass, treble, their rests also. . . . Seven whole notes form the fundamental scale of the Music of sound; an equal number of basic flavors are the scale of the Music of flavors.

Combinations of tastes within Poncelet's flavor scale (acid, bland, sweet, bitter, bittersweet, dry, spicy) yielded delicious harmonies in the same manner as musical chords: thirds, fifths, and octaves being the most beautiful. "Lemon with sugar, for example," he explained, "will give you a simple but charming consonance in a major fifth." The analogy is timeless; in 1994, cultural historian Theodore Zeldin compared cooks who prepare "food as an amusement, a form of permissiveness, a caress of the senses" to "jazz musicians improvising flourishes, never reaching a conclusion."

Casanova, ever the voluptuary, believed that a harmony of flavors corresponded to female physical types. For blondes, he selected delicate cheeses, greens, and fish cooked in butter; for more vivacious brunettes, peppered salami, stewed game, strongly colored vegetables, and pungent cheese; redheads, he accorded a mixture of sweet and spicy foods, on account of their pale skin and fiery disposition.

He did not record, however, what M. M. deemed suitable to serve a passionate Lothario, and merely described their meal as a "choice and delicious supper." Casanova ventured that the chef must be French. M. M. confirmed this guess. (His name was Duroisier; he had an equally talented brother, who cooked for the French ambassador to Switzerland.) The self-satisfied mutual admiration in this exchange nodded to the pair's sophisticated knowledge of *le haut goût*. The introduction to *Les dons de Comus* attests to the international dominance of the French culinary style, dividing it into two categories, *la cuisine ancienne* and *la cuisine moderne:*

The old cuisine is that which the French brought into vogue all over Europe, and which was generally practiced as recently as twenty years ago. Modern cuisine, based on the foundation of the old, with less confusion, less display, and with as much variety, is simpler, cleaner and possibly even more expert. The old cooking was extremely complicated, and extraordinarily detailed. Modern cooking is a form of chemistry. The cook's science today consists in dissecting, digesting, and extracting the quintessence of food, drawing out the light and nourishing juices, blending and mingling them together in a manner whereby nothing dominates and everything can be tasted; in short, in creating a harmony, such as painters give their colors, and blending them so homogeneously that from these different flavors there results but a single taste when they are reunited together.

Did M. M. and Casanova begin their meal with his favorite, *olla podrida?* Originally Spanish, this traditional spiced stew of mixed meats and vegetables had been made in French kitchens since at least the early seventeenth century. According to Barbara Ketcham Wheaton, by the mid-eighteenth century, it was one of the two most popular first-course offerings on French menus. Or did they enjoy a *potage de santé* (healthy soup), a lighter, restorative bouillon in the new style to fortify them for the amorous sport to follow? Casanova reveals nothing; but he so adored a good soup that while living in London some years later, he employed an English chef who knew how to prepare "very delicate French ragouts" and recorded, "People laughed when I said that I ate at home because at the taverns soup was not served." The high esteem that the ancien régime accorded to soup survives in the magnificent tureens produced to serve this important first course. Often engraved with impressive family crests, these vessels were sometimes modeled to look like a shell or a boar's head. They appeared in all manner of inventive sculptural forms. Soup tureens were, uncontestably, the most impressive, expensive, and glamorous objects on the eighteenth-century dinner table.

Les dons de Comus unequivocally stated, "It is true today, with all people of good taste, that the goodness of the meal—soups, hors d'oeuvres, entrées, entremets—is almost entirely dependent upon the substance of the stock, which is its foundation." Rich broths, simmered for hours and painstakingly clarified, also formed the underpinning for that other showpiece of French cuisine: an exquisite sauce, now free to swim over slick, porcelain plates. *Les dons de Comus* declared that it was the "spirit of sauces" which lay at the heart of "modern cooking," and Menon's 1755 edition of *Les Soupers de la cour* boasted recipes for seventy-four different types. Enlightenment logic, breaking the process of cooking into component parts, from the preparation of the stock, to the complex sauces created from it, lay beneath the fanciful menus of a wantonly flirtatious *souper intime*.

A bizarre cookbook called *Le Cuisinier gascon* (Amsterdam: 1740)—which, as Barbara Ketcham Wheaton points out, is neither by a Gascon, nor, in all probability, by a cook—captures, with its outlandishly whimsical recipes, the spirit of M. M. and Casanova's supper. Scholars attribute it to the Prince de Dombes, Louis-Auguste de Bourbon (1700–1755), a brother of King Louis XV, who, with fawning admiration and private amusement, dedicated it to himself. The recipes are arranged with the aristocratic unconcern of an elegant frock coat tossed casually aside in a moment of passion; their instructions are often quite as haphazard. Yet, how could Casanova and M. M. not have appreciated such naughty dishes as "Chicken in Panties," sauce "à la Demoiselle," egg hash "without malice," pigeon "à l'impromptu," or a lovely cream "à la Sultane"? Their very names are calculatedly suggestive.

Seduction at the table requires a menu that will temptingly inspire dissipation by offering luxuriant delicacies, if not outright aphrodisiacs. When Casanova later asked his own chef to prepare a dinner for two, sparing no expense, the menu included *gibier,* sturgeon, truffles, and oysters, all served on precious Meissen porcelain and accompanied by "perfect" wines. How mouth-watering it still sounds today! *Gibier,* the French term for small game of both the winged and furry varieties, was wildly popular among eighteenth-century gourmands, who consumed an unbelievable range of turtledoves, quails, thrushes, and robins, to name but a few, using separate terms to distinguish between the flavors of male and female, full grown and young. Rare birds were the most desirable; they had the lingering allure of a food forbidden to virgins and widows in Renaissance Italy because they were believed to stimulate too much carnal desire. What could be more tantalizing than a delicate game bird "à l'allure nouvelle" from *Le Cuisinier gascon,* stuffed with foie gras, butter, and *fines herbes* and braised with a small piece of ham in a white broth? Perhaps only decadent "Pigeons à la lune" from *Les dons de Comus,* prepared with truffles mixed into its foie gras stuffing and a decorative puff pastry heart garnish. (These recipes, like so many of the period, produce a dish with a purposefully fleshlike pallor; whiteness was admired in food as much as in porcelain in eighteenth-century Europe.)

Sturgeon, the mother fish of caviar, was equally regal. It was considered the queen of seafood, whether marinated, skewered, and served with a sauce; prepared in a savory pastry; braised; roasted; or glazed with *fines herbes.* Casanova's adoration of all kinds of fish is hardly surprising, since seafood is both subtle in flavor and light enough to invigorate a night of amorous sport. However, for a dinner of seduction, his chef chose the rarest variety for the allure of its sheer expense.

As the pièce de résistance, the chef proffered truffles, that most mysterious and elusive delicacy, hunted out of the ground by snorting pigs. Casanova favored black truffles from Périgord as well as the white truffles of Italy; Spanish *criadillas* he "loved to distraction." The truffle's reputation as an aphrodisiac dates to the ancient world, at least as far back as Galen, who wrote, "The truffle produces an overall excitement disposing one to sensual pleasures." In the eighteenth century, just as now, a small shaving to garnish a ragoût, or a more abundant flavoring for a dish, made a precious treat. However, a heaping mound of sliced truffles tossed simply with a bit of butter or oil was a dish worthy of the finest porcelain. Rococo cookbooks offer numerous variations of this recipe, dangerously capable of inspiring a gastronomic orgasm, or "Stendhal's syndrome" of the palate.

Oysters appeared more frequently than truffles at Casanova's intimate suppers, but he never tired of them. To his taste, the most delectable were purchased from the celebrated food purveyor, Count Bonomo Algarotti, and came from the area surrounding the Venetian Arsenal. M. M., he later noted, also enjoyed them keenly. Casanova's generation ate them before, during, and after almost any meal. They were eaten raw; cooked in stews, ragoûts, and forcemeats; and generously tossed over platters as a garnish. A purist, Casanova enjoyed his oysters unadorned or, one might say, as he did his women: naked and in great quantity. He once seduced a pair of young convent girls, Armelina and Emilia, at a playful supper that began with the arrival of a hundred oysters, which were opened before them to fill four large platters. The sight of the girls, "swimming in their liquid," charmed him enormously; as did Emilia's apt remark that "anything so delicious must be a sin." They consumed fifty with sparkling Champagne before supper, and the other fifty afterward. This was not at all unusual; Anthelme Brillat-Savarin (1755–1826) recalled of the ancien régime: "In the old days, a meal of note usually began with oysters, and there were always a good many guests who did not stop before they had swallowed a gross (twelve dozen, a hundred and forty-four)." In 1798 his friend Monsieur Laperte ate thirty-two dozen before sitting down to dine, "with the vigor and appetite of a man who had been fasting," a feat that impressed the worldly Brillat-Savarin.

FIGURE 8.4
Oysters, first half of
eighteenth century, by Le
Chevalier, from *Abrégé de
l'histoire des pesches et
pêcheries,* pen and ink in
autograph manuscript.

In his *Natural History,* Pliny called oysters "the palm and pleasure of the table." The Romans farmed them assiduously and imported them from locations as far away as Africa and Britain. The first oyster eaters lived much earlier; archaeologists have unearthed mounds of shells consumed in prehistoric times, and the Chinese have eaten them for millennia. The belief in the oyster's aphrodisiacal powers stretches back into the depths of ancient folklore and continues still. Its appearance, which some find suggestive of the female sex organs, partially explains the oyster's reputation. The culinary historian Lesley Chamberlain theorizes, "[F]ood is a pre-literate medium for sexual suggestion by association with its shape or place in animal life."

The study of aphrodisiacs intensified during Casanova's lifetime; the quest to reveal the secrets of inciting sexual prowess had links with his and others' experiments in black magic and alchemy. Even fashionable artichokes and asparagus were widely thought to have aphrodisiacal properties. The food historian Alan Davidson points out that almost every food known to man has, at some time and place, been considered an aphrodisiac, although medical evidence to support these disparate claims is scant. The Chinese prescribed herbal teas to restore sexual vigor as early as 3000 B.C.; the ancient Hindu *Kama Sutra* (a favorite text of Casanova's) suggests quite a number of aphrodisiacs; and Aristotle's star pupil, Theophrastus, wrote the guide *On Aphrodisiacs* about 310 B.C.

Casanova himself inspired imitators for his performance(s) after a cup of hot chocolate and an egg-white salad dressed with olive oil from Lucca and "Four Thieves" vinegar, infused with herbs. He, however, knew that seduction at the table is not so much a question of what one eats, as a matter of how one eats it. He used food as a toy, which helped him smooth the transition from eating to fondling and, he always hoped, to the bedroom. Oysters lent themselves marvelously to such antics, a potential he exploited mercilessly. He flirtatiously tossed them down the cleavage of a lover's dress, to be even more naughtily retrieved, and exchanged them mouth to mouth for hours, an activity he considered "the most lascivious and voluptuous game of all," his lover's saliva "the most beautiful sauce."

Sitting so close to M. M., watching her eat, fanned Casanova's desire. "[H]er appetite," he marveled, "was equal to mine." A vigorous lust for food suggested wantonness in other areas. "The appetite of women has always been one of my weaknesses," he admitted, and M. M.'s robust constitution had him swooning. M. M., however, remained firmly in control. She spoiled him, indulged him, flirted with him, but stayed ever so slightly aloof.

Wine added its intoxication to the dizzying enchantments of their supper. He remembered, "We drank nothing but Burgundy, and we emptied a bottle of *oeil-de-perdrix* champagne and another of some sparkling wine." Burgundies had been exported to Italy since at least the third century, but the new invention of mold-made bottles greatly improved both its durability and its ease of transport, allowing these lovers to sip ruby-red Burgundy in a Venetian *casino*. Burgundy was favored far above Bordeaux; the region's strict regulation of grapes, picking, and processing earned it a reputation for purity and quality that was second to none. Although far less durable and clear than the wine we enjoy today, it was the perfect companion to menus replete with roasted game birds, foie gras, and truffles. That they drank "nothing but" implies that they emptied more than one bottle.

Oeil-de-perdrix, a rosé-colored still wine from Villes-Allerand, was a highly sought-after luxury; the rococo aesthetic admired the appearance of pink in a glass as much as on upholstery.

Dom Pérignon had discovered the process of sparkling champagne around 1684, but it did not become fashionable until Philippe, Duke d'Orléans (regent of France, 1715–1723), served it at his famously licentious supper parties at the Palais Royal. His hedonistic aura clung to it—the fizz of its bubbles mirrored his frivolity—so serious oenologists continued to prefer their champagne still, rather than sparkling. For the same reason, Casanova and M. M. drank their bottle of the sparkling "for gaiety." They moved freely from one bottle to the next, without any need for interruption; in their culture of self-indulgent ease, delicate stem-glasses now sat easily within reach, chilling in rinsers of ice water, while bottles rested in portable, free-standing *rafraîchissoirs,* or sat in coolers placed directly on the table.

The supper unfolded with lingering, serpentine ease; each taste, each sip slowly savored by the warmth of the fire, the glow of candlelight on gilded porcelain, and the thrill of being alone together for the first time. Not knowing what pretext might bring them next together, they let the meal last as long as they could. Finally, there was a pause. The cutlery was set down; the plates were not replenished. It was time for a new diversion.

M. M., in her resplendent silks, rose and dressed the salad herself. We can imagine her blending composed vinegars with oil, perhaps adding a bit of hard-boiled egg and anchovies as a garnish. Her act communicated simplicity as it mimicked the French court, cued, yet again, by the Duke d'Orléans, who, reputedly, had personally cooked his renowned suppers. He probably refrained from complex preparations, perhaps just attempting an omelet shaved with truffles: fresh, simple, warm, inviting, a refreshing break from the formality of court life. Cookbooks offered numerous recipes that could be prepared at table in front of guests, such as partridge *à la bourgeoise,* luxuriously simmered in champagne. Sèvres produced porcelain cooking pans as the ultimate accessory for the highly born chef. But the sight of M. M. dressing a salad was even more preposterously irresistible. Here was a nun, imitating a lady of the French court, pretending to be a servant; this was artifice at its most sublimely unnatural! Casanova "could not but admire her knowledge, her skill, her grace. It was obvious that she had a lover who had taught her."

L'EPLUCHEUSE DE SALADE

M. M., however, was not quite finished. She rang the bell, and the serving woman reappeared with "dessert together with everything necessary to make the punch." This last course, of temptation rather than sustenance, could not be skipped on such a salacious evening; its sinfulness bathed them in prurient sugges-

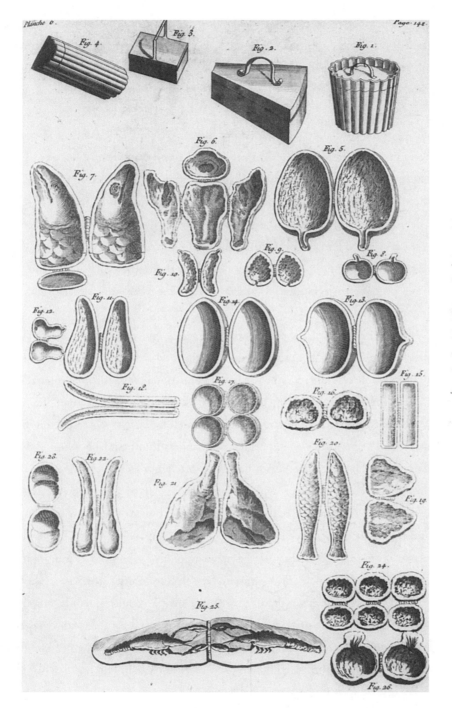

FIGURE 8.5 *(facing page)*
The Salad Washer, 1752, by
Jean-Firmin Beauvarlet,
engraving.

FIGURE 8.6
Diagram of ice molds, 1751,
engraving from Joseph
Gilliers, *Le Cannameliste*
français.

tion. When Casanova planned a *souper intime,* he asked his chef to bring "all the fresh fruits he could find, and above all, ices." Like the rest of his generation, he adored them; on a visit to Sorrento he sampled "ices flavored with lemon, with chocolate, with coffee," and thought "nothing more delicious could be imagined." Lusciously smooth, presented in impressive porcelain pails, ices were the showpieces of the rococo dessert; there were sorbets of fruit, ice creams, iced custards, and numerous iced cheeses (Parmesan was a particular favorite). The taste of sticky sweetness, eaten from a silver spoon, and the exhilarating, refreshing chill of ice on the tongue, inspired blissful decadence. Hothouse fruit, titillating in November, offered equal stimulation to the erotic appetite and imagination, as its juices sensuously dripped and slid down the back of the throat. A few romantically named pastries—such as *puits d'amour* (wells of love), puff pastry filled with fruit confitures, or *jalousies* (jealousies), a variant—would have been the perfect accompaniments to such provocative treats.

From England to Italy, an elegant meal rarely ended without punch. M. M.'s private supper for Casanova was no exception. M. M. mixed the punch herself with the same worldly panache she had demonstrated with the salad preparations. We can imagine her squeezing oranges with a decorative silver strainer and mixing her brew in a dazzling silver or porcelain punch bowl. No self-respecting hostess would fail to perform this important ritual in less than requisite style—the ingredients were far too costly. Punch had the exotic whiff of the colonies: rum, sugar, oranges or lemons, perhaps with a bit of nutmeg or another spice. To make his own version, Casanova once requested "lemons, a bottle of rum, sugar, a big bowl, and hot water . . . enlivened with a bottle of champagne." Taking great pains to plan a more sophisticated *souper,* he made a point of asking for "bitter oranges to give flavor to the punch," and "rum, not arrack," an inferior imitation.

M. M.'s precious elixir, prepared with her own enchanting hands, empowered and emboldened Casanova. After several cups, his mind turned, with renewed determination, to discovering the identity of his unseen host and rival. He noticed that M. M. was wearing a miniature, rock-crystal flask among her charms, identical to one he wore on his own watch chain.

I showed it to her, praising the essence of rose which it contained and with which a small piece of cotton was soaked. She showed me hers, which was filled with the same essence in liquid form.

"I am surprised," I said, "for it is very rare and it costs a great deal."

"And it is not for sale."

"That is true. The creator of the essence is the King of France; he made a pound of it, which cost him ten thousand *écus*."

"It was a present to my lover, who gave it to me."

"Madame de Pompadour sent a small flask of it two years ago to Signor Mocenigo, the Venetian Ambassador in Paris, through the A. de B., who is now the French Ambassador here."

Without knowing it, Casanova had stumbled upon the identity of M. M.'s lover; he was the Abbé François-Joachim de Pierre de Bernis (1715–1794), later a Cardinal, who had taken up his appointment as French ambassador to the Venetian Republic in October 1752. De Bernis was a close personal confidant of Madame de Pompadour, and while there is no record that he purchased porcelain from Vincennes, it is plausible that he might have received a set of plates as a gift from the royal mistress herself. Although he carefully sanitized his own memoirs of any mention of amorous adventures with a nun (quite the contrary, he proclaimed his own virtue amidst the general dissipation of Venice), there is not the slightest doubt that he was M. M.'s lover. Casanova had sniffed him out by instinct; the fine French furnishings, food, and wines, and particularly the royal porcelain and perfume, had been clues, narrowing the field of candidates. What Casanova did not yet know, but what M. M. would later reveal, was that de Bernis was secretly watching and listening to every word and every move, from behind the magnificent gilded mirrors of his *casino*. M. M. confirmed nothing and instead asked Casanova if he was acquainted with the ambassador.

The clock struck midnight. How thoroughly M. M.'s charming supper had distracted Casanova! He led her from the table to the fire, and, by his own admission, became "insistent." M. M. remained frustratingly implacable. If she surrendered too quickly, his desire would not have time to sufficiently ferment. Eroticism has been called "the art of cooking love well"; this young nun was a masterful chef.

Casanova's tactics became bolder. He suggested to M. M. that "if she would not yield to love she could not refuse nature, which must be urging her to bed after so fine a supper." He was exasperated; she would neither let him seduce her, nor permit him to retreat. Instead, she suggested that they sleep, fully clothed, on the sofa. He retorted:

> "In our clothes? So be it. I can even let you sleep; but if I do not sleep will you forgive me? Beside you, and uncomfortable in my clothes, how could I sleep?"
>
> "Very well. Besides, this sofa is a real bed. You shall see." With that she rises, pulls the sofa out at an angle, arranges pillows, sheets, and a blanket, and I see a real bed.

In a gesture, the little salon that had served as their dining room was transformed into a bedroom, a very convenient device when seducing at the table. Nevertheless, that night Casanova had to content himself with lying next to her, and holding and kissing her clothed body. He successfully maneuvered one trembling touch of her breast, but that was all.

The morning was hurried; they had no time to linger over a soothing hot chocolate, or even a rushed cup of coffee. The instant they awoke, M. M. rang for the serving woman to help her dress. As a parting pleasure, Casanova asked to watch. He was mischievously tickled to see her "disguised as a saint again." But in their last, stolen moment, M. M. wrapped her arms around him and asked when she should come to meet him for supper in Venice, where she promised they would "make each other completely happy." M. M. had cleverly deferred the pleasure of the final seduction, its planning, its anticipation, and its execution, to Casanova. And, she had instilled within him an urgent need to offer a repast as sinfully provocative as the one with which she had ensnared him.

And so it was that on an evening not long after, he met M. M. at Verrochio's

Statue of Bartolomeo Colleoni and brought her back to his voluptuous *casino* for a tempting supper of his own contrivance. When M. M. stood before him, her image infinitely reflected on his mirrored walls, he could hardly believe that she would soon be his to taste. But on this night she was more than compliant. She even offered to skip supper and go straight to bed, should he wish it. It was tempting, certainly; but then:

She felt cold. We sit down in front of the fire. She tells me that she has no vest on. I unfasten a heart of diamond brilliants, which kept her ruffle closed, and my hands feel before my eyes see that only a chemise defends against the air the two springs of life that ornamented her bosom. I become ardent; but she needs only a single kiss to calm me, and two words: "After supper."

It was such a simple phrase, only four short syllables, yet it sufficed to distract and delay the urgency of his desire. He knew he had her; the words were a promise. But now that his victory was assured, how could he let such a fine meal go to waste? And so, he did not hesitate, but rang for supper at once.

Chapter Nine

<u>Diplomacy</u>

Charles-Maurice de Talleyrand-Périgord at Table, Paris, Early Nineteenth Century

Culinary art serves as the escort to European diplomacy.

Antonin Carême, *L'art de la cuisine française*

GENERAL NAPOLEON BONAPARTE (1769–1821) defeated the Austrians at Bassano in September 1796; then, after a stunning series of victories through Italy and Austria, he marched straight into Vienna to demand peace on his own terms in April 1797. On 3 January 1798 (14 Nivôse, Year VI), Charles-Maurice de Talleyrand-Périgord (1754–1838), Chief Foreign Minister to the Directory, introduced France's new hero to Paris at a supper and ball for five hundred guests. Officially, Talleyrand's party honored Bonaparte's glamorous wife Josephine (1763–1814), but beneath this veneer of gallantry, it presented Napoleon as a shining alternative to the depressing corruption of the Directors. As the general later learned, this would not be the only occasion upon which Talleyrand would bring down a government even as he smilingly played host.

The party took place at Talleyrand's official residence, the neoclassical Hôtel

Galiffet, on the rue du Bac (the entrance is now on rue de Varenne); the building was begun before the start of the Revolution but not completed until 1792. The minister held his first big dinner party there only a month after taking office. His household was lauded for its "abundant luxury, sensual delicacy and spirit of elegance." For Josephine's ball, the hôtel had been transformed into a Roman temple,

lined with statues of Brutus allegorically representing the general's triumphant soldiering. The austere Doric columns of the building's façade lent their strength to this visual representation of military might. Bold tenting made the house look like an elegant army camp. Reproductions of the phenomenal masterpieces that Napoleon had pillaged in Italy hung on the walls, as a testament to French victory. Images of trophies and weapons covered every surface, inside and out. Such imagery could even extend into the pastry displays on the buffets and tables.

Immense chandeliers and wall sconces, dripping with ponderous crystal drops, blazed throughout the gilded and mirrored reception rooms. An elegant incense burner depicted on the frescoed ceilings suggests the thick scent that wafted though the air that night; rich amber mingled with sprigs of sweet myrtle hanging from the staircase and fragrant plants strewn through every room. Talleyrand's inordinate fondness for perfumes was renowned; a haze of cologne always alerted people to his approach.

The occasion marked an extraordinary return to elegance not witnessed since the Revolution. Although he is remembered for his liberal ideals, Talleyrand was born into one of the most elite aristocratic families in France. His great-grandmother, the Princesse de Chalais, with whom he lived as a small boy, taught him to entertain in the height of courtly style. She was a member of the noble Rochechouart-Mortemart family, a granddaughter of Jean-Baptiste Colbert, and could remember the glittering spectacles of Louis XIV's Versailles firsthand. Talleyrand reminisced: "He who has not lived in the years just preceding 1789 does not know the pleasure of living." His former lover and longtime friend, the outspoken writer Germaine de Staël-Holstein (1766–1817), noted that this "was a world that Bonaparte knew little about, but sought to know better in order to endow his dynasty with credibility from the first day." For those, like Madame de Staël, well acquainted with such fêtes, Talleyrand's party initiated a joyous return to civilized living not seen in the chaos of recent years.

The Reign of Terror, in 1793–1794, had sent thousands to the guillotine. Any aristocrats who had not voluntarily left France were forced into exile, including those, like Talleyrand, who had promoted revolutionary ideals. He only returned to Paris in September 1796 through the intervention of Madame de Staël, after spending several years in England and the United States.

The Paris Talleyrand returned to bore little resemblance to the city he had left. The Directory lacked both ideals and style. In former times, the minister had frequented the most exclusive aristocratic salons, run by women of delicate charm and keen wit such as Madame Adélaïde de Flahaut, his official mistress from 1783 to 1792. Under the Directory, the wives of the nouveaux riches dominated Parisian

FIGURE 9.1
Designs for making *(left)* a military trophy, *(center)* an ancient helmet, and *(right)* a modern trophy in spun sugar, 1815, by Antonin Carême, from *Le Pâtissier royal parisien.*

FIGURE 9.2
The Empress Josephine, 1805,
by Pierre-Paul Prud'hon,
oil on canvas.

society. Talleyrand mockingly dubbed them "les merveilleuses," ladies who "talked politics while dancing and sighed after royalty while nibbling ices and gazing at fireworks." The leaders of this group included Juliette Récamier, later lover to Chateaubriand, whose beauty was immortalized by Jacques-Louis David and François Gérard; Napoleon's wife, Josephine; and the exotic Creole Fortunée Hamelin, who created the irreverent fashion of wearing upswept hair and a red cord tied around the neck, a style called "à la victime."

Madame de Staël claimed that Napoleon once told a friend, "Madam, I do not like women who meddle in politics." To which his female conversant quite reasonably retorted, "General, you are right, but in a country where one cuts off their heads it is natural for them to want to know why." Talleyrand, who, according to Napoleon, "always had his pockets full of women," had no such prejudice against either their intelligence or political influence. The highly cultivated and subtle hostesses of ancien régime salons had taught him how a dinner party might be used to manipulate events and opinion; they had informed his diplomatic approach as each soirée fed the minister vast amounts of information critical to his political maneuvering. Talleyrand's objection to *les merveilleuses* was neither their sex nor their politicking but their absence of discretion and good taste. He was no prude, but he objected to their gauzy, semitransparent dresses that left nothing at all to the imagination. Under the Empire, Talleyrand told one woman who arrived to be sworn in for an Imperial Court appointment, "Madam, these are rather short skirts for an oath of fidelity."

Though not to Talleyrand's liking, these racy ladies had not left the capital devoid of entertainment. Indeed, the foreign minister noted, "Balls and spectacles and fireworks have replaced prisons and revolutionary committees." Even during the worst days of the Terror, much solace had been taken in the life-affirming pleasures of a decent meal (giving resonant meaning to the modern term "comfort food"). Louis-Sébastien Mercier's journal, *Le nouveau Paris,* declared, "[N]ever did one live with a greater proclivity for gourmandize than in those days of calamity and horror." However, the eccentric epicure, Alexandre-Balthazar-Laurent Grimod de La Reynière (1758–1838), complained that there was not a turbot to be found in Paris. Talleyrand's chef, Marie-Antoine (Antonin) Carême (1783–1833) declared, "Gastronomy marches supreme at the head of civilization; but she vegetates in times of revolution."

Parties there may have been, but Talleyrand's 1798 party was the first to offer delicacies of the highest quality, in an atmosphere of refined, pre-revolutionary glamour. He treated his guest of honor, Josephine, the scandalous marvel in a diaphanous dress, with the dignity usually reserved for a queen. Such regal courtesy, dispensed by a man whose family had attended every Coronation in France since the ninth century, had not been on public view for quite some years.

Talleyrand may have cynically dismissed the fashions set by the arrivistes, but he invited them all. And they came in droves, the ladies wearing fashionably revealing gowns *à la Diane* or tunics *à la Cérès,* some with a veil *à la Mi-nerva.* Thirteen-year-old Laure Permon, the future Duchess of Abrantès, dressed identically to her mother. Both wore "a white crepe gown trimmed with two bands of silver ribbon fringed in turn with an inch of pink gauze and silver lamé." In their hair each "wore a garland of oak leaves with silvered veins." Talleyrand accepted them as they were, although with such novice sophisticates he had felt compelled to explicitly state on the invitation: "I trust that it will be found advisable to ban the wearing of any English made article of attire." Everyone sported their finest, except for three of the five churlish Directors, who wore their drab office wear.

Nationalistic arias written for the occasion blared as General Bonaparte, dressed in an austere gray uniform that lent heroism to the intensity of his gaze,

Figure 9.3
*Charles-Maurice de
Talleyrand-Périgord,
Minister of Foreign Affairs,*
portrait engraving.

made a grand entrance with his wife, Josephine, who wore a diadem of antique cameos, and her daughter, Hortense de Beauharnais. This majestic treatment continued through supper, when the nobly born host stood behind Citizen Bonaparte's chair to serve him, as a royal steward would have assisted a king. As in the courts of old, only the ladies were seated while their gentlemen stood by chivalrously to attend them. Talleyrand admitted that he "experienced some difficulty on account of the vulgarity of the Director's wives, who of course enjoyed precedence over all other ladies." Nevertheless, even those who had never witnessed such regal courtesies could not miss the overt symbolism of these ancient practices. Talleyrand was creating a new French court.

The guests were as much transfixed by the charisma of their host as by his guests of honor. At a time when France was besotted by the mysteries of Egypt, Talleyrand embodied the Sphinx, immutable and silent. One foreign guest described him thus: "A figure pale as death, dressed in red velvet embroidered with gold. Dress coat, sword, ruffled cuffs, formal hairdo. It was the minister himself. What expression! Upon this ghostly frame lie the sensitive, lively features of the bishop of Autun." As Talleyrand's portraits by Pierre-Paul Prud'hon record, the Minister of Foreign Affairs comported himself with stately hauteur at all times. The ritual of his morning *levée,* when he received visitors in princely fashion as his servants powdered and dressed him, was reckoned to be one of the marvels of Paris. However, what mystified observers the most was that this worldly, arrogant statesman was a consecrated bishop of the Catholic Church.

Talleyrand never hid nor apologized for his dissipated behavior. Even as a young seminarian at Saint Sulpice, he had openly walked through the streets with a mistress. His parents had thrust an ecclesiastical career upon him out of shame that he was club-footed. Although his condition was the result of an accident sustained when he was a toddler, they felt his deformity tainted their noble blood. In April 1775, Talleyrand took his priestly vows, and in 1789, was appointed Bishop of Autun. He spent just one month in his diocese, never bothering to open all of the congratulatory gifts he received, but he made a lasting and favorable impression by feasting the congregation daily on delicate fish imported from Dieppe.

As a young priest in Paris, dinner parties with the most worldly and sophisticated minds occupied him more than spiritual concerns. When Talleyrand's grandmother wished to send him some fine Burgundy, his governess warned, "I am afraid that if the wine is a good one, it will not stay around long. Monsieur l'abbé is extremely generous and will want to treat his friends to it." Frequent guests included Gabriel, Count de Mirabeau, the inspired orator of the Constituent Assembly; Louis, Count de Narbonne-Laru, a handsome, womanizing, bastard son of the King; and his closest friend and former childhood playmate, Auguste, Count de Choiseul-Gouffier. Looking back, Talleyrand fondly recalled that as they sat around his table, the group "touched on every subject with the greatest liberty," for conversations, "both pleasant and instructive." It was Choiseul-Gouffier's uncle, Étienne-François, Duke de Choiseul, a bon vivant who replaced the Abbé de Bernis as Louis XV's Minister of Foreign Affairs, in whom the youthful cleric found a mentor. Choiseul's luxuriant gourmandise and his diplomatic strategies both inspired the future diplomat, who called him "the man with the clearest insight into the future."

Talleyrand had an unfailing sense of smell that included an astute ability to sniff the subtle winds of political change. He chucked out his holy vestments on the eve of the King's order that the Estate dissolve itself and stepped into the political arena to which he was innately drawn. It was the Bishop of Autun who proposed the scandalous motion that the State confiscate all church property, an act for which many never forgave him. As President of the Constituent Assembly, he was also the first to propose public education, the emancipation of the Jews, the abolition of the royal lottery, and an Anglo-French Conference to standardize weights and measures.

Despite the monumental upheaval of the Revolution and his intense participation in it, the whirl of Talleyrand's social life continued unabated, at least for a while. After Talleyrand officiated at the "altar of the Nation," saying mass to a crowd of three hundred thousand for the first celebration of Bastille Day, he spent the evening at the gaming tables and then enjoyed a superb dinner hosted by the glamorous Viscountess de Laval. It was not until the mobs invaded the Tuileries on 20 June 1792 that the world of aristocratic salons and dinner parties came to an end. At the time, Talleyrand was already employed as a diplomat in England, but when he came back to France that summer, he realized it was time to leave.

When Talleyrand returned to Paris in 1796, he was determined to revitalize his nation, if for no better reason than to enjoy dinners as elegant as those he had known before. His ball for Napoleon created such luxuriance even as it promoted a leader whom Talleyrand believed capable of restoring France to her former glory. The Foreign Minister had met Napoleon for the first time only one month earlier, although they had been corresponding since the summer. Though the ambitious young general, who always ate with soldierlike speed and simplicity, could not have been more different in character from the languorous diplomat, the pair felt an immediate mutual admiration. Talleyrand saw in Napoleon a shared desire for peace and a respect for the solidarity of other nations, which provided the underpinning to flourishing economic trade, the necessary prerequisite for civilized life.

Even Madame de Staël, later exiled by the Emperor as one of his most vociferous critics, was smitten with the young general, telling Talleyrand, "I want him made Director very soon." She enjoyed her role as a political muse and hoped to catch Napoleon's eye. She was so enamored that at Talleyrand's ball she grossly placed her urgent wish to meet her hero above the success of her friend's carefully orchestrated event. Insisting upon a private conversation with the general, she badgered his escort at the foot of the stairs until her wish was granted. Face to face with the bewildered object of her desire, she asked, "General, who represents your ideal of a wife?" When Napoleon tartly replied, "Mine!" she obstinately refused to drop the subject, until she had thoroughly offended the guest of honor. Talleyrand never received her again, despite the invaluable help she had afforded him in securing his return to France.

Nevertheless, the evening succeeded magnificently. Celebrants danced Paris's first waltz. More important, all of Paris saw Napoleon as a radiant alternative to the seedy Directors. Nor was the acting government indifferent to what had transpired; from that night forward it actively sought to discredit the minister. Talleyrand, however, was a patient man. Just as he never ate during the day, preferring to build his appetite for one lingering meal that began at six o'clock, he could bide his time and allow events to simmer slowly until, like a tender braise, they would break at the slightest touch.

In July 1799 Talleyrand resigned from the ministry, convinced that the government had sufficiently stewed itself. On October 16, Napoleon marched triumphantly into Paris, where cheering crowds thronged to greet him. Talleyrand and other collaborators met secretly with the general the next night. Jean-Jacques-Régis de Cambacérès, a leader in the Directory government, took charge of creating a new constitution. On 18 Brumaire (November 9), Napoleon staged his historic coup d'état. Talleyrand effectively managed his appointed task of forcing Barras to resign his post. Three million had been donated as a potential bribe, but so skillfully did Talleyrand negotiate that he was able to keep the money for himself. (The foreign minister never hesitated to take a bribe, often taking payments from conflicting parties at the same time. This helped defray the expense of his table but never altered his course of action.) Napoleon, however, nearly bungled the entire plot with his inept handling of the Council of Five Hundred. The following day, the Council readied itself to bring down the plotting general. Only the eloquence of his brother Lucien Bonaparte, Council President, swayed events yet again to bring the coup to its successful completion. The Consulate was born. With a sigh of relief, Talleyrand declared, "My friends, it's time for dinner."

By November, Talleyrand moved back into his official residence on the rue du Bac in his former position as Chief Foreign Minister. Still enchanted by the ball held in his honor nearly two years earlier, Napoleon considered official entertaining primary among his Foreign Minister's duties. Talleyrand readily complied with the First Consul's wishes. Almost immediately, he purchased an enormous villa in the suburban town of Neuilly. There, on 25 February 1800, he held an enormous

FIGURE 9.4
*Portrait of Catherine
Worlée, Princesse de
Talleyrand-Périgord,* by
François-Pascal-Simon
Gérard, oil on canvas.

party, whose purpose was to legitimize the nascent regime. Former aristocrats mingled with new leaders of government and finance. The following February, Talleyrand organized the grandiose fête to celebrate the signing of the Treaty of Lunéville with Austria, which extended the French border into the Rhenish frontier, even though the First Consul had not bothered to include his Foreign Minister in the negotiations. When the Duke and Duchess of Tuscany, the first two Bourbons to return to France, arrived in Paris, Talleyrand transformed his house into a model of the Palazzo Vecchio for a brilliant supper and ball at which two famous prima donnas were brought from Italy to serenade the guests. And when Napoleon wished to have the delegates to the Cisalpine negotiations elect him President of the puppet Italian Republic, he sent Talleyrand to Lyon to take care of it. The Foreign Minister spent thirty-two million francs on just over a month's rent for the most opulent house he could find and another seven million on food and servants, and set about entertaining the delegates over nightly dinners. When it came time for the vote, Talleyrand congratulated the envoys on the Italian candidate initially selected; with deliberate emphasis, he then suggested they might make an even better choice. The well-feasted delegates took the hint and voted for Napoleon.

The First Consul delighted in his minister's ability to manipulate events with his gracious repasts. With his own brusque manners, how could he fault Talleyrand's inimitable hospitality? Nevertheless, he complained that some of the ambassadors' wives refused to visit the Foreign Minister because he was living in sin with a woman of notably dubious reputation. Although Talleyrand exhibited detached, unprejudiced discernment in selecting both his wines and his governments, he inexplicably succumbed to Madame Grand, née Catherine Noëlle Worlée (1762–1835). She was a blond, blue-eyed stunner, immortalized on canvas by Élisabeth Vigée-Lebrun and Gérard, but in contrast to the highly cultivated women with whom the bishop habitually cavorted, Madame Grand was as stupid as Talleyrand was witty. At one legendary dinner she purportedly mistook the guest of honor, Sir George Robinson, for Robinson Crusoe and politely inquired after the health of Friday.

After Napoleon signed the 1801 Concordat reinstating the Catholic Church with its former privileges, he began to demand that Talleyrand do something about his embarrassing domestic situation. The fact that a lapsed bishop had been among the chief negotiators of this act had proven awkward enough. Napoleon hoped that his Foreign Minister might rid himself of this fallen woman, rejoin the church, and even become a cardinal. This, however, was even more of a pipe dream than his vision of a pan-European empire. Alternatively, he demanded that Talleyrand marry Madame Grand, and in a weak moment, his minister complied. The Pope had granted Talleyrand dispensation to wear secular attire but not permission to marry. This was simply ignored. On 9 September 1802, the marriage contract was signed and a civil ceremony took place. Talleyrand later regarded this as the biggest mistake of his life, not because it constituted a sacrilege against the Church but, worse, because it was "a sin against good taste."

Napoleon, however, was pleased and placated and so rewarded Talleyrand with increased prestige and power. Those who had hitherto shunned the Foreign Minister's hospitality paid congratulatory calls on the new Madame de Talleyrand in a house glittering with dignitaries and diamonds. One visitor recalled, "The courtyard at the ministry of foreign affairs was so jammed with carriages that some had to leave before one could enter. Arriving inside, I mounted the staircase which was blazing with light and studded with flowers."

On 18 May 1804, Napoleon declared himself Emperor; at his Notre Dame Coronation seven months later, he grabbed the crown out of Pope Pius VII's hands to place it on his own head during the ceremony. To establish a suitably Imperial atmosphere at his new court, he turned to his noble Foreign Minister. Talleyrand was promoted to the position of Grand Chamberlain, and stood behind the Emperor's chair during meals, just as he had playfully done at his ball six years earlier. The majestic spectacle of the *grand couvert,* the formal dinner served to French kings before an audience of courtiers, was revived. At Napoleon's imperial banquets, an enormous silver-gilt nef, a container in the form of a ship to hold a sovereign's napkin and utensils that in medieval times symbolized the monarchy, was placed to the right of both the Emperor and the Empress, as had not happened in France since Louis XIV had declared the practice antiquated and had relegated his nef to an antechamber (courtiers, nevertheless, had to pay homage to it). Although Talleyrand found Napoleon's new title pretentious, reinstating such vestiges of the old, royal protocol, which lent an air of legitimacy to the fledging Empire, and enticing former aristocrats to join the Imperial Court to enact these with aplomb were principal among his duties as Grand Chamberlain.

At the end of December 1805, Napoleon rewarded Tallyrand with the title of Prince of Benevento, six months later transferring to him the corresponding territories, which had formerly been a minuscule papal territory. The title was but small compensation for what was becoming an increasingly difficult job. As Talleyrand wined and dined the ambassadors of Europe, the Emperor stormed and battled with increasing belligerence. Not quite two months before Talleyrand received his elevation, the English fleet humiliatingly defeated the French at Trafalgar. Talleyrand, who valued civility above all else, urged the Emperor to act with restraint and to offer an honorable peace to the Austrians and Russians, whom the French defeated at Austerlitz. The Emperor ignored him completely. Worse than that, Napoleon made Talleyrand traipse around the military camps; New England almost seemed preferable. From Brno, Talleyrand complained that the stench of death was everywhere and asked to be sent some "Malaga wine, very dry and the least liqueur-like possible" to ease his distress. After the hard-fought Battle of Eylau in February 1807, Talleyrand, camped on the banks of the Neman, pleaded with Stendhal's cousin Daru to aid his pitiable plight: "My dear Daru, of one thing I am certain: when you were translating Horace and came to that delightful ode beginning 'Nunc est bibendum' (Now let us drink) you never thought Horace was recommending water; yet that is just what I am reduced to unless you send me some of the provisions furnished to the Emperor." Certainly, he considered such luxuries wasted on Napoleon, who gloried in the military life of the camps.

Deprived even of decent bread and wine, the most fundamental elements of European civilization, and with his pleas for moderation thoroughly ignored,

Talleyrand became disillusioned with the man whom he had so hopefully introduced to Paris. When Napoleon forced unreasonable concessions from the Austrians with the Treaty of Pressburg, Talleyrand felt sickened. The Austrian diplomat Prince Klemens von Metternich noted, "During the campaign of 1805, M. de Talleyrand determined to bring all his influence to bear against Napoleon's ruinous projects. . . . We are indebted to him for the slight, more or less favorable modifications in the Pressburg negotiations." Talleyrand always maintained that "[a] genuine balance of power could have made war impossible. Proper organization would have brought the highest degree of civilization to all nations." Nevertheless, the Emperor continued his stomp through Europe. By late November, when Napoleon tyrannically vowed to destroy the Spanish Bourbons, Talleyrand "secretly swore at any cost to cease acting as his minister as soon as we returned to France."

The Prince of Benevento contemplated his situation with languorous deliberation; his feline sensuality and pragmatic realism deterred him from martyring gestures that accomplished nothing. In August 1807 Talleyrand officially resigned from his post in the ministry, stating, "I do not wish to be Europe's executioner." Nevertheless, he continued to attend Imperial Council meetings and accepted the title of Vice-Grand Elector. (Napoleon's vicious Minister of Police, Joseph Fouché [1759–1820], quipped that this "was the only vice that Talleyrand lacked.") He decided to maintain his position as the Emperor's Grand Chamberlain in part because Napoleon's largesse helped fund his grandiose lifestyle, but also because as he stood behind the Imperial table, he could more effectively engineer to bring down the man he had so assiduously plotted to raise up.

Even before Napoleon became Emperor, he told Talleyrand, "I want you to buy a fine estate, to give brilliant receptions for diplomats and foreign dignitaries; make people want to come there, make them feel that an invitation is a reward to the representatives of sovereigns with whom I am pleased." With Napoleon's financial assistance, he purchased the Loire Valley's magnificent Château de Valençay. Complete with turrets, a moat, twenty-five master bedrooms, a fifty-six-meter (184-foot) long gallery leading to the family chapel, and an enormous park, the château embodied the glory of ancien régime culture. When, in May 1808,

Napoleon kidnapped Fernando, Prince of Asturias, heir to the Spanish throne, together with his brother, the Infante Don Carlos, and uncle, the Infante Don Antonio, and forced them to renounce any claim to the Spanish throne, Valençay became a royal prison and Talleyrand a jailer. It was a role that this consummate diplomat fulfilled with the deepest tact, so that the princes might consider themselves honored guests. Spanish flags waved respectfully as the royal prisoners, with a retinue of advisors and servants, arrived at their well-appointed cage. Talleyrand amused them with daily hunts and diversions, allowing them to irrigate miniature gardens in their rooms. The diplomat later recalled that his master chef even graciously "put all his skill and all his heart into making them bad Spanish stews." Valençay's dining room, with commodious built-in sinks and covered dish warmers, provided a princely setting for these daily feasts. A Spanish guitarist soothed the captives with boleros in the garden, while her Serene Highness, as Madame Grand was now called, entertained them at the piano in the silk-lined music room after dinner. (For once, she proved to be an asset and helpfully seduced Fernando's chief advisor, the Duke of San Carlos, which capped off the mission's success.) The princes grew so fond of their host that when he left at the summons of the Emperor, with tears in their eyes, they presented him their treasured prayer books as a souvenir.

Napoleon called his Grand Chamberlain to assist him in bridging an alliance with his former enemies, Czar Alexander I (r. 1801–1825) and the myriad German sovereigns, at a conference that amounted to an international public relations campaign. The Convention of Erfurt in the autumn of 1808 at last gave Talleyrand greater scope to maneuver on behalf of civilization over empire. Talleyrand brought the Comédie Française to perform Corneille, organized grand dinners, and on the Emperor's command, spent as much time with the impressionable Czar as possible. Although Napoleon had ordered him to "promise everything and concede nothing," it was Metternich to whom Talleyrand revealed the full extent of his tableside conversations with Alexander. The endless round of banquets offered Talleyrand the opportunity to secretly ally Austria and Russia. His actions were later dubbed "the betrayal at Erfurt"; however, Talleyrand remained proud of his efforts to free

Europe from a tyrant who threatened to destroy everyone's enjoyment of a peaceful meal.

Although officially released from all but his court duties, when Talleyrand returned to Paris in mid-October Napoleon ordered him to hold four dinners a week, each for thirty-six guests. The Emperor personally selected the guest lists and instructed his Chamberlain to bring together councilors and ministers so that he might "get to know the principal ones and mold their frame of mind." Napoleon relied upon the fact that anyone lucky enough to receive a coveted invitation to Talleyrand's table would not decline. The gastronomer Louis, Marquis de Cussy, an old-world aristocrat who became Prefect of Napoleon's Imperial Palace,

ranked the Prince of Benevento first among those who restored French dining to its former glory.

Cussy described Carême, who labored in Talleyrand's kitchens, as the greatest culinary artist of all. Alexandre Dumas, likewise, dubbed him "the apostle of gastronomes." However, this master of French cuisine did not join Talleyrand's household until 1804, and when he arrived, began as a pastry chef in the *office,* working under the supervision of the head chef, Boucheseiche, called Boucher, who had cooked for the Prince de Condé before the Revolution. Carême dedicated his first book, *Le Pâtissier royal parisien* (1815), to Boucher: "[U]nder [his] supervision, for the splendid dinners given by His Excellency to the ambassadors, I have made great progress in my art." It was Boucher who created Talleyrand's exquisite dinners, for which he received a princely salary.

Talleyrand always worked in tandem with

his staff to achieve astounding results and thoroughly appreciated their efforts. According to Carême, the Foreign Minister spent an hour every morning reviewing instructions from the kitchen:

> He would listen to everyone's news, flirt with the serving girls, inquire what the waiters might have heard from the guests of the previous evening. His knowledge of food was of the first order. He knew how to select the most succulent and appropriate dishes to appear at table according to the seasons. He differentiated with subtlety between the numerous pâtés in his reserve; goose liver pâté from Strasbourg, duck liver pâté from Toulouse, *terrine* from Nerac, mortadella from Lyon, sausage from Arles.

The same menu never appeared twice in the year, dishes varying according to every nuance of the season and the occasion. Câreme recalled the heroic effort required to produce these daily feasts:

> The moment for service is beyond any expression of pain or fatigue. We are at the hour, and at the minute, and we cannot defer the moment of service. Honor commands us (witness Vatel). One must obey her, even when physical strength is lacking, but it's the coals that kill us. Imagine being in a *grande cuisine* (like that of the Minister of Foreign Relations before his great dinners), and you will see about twenty cooks at their pressing tasks, coming, going, and in action, all pressed one against the other; *eh bien!* All this famously happens in this abyss of heat. Look at the path of coals blazing over straw; one for the *entrée* cook, another row of coals on the stove for the soups, *sautées, ragoûts, fritures,* and the *bain-marie;* add to that . . . blazing wood in front of which four spits rotate, on one a piece of sirloin weighing 45-60 pounds turns, the other has a quarter of weighty veal, poultry, and game. In this pit of heat it is necessary for the man in charge to have a strong and quick head, and the demeanor of a great administrator. He sees everything, taking actions all at the same time; he asks successively for the large roasts and

the *entrées,* and also places them in line for serving. Oh yes! Can you believe it! In this brazier, everyone acts swiftly, a breath cannot be heard; only the chef has the right to make a sound, and all obey his voice. In fact, to heighten our suffering, for about half an hour, the doors and windows are closed, so that air will not chill the food: one can breathe only painfully, and is in the most complete sweat.

When Carême joined Talleyrand's household in 1804, twenty people worked in the kitchens; by 1808 the number had doubled, and when Talleyrand moved to an even grander residence on the rue Florentin, quadrupled. Carême described

them as the most talented and best salaried staff in Paris. Like an army, they were delineated into ranks: ordinary chefs, extraordinary chefs, inspectors, and masters right down the line to simple assistants, kitchen boys, and dishwashers. Old-world aristocrat that he was, in his kitchens Talleyrand kept the traditional distinction between the staff of the *office,* who prepared desserts, pastries, and decorative presentation pieces, and that of the *cuisine,* who cooked the main courses. Within these divisions there were specialists who prepared roasts, stocks, sauces, and fruit, and who supervised the wine and plate.

After the Revolution, such elaborate private kitchens became increasingly rare. However, talented chefs who once labored in the grandeur of aristocratic kitchens found new opportunities to work in the burgeoning restaurant industry, providing high-quality meals to those who might not be able to entertain so lavishly at home. Despite the upheavals French society had endured, Carême considered the general public of 1815 more knowledgeable about food than ever before. Gastronomy flourished as a serious topic for writing and discussion. In 1803, Grimod de La Reynière began to publish his *Almanach des gourmands,* the first serialized food journal; his *Manuel des Amphitryons* appeared in 1808. Yet, Carême flippantly dismissed Grimod's contribution:

> Grimod . . . has no doubt done some good for culinary Science, but he counts for nothing in the rapid progress that modern cooking has made since the renaissance of the art. . . . It is to the great dinners given by the Prince de Talleyrand during his ministry of foreign affairs and to the famous Robert that we owe the growth of modern cuisine, and not to the famous author of the *Almanach des gourmands.*

This was also the generation of Brillat-Savarin, a cousin of the *merveilleuse* Madame Récamier, whose *Physiologie du goût* (1826) remains the most widely read culinary text of the period. However, Carême and Cussy both discounted Brillat-Savarin's gourmandise; Cussy stated that the purported epicure "ate copiously and badly," while Carême accusingly claimed, "At the end of a meal his digestion absorbed him; I have seen him fall asleep!" Talleyrand's rival in politics, Cambacérès, also competed with the Grand Chamberlain in the splendor of his table. Here, Brillat-Savarin himself agreed with both Cussy and Carême that the Archchancellor was "much less a gourmand than a big eater." In this world of gastronomic competition, Talleyrand was considered the unrivaled epicure.

One of the most heatedly debated topics amongst the gastronomes was whether a meal should be presented in the traditional *service à la française* (numerous offerings served in the center of the table from which diners picked what they liked) or in the newly fashionable *service à la russe* (individually plated portions of the same food, arriving consecutively in courses). Grimod de La Reynière thought the method of serving plate to plate was an immense refinement to the art of living because each dish could be enjoyed at its optimal moment: hot, fresh, and without

FIGURE 9.6
Meeting of a Jury of Gourmand Tasters, 1807, engraving by Dunant, printed by Maradan or Mariage, frontispiece from A.B.L. Grimod de La Reynière, *Écrits gastronomiques: Almanach des gourmands,* third year.

any distraction from its succulent perfection. However, Carême, who used the Russian method when he later worked for Czar Alexander, maintained that the traditional French method was more luxuriant. He loved the sumptuous effect of "rich, elegant vermeil platters, ornamented with perfectly sculpted figures; antique vases, elegant chalices, beautiful gilded candelabra, stunning crystal for drinking our excellent French wines, gorgeous desserts composed of our exquisite fruits, flowers and sweets; then, there is the service of the food, which, uncovered at the moment when the gentlemen sit at table, diffuses a gentle fragrance perfumed by fine cuisine."

FIGURE 9.7
Diagrams for aspics and molded aspics *à la moderne,* with, in the center row, *(left)* trout and *(right)* perch *historiées,* 1828, engraving by Antonin Carême, from *Le Cuisinier parisien.*

The guest welcomed to a dining room such as Talleyrand's and served *à la française* could not help but have his senses overwhelmed in one stunning moment. The porcelain, the silver, the glass appearing simultaneously with a breathtaking display of France's finest cuisine covering the table, as it had since the days of Vatel's banquet at Vaux-le-Vicomte, crystallized the glories of France. The poet Alphonse de Lamartine stated, "Opulence, for Monsieur de Talleyrand, was a policy as much as a style of life."

For a simple party of ten or twelve people, Talleyrand began with a choice of two soups; the tureens were then replaced by two platters of *relevées* (removes, often galantines or aspics); followed by a fish, four *entrées* (substantial sidedishes such as ragoûts or fricassées), two roasts, four *entremets* (accompaniments), and a dessert. As the number of guests grew in quantity or importance, so too did the menu. One particularly grand event offered eighty-five different *entrées* and numerous presentation platters of fancy roasts. Cussy underlined that the guiding principle for any important feast, as in the army, was to have abundant stores of reserves on hand: for an Imperial Banquet, fifty legs of lamb, or fifty turkeys, or two hundred chickens, fifty pâtés, and lots of savory roast hams.

Talleyrand's grandeur was, nevertheless, marked by a tasteful restraint. He upheld that "[e]legance and simplicity combined are, for all things and all persons, the hallmark of nobility." Like the severe lines of the vermeil tureens expertly created by the Empire's master silversmiths, such as Henri Auguste, Martin-Guillaume Biennais, and Jean-Baptiste-Claude Odiot, the soups that went into

them represented a purification and reinvention of antique forms, a style that emerged from the neoclassicism of the second-half of the eighteenth century. Carême declared:

> The creation of the great houses of the Empire gave a golden age to our art. We created perfect things; it was only for that moment that a few houses reliably spent what was correct and required. Sauces became more velvety, more sophisticated. Exquisite soups and stocks for braising were adopted. The most judicious novelties appeared everywhere and our beautiful cuisine scented the air of every *quartier* of Paris.

By the time Carême left Talleyrand's employ, he knew how to make 190 French *potages,* and 103 of foreign origin. Like the opening act of theatrical spectacle, a selection of two or three soups, subtle but rich recipes such as *potage aux marrons à la*

FIGURE 9.8
Diagrams for game and salmon encased in pastry and garnished with decorative skewers on pastel-colored lard bases, 1828, engraving by Antonin Carême, from *Le Cuisinier parisien.*

lyonnaise served in gilded tureens grounding either end of the table, grabbed the diner's attention and hinted at what might follow. Then, came the lighter removes: perhaps a delicate fish, stewed sweetbreads, or small galantines. This prepared the palate for heartier *grosses pièces,* such as a grand beef tenderloin, garnished triumphantly with spear-like skewers stuck copiously into the surface. The protruding ends of the skewers held bits of pastry, sweetbreads, or crayfish, capped by trophies or helmets. On fish days, which returned, to Carême's great joy, after France's reconciliation with the Church, a beautiful salmon or an entire sturgeon might take pride of place. These dramatic *grosses pièces* provided the pivotal focal point to Talleyrand's meals, to which numerous side dishes were added. Cussy fondly remembered succulent pastries of fish and vegetables served hot at the Foreign Minister's table as well as chilled timbales. But the glory of French cuisine, the secret weapon that the Foreign Minister relied upon to smooth over contentious politics, was the exquisitely delicate sauce that accompanied these dishes, served in

FIGURE 9.9
Diagrams for boar's head *en galantine,* garnished with skewers *à la royale,* and for piglet *en galantine,* garnished with skewers *à la moderne,* both on lard bases decorated in pastel colors with pastry and sugarwork, 1828, engraving by Antonin Carême, from *Le Cuisinier parisien.*

silver sauceboats with handles standing at attention *à l'antique* in honor of their precious contents. One of Talleyrand's greatest complaints about his exile in the United States was that "[t]he Americans have thirty-six religions, but alas, only one sauce." The deceptive simplicity of Carême's recipe for *sauce à l'éspagnole* required four days to prepare. His béchamel, the most sophisticated rendition ever produced, subtly harmonized the rich nuances of beautiful clear stocks.

Carême advised, "Adopt in the service of the meal, the style of the Empire—which is male and elegant." His *Le Cuisinier parisien* illustrated examples of the newest styles of plate and advised readers to consider "the tone and elegance that this new silver gives our opulent tables," particularly when the second service is presented, elegantly covered, while silver casseroles and cassolettes already adorn the table with the side dishes. Gilt was the requisite finish for tableware; shapes should be round and oval. Antique lines were given bold, militaristic themes; the blades of dinner knives were sabre-shaped, the ends of French tablespoons pointed aggressively.

Even the fragile porcelain plates produced at Sèvres, formerly the royal porcelain manufacturer, carried battle scenes and a glossy imperial gilding. The Emperor's personal service meticulously re-created moments such as General Cafarelli ready to drown himself at the isthmus of the Suez. Napoleon was extremely particular about the themes he considered appropriate. He rejected a scene proposed by the factory for "St. Louis, a prisoner in Africa, chosen as judge by the men who defeated him." When he saw David's painting *Léonidas aux Thermopyles,* now at the Louvre, he likewise quipped, "Not a good subject for painting, Léonidas lost." Exceptionally, Napoleon's most famous porcelain service commission, intended as a "divorce gift" for Josephine, illustrates sites from the failed Egyptian campaign, complete with centerpiece temples with hieroglyphics and obelisks.

The survival of Sèvres through the tumultuous transition from the reign of Louis XVI (r. 1774–1792) to Napoleon's Empire bears testimony to the unflappable ability of France's preeminent institutions to adapt and reemerge, like a phoenix from the ashes, under the most daunting conditions, much like Talleyrand himself. Somehow, during the worst years of the Revolution, the factory continued to produce exquisite objects. There were difficult years; when the government declared them state property in 1793, all molds with royal subjects were destroyed. Rival Paris factories competed openly with Sèvres after its royal monopoly on gilding was nullified. The staff was reduced and production almost, but not quite, stopped. Then on 25 Floréal, Year VIII (14 May 1800), Napoleon's brother Lucien, as Minister of the Interior, appointed Alexandre Brongniart to reorganize the failing concern. In 1804 the production of soft-paste porcelain ended in favor of a hard-paste formula with an extremely shiny surface, utterly appropriate for the racy, new society. An innovative range of colors was developed, imitating antique bronze, marble, and Wedgwood blue. A mirrorlike gilding, which could be also be burnished and chased, one layer over another, was implemented and used without restraint. Brongniart revitalized the factory into a thriving business, meticulous in its quality, but utterly different from what it had been before.

There is no record that Talleyrand, conservative in his tastes, and often short of cash, ever purchased a Sèvres dinner service for himself. He did buy an extensive Sèvres dessert service, in *beau bleu,* as well as numerous unglazed "biscuit" figures. Many aristocrats still preferred to dine off silver plates polished to a soft patina, reserving the use of delicate porcelain for dessert. Talleyrand, the refined nobleman, never went in for the showy gilding or the overtly militaristic themes. While Napoleon liked to dine surrounded by scenes of battle, his chief diplomat ornamented his table with sculptural groups such as *Peace Restored by Victory,* modeled in 1798 to commemorate the peace of Campo Formio. Such figures sat on a mirrored plateau placed in the center of the table. Table decoration was a weapon in the Foreign Minister's arsenal to be consciously deployed as the occasion dictated. Carême believed:

One should, it seems to me, match the decorations to the gatherings at the tables we are serving. For example, for a military meal, helmets and trophies; for musicians, the lyre and the harp; for a marriage, the temple of hymen; for philosophers, pavilions and cottages; for novelists, ruins, waterfalls, fountains, towers, forts, rocks and torrents; something to satisfy everyone.

Tall, gilded candelabra towered over elaborate centerpieces so that their beauty might be admired and their message ingested along with the incomparable sauces. Even the names of the dishes evocatively argued on behalf of policy. Sturgeon, that most regal of fish, could be prepared *à la Napoléon* as a tribute to the Emperor, or *à la romaine* to imply that France was as glorious as ancient Rome.

Dessert provided the grand finale to the meal. Carême, who began his career as a pastry maker, considered his branch of cooking to be the noblest area of culinary art. Cussy credited him with inventing such delicious sweets as *gros nougats, grosses meringues, croquantes,* and babas, although these all, very likely, had earlier precedents. Carême's true combination, however, lay in his pastry and sugar centerpieces called *pièces montées;* a form that, similarly, he did not introduce, but elevated to its most staggering. For fancy balls he dazzled guests with even more elaborate creations: *les extra, les beaux extra,* and *les grands extraordinaires.* Among his favorite compositions was a large fountain of Parnassus: "I executed it twice at my grand dinners; it produced the same effect I anticipated. This dish is mounted in the shape of an ancient fountain, crowned with a palm wreath and two laurel wreaths decorating the sides of the piece. In these crowns I placed the names of Sophocles, Schiller, Shakespeare and Racine. . . . I made these large centerpieces yet again for another grand dinner, and in the four crowns I put the names of four great poets: Homer, Virgil, Dante, Milton." The names and decorative flourishes could be adjusted as appropriate to the guests: great generals in history for a field marshal's table, or historic ministers for that of a minister, and so on.

In *Le Pâtissier royal parisien,* Carême wrote more than a hundred pages of ideas for such decorations: moss-covered grottoes made of sweetmeats with small cakes colored to resemble granite, ocean waves and waterfalls of spun sugar, and trophies of gum arabic and sugar, colored to imitate the patina of antique bronze. He also used sugar and lard to create intricate edible bases on which to serve the dishes of the main meal. Cussy called Carême "the Palladio of the kitchen." The chef himself declared pastry "the highest form of architecture." He spent Tuesdays and Fridays at the Louvre copying designs by Tertio, Palladio, and Vignola. His *Pâtissier royal parisien* included a treatise on the five orders of architecture. While

Napoleon's favorite architects, Percier and Fontaine, erected the Arc de Triomphe du Carrousel, Carême produced edible monuments to sit on the table. With the use of resilient materials, occasionally even marble dust, these centerpieces could be made durable (once, he preserved a military trophy for six years). But the most difficult versions were made entirely in pastry, which, Carême noted, could not be made more than two days in advance. His food sculptures marked the pinnacle of the form, which found its roots in the colorful subtleties of the Middle Ages. Carême bemoaned the younger generation's reliance on shortcuts, especially the easier method of working in almond paste rather than pastry, which brought his special art into decline. As kitchen staffs shrank and service shifted to the new Russian style, never again would such intense labor and meticulous detail be applied to the creation of ephemeral sculptures.

FIGURE 9.10
Designs for sugar and pastry *pièces montées* in the form of ships, 1815, from Antonin Carême, *Le Pâtissier royal parisien.*

217

Talleyrand swathed his guests in luxury beyond anything they had ever experienced. Exquisite wines, perhaps a perfect Chambertin popular in the period, served in delicate cut-crystal glasses lowered their defenses. From another room, Talleyrand's staff of musicians—a Bohemian pianist named Dussek, a violinist, and a harpist—played lulling chamber music. Mozart and Haydn were among the Foreign Minister's favorites. However, without Talleyrand's firm command of his table, his dinners would have accomplished nothing beyond imparting a pleasurable experience.

The Foreign Minister watched over his dining room with the focused clarity of a military strategist. While Boucher and Carême glorified French civilization with

Grand Buffet de la Cuisine moderne.

their sublime creations, Talleyrand changed the fate of nations with his mastery as host. His greatest talent, a gift commensurate with Carême's cooking, was the art of conversation. Such sophisticated table talk, "in which there is perfect harmony in all that is felt and expressed," was what Madame de Staël missed the most after

218

her exile from the Empire. "French conversation," she wrote, "exists only in Paris, and conversation has been my greatest pleasure since childhood." Even Napoleon enjoyed the charms of the postprandial discourse at Parisian tables, telling his captors on Saint Helena, "If I were an Englishwoman, I should feel very disconcerted at being turned out by the men to wait for two or three hours while they were guzzling their wine." Talleyrand was the unrivaled master. Long after Madame de Staël considered him her enemy, she admitted, "If the art of conversation could be bought, I would go to the poorhouse to acquire his."

Napoleon, who likewise credited Talleyrand as being "Europe's master at the art of conversation," once purportedly inquired as to his secret. His Grand Chamberlain equated his strategy to the manner in which the Emperor always selected his battlefield in warfare and explained:

> Well, sire, I select the field of conversation. I venture only where I have something to say. I ignore all the rest. Ordinarily, I never allow myself to be questioned, except by you; if someone asks me something, it is because I myself have suggested the question. When I used to hunt, I would always fire at a distance of six paces and rarely bagged anything. I never took chances. In a conversation, I let everything remote go by about which I can offer only banal comments; but when something crops up right under my nose, I never miss.

FIGURE 9.11
Grand Buffet de la Cuisine Moderne, 1822, engraving by Antonin Carême, from *Le maître d'hôtel français.*

Politics were never overtly discussed in the refined atmosphere that reigned at Talleyrand's table. Lady Frances Shelley remembered one such evening: "During the whole repast, the general conversation was upon eating. Every dish was discussed, and the antiquity of every bottle of wine supplied the most elegant annotations. Talleyrand himself analyzed the dinner with as much seriousness as if he had been discussing some political question of importance." It was a rare occasion on which the Foreign Minister offered any distinct opinion. He believed in listening to everything and saying as little as possible. A German princess, who called in numerous favors to obtain a coveted seat next to the minister, complained afterward that he never said one word to her. Such unnatural silence heightened the weight of the sparse and carefully chosen words he did speak. Hortense de Beauharnais described the Foreign Minister's mesmerizing charm:

> The attentions of a man who rarely confers them are always effective. I am certain that his reputation for great cleverness is due not so much to anything unusual he does, but to the fact that he says so little, but says it so well. . . . The vanity of people is what makes Talleyrand so attractive to them. I was a victim of this myself. When he unbends to the extent of speaking to you, he seems utterly charming. And if he goes so far as to inquire about your health, you are prepared to love him forever.

Another observer commented that Talleyrand "possessed the art of concealing his thoughts or his malice beneath a transparent veil of insinuations, words that simply imply something more than they express. It was the most savory conversation of an era when conversation was uniquely a function of intelligence. . . . Only when absolutely necessary did he inject his own personality."

Talleyrand encouraged his guests to stay long after the last of dessert had been cleared away, sipping Cognac or nibbling biscuits dipped in Madeira, often inviting additional visitors to arrive for a reception at eleven, sometimes with dancing, followed by a midnight supper and gaming into the early hours of the morning.

These dinners bridged relationships and sounded out policy, but business was always hidden beneath a veneer of politesse. Talleyrand could weather outright hostility; what offended him above all else was lack of manners. The pretentiousness of the Empire increasingly grated the Foreign Minister's blue-blooded nerves. He later quipped that "[l]uxury at the courts established by Napoleon was a mockery. Bonapartist luxury was neither German nor French, it was a mixture, a studied luxury acquired from all over. . . . The most salient feature of this type of luxury was its absolute lack of decorum, and in France, any serious departure from decorum invites ridicule." He was forced to contend with boorish guests who vulgarly downed his aged Cognac in a single gulp. He did not hesitate to correct one such visitor, instructing him in the simplest terms: "Cup the glass in your hands, warm it, agitate it gently in a circular direction so that the liqueur gives off a bouquet. Then breathe it . . ." The frustration of being asked "Then what?" tried his patience to the limit. The minister replied tartly, "Then, sir, put down the glass and converse."

The problem stemmed from the bombastic Emperor himself. Napoleon once complained to his Grand Chamberlain: "I invited a lot of people to Fontainebleau. I wanted them to enjoy themselves, I organized all the amusements; and everyone had long faces and looked worn out and gloomy." Talleyrand responded as simply as if he were speaking to a small child: "That is because pleasure cannot be regulated by drums, and here, just as in the army, you always seem to be saying to each of us, 'Now then, ladies and gentlemen, march.' " Napoleon had learned his social graces on the battlefield. Talleyrand lamented, "There was debauchery before the Revolution, but there was elegance. There were rogues, but they were witty. Today, debauchery is vulgar and rogues are a bore."

When Napoleon's deteriorating position in Spain sufficiently weakened his hold over his beleaguered citizens, Talleyrand was ready to strike. On 20 December 1808 he hosted one of his most magnificent receptions. Who could refuse such a promising invitation? He waited until they all arrived: aristocrats, government officials, diplomats, bankers, and, *bien sûr,* the "merveilleuses." He wined them on the best vintages of his cellar, dined them on the magnificent creations of his kitchen, and entertained them with his gifted musicians. Then, when even the stragglers had been lured into his enticing pleasure palace, a hushed, uncomfortable silence fell over the room. Talleyrand let it hang in the air, almost, but not quite, too long. He wanted to be sure that no one missed the importance of the moment.

On cue, the Grand Chamberlain's archenemy Joseph Fouché was announced. He stood, smiling in the threshold, for dramatic effect. The guests could hardly believe their eyes. Prior to this occasion, the Prince of Benevento openly hated Napoleon's vulgar, conniving Minister of Police, who had unforgivably sentenced many to the guillotine during the Terror. Once, when someone remarked that the chief of police held all of humanity in the utmost contempt, Talleyrand quipped that this was because he had "examined himself thoroughly." Amidst the aristocratic splendor of Talleyrand's party, the dazzling edible sculptures glistening under crystal chandeliers, Fouché's garish presence at the entryway must have seemed like a mirage. It was not.

With the full majesty of his noble heritage and ecclesiastical training, the host limped over to personally greet and welcome his most recent arrival. Arm in arm, Talleyrand and Fouché then proceeded to circulate through every room of the party, never speaking a word, but eloquently announcing their new alliance with every step. When they completed their tour, they withdrew into a corner where they could be seen, though not overheard, whispering together. The act was as symbolically charged as the glittering feast that united the warring young kings Henry VIII of England (r. 1509–1547) and François I of France (r. 1515–1547) for the momentous, truce-making banquet at the Field of the Cloth of Gold in 1520.

The meaning of this theatrical display of friendship meant only one thing: these disparate characters had united against a common enemy, whom they abhorred so thoroughly that plotting his downfall outweighed the personal enmity each felt toward the other. Only one man was powerful enough to warrant such an occurrence: the Emperor. Talleyrand and Fouché had publicly declared war on Napoleon. Their march of solidarity issued a call for other dissenters to join in. Never, of course, was a disloyal word uttered.

Napoleon was livid. While he may have lacked decorum, he was no fool. When he returned to Paris just over a month later and called his Council to a meeting, he exploded at Talleyrand in one of his infamous rants. The death penalty seemed almost inevitable, but the diplomat stood implacably tall and aloof. Napoleon was reduced to shouting, "What about your wife? You never told me that San Carlos was your wife's lover?" With perfect equanimity and princely hauteur Talleyrand calmly replied: "Indeed, Sire, it did not occur to me that this information had any bearing on Your Majesty's glory or my own." Flustered, Napoleon stormed out of the room. When he was gone, Talleyrand sniffed, "What a pity, gentlemen, that so great a man should be so ill-mannered." Talleyrand lost his post as Grand Chamberlain, but he was not arrested. Napoleon, even in exile, never lost his awe for the

Foreign Minister who had opened the doors of Paris and its hidden world of glamour to him so many years before.

Talleyrand's grand reception presaged a shift in the winds of Napoleon's fortunes. News of his startling promenade with the chief of police spread swiftly to the Emperor's numerous foreign enemies, allowing Talleyrand to gain their confidences and easing his reconciliation with the exiled monarchists. Although it took several more years of plotting to bring Napoleon down, when the time came, Talleyrand personally invited them to take Paris. On 30 March 1814 Czar Alexander and the allies toppled Paris by midday; the younger brother of Louis XVI was declared Louis XVIII (r. 1814–1824). Civilized life could continue at last.

Fearing that Napoleon might have planted mines in the Elysée Palace, the Czar chose to stay with his ever-hospitable friend Talleyrand. His obliging host organized a celebratory dinner and a trip to the opera. Alexander was so impressed with Carême's cuisine that he requested that Talleyrand release the chef to serve him once he was installed at the Palace. The Czar later brought Carême with him to Russia.

As President of the provisional government, one of Talleyrand's first acts in office was to organize a grand dinner for the allies who liberated Paris from the tyrant and the senators who voted in the new regime. Carême eagerly commenced preparations, but the senators proved less cooperative and refused to bow to the allied rulers. Talleyrand would not have his vision thwarted by such a minor problem. He hired and rehearsed actors to replace his senators, who obliged him by lifting to toast Louis XVIII on cue. Talleyrand understood that dinner is living theater.

The greatest challenge to Talleyrand's astute diplomatic talents came at the Congress of Vienna, which began in late September 1814. As the representative of a defeated nation, he arrived without a voice in the negotiations. When Louis XVIII anxiously inquired whether Talleyrand needed additional staff, the reply came back: "Sire, I need cooks more than diplomats." Nevertheless, the experienced diplomat had come prepared; Carême tackled the kitchen and Talleyrand's charming mistress (his nephew's wife), Dorothée, Duchess of Dino, assisted the host in the dining room. The aging diplomat rented the most opulent house on the market, and with his glamorous companion welcomed the Congress to enjoy his hospitality.

One evening at the end of dinner, the conversation turned to cheese and each ambassador defended the superiority of his own nation's specialty. Lord Castlereagh extolled English Stilton, the Swiss representative, Emmenthal, and so the discussion continued while Talleyrand graciously held his tongue. As if on cue, a valet interrupted them to announce that the courier had arrived from Paris with a packet of court dispatches and a case of Brie. Talleyrand asked that the cheese be placed on the table and announced: "I refrained from taking part in the discussion and, as your host, crying up a product of French soil, but it is here. Judge for yourself, gentlemen." It was a triumph of diplomacy at the table.

Brie was Talleyrand's favorite cheese; he called it the "king of cheeses." There were those who wryly noted that it was "the only king he did not betray." Metternich, who so frequently enjoyed the bounty of Talleyrand's table, more aptly penetrated his friend and colleague's interior: "As an individual and as a symbol, M. de Talleyrand truly represents France as she is, whereas the majority of foreign envoys only represent a political party at best and very often just themselves." Civilization, embodied nowhere more fully for Talleyrand than by the refinements of the French table, held more importance than any government, especially if that government threatened the health of this sacred institution. Brie was, indeed, the king whom Talleyrand would never betray. Carême by no means exaggerated his contribution to his employer's diplomatic tactics when he wrote, "Our art escorts the diplomat, and every Prime Minister and his councilors. To preside over a political body or hold an ambassadorship is to take a course in gastronomy."

As the Congress of Vienna progressed, Talleyrand convinced Metternich to allow him to actively participate in the discussions and became one of the most influential voices of the group. But when Napoleon stormed back into France in February 1815, Talleyrand's hard-won gains were erased. Nevertheless, the diplomat, and his dinners, continued unabated through several successive governments. Although his tenure as Prime Minister to Louis XVIII was brief, when Charles X

(r. 1824–1830) became King in 1824, Talleyrand organized the Coronation. Five years later, he had lost neither his smell for the political nor his taste for the high life; when the King replaced his cabinet with the least popular men in France, Talleyrand wrote to Louis-Philippe (r. 1830–1848) and encouraged him to come to Paris. A year later, the grateful Monarch rewarded his subject with the ambassadorship of London. At the age of seventy-seven, Talleyrand established a new address of note, where, the Duchess of Dino wrote, they were "making gastronomic history in London." It was the Foreign Minister who taught Carême that "[t]he ambassador who wishes to serve his country well should have a succulent table; his diplomatic position imposes upon him to sacrifice his fortune, if his country does not understand the importance of his noble mission."

Chapter Ten

Family

BERNARD SHAW'S
SUNDAY SUPPER WITH
WILLIAM MORRIS AND FAMILY,
LONDON, JULY 1884

[T]he Morris meals were works of art, almost as much as the furniture.

George Bernard Shaw, "Morris As I Knew Him"

*I*T WAS A SUNDAY EVENING IN JULY 1884 when George Bernard Shaw (1856–1950) first crossed the threshold of Kelmscott House, in the Hammersmith section of London. William Morris (1834–1896) had invited him home for Sunday supper with his wife and children, whom the future playwright had never met. Shaw knew his host—the designer and managing partner of Morris & Co., famous for its luxuriant floral patterns and finely crafted furniture—only as the "Great Man" of the Social Democratic Federation, of which he was also an active member. After joining the party in 1883, Morris became so thoroughly involved in the movement that he converted his coach house into a lecture hall, where he arranged for speakers to hold forth every Sunday night. He had asked the young activist to deliver a lecture, "On Individualism," and, as was his habit, invited the speaker to join him afterward for supper at the

227

FIGURE 10.1
Peach Wallpaper, designed
by William Morris.

house. This was the means, Shaw recalled, by which he "penetrated the Morris interior."

The gaunt, auburn-bearded Irishman, at the time, very much embodied the title of his most recent novel, *An Unsocial Socialist,* published in serial form earlier that year. Though Morris had read it with relish (which had, in fact, spawned his interest in the younger writer), the public largely ignored it. The future Nobel Prize winner had gained a reputation as a charismatic speaker for biweekly political lectures delivered on street corners throughout London, but he still lived at home with his mother, earned a meager living as a journalist, and had four other unpublished novels to his name. With little to show for himself but a frayed suit and a thorough irreverence for respectability, Shaw confessed that in these years he "avoided literary and artistic society like the plague."

The prospect of supping in Morris's elegant, upper bourgeois home with the family man and the capitalist, rather than the social agitator, must have given Shaw a measure of ambivalence. Although Shaw applauded his host's politics, he was somewhat disparaging about socialists from privileged backgrounds like Karl Marx, Ferdinand Lassalle, and Morris himself. He attributed Morris's famous temper tantrums wholly to his childhood in a rich household, "where he had not been sufficiently controlled or forced to control himself," while equally decrying the social snobbery and pretensions evinced by his own shabbily gentile family. Shaw universally loathed any form of what he viewed as moral hypocrisy. As the son of an alcoholic father and a deserting mother, Shaw did not share the prevalent Victorian sentimentality over family life. He was well aware that the domestic meal could be as much a battleground as a forum to strengthen the bonds of kinship, less sure what participating in the Morrises' supper might yield.

Morris, however, had no reservations about bringing his young comrade into his inner sanctum. In contrast to the studied politeness of his class and time, Morris behaved with gruff naturalness, always buzzing with ideas and enthusiasm for his myriad projects as he ran his fingers through his wildly unkempt hair. Nor, in a time when Queen Victoria (r. 1837–1901) was nicknamed "Mrs. Brown" for her love of domesticity, did Morris consider his family table a sacred haven to be safeguarded against intrusion. Victoria's consort, Prince Albert, had brought the German Christmas tree to England in 1840, whereupon the custom became wildly popular as an "invented" tradition, but Morris declared, "How I do hate Easter: second only to Christmas. . . ." Shaw later recalled that his friend "never discussed his family affairs" with him: "[A]nd I am not sure he ever discussed them with his

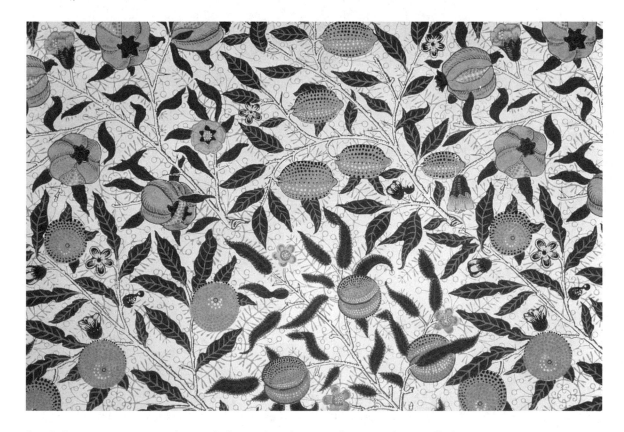

family." Unpretentious and straightforward in his speech, gesticulating all the while, Morris welcomed his guest from the lecture hall into the house without ceremony.

The brick Georgian exterior of Kelmscott House had not prepared Shaw for the transformation he discovered its owner had rendered on its interior. To Morris's daughter May (1862–1938), set loose to play amidst the gardens of their many-gabled country house, Kelmscott Manor, Kelmscott House was merely "a convenient and seemly shelter from the weather." Shaw, however, deemed it "magical." He admired the "extraordinary discrimination" with which Morris had furnished it. The upstairs drawing room was hung with woven wool "bird" fabric, made by Morris's company under the supervision of Thomas Wardle, who produced dyes from vegetables and other organic materials by a careful study of ancient herbals. Morris himself had designed the pattern of abstracted birds in a rich background of flowers and vines after Verdure tapestries hung in medieval halls. A painted settle—a sturdy wooden bench and backed storage trunk based on Gothic examples—dominated the room's judicious furnishings. The object had originally been made for the dining room of Morris's Red House, which Philip Webb (1831–1915) designed for him in 1859 as a home for his new bride. Morris's Pre-Raphaelite Brothers, including Edward Burne-Jones (1833–1898) and Dante Gabriel Rossetti (1828–1882), had helped him decorate it. It was the project that gave birth to the firm of Morris, Marshall, Faulkner, and Company, Fine Art Workmen in Painting, Carving, Furniture, and the Metals. When the Red House was sold in 1865, and the family moved to quarters above the firm's workshop at Queen's Square, the settle went with them; so too, it moved with them to Kelmscott House in 1878, as a vestige of their lost, lyrical Camelot.

Shaw claimed that when he met Morris, he was unacquainted with his friend's past: "Of William Morris of the Red House, head centre and organizer of a happy Brotherhood of artists who called him Topsy and thought of him as a young man, we knew nothing. The small minority of us who had any contact with the newest fashions in literature and art knew that he had become famous as the author of a long series of poems called 'The Earthly Paradise' which few of us had read, though the magic line 'the idle singer of an empty day' had caught our ears somehow." For Shaw, the Red House settle held no memories or nostalgia; it was simply a handsome object, well made, and extremely functional. Even as a boy, Shaw evinced a particular interest in aesthetics, and was far more likely to be found wandering through the National Gallery in Dublin than tending to his homework. From 1885 to 1889, he worked as an art critic for *The World,* and even before his later fame, his wry, Irish wit could not be quelled from expressing his firm opinion on any subject. His friend and employer, William Archer, recalled, "He didn't know much more about painting than I, but he thought he did and that was the main point." The elegant restraint with which Morris appointed his home impressed Shaw immensely. In contrast to the knickknack-crammed interiors found in Victorian homes, Shaw approvingly noted, "Nothing in it was there because it was interesting or quaint or rare or hereditary, like grandmother's or uncle's portrait. Everything that was necessary was clean and handsome; everything else was beautiful and beautifully presented."

The interior of Kelmscott House reconciled Shaw to the paradox of Morris's radical politics and his position as a prosperous tradesman and owner of a factory that produced high-quality objects for the upper middle class. The integrity of a polished, solid wood floor, a hand-woven tapestry, or a sturdy but portable chair embodied the designer's golden rule of aesthetics: "Have nothing in your houses which you do not know to be useful or believe to be beautiful." The decor visually espoused Morris's belief that "civilization meant the attainment of peace and order and freedom, of goodwill between man and man, of the love of truth and the hatred of injustice . . . not more stuffed chairs and more cushions, and more carpets and gas, and more dainty meats and drink—and therewithal more and sharper differences between class and class."

The pleasure Shaw took in looking over the objects and furnishings was slightly marred by his anxiety about meeting his hostess, who had not yet made her appearance. Shaw believed that he "knew that the sudden eruption into her temple of beauty, with its Pre-Raphaelite priests, of the proletarian comrade who began to infest the premises as Morris's fellow-Socialists, must be horribly disagreeable to her (I knew how my mother felt about the more discordant of them); and as a rag-and-tag-bobtail of Socialism I could not expect her to do more than bear my presence as she might." He was, in general, somewhat overawed by women, fearful of the power they might wield over him, and he recoiled from intimacy throughout his life.

Although Shaw claimed ignorance of the details of his host's earlier career, he admitted that the stunning features of his hostess had been indelibly burned into his imagination through her portraits by Rossetti, which he had recently seen on exhibition at the Burlington Arts Club. Jane (née Burden, 1839–1914), or Janey, as she was called by those closest to her, embodied the Pre-Raphaelite ideal, with hypnotic, deep-set eyes, a forceful jaw and brows, and endlessly long waves of ebony hair that cascaded down the length of her languorous figure. Whistler was

said to remark that "without Mrs. Morris to supply stained glass attitudes and the lissome beauty of an angel, the Pre-Raphaelites would have long since gone to dust and been forgotten." Rossetti rendered her in mythic terms, like a Gothic princess sprung to life from Malory. Her image had become so iconic that it became difficult for those in aesthetic circles to see her as a real person, who dwelt among breathing mortals. A quarter of a century after Rossetti and Burne-Jones discovered this "stunner" at a performance of the Drury Lane Theatre in Oxford, Jane's life story was equally legendary. At work on the Oxford Union murals, the Brotherhood adopted this humble daughter of a stable hand as their muse, painting her as Guinevere. Morris, transfixed by her, had proposed. "I cannot paint you; but I love you," he purportedly said. They married in 1859; then followed the happy years at the Red House. But, like the queen they cast her as, she betrayed her husband with his trusted friend. Though the public was never completely sure, Rossetti's portraits of Jane had immortalized their love for all to see.

Shaw records how, on that evening, suddenly, the fabled beauty appeared before him in the flesh.

When she came into the room in her strangely beautiful garments, looking at least eight feet high, the effect was as if she had walked out of an Egyptian tomb at Luxor. Not until she had disposed herself very comfortably on the long couch opposite the settle did I compose myself into an acceptance of her as a real woman, and note that the wonderful curtain of hair was touched with grey, and the Rossetti face ten years older than it was in his pictures.

Shaw was an inveterate, almost shameless charmer, renowned for his excessive yet amusing conversation. Just one month after this visit to Kelmscott House, Edith Nesbit described him as having "a fund of dry Irish humor that is simply irresistible." She said, "He . . . is the grossest flatterer I ever met . . . [and] is horribly untrustworthy as he repeats everything he hears, and does not always stick to the truth." Janey, however, was not having any of it. As engaging and complimentary as he tried to be (and we can only imagine that the man who would write *Pygmalion* must have been sincerely fascinated by her), Janey remained implacable. He later declared, "She was not a talker at all; in fact she was the silentest woman I have ever met. She did not take much notice of anybody, and none whatever of Morris, who talked all the time." (Years earlier, Henry James had fared no better and described her as "a dark, silent medieval woman with her medieval toothache.")

In spite of Morris's affable demeanor, home life was not happy. It had been nearly twenty years since the Morrises had sold the Red House, which Rossetti had described as "more a poem than a house, but admirable to live in too." May, who was only a toddler when they left, recalled:

Laughter sounded from the half-finished room where the young people painted the walls with scenes from the Round Table histories; laughter sounded from the fragrant garden as the host, victim of some ingenious practical joke, fulfilled the pleased expectation of his guests by conduct at once vigorous and picturesque under the torment; laughter over the apple-gathering; laughter over every new experiment, every fantastic failure of the young housekeepers.

FAMILY

With the sale of the Red House, where Morris and Jane had been painted on a mural as the king and queen entertaining their guests at a medieval banquet, went the relaxed dinners at their round table: the beautiful sight of "Morris coming up from the cellar before dinner, beaming with joy, with his hands full of bottles of wine and others tucked under his arms" and Janey playing old English songs late into the evening from the book given to her as a gift from her husband on the piano decorated by Burne-Jones.

Georgie Burne-Jones, married to Edward and friend to Janey, recalled there were weekly "family" dinners reuniting the partners of "The Firm" for some time after the Morrises took rooms over the workshop in Queen's Square in 1865. But Jane's health declined; she went away to convalesce, a pattern that continued from that time on, though the cause of her illness is unknown. Perhaps she was merely depressed; the affair with Rossetti began not long after her return from the spa. Sometimes the Morrises gave full dress dinners for up to eighteen guests. At one, a duly impressed attendee wrote "The Earthly Paradise" atop the menu card; but that had been in 1868.

As the affair had blossomed, Rossetti (whose eccentric antics Lewis Carroll [Charles Lutwidge Dodgson] claimed as the inspiration for the Mad Hatter's tea party in *Alice's Adventures in Wonderland*) had taken to publicly courting his muse at such gatherings. At one dinner, he spoon-fed Jane strawberries, carefully wiping the cream from each one to protect her fragile health, while his stupefied friends, including Morris, looked on. At another, the host, painter William Bell Scott declared Rossetti "acts like a perfect fool if he wants to conceal his attachment." There was gossip. The mirthful dinners of the Brotherhood became painful, and had finally dropped off.

As the years passed, Jane became increasingly withdrawn and passive, so Morris, heartbroken, threw himself ever more fully into work. Jane spent long stretches of time in the Cotswolds at Kelmscott Manor, the country house which Morris had at first leased with Rossetti in 1871, ostensibly for Janey's health, but implicitly so the lovers could discreetly meet. When the affair ended in 1874, Morris bought the house, and Jane continued to go there with the children.

FIGURE 10.3
*William Morris with Jenny
and May Morris,* ca. 1865,
lost drawing by Edward
Burne-Jones, photographed
by Emery Walker.

Even more painful than this marital discord, to which Morris simply turned a blind eye and a patient heart, was the tragic diagnosis of epilepsy thrust upon their elder daughter, Jenny (1861–1935), in 1876. In Victorian England the disease was thoroughly misunderstood, considered akin to insanity and duly stigmatized. The violent spectacle was to be hidden. By the time of Shaw's first visit to Kelmscott House in 1884, Jenny's condition had deteriorated to the point of requiring frequent institutional care. While it is not known whether Shaw met Jenny that evening, he never mentioned her.

Despite Jenny's painful disease, open-house Sundays at Kelmscott House continued to be held. The old crowd came less frequently, but members of the Social Democratic Federation, like Shaw, poets, and others who shared interests with the master of the house, were often invited to stop by. Janey had few friends to speak of, but her husband had many. The awkwardness of his marriage and his sadness about Jenny must have made the presence of these outsiders a blessing, easing his loneliness and his wife's uncomfortable silence.

May looked skeptically at first-time guests because her father had an unfortunate habit of extending his hospitality to a number of "bores" who, once ensconced, settled in for the whole evening. "Minor poets pounced most often," she claimed. The invasion was tolerable in the drawing room, where she and her mother busied themselves with their embroidery. However, she dreaded the moment when her father would look at them plaintively and whisper, "My dears—a BORE—can't get rid of him! Afraid he'll stay to supper!" She complained that "more often than not, on returning to his Bore, he could not, as the hour of Sunday supper drew near, bring himself to use the accustomed wiles of civilized man that lead gracefully to leave-taking, but felt bound to give an outwardly cordial invitation to join the company at the long dining-table."

As Shaw sat with the Morris women awaiting supper in their drawing room, it must have been excruciatingly awkward for all concerned. With his acute perception, the guest, in particular, must have sensed the complex Morris history and its secrets, which could neither be addressed, nor ignored, nor known. But where his attempt to smooth the introduction over with boundless anecdotes and compliments had failed to soften his hostess, her daughter, for once, found herself entirely charmed. Shaw, likewise, always remembered that "among the many beautiful things in Morris's two beautiful houses, was a very beautiful daughter, then in the flower of her youth." May had been well educated at the Notting Hill High School, had trained at the South Kensington School of Design, and was by then a self-possessed professional in the embroidery division of her father's company. She was forthright and opinionated, a zealous proponent of her father's socialist causes, as simply dressed as plainly spoken, and without a shred of pretense. For Shaw, who considered himself too poor to marry—and certainly to a daughter of the illustrious William Morris—May held the fascination of being simultaneously engagingly present and beyond reach.

May's eagerness to speak with her new guest enlivened the atmosphere, yet her polite demeanor was overshadowed by the presence of the third lady of the family, Miss Mary de Morgan, sister of the pottery designer William de Morgan (1839–1917), who, Shaw wryly said, "was by no means either silent or consecrated to beauty." She was not, strictly speaking, a relation but part of the old circle who willfully remained a fixture within the Morris home. Shaw could not understand how or why they tolerated her at all. Before meeting her that evening, the scathing criticism he had heard about her, accusations that she fostered mischief-making gossip to break homes and friendships, embroiled herself in everyone else's personal affairs, and offended every host by bossily ordering everyone around, firmly predisposed him to loathe her. Although he later credited her with an ability to make herself indispensable in difficult times, as he awaited the dinner bell, convinced as he was "that she must be the most odious female then alive," the prospect of listening to her through an entire meal, while the lovely Miss Morris could not get a word in edgewise and his hostess glared at him stonily, must have seemed unbearable.

In spite of his short temper, Morris, for his part, continued to chat animatedly without letting Miss de Morgan upset him. When Jane's unmarried sister Bessie Burden had lived with the family he had not been so forgiving. He complained, "I must say it is a shame, she is quite harmless and even good and one ought not to be irritated with her, but O my God what I have suffered from finding her always there at meals and the like!" She had not been invited along when the Morrises moved to Hammersmith in 1878. Shaw could not know this, but he had witnessed enough of Morris at their meetings to remark upon "his habit, when annoyed by some foolish speaker, of pulling single hairs violently from his moustache and growling 'damned fool!' "

Nevertheless, without incident, the hour for supper came, and he was escorted into the dining room. Bewitching, yet utterly restful, the room was described by one guest as having "more than a touch of the Thousand-and-one-Nights." This magical atmosphere emanated from an enormous antique Persian carpet, swirling with color and pattern, which, instead of covering the handsomely polished wood floor, had been hung like a swooping canopy from the wall to the ceiling above the table. Shaw thought it "so lovely that it would have been a sin to walk on it." Those who sat beneath it were caught within its spell.

In contrast to the textile hanging overhead, Shaw noted that "[o]n the supper

FIGURE 10.4
The dining room at
Kelmscott House,
Hammersmith, London,
showing the Persian carpet,
1896, photographed by
Emery Walker.

table there was no table cloth: a thing common enough now among people who see that a table should be itself an ornament and not a clothes horse, but then an innovation so staggering that it cost years of domestic conflict to introduce it." Although it was fashionable in England to remove the cloth before dessert and reveal the slickly polished veneer of a mahogany table, to dine without linen, as Shaw points out, was radically modern. Long before cutlery, or even plates, arrived on the European table, exquisite table linen demarcated the hallowed space set aside for the purpose of dining. As the picnic blanket spread on the grass makes clear, a cloth without the table is sufficient to define the boundaries of an area in which to eat. In the great age of the Gothic, which Morris revered as a lost world of both chivalry and craftsmanship, staggering sums were spent on linens, the best damask imported from Syria. Morris's undraped trestle table, of solid, scrubbed oak, not veneer, daringly straddled tradition and innovation.

Morris considered it his mission as a designer "to beautify the familiar matters of everyday life." He was waging a battle against the proliferation of cheaply made, overly decorated objects that cluttered high Victorian tables. As the fashion for *service à la russe* spread from France through Europe and the United States in the 1870s and 1880s, popularized, as it was, through translations of chef Urbain Dubois's cookbooks, the stunning platters and pyramids of food that once visually dominated the table disappeared. Instead, individual place settings became more complex, with objects designed specifically for each course or food: fish forks, salad forks, pastry forks, oyster forks, snail forks, even terrapin forks and ice-cream forks; matching sets of crystal stemware for each wine and water; cut-glass finger bowls; and ludicrously tall flower arrangements and candelabra. How could the standardized, logical flow of serving numerous courses consecutively, each with its own set of tools, fail to appeal to the generation of the Industrial Revolution and the assembly line? Tableware was bigger, heavier, and more decorated than ever before. The invention of silver electroplating in 1840 and the discovery of new silver deposits in the subsequent decades, lowered the price of the actual metal, expanding popular access to silverware. Inferior production values necessitated the invention of some of the new utensils. Fork tines that had not been hammered by hand

239

to compact the soft metal frequently bent or broke when confronted by a crisp leaf of lettuce or a thick pastry crust: hence the invention of variations to perform these functions, sporting a wide, reinforced tine. Most of these objects, however, merely fed the demand of the burgeoning industrial class, who vied with one another to have the very latest, most extensive dinner services. Just six years before Shaw's first supper at the Morris residence, one of the largest and most ornate Victorian flatware sets, the Mackay Service, commissioned by the owner of the Comstock Silver Mine in Nevada as a gift for his wife and made from his own silver by Tiffany and Company in New York, had been exhibited at the American Pavilion of the 1878 Paris Exposition. The service for twenty-four included more than 1,250 pieces; even scholars of the period expressed their bafflement as to the utility of all these pieces.

Decades before Emily Post was driven to write "queerly shaped pieces of flatware, contrived for purposes known only to their designers, have no place on the well-appointed table," Morris rebelled against this aesthetic of "more is more," and strove to make every cup and every knife both practical and a work of art. He privately joked with his daughter that he wished he could advise his clients to whitewash their walls and leave everything bare except for a fine Arras tapestry. Such recommendations, he realized, would put him out of business.

He chose instead to lead by example, setting his own table with a judicious selection of useful, honest, carefully crafted, and beautifully ornamented objects so that it appeared restful. Morris engaged the obnoxious Miss de Morgan's brother to handcraft for Morris & Co. at his Merton Abbey workshop earthenware vessels and tiles, which Morris not only put on his own table but also offered for sale. De Morgan revived ancient glazing techniques to decorate these wares in saturated greens and blues, and with iridescent luster effects. Inspired by fifteenth-century Hispano-Moresque, Iznik, and Persian pottery, the patterns were as rich as those on the dining room carpet.

Morris describes his ideal table décor in his last literary work, the utopian novel, *News from Nowhere* (1892), in which his vision of the future very nearly resembles the Gothic past:

> The glass, crockery and plate were very beautiful to my eyes, used to the study of medieval art; but a nineteenth-century club-haunter would, I daresay, have found them rough and lacking in finish; the crockery being lead-glazed pot-ware, though beautifully ornamented; the only porcelain being here and there a piece of old oriental ware. The glass, again, though elegant and quaint, and very varied in form, was somewhat bubbled and hornier in texture than the commercial articles of the nineteenth century. The furniture and general fittings of the hall were much of a piece with the table-gear, beautiful in form and highly ornamental, but without the commercial "finish" of the joiners and cabinet-makers of our time. Withal, there was a total absence of what the nineteenth century calls "comfort"—that is, stuffy inconvenience; so that, even apart from the delightful excitement of the day I had never eaten my dinner so pleasantly before.

FIGURE 10.5
Frontispiece, 1892, designed by Charles March Gere, with lettering by William Morris, showing the entrance to the Kelmscott Manor, from William Morris, *News from Nowhere.*

Morris's taste for the variegated texture of goods produced by gifted artisans extended from the earthenware on his table to the food he liked to eat. His narrator enjoys a breakfast "which was simple enough":

> But most delicately cooked, and set on the table with much daintiness. The bread was particularly good, and was of several kinds, from the big, rather close, dark-colored, sweet-tasting farmhouse loaf, which was the most to

241

my liking, to the thin pipe-stems of wheaten crust, such as I have eaten in Turin.

The aesthetic espoused in *News from Nowhere* governed Morris's real-life home. On a visit to Kelmscott House, Helena Sickert, sister of the artist Walter, admired a plain trestle table, a dresser with blue-and-white crockery, honey, and homemade bread, as well as "the exquisite cleanliness of the house." The aesthetic equally pleased Shaw, who declared the Morris meals "works of art almost as much as the furniture."

Credit for the organization of the household and the supper must be given to Jane and not her husband, who imposed his taste upon home décor but did oversee its day-to-day operation. Helena Sickert specifically made note of the fact that Mrs. Morris enjoyed a reputation as an exemplary housekeeper. Jan Marsh, Jane's biographer, thinks it very probable that after her engagement she was sent to a finishing school or ladies' seminary for education in proper manners, speech, and household management. Even in the first years of married life, Jane had a cook and a housemaid, as well as a groom and a nanny to help her in her duties. Although catapulted upon marriage from extreme poverty into privilege, Jane was never tempted toward excess. She ran a well-ordered home and minimized expense, almost to the point of frugality. Although Shaw was not taken by her melancholic silence, he conceded that "she had a certain plain good sense which had preserved her sanity perfectly under treatment that would have spoiled most women."

As Jane was preparing for her marriage, Mrs. Isabella Beeton's *Book of Household Management* (first published 1861) appeared in serialized form. This phenomenally popular resource book, reprinted for decades, addressed women who undertook the cooking and cleaning themselves, as well as wealthier wives, who managed housekeepers, cooks, butlers, and servants. Beeton stressed the importance of economy to all classes of women, especially with regard to the family meal. When preparing "[a] Family Dinner at Home," she counsels, "it will be found, by far, the better plan, to cook and serve the dinner, and to lay the table-cloth and the sideboard, with the same cleanliness, neatness and scrupulous exact-

ness, whether it be for the mistress herself alone, a small family, or for 'company.' "
Mrs. Beeton believed that

> there is no more fruitful source of family discontent than a housewife's badly
> cooked dinners and untidy ways. Men are now so well served out of doors—at
> their clubs, well-ordered taverns, and dining houses, that in order to compete
> with the attractions of these places, a mistress must be thoroughly acquainted
> with the theory and the practice of the art of cookery, as well as perfectly con-
> versant with all the other arts of making and keeping a comfortable home.

While Jane lacked the wifely desire to entice her husband to stay home more often, she followed the letter, if not the spirit, of Mrs. Beeton's advice. The Morris
household offered abundant, unpretentious hospitality that Mrs. Beeton would
have found exemplary.

Janey, like Mrs. Beeton, placed a good joint of meat at the center of the domestic
dinner table. In her menu recommendations for a "Plain family dinner" for a winter Sunday, Mrs. Beeton suggests oxtail soup, followed by roast beef and Yorkshire
pudding, accompanied by broccoli and potatoes; for the same event in summer, a
vegetable-marrow soup to start, with roast quarter of lamb accompanied by mint
sauce, French beans, and potatoes as the main course. These were simple, honest
menus, as solid as the Morrises' oak dining table. Although the potatoes were a
New World import, gradually assimilated into the native diet, and only fully popularized during the nineteenth century, nothing could be more quintessentially
English, from the Saxons to Victoria, than a hearty roast served up at dinner.

Morris adored a big beefsteak, sometimes even in the morning. On a trip to
Iceland in 1871, he enjoyed huge breakfasts of "beefsteak and onions, smoked
salmon, Norway anchovies, hard-boiled eggs, cold meat, cheese and radishes and
butter, all very plenteous." Shaw professed, "There is no sincerer love than the love
of food," an adage to which Morris clearly subscribed. He was quite chubby, even
as a youth. On that same expedition to Iceland, he had learned to cook, relying
upon newfangled innovations like tins of preserved meat and canned carrots, as

well as older conveniences such as bouillon cubes to sustain him. He had no use, however, for pretentious French delicacies or overly rarified sauces. Given his druthers, he was a man who liked a quality cut of meat, fresh, garden-grown vegetables and fruits, and the grainy texture of home-baked country bread.

We can imagine Morris slicing into a beautifully crusted roast with the elegant flourish described in the 1508 *Boke of Kervynge*. The act of carving at the family table holds the last vestiges of the great noble perquisite of gaming rights and the faint traces of the hunting tribes who were the ancestors of northern Europe's aristocracy. By the late nineteenth century, when the sight of an entire hunk of meat evoked barbarism rather than splendor, the elaborate ritual once performed by noble sons with solemnity and flair was hidden from view at grand formal banquets. But within the middle-class family homes of Victorian England, and often still, the head of the household continued to "do the honors." In Morris's Gothic-inspired house, nothing could have been more fitting.

Morris's interest in the Middle Ages extended to ancient dining customs. He explained to Eiríkr Magnússon:

[T]rencher in English is a mere flat square-board, on which the carver put slices of flesh-meat, and which would not hold any liquid. I have seen the blue-coat-school boys eating off them when I was a little boy, and noticed their devices (with much interest) for banking up a little soup with a potato toft. It seems our forefathers when they had flesh-meat, usually boiled it up with dough puddings. They ate the puddings first to dull the edge of appetite, then supped the brewis (from cups) & then came to the *pièce de résistance*. This was the custom of country places almost in my young days.

Although Morris was not particularly sentimental toward his children, he did speak nostalgically about his own boyhood. The scent of balm reminded him of "the very early days in the kitchen garden at Woodford, and the large blue plums which grew on the wall beyond the sweet-herb patch." More than his personal memories, however, he was concerned with preserving the dying traditions of

Merry Old England. As a girl, May listened with wide-eyed fascination to her father's storytelling:

> Christmas was fine, but Twelfth Night was always the most entertaining anniversary, with its Saint George play and all the rest of it. And delicious rum-punch was brewed and given to everyone, children and all—half a tumbler of it! (Surely we don't know how to drink now.) They had jolly 11 o'clock lunches, too; cake and cheese and a glass of small beer brewed at home; the cake was "nicer than anything of the kind he has tasted since."

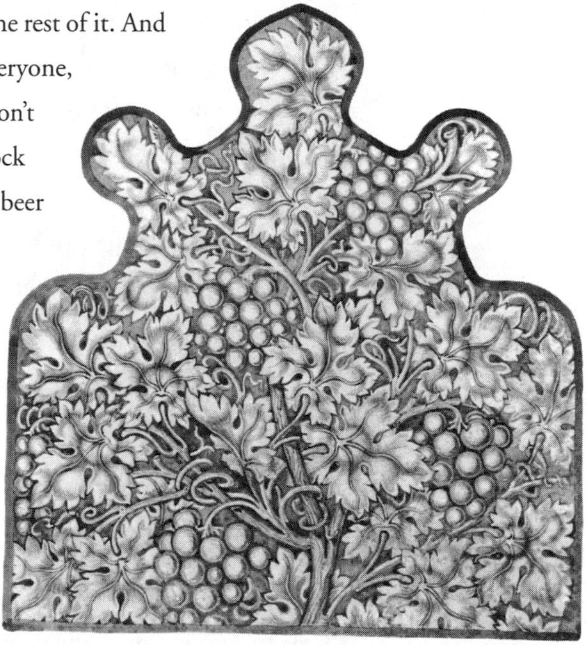

While Morris reminisced about the cakes of his youth, he gave up the old English tradition of home-brewed beer in favor of vintage red wine, preferably French. *News from Nowhere* placed a good bottle of Bordeaux on the crockery-laden table of the utopian dining hall. In 1867, one of his associates worried that Morris was spending all his capital on books and wine. As a burgeoning Socialist, he took even more pleasure in offering glasses around to his friends than he did in drinking it himself. Though he may have tippled beer as a child, as an adult, rather than raising a tankard of beer or ale to his mouth, Morris could occasionally be found drinking tea from an enormous vessel that, Shaw later recalled, "he had purchased to enable him to keep a promise made to his doctor that he would never exceed a single cup."

If only Morris had been serving tea at dinner that night, poor Shaw would have had a much better time of it. Shaw explained:

> To refuse Morris's wine or Mrs. Morris's viands was like walking on the great carpet with muddy boots.

FIGURE 10.6
Design for the head of one of the lights in a stained glass window in Jesus College Chapel, Cambridge, showing a vine and grapes, 1872–1874, by Morris & Co.

Now, as it happened, I practice the occasional form of Yoga: I am a vegetarian and teetotaller. Morris did not demure to the vegetarianism: he maintained that a hunk of bread and an onion was a meal for any man; but he insisted on a bottle of wine to wash it down. Mrs. Morris did not care whether I drank wine or water; but abstinence from meat she regarded as a suicidal fad. Between the host and hostess I was cornered; and Mrs. Morris did not conceal her contempt for my folly.

In Jane's world, vegetarianism was extremely avant-garde, for although the practice of abstaining from animal flesh goes back to the ancient world, the English term only came into common use after the formation of the Vegetarian Society at Ramsgate in 1847. In a country where Beefeaters guarded the Queen, how could such a diet fail to seem at least slightly subversive? Especially when practiced by a scraggly, agitating Irishman dragged unwanted into one's home.

Shaw had given up meat three years earlier, ostensibly to cure recurring migraine headaches, but he developed a firm ethical abhorrence to the consumption of animals. After being asked why he had chosen this diet in an 1898 interview for *The Vegetarian,* he replied, "Oh come! That boot is on the other leg. Why should you call me to account for eating decently? If I battened on the scorched corpses of animals, you might well ask me why I did that." As an old man, he attributed not only his good health but his extraordinary success to being a vegetarian, stating without the slightest shred of modesty, "It seems to me, looking at myself, that I am a remarkably superior person, when you compare me with other writers, journalists, and dramatists; and I am perfectly content to put this down to my abstinence from meat. That is the simple and modest ground on which we should base our non-meat diet." He was, as a personality, nothing short of the incarnation of resolve, believing, "The reasonable man adapts himself to the world; the unreasonable man persists in trying to adapt the world to himself. Therefore all progress depends on the unreasonable man."

With only his sense of moral superiority to sustain him, Shaw somehow muddled through the "positively painful" supper. The meal must have seemed interminable as his convictions forced him to decline each course offered by his intimidating hostess. "Fortunately," he noted, "she did not take much notice of me." The fact that he carried away an impression of Miss de Morgan as "by no means silent," implies that she made up for Jane's lack of conversation. At least Shaw had Morris's gregarious enthusiasm to distract him, and the lovely Miss Morris to gaze at. It is hard to imagine that May, seated with Miss de Morgan, Morris, and Shaw himself, had much opportunity to speak.

Shaw must have been ravenous at the end of the meal, if Janey's menu resembled those of Mrs. Beeton, having eaten only a few potatoes (if they had not been roasted with the drippings) and a bit of vegetable. With relief, he watched as the dessert was presented. It was, of course, a fine English pudding. As far back as the 1690s, even the French took note of the English predilection for pudding; François Maximilien Misson wrote:

> They bake them in an oven, they boil them with meat, they make them fifty several ways: blessed be he that invented pudding, for it is a manna that hits the palates of all sorts of people; a manna, better than that of the wilderness, because the people are never weary of it. Ah, what an excellent thing is an English pudding! To come in pudding-time, is as much as to say, to come in the most lucky moment in the world. Give an English man a pudding, and he shall think it a noble treat in any part of the world.

A century earlier, *A Book of Cookrye: very necessary for all such as delight therein* published recipes, including "How to boyle a Cony with a Pudding in his Belly," "How to make white Puddings of the Hogges Liver," "How to make a pudding in a Turnep root," and "A pudding in a Cowcumber." Pudding was the most ancient of English accompaniments and desserts; the origin of the word is believed to be Celtic.

Shaw's eyes lit up at the sight of the beautiful specimen, noting, "[T]he pudding was a particularly nice one." With delight, he remembered, "my abstinence vanished and I showed signs of a healthy appetite. Mrs. Morris pressed a second helping on me, which I consumed to her entire satisfaction." With pleasure, he thought he was finally breaking through Jane's reserved exterior by the delight he took in the delicate treat she extended to him. For the first time all evening, she seemed almost to be smiling.

After he finished the last bite and put down his spoon, she remarked, "That will do you good: there is suet in it." It was Janey Morris's triumph at the table. Shaw's resolve proved no match for her own. He claimed, "[T]hat is the only remark, as far as I can remember, that was ever addressed to me by this beautiful, stately and silent woman, whom the Brotherhood and Rossetti had succeeded in consecrating." Not surprisingly, the two never did get along.

Jane's silent duplicity in the matter of the suet pudding was certainly an act of antagonism. Nevertheless, Shaw displayed a certain, perhaps hopeful, naïveté regarding the contents of this tempting dessert. So-called Suet Pudding is a savory dish to accompany a roast, which Morris had recalled seeing served on square trenchers. Though Morris described the practice of offering the pudding before the roast as a dying rural practice of his youth, Mrs. Beeton recommended it. The note published with her recipe for suet pudding perpetuated the tradition: "Where there is a large family of children, and the means of keeping them are limited, it is a most economical plan to serve up the pudding before the meat: as, in this case the consumption of the latter article will be much smaller than it otherwise would be." Shaw was by no means confused as to the difference between savory foods and sweet. However, an overwhelming percentage of Mrs. Beeton's numerous recipes for dessert puddings also contain suet as a primary ingredient. In addition to perennial classics like "Christmas Pudding" and "Plum Pudding," suet is used in "Aunt Nelly's Pudding" with treacle and lemon rind, "Rich Sweet Apple Pudding," the author's own "Baroness Pudding," and more traditional "College Pudding" filled with currants, candied peel, nutmeg, and brandy, as well as "Lemon Pudding," "Brown Bread Pudding," "Baked or Boiled Carrot Pudding," "Boiled Gooseberry Pudding," "Hunter's Pudding," and "Roly-Poly Jam Pudding." The list continues on and on.

The use of suet as a primary ingredient to make pudding, whether savory or sweet, was as ancient and widespread as the English love of pudding itself. Suet was required in recipes for "Rice Pudding" and "Hasty Pudding," "Black Pudding" and "White Pudding," as well as "Oatmeal Pudding" published by Joseph Cooper in 1654, just as it appears in the earlier recipes set down by A. W. in 1587. Though Jane failed to identify suet as an ingredient in her pudding, the fastidious Shaw should have guessed it would have been used. Perhaps he was deluded by hunger and the mesmerizing spell of the magic carpet.

With her polite offer of a tasty dessert, Jane had deftly used her position as hostess to insult the unwanted visitor, and thereby her husband, who had invited him into her private realm. Surrounded by loquacious conversationalists, her actions, indeed, spoke louder than any of their words. In a short instant, Shaw had felt the full brunt of her years of dissatisfaction thrust upon him.

Despite this unpleasantness, the act of breaking bread with these strangers had transformed Shaw into a surrogate relation, enmeshed within their troubled history, which, hours before, he had known little to nothing about. It was an evening he never forgot; fifty years later he wrote about it in his commemorative essay "William Morris As I Knew Him."

Shaw became a habitué of the Kelmscott House Sunday suppers. On one such night, as he was preparing to take his leave, lovely May walked with him from the dining room into the hall. For a moment their eyes met and they gazed at one another. Not a word was spoken, but Shaw considered them irrevocably joined in a "Mystic Betrothal." Although the Morris meals did not conform to the sentimental Victorian ideal, family, with all its complexity, had been forged at the Morris table.

Chapter Eleven

Eat, Drink, and Be Merry, for Tomorrow We Die

The Secession Banquet, Vienna, 19 January 1900

Serenely full, the Epicure would say,
Fate cannot harm me,—I have dined today.

Sydney Smith, *Lady Holland's Memoir*

$\mathcal{A}$T THE DAWN OF THE TWENTIETH century, 19 January 1900, the members of the Vienna Secession held a banquet to toast their cresting ambitions for the new era and to stave off their fears as the Austro-Hungarian Empire crumbled around them. Carl Moll (1861–1945), a co-founder of the movement, contributed his studio and home at No. 6 Theresianum-gasse, near the Ringstrasse. Moll's convenient and spacious rooms often acted as their unofficial meeting place. Although not as artistically gifted as the group's renowned cofounder, Gustav Klimt (1862–1918), Moll contributed enormously to the promulgation of Secessionist ideals as both a painter and dealer, and especially through his role as host. For this "official" banquet for thirty-six men and three women, however, the talented membership divvied up the myriad responsibilities of organizing a feast to cocoon them in aesthetic splendor.

Later in 1900 the Secession journal, *Ver Sacrum,* argued: "Those who have attained the heights of civilized refinement in their daily life, even if they have otherwise little time for art, make certain demands upon the things which serve them, upon their whole environment, demands which can only be satisfied with the aid of art." Their January banquet actualized this theory and proved what they had declared two years earlier, in the very first issue of their magazine: "And suppose one among you says 'But why do I need the artist? I don't like pictures,' then we shall reply, 'Even if you do not like pictures, let us decorate your walls with beautiful hangings; would you not care to drink your wine from an artistically fashioned glass? Come to us, we shall show you the design for a vessel worthy of the noble wine.' " From their inaugural exhibition, the Secessionists placed as much importance on the design of decorative objects as they did on paintings and sculpture.

The invitation cards designed by Koloman Moser (1868–1918) set the tone for the banquet before it had even begun. The name of the group, "VEREINIGUNG BILDENDER KÜNSTLER OESTERREICHS," appears on the upper left, and "WIEN" and "19. JANUAR 1900" at the lower right. The card was left sparse, except for a square filled with a luxuriantly scrolling art nouveau vase in the upper right. In addition to Herr Professor Moser, various members and friends of the group, including the architect and designer Josef Hoffmann (1870–1956), the writer and literary critic Hermann Bahr (1863–1934), and Dr. Max Burckhard (1854–1912), director of the Burgtheater, added their signatures. The architect Otto Wagner (1841–1918) signed, "To the lady of the house" on the card they presented to Moll's beautiful stepdaughter Alma Schindler (1879–1964), later known as the "muse of Vienna."

Ravishing, intelligent, and vivaciously self-possessed, Alma cultivated her natural gift for enrapturing the men around her; her childhood dream had been to "fill her garden full of geniuses," and she eventually fulfilled that ambition in her marriages to the composer Gustav Mahler, the architect Walter Gropius, who founded the Bauhaus, and the author Franz Werfel. Her stepfather's incessant dinner parties with the leading Secession talents offered her a fantastic venue to scout for potential candidates. Although Alma was more zealous in her pursuit of men of genius than might be considered suitably demure for a polite Fräulein, there was nothing improper about flirting at dinner, whether in the haute bohemian Moll household or in more conservative Viennese residences. The dinner table provided a socially acceptable forum for young ladies to meet eligible members of the opposite sex, which, after all, was what their society asked of them. The entire experience—the flattering glow of candlelight, the perfume of the flowers, the savor of good food, and the loosening exhilaration of the wine taken amidst lilting music—purposefully conspired to show off these elegantly dressed beauties in the most attractive light. On this occasion, however, Alma's mother, Anna Schindler Moll (1857–1938), insisted that Alma and her younger half-sister, Gretl, stay upstairs and out of the way.

Some time earlier, in her first attempt to catch a genius, Alma had set her sights on Gustav Klimt, and the rakish, bohemian painter had not behaved appropriately. What began as mild flirtation within the twinkling banter of Secession dinner parties grew into a full-blown attempt at seduction. Games like trying to touch Alma's leg under the table escalated into a public grooming of her latent sensuality. At one dinner, Klimt gave Alma the idea of shaping her bread into a heart. He then turned a toothpick into an arrow, plunged it into the bread, and poured wine into the wound until it flowed like blood before presenting this creation, she recorded, to another of her admirers as "my wounded heart." Alma was smitten by the "Byzantine delicacy" of this artistic luminary, who, "sharpened and deepened

FIGURE 11.1
Invitation card for the
Secession banquet of
19 January 1900, by
Koloman Moser.

the 'eyesight' I had learned from Papa." Moll, however, while lauding the feline eroticism of his paintings, did not wish Klimt upon his virginal stepdaughter. Anna read Alma's dairy and discovered that the painter, known to be living in sin with his sister-in-law, had followed the family to Italy and enticed her into sneaking away to meet him; he had kissed her passionately in Genoa and had boldly proposed she sleep with him in Verona. Moll confronted him and begged him to retreat; Klimt complied without protest; and Alma felt betrayed and heartbroken. In the long months since this disaster, she had seen him only once, in passing, just two days before the dinner.

Moll could neither exclude the movement's first president from this official banquet nor allow his stepdaughter to be exposed to him. And, because the party was specifically for the members of the Secession and their honored guests, there was no reason why Alma should be permitted to join them. Consumed with the possibility of seeing Klimt, yet not daring to ask her parents if the artist even planned to attend, Alma confessed her mounting excitement and anxiety in her diary. Would he come? Would she be able to see him? What would it be like if she did? Being banished from the table only added to the banquet's allure.

Her diary recalls that on the eve of the party, Hoffmann and the more academically inclined painter Wilhelm Bernatzik (1853–1906) sat in Moll's studio consulting as to how they should decorate. These disparate artists inhabited a city struggling to assimilate the modernity erupting within its inherently staid conservatism, and as in their metropolis, these contrary impulses battled within them. No single style defined Secession; its members were united only by their 1897 resignation from the Kunsterhaus and the motto "To the age its art, and to art its freedom" emblazoned beneath the gilded, cabbage-like dome of their exhibition hall. They swathed their art of rebellion in a richly textured sensuality that aimed to transform life itself into a totally aesthetic experience, bringing Richard Wagner's ideal of the *Gesamtkunstwerk* into the everyday world. For the banquet at Moll's studio, they borrowed tapestries and Empire furniture from the interior decorator Otto Schmidt to add extra magnificence to the already luxurious space.

It was an old-world studio, filled with exotic vases and plants that exuded the dripping romanticism of the previous century. Moll had been a student of Alma's father, Emil Jakob Schindler, and the popular court painter Hans Makart, whom Alma remembered giving "the most lavish parties, inviting the loveliest women and dressing them in his genuine Renaissance costumes. Rose garlands trailed from the ballroom ceiling, Liszt played through the nights, the choicest wines

FIGURE 11.2
Facing the Banqueting Hall,
ca. 1899, by Carl Moll,
oil on canvas.

flowed, behind each chair stood a page clad in velvet, and so forth to the limits of splendor and imagination." Despite Moll's embrace of Hoffmann's sleek modernism, he never shed his taste for imperial Viennese opulence. Even after Moll moved his family into a villa designed for him by Hoffmann, Oskar Kokoschka (1886–1980) described the interior as feeling neoclassical/mid-Victorian in its decor, recalling, "I liked the atmosphere of the house, although its slightly Oriental magnificence was less reminiscent of Schindler's time than of the age of Ingres and Delacroix (or Makart, whose pupil Moll had also been): Japanese vases, great sprays of peacock feathers, Persian carpets on the walls. The table was elegantly laid; there were always flower arrangements, gleaming silver, sparkling glass—and good wine."

Although Alma was not invited to attend the Secession banquet, she helped to lay the tables and arrange the decorations. As the grown-up daughter of the house, she often assisted her mother in planning menus and setting out the place cards that determined the all-important question of who sat next to whom at Moll's frequent parties. Moll had painted Alma peeking out from behind their long banqueting table, which was splendidly arrayed with pristine rows of porcelain dishes, flatware, and delicate stemware. She is hardly noticeable next to an exuberantly tall floral centerpiece that reaches up to the fringed lamp overhead and a pair of towering candelabra wrapped in a profusion of flowers. She carefully recorded the table decorations after a Secession banquet in November 1898:

> We had girandoles and, as a centerpiece, a fruit bowl surrounded with flowers—and garlands, with which they later decked me out. On the table for the older guests, the centerpiece was Hellmer's water-nymph—also surrounded with flowers and garlands, and all the ladies had large bouquets of violets. Attached to each bouquet was a card inscribed with a little poem, which was passed round and signed by each guest in turn.

For the January 1900 event Hoffmann was in charge of the décor. He selected traditional Viennese earthenware for the table rather than highly finished porcelain. Later that year, the Secession exhibited objects by Charles Rennie Mackintosh and Charles Robert Ashbee, but the influence of the British Arts and Crafts Movement could already be seen in the party the artists held privately for their patrons and critics. Hoffmann, who in 1903 founded the workshops of the Wiener Werkstätte with Moser, aimed to coordinate every object, from the utensils, to the crystal, to the table and the chairs around it, into a unified aesthetic that promoted a streamlined modernity. In an article summarizing the aims of the program, Hoffmann argued: "It cannot possibly be sufficient to buy pictures, even the most beautiful. As long as our cities, our houses, our rooms, our cupboards, our utensils, our jewelry, as long as our speech and sentiments fail to express in an elegant, beautiful and simple fashion the spirit of our own times, we will continue to be immeasurably far behind our forefathers, and no amount of lies can deceive us about all these weaknesses." In 1906, the Werkstätte held a special exhibition, "Der gedeckte Tisch," which displayed table settings with Moser's glassware and Hoffmann's silver flatware, in chic black and white rooms, to the Viennese public. The critic Joseph August Lux extolled their avant-garde aesthetic:

Dear God, every servant girl thinks she knows how to set a table. I have even got a book about this particular art, with numerous illustrations, for example, of how one folds napkins into various "pretty," that is, absurd, patterns. And with tips on how to "bestrew" the tablecloth with living flowers, presumably in order to conjure up the mood of a Roman orgy—specially for Grandma's birthday. . . . Hoffmann and Moser have quite different views. And other forms of inspiration. . . . Hoffmann's cutlery is as carefully designed as the precision instruments of the scientist, and a flower piece by him is so finely conceived, according to its form and purpose, that the same amount of mental energy would suffice to design a monument. On one of the tables, the usual, obligatory four types of glass. But normally, of course, one finds oneself confronted with four different designs of glass, of four different heights—nothing more disturbing, than a glance over the glassware of a "correctly" laid table. Moser has set himself the problem of creating a set of glasses of the same height and of one single design. A problem which he solves in the simplest possible way: by differing lengths of stem and different volumes. So simple, that you might smite your brow when confronted with this kind of novelty. . . .

And how many people are unacquainted with Hoffmann's silver cutlery? When they first turned up in the Secession exhibitions, a tremor ran through the eating world. People maintained it was quite impossible to eat with it, not eat properly, and certainly not in the "English" manner! Herr Wärndorfer was the only person to buy it, and since then I myself have eaten with it, as English as an Englishman and found it all extremely practical.

Hoffmann's striking designs for silver flatware, with their stark geometry, his elongated checkerboard breadbaskets and vases, brightly patterned glasses and rippling coffee services boldly broke away from the heavily ornamented patterns popular with the majority of the gilded generation. But streamlined design did not eliminate the plethora of gleaming utensils lying in rows at the elegant place setting. Hoffmann created sardine forks, escargot forks, sandwich servers, soda water stirrers, cheese and butter knives, and even special cutlery for children to gratify the fin de siècle predilection for specialized flatware. Nor did Hoffmann and Moser eliminate purely decorative elements; one table at their exhibition had long, lush swags of foliage draped over Hoffmann's silver baskets and a tall figure of a kneeling youth by George Minne as the centerpiece. The use of colorfully decorated Viennese crockery at their 1900 banquet added rustic flavor and informality to the event and placed the membership of the Secession within the tradition of local Austrian craftsmen.

When the party began, Alma and Gretl were permitted to stay in the upstairs anteroom with their mother to greet the arrivals—even Klimt, Alma noted. If the girls were forbidden from joining the artists down in the studio, Moll had not banned his colleagues from paying court to the ladies in the apartment above. Soon, Franz Hancke, secretary of the Secession, presented a menu card to the ladies; Moser followed with another. They had gallantly added their signatures beneath the drawings, including one that playfully depicted, as Alma described it, "us peeping through a chink in the door." Hoffmann offered Frau Moll a card amusingly illustrated with smiling and frowning flowers dancing on long, thin stems. These cards were more than program guides to let diners know what to look

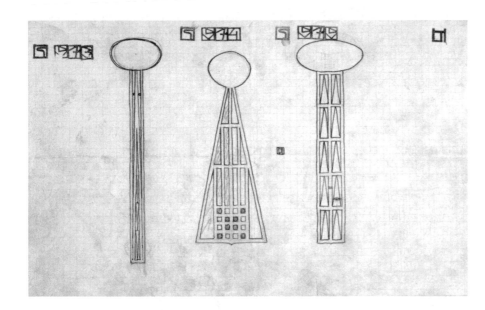

FIGURE 11.3
Design for three spoons,
1905, by Josef Hoffmann.

FIGURE 11.4 *(below)*
Design for oyster fork and
cutlery for fish and crab,
by Josef Hoffmann.

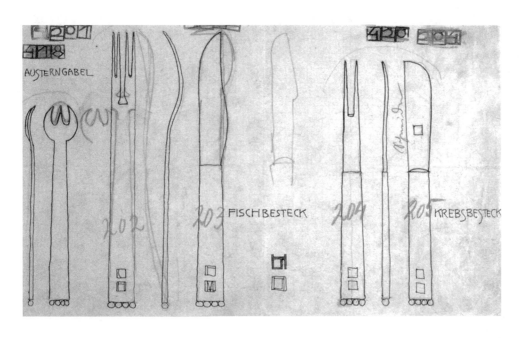

AUSTERNGABEL

FISCHBESTECK

KREBSBESTECK

forward to; they were commemorative souvenirs of the occasion. Alma sentimentally pasted the cards into her diary to treasure the evening, just as in 1898 she had been pleased when she noticed that Klimt kept his place card, which she had written out, as well as hers, in his wallet as a reminder of a dinner when they had been seated next to one another.

When it came time for the meal, Alma and her sister ate in the family dining room while the members of the Secession took their places at the table in the studio. The five-course menu printed on the cards was more extensive than an everyday dinner of chicken with paprika that Anna Moll later offered Gustav Mahler on his first visit to her home, but considerably less elaborate than the nine-course, French-styled meals that Emperor Franz Joseph (r. 1848–1916) dined on as an abridged menu when he was alone at the palace. Like Hoffmann's refined flatware, the food was simple yet elegant, plentiful but not gluttonous, and most important,

eminently possible to produce successfully for forty-odd diners in a bourgeois kitchen. To begin, there was cold trout, the succulent local offering of the Danube, garnished with the belle époque favorite, shimmering, gelatinous aspic. Then came fried chicken with vegetables on the side. Without overtaxing the talents of the cook, these reassuring dishes could be delicious if prepared with the same attention to high-quality materials and masterful execution that the Secessionists demanded in their art. On this winter night, they continued with a hearty course of rich venison, worthy of the tapestries surrounding them, served with a salad to balance heaviness with lightness. The customary cheese and fruit followed. To complete the menu, despite the season, they had fashionable ices, which were often molded into decorative, geometric forms, and served in a swirl of whipped cream or fruits stewed in liqueur to lend a bit of glamour to the finale of their feast.

It was just the sort of unpretentious, yet appealing meal that Franz Joseph snuck away to share with his longtime mistress, Katharina Schratt (1855–1940). She was the most famous actress of the day, immortalized by Klimt in his prize-winning painting of the Burgtheater in 1890, but like any good Viennese woman of her middle-class upbringing, she carefully shopped for food for her illustrious consort herself at the local markets, and baked him fresh *Gugelhupf*, filled with nuts and raisins, each morning. In her autobiography, Alma recorded that Schratt's ability to cater to the Emperor's appetites had saved her friend Burckhard's career. According to Alma, the prominent intellectual and creative talent accidentally learned that because of a bureaucratic error, he was listed in the government files as "Chief Presumptive of the Land Credit Institute." In desperation, he promptly took a cab to Schratt's villa, hoping she would intervene on his behalf. As Alma told the story:

> La Schratt, who liked Burckhard, sent him right back to a famous Vienna pastry shop, to order some nut and poppy-seed crescents. "Bring them here when they're ready," she said. "The emperor is coming to dinner; they're his favorite dish. When he gets that, he'll sign anything. Just imagine such a silly blunder!"

FIGURE 11.5 *(facing, left)* Menu card for the Secession banquet of 19 January 1900, with signatures of Moser, Hancke, and König, by Koloman Moser.

FIGURE 11.6 *(facing, right)* Menu card from the Secession banquet of 19 January 1900, presented to Anna Moll, attributed to Josef Hoffmann.

261

So, on the very next day, the Burgtheater got its new director, the man who introduced Ibsen and Hauptmann to Vienna—over protests of the court—as well as the greatest Viennese actors of the period.

A recipe collection that belonged to Schratt, dated 1905, filled with Hungarian and French-styled recipes, such as "Transylvanian Goulash" and "Little Croustades à la Talleyrand," illustrates the divergent flavors and cuisines available in the capital of the Empire. Other recipes, such as "Japanese Goulash," made with cubed goose breast and in no way even vaguely Asian, reveal that the taste for foreign cultures did not necessarily extend beyond an exciting name. The Secession menu at the Moll residence in 1900, however, was neither pretentiously French nor exotically provincial; it was good, fresh, local Viennese cuisine. Franz Joseph would have approved immensely.

As the banqueters sat down for dinner, a string quartet led by Albert Bachrich, principal violinist of the Vienna Philharmonic, began to play. In the European capital of music, the city of Mozart, Schubert, and Strauss, no dinner would be complete without it. Alma, a gifted musician, studied composition with Alexander von Zemlinsky, another of her lovers, who also taught Arnold Schönberg, and devotedly attended the musical events of her city. Her mother had been an operetta singer, and even her painterly stepfather adored the sound of music filling the house. Alma often performed Wagner for guests after dinner. However, on this occasion, the Secessionists were serenaded, Alma noted, with "lively Viennese dance-music," as colorfully rustic as the crockery and the menu.

After finishing their meal, the guests began to wander from their seats. The party was only just beginning. Anna came up to fetch the punch bowl with Burckhard, who lingered to chat with Alma. He was an older admirer and mentor, on familiar terms with the family, who had given Alma laundry baskets of classic editions of literature, groomed her taste for Rilke and Nietzsche, and taken her to concerts and plays as well as country picnics with "French vintage champagne, partridges, and pineapples—whatever was good, and, accordingly, expensive."

They stayed in the anteroom, where wine was being poured. One by one, diners trickled in for a glass and a chance to flirt with young Fräulein Schindler. Hoffmann and Moser made repeated visits with trays of fruits and sweets. If Vienna was the city of music, it was also the capital of pastries and scrumptious desserts: dark, rich Linzer torte, with a thick layer of jam and the bite of cinnamon and lemon rind; cream-filled custards; and the renowned Sacher torte with apricot jam and almonds under a layer of chocolate, from the fashionable Hotel Sacher across from the opera, a favorite spot of Alma's for afternoon tea. Dinner had been modest, although filling, but bite-size chocolates and dainty desserts circulated late into the night as the music played on.

From her vantage point in the anteroom, Alma had a clear view of Klimt down below. He could watch her as well, she claimed, so she made sure to put on a good show. Moser introduced her to Joseph Auchentaller, who created flowing *Jugend-stil* illustrations for *Ver Sacrum*. She knew she was succeeding when she overheard

FIGURE 11.7 *(facing, left)* Menu card for the Secession banquet of 19 January 1900, presented to Alma Mahler, by Friedrich König.

FIGURE 11.8 *(facing, right)* Menu card for the Secession banquet of 19 January 1900, presented to Alma Mahler, by Friedrich König.

him tell Hoffmann, "I say, she's pretty." As the Scarlett O'Hara of Vienna, Alma played the coquette and encouraged the admiration of the artists who flocked upstairs to pay their respects. Moser watched closely the entire evening (he eventually proposed to her a dozen times and made her a gift of an enormous brooch).

The drinks flowed faster to keep pace with the music. The earnest discussion of aesthetics among the distinguished gentlemen below could not compete with the youthful vigor of the local music and native beauties. The table was gradually deserted as more and more of the banqueters investigated what was happening in the anteroom. Finally, Alma recalled, they begged to dance just one waltz with the Schindler girls. Hoping that Moll would be too preoccupied to notice, they discreetly went into the dining room and rolled up the carpets to make an impromptu dance floor and, swept up by the vigorous waltzes, "danced for all we were worth."

Johann Strauss II, "the Waltz King" of Vienna, had died only the previous June. His dance music, most famously "The Blue Danube," written in 1867, was just old enough to be indelibly ingrained in their memories as a timeless classic, synonymous with the gilded life of their city. His melodies had become as organic to their culture as the local crockery. At the time of Strauss's death, Alma had gushingly declared "such effervescence, such grace and elegance—words cannot define the essence of his waltzes." The dizzying speed of the circular dance, spinning them around and around in three-quarter time, impelled them further into the frenzy of their celebration. The waltz was a reassuring assertion of imperial pride; as long as it played, they felt sure of the glory of Vienna.

Carried away by the rush of the wine and the dancing, they did not see Moll come in. He had forbidden the girls to stay downstairs on the parlor floor, and when disobeyed, he could be severe and humorless. The girls ran and hid from him like children in the *office* while his Secession colleagues, Alma claimed, "lifted him up bodily and carried him out." The sweeping energy of the dance was stronger than he; caught in its hypnotic spell the revelers would not be stopped.

Nevertheless, Alma and her sister felt, if not chastened, then momentarily fearful, so they stayed hidden and out of the way upstairs, at least for a while. Burckhard gallantly kept them company so they would not feel completely neglected. In spite of his distinguished age and position as a serious writer, critic, and director, he soon helped them sneak back down again. Life seemed too short not to let them enjoy the moment.

Burckhard rejoined his colleagues in time for the high-blown speeches required to make the occasion suitably "official," while Alma and her sister looked on from their perch up above. The painter and designer Josef Engelhart spoke on behalf of the membership, welcoming their guests, with particular deference and appreciation extended toward Alfred Lichtwark, a patron and influential aesthetician who founded the Hamburger Kunsthalle in 1868. Lichtwark, in turn, rose and offered grandiloquent words of hope that the new trend in Viennese art would hold sway for many years to come, and that within a decade a new style would arise that would rival that of Paris. (Alma cynically noted that "his speech was neither persuasive nor eloquent.") In response, Friedrich Viktor Stadler, who, as a member of the Ministry of Education, acted as the official government spokesperson of the evening, spoke, Alma recalled, "warmly and amiably." Although the Secession had broken from the conservative academics, the group's exhibitions had been an enormously popular success and crowds flocked to see them.

Things took a turn for the worse when Hermann Bahr took the floor and seemed determined to hold it forever. For fifteen minutes he deluged them with a ponderous denunciation of the bureaucracy and the lack of public taste, "beating his breast" all the while. His unrelenting droning managed to offend everyone. Their feast was a celebration, an aesthetic tribute to avant-garde Viennese pride, meant to keep the troubles of the world at bay. Moreover, following the gracious words of the imperial representative, Bahr's diatribe struck the group as utterly tactless. Stadler dramatically rose to his feet and walked out, telling Moll, "You know I really should have responded, but I didn't want to spoil the fun."

Alma triumphantly reported that neither Bahr nor Stadler succeeded in ruining the party. Captivated by her sybaritic charms, Alma's admirers soon forgot the ranting of an old man and rejoined her in the crowded anteroom. Alma was pleased when Burckhard managed to offend Hancke as he entered, saying, "Do come in, dear Hancke. You can stand between us if you like, you still won't be able to separate us." The artist turned around and walked straight back out.

Klimt skirted around the edges of the group. Wilhelm List called him over and asked him to join, but after briefly shaking hands, he left. From outside the door he playfully tossed a rose at Alma. He missed and it hit the lintel, so he threw it again, this time successfully dropping it at her feet. She was delighted when another member of her coterie gallantly stooped to pick it up for her. When she stuck it in her hair, Klimt, she noticed, smiled "a wicked frivolous smile."

Wagner and Lichtwark made their way into the room, and the distinguished aesthetician asked Alma for a dance. She insisted she was not allowed to. He continued to beg for just one turn, telling her, "I'll take full responsibility." Everyone laughed when Alma finally relented and told him, "You'd better ask Carl. By the way, do you have any idea who Carl is?"

The stiff formality of the speeches was drifting into the past. Now that they had eaten well and the wine and the music were having their effect, the atmosphere took on a more lighthearted gaiety. With Lichtwark on the hunt for Carl, Wagner asked, "Please, Fräulein, would you care to walk round the studio with me? Give the other guests something pretty to look at, just one round?" When Alma was forced to say that her stepfather wouldn't approve, her assembled audience thought this even more hilarious than her retort to Lichtwark. He tried to coax her, insisting that as a fifty-six-year-old grandfather, surely he might be trusted to escort her safely through the band of artists.

Lichtwark triumphantly returned and announced, "Well, Carl has given us permission, but only in the dining room, where nobody can see us, not even he." Moll's indulgence betrayed a very fin de siècle policy that could be summarized as "what you can't see, won't hurt you, even if you know about it." So, the carpets were rolled up again, and they danced without fear of discovery until they were worn out, at which point everyone trundled upstairs for a break.

Burckhard teased Alma about the eyes he had seen Klimt making at her and called himself "the wall" for guarding her from these advances. But then Klimt called from the stairs looking for him, made a face when he saw Alma, and gruffly told her to send Burckhard downstairs. Alma shook Klimt's hand stiffly and said good night. Later that evening she decided Klimt had just been a youthful crush; one from which she had recovered: "His behavior is childish, his smile vulgar. He has no business to smile at me. And throwing the rose—that was entirely inappropriate."

Her mother called from downstairs for everyone to come and watch. The artists Franz Hohenberger and Maximilian Lenz had dressed themselves up *à la japonaise,* sporting lampshades on their heads, and were quite uproariously performing a mock Japanese-style dance. They had both written essays on Japanese art for *Ver Sacrum* in 1899, and the newest Secession exhibition was devoted to it. At 3:00 A.M., Alma finally called it a night and went to bed, although the others kept at it until 5:00.

There was a frantic urgency to the dinner, a need to draw out its pleasures and make them last as long as possible. It was no accident that this was the city and the year in which Sigmund Freud published his *Interpretation of Dreams.* Nevertheless, this glittering capital of neurosis was not interested in Freud's ideas; it took seven years to sell out the first edition of six hundred copies. Instead, the waltzes played faster and the champagne glasses clinked a bit more sharply. The painstaking efforts the Secession artists made to seal themselves hermetically within an aesthetic shell masked their terror of the world collapsing around them. Vienna in 1900 subscribed to the ancient adage "Eat, drink, and be merry, for tomorrow we die."

Alma was only a girl when the newspapers reported that Crown Prince Rudolf, about to take her father on an expedition, had killed himself in a double suicide with his mistress in January 1889, but even she, beneath her soaring ambitions and self-absorbed flirtations, understood that the good times needed to be grasped while they could. As far back as 1 December 1898, after the torchlight procession for the Kaiser's jubilee, Alma bitterly noted in her diary, "The Viennese are quite right to illuminate the streets: it's their way of thanking the Kaiser for all the stupid things he's done for them. His entire term of office has been nothing but a series of blunders, which he attempted to put right, and, in the process, only made worse. Austria is not far from collapse. In truth the Viennese are probably quite right to illuminate the streets." How long could it go on? What would happen? Rather than look too far into the abyss, they feasted and waltzed in the present tense, stretching out its sumptuous luxury as far and as long as they could.

A dozen years later they were still at it. The golden age of the Secession had passed; Moll, Klimt, Hoffmann, and Moser had withdrawn from the larger movement, but stuck together as friends. Moll had moved from the center of the city to the utopian artists' colony of the Hohe Warte, in the hills northwest of the city, almost out to the villages of Grinzing, Heiligenstadt, and Neustift am Walde, where quaint *Heurigen* taverns dispensed the new vintages of local wine. Moser was his immediate neighbor; their villas shared a contiguous wall. Both residences were designed by Hoffmann as part of a complete Secession universe, where the inhabitants lived an aestheticized version of traditional village life with a view of the city always before them. Each of the Hoffmann houses in the Hohe Warte had a high, glassed tower, a salon in the air, lit with electric light that made it appear as a beacon of modernity. Half-timbering on a stucco façade bowed to rustic materials, but sleek, thin lines and checkerboard detailing imposed a sophisticated ornamental elegance. The nearby Haus Brauner exemplified the preciousness with which Hoffmann's village was rendered: "For the whitewash, ground marble has been used instead of sand, imparting its own chastity to the whiteness."

Moll and his friends became as hypnotically complacent within their miniature city on a hill as the ambivalently sensuous figures in Klimt's gilded, friezelike paintings. Later, Moll fondly recalled that almost every evening Moser, after his mother and sisters went to bed, would leap over the garden fence between their houses for cigarettes, schnapps, and conversation. The inhabitants of Hoffmann's colony were like the languorous habitués of an opium den, no longer capable of seeing through the thick haze of the drug.

On 12 April 1912, Alma greeted the familiar faces arriving at Moll's door. She was by this time a widow, resplendent in her mourning, not quite a full year after Mahler's death. During the decade of her marriage, while the old crowd had continued their gatherings, she had been out of circulation. She had met and charmed Mahler at a dinner party held by her friend, the avant-garde journalist and socialite Berta Zuckerkandl, but she discovered that being married to a genius was much less fun than seducing one. Mahler expected that the moment he rang the bell downstairs, his soup would be brought piping hot to the table, reaching his place just as he ascended the four flights up to their apartment. Theirs were silent meals; the composer could not bear extraneous noise while higher thoughts of composition occupied his mind. Just as her stepfather and his cohorts had grown numb in their prosperity, after the long and often painful years, Alma felt exhilarated in her widowhood.

A full-blooded new arrival burst into Moll's placid and fastidiously groomed surroundings: Oskar Kokoschka. Klimt called him the greatest talent of the younger generation, and Moll suggested that Alma might like to meet him, after having his own portrait painted by him. Kokoschka had rendered Moll with exaggerated hands that seemed to tremble and a nervous expression, capturing the demons simmering beneath his elegant veneer. If Moll realized there was something jeopardous, even masochistic, about welcoming such an artist into their midst, he did not show it, and greeted Kokoschka with flowery Viennese politesse.

Alma knew Kokoschka's work from the controversial Kunstschau of 1908, where he had exhibited alongside Klimt, whose pivotal masterwork, *The Kiss,* was seen there for the first time. Kokoschka's corner of the exhibition had been dubbed "the chamber of horrors," and the public outcry against him resulted in his expulsion from the *Kunstgewerbeschule.* The works he presented there included *Warrior,* a skull-like head in sickly blue, jangling with exposed nerve endings, which he called "a self-portrait with open mouth, the expression of a wild cry . . ." as well as illustrations from his nursery rhymes gone awry, *Die träumenden Knaben,* published by the Werkstätte:

> little red fish
> red little fish
> let me stab you to death with my three-pronged knife
> tear you apart with my fingers
> put an end to your mute gyrations

little red fish
red little fish
my little knife is red
my little fingers are red
in my dish a little fish sinks down dead

He entered Moll's luxuriant world very much the embodiment of his self-portrait; Alma remembered that his shoes were torn, his suit in tatters, and his manners coarse. George Grosz, famous for his interwar paintings of cripples and prostitutes, never forgot the sight of Kokoschka in these years, wandering through the balls of Vienna, "gnawing on a real ox-bone, dripping with blood." Amidst the cool order of Moll's Secession table, the angry rebel ate with a bestial tearing of the flesh—a destructive, animal act, in German *fressen,* rather than the human *essen,* that exposed the primal violence and fear lying beneath good manners.

The luxe, white walls of the villa could not protect Moll and his friends from the lurking fears that Kokoschka's brutality called to the surface. The Expressionist's friend, the architect Adolf Loos, congratulated him for "[s]ounding the death-knoll for Viennese aestheticism." Yet, it was the Secessionists who had invited him to their table. As they dined with familiar faces in the placid tranquility of the Hoffmann interior, the newcomer alone could express the urgent sense of impending doom. The rest of them poured Moll's fine wine a little faster, helped themselves to seconds, and perhaps laughed a bit too shrilly, living by their mantra "Eat, drink, and be merry, for tomorrow we die."

The widow Mahler found Kokoschka darkly mesmerizing. She planted her riveting blue eyes upon the young painter, seven years her junior. Kokoschka recalled, "How beautiful she was, and how seductive she looked beneath her mourning veil." When she was a young girl, her father had told her, "Play to allure the Gods," and so she did.

What transpired at the dinner, they did not record. But by the time the banqueters had eaten, Alma had worked her spell. Leaving the others behind, she took her new friend by the arm and led him into the next room where she played

Wagner's *Liebestod* (Love in death) to him on the piano. It was her favorite piece from her favorite opera, *Tristan and Isolde.* She called it "the opera of operas. With its continuous flow, its mad passion and boundless longing. Longing for something that exists but which we cannot recognize. Wagner had a presentiment of it." She knew its value in the drama of her own life. She had played it in December 1899 after a lingering lunch, when she thought Joseph Olbrich might be her genius and wrote "Everyone was enraptured, kissed me, and looked sad. I'd never played more beautifully in my life and never shall again. With every note I was recalling my lost friend Olbrich." Mahler had conducted it for his premiere at the Metropolitan Opera in New York City, on New Year's Day 1908, a performance that began late because he accidentally ripped the train of her gown and stayed to help her repair it. But in her widow's veil, with Kokoschka looking on, she captured the piece to its fullest. Alma, operatic in life, understood that this dinner was her ultimate *Gesamtkunstwerk.*

Kokoschka sat and drew her, his reddened fingers flying over the page as her hands ran over the piano. In her telling of the story, he coughed up blood as he stared intently at her. Abruptly he stopped, kissed her passionately, and ran out of the house. Nothing would ever be the same again. Alma described the next three years of her life: "[O]ne fierce battle of love. Never before had I tasted so much tension, so much hell, so much paradise." Kokoschka encapsulated their love affair, the passion that called up the festering brutality about to overtake Europe, in a masterpiece of Expressionist art, a painting of the two of them embracing in a swirling storm. He had intended to call the picture "Tristan and Isolde." But his friend, the poet Georg Trakl, arrived at his studio agitated, emaciated from drugs, and soaked with rain; drank a few glasses of cheap red wine while gazing at the painting; and began to recite an eerie poem—"drunk with death the glowing tempest plunges over blackish cliffs. . . ." The painting became known as *The Tempest.*

Chapter Twelve

Shocking the World

Caresse Crosby's Surrealist Picnic, The Moulin de Soleil, Forest of Ermenonville, Early July 1932

A giraffe is gorging himself on your lace garters a Parisian doll is washing herself in my tall glass of gin fizz while I insist on their electrocution on the grounds of indecency.

Harry Crosby, "On the Grounds of Indecency"

*I*T WAS QUITE EARLY, ESPECIALLY FOR A Sunday, when German artist Max Ernst (1891–1976) and his wife Marie-Berthe picked up the American art dealer Julien Levy (1906–1981) in Paris to drive him to a wild, all-day-until-who-knew-when picnic at the Moulin de Soleil on a July morning in 1932. Julien had only arrived from New York the previous week and was celebrating the end of a triumphal debut year for his gallery. The previous evening he had been on a tear through Paris that began with Cinzano *à l'eau* at the Flore; followed by dinner and a festival of cheeses at a local bistro; and then drinks and dancing at the Jockey, the Bœuf-sur-le-Toit, and, finally, Zelli's in the wee hours of the morning. Nevertheless, he was thirsting to lap up the next event. Julien considered his escapades of the night before not only typical of his Paris visits but a requisite fringe benefit of his occupation, writing, "Artists are often good

273

procurers, finding and sharing women, food, wine; and usually they are good company with high standards for all the sensual things of life."

He adored a good party, and the City of Lights never disappointed him. The very night he arrived in Paris for the first time in 1927 he found himself drinking highballs at Peggy Guggenheim's apartment on the Île Saint Louis, with her guests, Ernest Hemingway, Ezra Pound, Jean Cocteau, Kay Boyle, and an aging Isadora Duncan, draped fleshily over the couch, a vision of hennaed hair and plum-colored silk. The food was nothing to write home about—Peggy preferred to scrimp for her art collection—but the cocktails flowed freely. They were modern, sleek, and ultra-American. Paris had been mad about American cocktails since the dwarfish Henri de Toulouse-Lautrec, wearing a waistcoat made from an American flag, served two thousand bizarre concoctions such as sardines in straight gin, tinged bright reds, pinks, yellows, and peevish greens, at the 1895 house-warming party of Thadée Natanson, editor of *La Revue Blanche,* and his wife, Misia. Alfred Jarry, Félix Fénéon, Pierre Bonnard, and Édouard Vuillard had been among the "casualties" who had to be carried away horizontally into a makeshift "emergency ward." Gin, consumed in great quantity, linked the frenzy of Misia's soirée to Peggy's. André Gide (1869–1951), an attendee of both events, incited revelers to the *acte gratuit* (gratuitous act) in his novel *Les Caves du Vatican;* gin braced them to perform it.

At Peggy's, Julien heard someone say, "Try some of this gin, my dear. It's prohibition gin imported from the United States. It gets you drunk *rapidly*." From the other side of the room Marcel Duchamp playfully retorted, "Il faut de l'eau forte, pas trop d'effort." The bohemian poet Mina Loy (later Julien's mother-in-law) jumped in, "Speak easy? Why if I ever tried to speak easily some policeman would come up and give me a really hard sentence." Puns, both verbal and visual, lay at the heart of the Surrealist spirit, tapping into the subconscious meanings beneath the surface of the material world. Julien later explained "SURREALISM attempts to discover and explore the more real than real world behind the real." More than a poem or a painting or a play, the movement was an attitude and a way of life encapsulated in the raucous merry-go-round of such carnivalesque parties where accident and automatism abounded.

Julien had never been to visit his fellow American, Caresse Crosby (1892–1970), but he knew that the Ernsts and Salvador Dalí (1904–1989), with his mistress and future wife, Gala Éluard (1895–1982), took the forty-eight-kilometer trip northeast of Paris almost every week because, whatever might take place, Caresse's Sundays were dependably unpredictable. Dalí later reminisced, "A mixture of Surrealists and society people came there, because they sensed that in the Moulin, *things were happening.*" Caresse traveled in the same mixture of New York, Boston, and Paris that Julien did. He remembered her as "a heady mixture of champagne bubbles and poésie, with a body solid, almost plump," but did not know her well. Slightly older, certainly wealthier, and on her mother's side descended from the cream of American society, Mary Phelps Jacob, as Caresse was christened, lived in a more glamorous realm than Julien's, but he was just near enough to be dazzled.

As a student at Rosemary Hall, she had been the original Girl Scout; as a debutante, she invented the brassiere as an alternative to the whalebone corset, a patent she later sold to Warner & Co.; but it was her passionate, over-the-top marriage to Harry Crosby (1898–1929), almost seven years her junior, that made her a legend. After moving to Paris, Harry and Caresse, as she reinvented herself, committed themselves to avoiding what Harry deemed the great crime of "ending life the way so many people do, with a *whimper.*" Every day became a festival of creative endeavor, parties, and lovemaking that blurred inseparably. They wrote poetry— "Our *One*-ness is the color of a glass of wine"—and hired the master printer Roger Lescaret to publish it for them in lusciously tactile beauty. Their enterprise became the Black Sun Press, which brought out exquisite limited editions by cutting-edge authors such as D. H. Lawrence, Hemingway, and James Joyce. Paris remembered them most for their outlandish appearance at the 1924 Incan-themed Quatre Arts Ball. Harry, with his body painted ochre and wearing a necklace of dead pigeons, carried a bag of live snakes, and Caresse, as an Incan princess in a blue wig, hoisted into the jaws of a paper dragon, displayed her bare breasts as if she were the figurehead of a Viking ship. The evening had begun with a dinner of free-flowing champagne at the Crosby apartment, and it ended with seven in their bed. Then, in December 1929, on the last day of a visit to New York, Harry shot himself with a mother-of-pearl-encrusted silver-handled pistol in a double suicide with his nineteen-year-old society mistress. A mutual friend had taken Caresse to a party at Julien's apartment on the evening before the bodies were discovered. The young art dealer had not seen her since.

After Harry's death, Caresse made herself sleeker, chicer, and even more conspicuous in an effort to drown out the pain. Her Parisian fêtes were so famous that the American wire services wrote about them. Caresse personally avowed, "I love to entertain my friends and even at times my enemies—but entertain I must—I am very apt when someone calls me on the telephone to ask me to lunch, cocktails, or dinner, to reply, 'Please come to me instead.' "

Julien was excited to see Caresse again and enter into her exclusive circle. But as he chatted with Max and Marie-Berthe on the drive, he mentioned that he had brought along a small movie camera with the hope of making a series of documentary artist portraits, starting with Max, if he would agree to it. Marie-Berthe, Julien recalled, cooed with delight, clapped her hands, and decided they should begin that very minute. Julien's fears of keeping his hostess waiting were met only by Max's observation that the light was good. Spontaneity, showmanship, and shock value were essential to the Surrealist banquet; showing up on time was not.

Max pulled his "surplus property" Dodge straight over to the side of the road. Whether it was accident or intuition, the car stopped beside the crumbling ruin of what Julien conjectured to be an ancient priory or factory, perhaps even a Roman aqueduct. This evocative scene of architectural decay—towering arches leading nowhere and eroding back into nature—provided a ready-made set. Within moments they improvised a scenario, and Julien began to shoot. Marie-Berthe ran in and out of archways and tree trunks, waving a glove and scarf as Max chased her, until she vanished for the last time, leaving only these fetishistic objects for her pursuer to capture. Max was the star; Julien credited him with an extraordinary ability to instantly compose himself into every frame. Playing oneself was essential to the Surrealist artist, whose every action constituted a part of his oeuvre. Fifteen minutes later, they tumbled back into the car and continued along on their way.

Julien need not have worried about the delay in their arrival. At the Moulin, pretense was banished and formalities kept to an absolute minimum in favor of playful impulse. Caresse's rules for entertaining were embodied in the song "Anything Goes," written by her first date, Cole Porter. As soon as Julien and Max told their hostess about the film, she insisted they continue work on it immediately and that she be allowed to join in. Anaïs Nin described Caresse as "a pollen carrier" who "mixed, stirred, brewed and concocted friendships together, who encouraged artistic and creative copulation in all its forms and expressions, who trailed behind her, like the plume of peacocks, a colorful and fabulous legend." Caresse could not have been more pleased than to transform her party into an artistic project. She abandoned her guests to the quadrangle of the garden, asking them to rearrange things as they liked, while she raced off to find an appropriate costume for the film.

Harry and Caresse had created the Moulin de Soleil from the ruins of a dilapidated mill at the edge of an extensive Anglo-Chinese garden on the property of their friend Armand de La Rochefoucauld's château in the forest of Ermenonville. It had once been the stomping ground of Jean-Jacques Rousseau, whose tomb rests there, together with such evocative neoclassical follies as the "Altar of Dreaming." From the gate of the Moulin, signs pointed to myriad pathways through the garden and the woods; one led to the "Tomb of the Unknown," created for an unrequited lover who had long ago committed suicide in the park. Sometimes guests stumbled upon Armand's private secretary, a nudist, who romped stark naked through the gardens with his friends.

The Moulin and its enchanting surroundings offered Julien

and Max a rich field of cinematic potential. It was the physical incarnation of the castle, "half of which not necessarily in ruins . . . in a rustic setting not far from Paris," which André Breton (1896–1966) had described as the metaphoric home of the Surrealists in his famous 1924 *Manifesto.* "The spirit of *demoralization* has elected domicile in the castle . . ." he wrote, "but the doors are always open, and one does not begin by 'thanking' everyone, you know. Moreover, the solitude is vast, we don't often run into one another. And anyway, isn't what matters that we be masters of ourselves, the masters of women, and of love too?"

A white fence separated the three ancient stone buildings and garden quadrangle of the Moulin from the encircling woods. On one side, the Crosbys had added a racing course for games of donkey polo; on the other, near the waterfall, they had built a small swimming pool. According to legend, Cagliostro had transported the ancient pillar standing in the stone-paved courtyard from Chalis when he went into retreat at the nearby abbey (D. H. Lawrence's favorite spot to sun). So too, the wizard reputedly concocted his magic formula beside the millstream. The stream had long ago slowed to a mere trickle, and the ancient water wheel had disappeared; but an enchanting spell hung over the property all the same. Caresse observed small fish that mysteriously leapt twenty feet into the air to land in the pool above; a flock of sheep that managed to cross through her thrice-barred gate; and thunderstorms that broke out suddenly, only to disappear just as quickly. She later recalled, "The millstones like mantic rings still waited on the granary floor. Honeysuckle choked the entrance. Four-leaf clovers pushed their way through the cobbles in the paved courtyard, doves circled about the tower eaves and the soft thunder of the waterfall made the lovely enclosure seem distantly removed from the outer world across the castle moat."

The antiquated village stagecoach, emblazoned "Ermenonville-Pailly," stood pushed against the shed in the courtyard. For special occasions Caresse brought the bartender from the Ritz to serve cocktails through its window. Next to the caretakers' rooms, the old washrooms and cellars had been converted into a large kitchen. The rest was furnished in a style that Caresse considered reminiscent of "Adirondack camps and Arizona ranches." There was only one small bathroom

FIGURE 12.4
Max Ernst's painting on the wall at Caresse Crosby's Moulin, film still from Julien Levy and Max Ernst, *Weekend at Caresse Crosby's,* July 1932.

FIGURE 12.5
Max Ernst in Caresse Crosby's swimming pool, film still from Julien Levy and Max Ernst, *Film illogique,* July 1932.

FIGURE 12.6
Max Ernst in Caresse Crosby's swimming pool, film still from Julien Levy and Max Ernst, *Film illogique,* July 1932.

and no electricity or telephone. Entertaining generally took place in the central mill tower, whose ground floor, with its original rafters and hay boxes, served as the dining room, both for humans, who sat on logs hewn from neighboring oaks, and for Caresse's eight donkeys, who ate from mangers. The room also contained a solid brass marine cannon that was rolled out and fired when special visitors arrived or left. By the chestnut stairway leading to the loft, a whitewashed wall served as a guest book and was covered with the brightly painted signatures of all who had passed through.

Later that evening, Caresse invited Julien to add his name to the roster of illustrious predecessors such as D. H. Lawrence, Douglas Fairbanks, and the future George VI, who signed simply "GEORGE of England." Ernst had signed with a painting, in addition to his name. When she handed Julien the box of colored paints reserved for this important ritual, she asked if she might publish his book. He was flabbergasted and wondered, "What book?" "Why, the book you will write, of course," Caresse replied, and in 1936 the Black Sun Press brought out *Surrealism* by Julien Levy, an anthology defining the movement as a way of life, from painting, to poetry, to psychology. In it, under his pseudonym, Peter Lloyd, he set forth proper Surrealist etiquette for the guest arriving at just such an occasion, advising:

When invited to a party, unless the contrary is expressly stated, the Guest must assume that he is expected to make love eventually to the Hostess; for a party without love, is a snare without delusions, wrack without ruin, or as rough without a tumble. The Hostess is considered as the mistress of the house. If, for any reason, this should be distasteful to the Guest, he must make his attitude clear at the outset. On entering the drawing room, pay your respects, immediately to the Hostess, then say, "I have no intention of sleeping with you tonight."

She will reply with some expression of polite surprise, such as "Why not, Mr. X?" The Guest must be prepared to explain why, or more exactly, why not, as truthfully as possible.

Such an abrupt greeting may not have been entirely out of place with Caresse acting as hostess; she reputedly had more than two hundred lovers in her day. However, she had so swiftly and brashly inserted herself into his film that it was he who was taken aback.

Max wasted no time setting up their improvised shoot. Perhaps because the pool, which had not yet been filled for the summer, provided a ready-made stage set, or possibly because, on this sunny day, the horseshoe-shaped refectory table that normally stood in the dining room had been placed next to it with inviting bowls of wild strawberries and champagne, Max decided upon the empty pool as a base of operations. (Caresse could always be counted on for plenty of champagne; sometimes she enlisted Harry's cousin, Nina de Polignac, to send magnums of Pommery Nature.) Max gathered zebra- and leopard-skin rugs from the tower's loft, as well as cushions and stray pieces of clothing to decorate his improvised stage set. Rugs, old chairs, and pillows were spread over the grass and cobblestones of the surrounding courtyard, offering respite to Caresse's numerous Afghan hounds and whippets, while her donkeys, a cheetah, a parrot, and fifteen pigeons strayed freely about the premises.

Caresse reappeared in safari boots and white riding pants, demanding that she be allowed to fire both her shotguns. While she permitted her new guest to introduce his film project into her picnic, Julien had to relinquish control of the movie as she and Max brought their ideas into the mix. He later wrote, "This was all as it should be, of course, in a Surrealist scenario, which now continued in a fugue of complete free-association, each participant contributing his secret whim in defiance of all continuity." It began, Julien recollected, with Max in the pool,

> . . . as a hunter stalking an invisible object. He raised a gun to shoot. At the same time Caresse appeared on a balcony overlooking the swimming pool,

FIGURE 12.7
Caresse Crosby shooting from the tower of the Moulin, film still from Julien Levy and Max Ernst, *Film illogique,* July 1932.

FIGURE 12.8
Max Ernst "as a hunter stalking an invisible object," film still from Julien Levy and Max Ernst, *Film illogique,* July 1932.

FIGURE 12.9
Julien Levy, Max Ernst, and an unidentified guest in the courtyard of the Moulin, film still from Julien Levy and Max Ernst, *Weekend at Caresse Crosby's,* July 1932.

raising her gun and shooting Max. Ernst was "wounded." The glove and the scarf materialized in a concrete corner near the drain, and the plot, if it was a plot, proceeded. Stains of blood appeared to drench a bodiless chemise which floated down from nowhere. Max gently picked it up and, carrying it on the hood of his car, hung it over the radiator cap.

Other guests arrived while the filming was in full swing, so they helped themselves to champagne and sat by the edge of the pool to watch. Armand de La Rochefoucauld dropped over from the château. Antoine de Saint-Exupéry (1900–1944), whose English edition of *Night Flight* was then appearing for the first time in Caresse's Crosby Continental Editions, arrived with his exotic bride, Consuelo Gomez Carillo, whom he had recently brought back from his flying adventures in South America. Caresse's good friends and fellow puritans in exile— Peter Powel, engaged in "doing exciting professional photography in a very unprofessional manner," and his Texan wife, Gretchen—brought the young Henri Cartier-Bresson, who had received his first camera as a gift from Harry after a three-day visit to the mill. No one minded in the least that the picnic was delayed for the completion of *Film illogique,* as it was later titled. When the pope of Surrealism himself, André Breton, showed up with Dalí and Gala, the informal picnic became an official happening.

Breton paid absolutely no attention to the hostess, her guests, the film, or the bubbly. In a "soft, green fishing hat and green glasses," he went off by himself for the afternoon, as was his habit. Caresse always retained the image of him earnestly fishing on the rustic bridge beyond the sheep pasture, "where there were no fish," dressed in a "dark, double-breasted suit, with high, black button shoes, a stiff collar, and a flowing tie." It

was an appropriately surreal pastime for the author of *Soluble Fish* and a suitably distant stance for the self-proclaimed leader of the Surrealists; he blessed them with his presence but did not deign to let the mere mortals come too close.

Dalí, Breton's current acolyte, similarly ignored the film, since he was not its star. He and Gala liked to sit by themselves along Caresse's garden wall. In these years, Caresse described the painter as young, very naïve, and extremely hard up for money, receiving a monthly stipend from her and a few of her friends. Although Dalí was already quite colorful in dress, favoring orange shoes and crimson ties with a black shirt, Julien recalled, "Dalí, when I first met him, offered no confirmation of my preconceived notion that he might be slick or pandering." This was the artist's period of greatness, before Breton renamed the painter "Avida Dollars," for the ridiculous caricature of himself that he later became. His *Persistence of Memory* had been the star of Julien's seminal exhibition, *Surréalisme,* that January.

Fueled by a steady supply of alcohol, the complicated sexual and creative interrelationships of this tightly knit group threatened to explode. Dalí especially wished to ignore the attention being paid to Max, because Ernst had been Gala's lover, living with her in a ménage à trois with her husband, the poet Paul Éluard (1895–1952), before Dalí met her. Conversely, Marie-Berthe, who had encouraged Max to physically attack Éluard over Gala, felt no goodwill toward her former rival. As a group, they purposefully cultivated and courted such emotional tumult. Julien later advised that proper Surrealist party conversation "should be such as to irritate others, for the faculty of irritability is a coefficient to life, to which end the subject of it should be appropriate to the time, place, and company, and we should bend our most astute efforts to discovering as rapidly as possible the vulnerable emotions of those who listen to us." As an ideal example of this, he cited their cult hero, the poet Arthur Rimbaud, who, when invited to dine with his lover, the poet Paul Verlaine, one evening, refused to speak except to demand bread or wine as if in a restaurant and, after a few glasses of Burgundy, became surly and aggressive, brandishing his dessert knife like a weapon.

On this occasion, Caresse was eager to convince Julien to give Dalí a one-man show in New York, or more precisely, to talk Dalí into the idea of going to Amer-

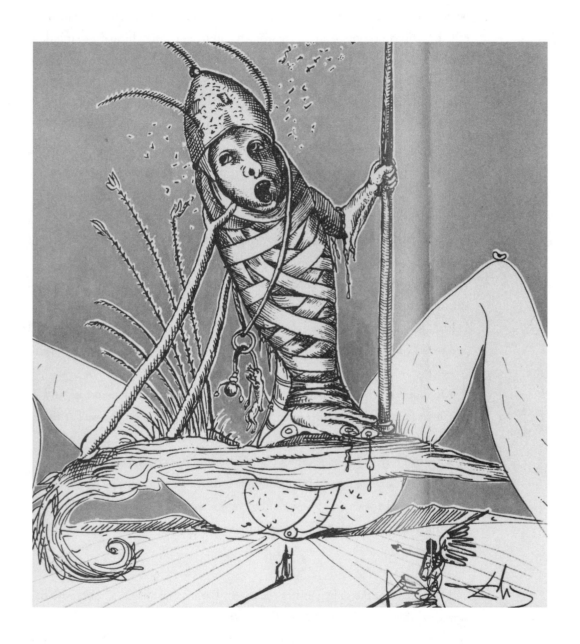

ica. The fact that she and Julien were preoccupied making a film portrait of Max when Dalí arrived seemed to bode poorly for Caresse's secret project. Julien recalled, "This collection of attractive women and talented men brought to mind, in the luxurious rustic setting of the moulin, such a gathering as Marie-Antoinette might have assembled at her milkmaid cottage. So, too, the intricate feuding and flirting everywhere sparking and sputtering out." Indeed, Caresse fondly recalled that at these Sundays she was "Queen Mistress of my own small realm."

The ghosts of the self-willed dead, those who had found such intensity in life too exhausting, also added their spirits to the party. The balcony on which Caresse had appeared to gun down Max had been Harry's special place to get in touch with the Sun God, Ra. Max flung a "blood-stained" chemise up over the villa-style roof, where Harry had placed the dove gray marble marker, engraved with the cross of the Crosbys combined names and their birth and projected death dates. After Harry's suicide, when, in Caresse's words, he had "gone to seek the sunvast splendor through negation," the marker mysteriously shattered into pieces. Now, Harry's ghost danced through the party, which echoed the events he had hosted and recorded in his diary:

Mobs for luncheon—poets and painters and pederasts and divorcées and Christ knows who and there was a great signing of names on the wall at the foot of the stairs and a firing off of the cannon and bottle after bottle of red wine and Kay Boyle made fun of Hart Crane and he was angry and flung *The American Caravan* into the fire because it contained a story of Kay Boyle's (he forgot it had a poem of his in it) and there was a tempest of drinking and polo *harra burra* on the donkeys, and an uproar and a confusion so that it was difficult to do my work.

Harry was not the only ghost in the tower. Earlier that spring, Crane, who had stayed in the tower loft to finish *The Bridge,* had jumped off a steamship from New York to Mexico. And there was the anarchist and frequent Moulin visitor Jacques Rigaud, whom Breton lionized for writing "Suicide should be a vocation."

284

The visitors brought their own ghosts with them: Julien, the haunting figure of Arthur Craven, the poet-boxer who, while married to Julien's mother-in-law and muse, Mina Loy, had sailed off into the Gulf of Mexico never to be seen again; Breton, his old friend Jacques Vaché, who had died with a companion after smoking forty grams of opium. Suicide was high fashion with the Surrealists; the first edition of their magazine, *Littérature,* contained a questionnaire, "Is suicide a solution?" For those who took the ultimate step, it was, in Julien's view, "another experimental entrance into the unknown world of the subconscious and the womb."

As a grand, final gesture, Max appeared to hurtle from the parapet of the Sun Tower, and Caresse remembered, "his shirt and trousers, empty of the body, went swirling through the air to lie limp upon the cobblestones below. The shirt was kicked aside into the pool while the trousers walked disconsolately away into the forest, presently Max's arm, back in the shirt, beckoned to us from a watery grave." Julien wondered if it was a "symbolic suicide," a death hanging over their sun-drenched afternoon.

Filmmaking and frolicking came to a halt as Monsieur Henri, the local gravedigger, and his wife, whom Harry had engaged as caretakers, appeared with steaming heaps of fiery red lobsters. The late appearance of the food in the sequence of events followed Caresse's priorities for entertaining. In her opinion, "The main requisites in party giving are (1) guests, (2) drink, (3) entertainment . . . food is last, but should be as exotic as possible, so no one knows the difference, and copious." In her early days in Paris she favored serving American dishes such as mashed sweet potatoes, tomato-cheese salad, or marshmallows with hot chocolate sauce, not daring to compete with the French at their own cuisine. She taught her Cordon Bleu chef to make fried chicken and cornpone, creamed codfish and New England clam chowder, brown betty and prune whip. (Guests did not attend for the food but to participate in the decadent antics; she and Harry typically served dinner in their bedroom and invited attendees into their large bath.) Beyond her garden fence at the Moulin she even grew corn to serve on the cob for authentically Yankee picnics.

Caresse offered lobsters to her epicurean visitors as a more luxuriant bow to her first marriage to a Peabody on the North Shore of Boston than her suspicious-looking casseroles. Like caviar, her other favorite, lobsters bespoke opulence, but required little in terms of preparation, providing foolproof success. As a rule, she never asked the chef what anything cost, as long as the bills were paid. She explained, "You see, if you tell a French cook what you want and what she can spend per week, you will get all you desire, but if you order plainer food to economize, the accounts remain the same and she will grumble. They always spend the limit, good or bad."

She knew that her guests that Sunday, however eccentric in behavior, demanded to eat well, and in their Parisian view, that did not mean marshmallows with chocolate. The expatriates adopted gourmandizing standards as exacting as those of the natives. For one of Caresse's subsequent parties, Max Ernst took no chances: he personally drove to Marseille to select the lotte, mussels, lobsters, and prawns; searched Paris for saffron in sufficient quantity to make bouillabaisse for one hundred; and left explicit instructions with her chef for the preparation of bushels of tomatoes before he arrived with the fish shimmering and flailing in the backseat of his car.

Julien developed a similarly French epicurean bent under the tutelage of his artists. Man Ray introduced him to a bistro on the Avenue de Maine, a favorite of Robert Desnos, André Masson, and Breton, and otherwise frequented by gravestone sculptors, that specialized in a diverse cheese board offered as a first course before the meal, "all you could eat for five francs."

However, it was the Romanian sculptor Constantin Brancusi who truly groomed the young dealer's Francophile palate as much as his eye. Julien remembered, "He wouldn't talk of his sculpture; Brancusi was proud of his cheese. It was only when I walked with him in the market that I began to see how his play and his work were linked. For there we found cheeses, and sausages too, formed every one with some exotic relation to their taste. They hung in formal ranks, a luxurious jingle of traditional and informative shapes, while Brancusi's studio was filled with their glorified replicas in marble and brass and wood. . . . Since knowing Brancusi, I have enjoyed more fully the gardens of the world, bouquets of carrots, piles of cabbages, sacks of dried and uniform beans, rice, coffee, in which I would bathe my hands."

Dalí also exerted his influence upon Julien, who recorded that the Spanish artist "likes cheeses too, but not the outer shape with its red, white, gray, or green skin of mold. He loves vivisected cheese, coulant, *pungent,* walking by itself. This is because Dalí approves of what he calls the 'visceral' the organic and the animal. . . . So, from Dalí I learned to enjoy jellyfish, tripe, the morphology of a drop of water, ogee curves, and long before it became a cult, Art Nouveau." Dalí began his autobiography by stating "At the age of six I wanted to be a cook." He believed, "One can choose not to eat, one cannot accept to eat poorly." Eating well fed the machinery that housed his creativity. He declared, "In my daily life every move becomes ritual, the anchovy I chew participates in the shining light of my genius. Being a genius I have to care for the body that harbors it, I therefore accept this obligation, I accept with joy this holy inquisition."

At the time of Caresse's picnic, Dalí was at the height of his "food phase," painting edibles into compositions such as *Anthropomorphic Bread* and *Eggs on a Plate Without the Plate,* themes which could be combined together as *Ordinary French Loaf with Two Fried Eggs Without a Plate* or added to, for example, as *Average French Bread with Two Fried Eggs Without the Plate Trying to Sodomize a Crumb of Portuguese Bread.* Dalí rendered the ordinary baguette wrapped in a napkin, the staple of any French bourgeois meal, so that it appeared distinctly like an erect penis wearing a condom. He depicted the staff of life in Freudian terms not only for its shape but also because the metaphor of rising yeast has inherently sexual connotations in numerous cultures: in English, for example, the "bun in the oven." Nor did Dalí, who painted themes such as *The Last Supper* and *The Host,* overlook the Catholic overtones of bread as the body of Christ, or fail to enjoy the sacrilege of painting it in overtly sexual terms. (His compatriot, Luis Buñuel, believed that the Spanish made especially good Surrealists because they had such a keenly developed sense of sin.) Dalí considered the egg, ancient symbol of fertility and femininity, a metaphor for his eroticism; it recalled sneaking into the family kitchen as a child (a forbidden pleasure) where he was fascinated to observe that "[t]he beaten white of an egg, caught by a ray of sunlight cutting through a swirl of smoke and flies, glistened exactly like froth foaming at the mouth of panting horses rolling in the dust and being bloodily whipped to bring them to their feet." He compared his most famous symbol, the soft watch, to Camembert cheese "running like sore" because "they are also mystical, Saint Augustine having said in the Psalms of the Bible, that cheese can be assimilated to the body of Christ." Dalí, in fact, envisioned Jesus as a "mountain of cheese." However, of all the foodstuffs in

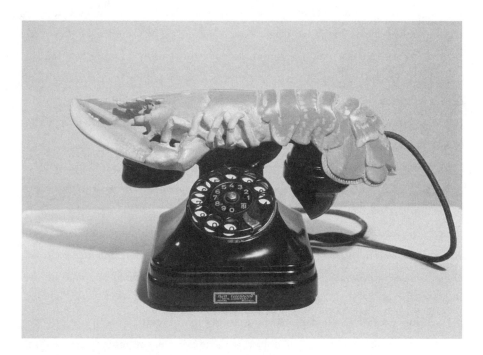

FIGURE 12.11
Lobster Telephone, 1936,
by Salvador Dalí, plaster
and telephone.

the lexicon of Dalinian imagery, lobsters were his absolute favorite, which Caresse must have known when she chose her menu.

Decades later Dalí published a cookbook, *Les dîners de Gala,* where, in his introduction to the "Spirito-Mystic-Monarchic, Catholic, Apostolic, Romanism of DALINIAN GASTRO ESTHETICS," he asserted: "I only like to eat what has clear and intelligible form. . . . I love eating suits of arms, in fact I love shell fish. . . . [O]nly a battle to peel [it] makes it vulnerable to the conquest of the palate." He considered lobster a symbol of female genitalia and wrote: "I have a predilection for young girls and lobsters. Like lobsters, young girls have exquisite exteriors. Like lobsters, they turn red when one wants to make them edible." They adorned the mermaid skirts for his "Dream of Venus" pavilion at the 1939 New York World's Fair; one appears as a headdress on a portrait of Gala; and another as the receiver for his *Lobster Telephone*. Before Dalí, Alfred Jarry had plumbed the rich imagery of boneless lobster protected by a thick shell in his poem *Fable,* which Breton republished as an example of "pure objective humor"—Surrealism at its best.

> A can of corned beef, chained up like a lorgnette,
> Saw a lobster pass by, which resembled it fraternally.
> It protected itself with a hard shell
> Upon which it was written that inside, like the can, it was boneless,
> *(Boneless and economical);*
> And under its curled-up tail
> It probably hid a key intended to open it.
> Overcome with love, the sedentary corned beef
> Declared to the little self-propelling can of living preserves
> That if it would consent to acclimate itself
> Next to it, in earthly shop displays,
> It would be decorated with numerous gold medals.

While Dalí had paid no attention to the film, the lobsters could not be ignored. The heaping platter of these creatures, plunged to their deaths into a pot of boiling water to nourish the living, brought even this narcissist into the fold. The group sat on blankets, cracking shells, nibbling the meat with their bare fingers, and sucking the juice out of the legs with the brutal vigor of Lautréamont's *Chants de Maldoror,* with its violent fantasy of killing a child by plunging overgrown fingernails into his breast. Harry used to read the passage aloud to guests: "Then you drink the blood, passing your tongue over the wounds; and during this time, which should last as long as eternity lasts, the child weeps. There is nothing so delicious as his blood, extracted in the manner I have described, and still warm, unless it be his tears, bitter as salt."

Just as Caresse had rejected the whalebone corset, she rebelled against the rigid code of dining etiquette and the mania for cutlery in which she had been raised, a world in which even bread and sandwiches were picked up with forks designed solely to perform this service, and asked her guests to plummet to the depths of their most primal urges by eating with their hands. The Surrealists did not always forgo cutlery; spoons, especially, but also knives and forks appear almost as frequently in Dalí's paintings as eggs, bread, and lobsters. Symbolically, Freud, whom they revered, considered the round, soothing shape of the spoon, an object used to feed babies, to be the mother; the long, bladed, warrior-like knife as the father; and the fork, the male child of the two. Within the Moulin coterie, René Crevel had recently published his own psychosexual flatware vision, *Miss Fork, Mr. Knife,* with the Black Sun Press with illustrations by Max Ernst; it tells the story of a young girl's fantasy that her knife is her father and her fork, Cynthia, the beautiful redhead he has left with. As the child plays, grasping at words her mother will not explain to her, Mr. Knife tells Miss Fork, "You are not at all like other women. You are much more beautiful. You are like death, Cynthia, you are a whore like death." In the Surrealist imagination, even cutlery could be imbued with sexual nuance and the fascination with mortality. (Three years later, Crevel joined the long roster of Surrealist suicides.)

When Caresse served up lobsters without tools designed to make the process of eating them less messy, her Yankee ingenuity provided a no-fuss solution for meeting the Surrealist aesthetic for surprise and brutality, metaphor and tactile pleasure. In the long centuries since the wife of the Doge of Venice lasciviously plucked her mulberries with a fork, the utensil's magical sensuality had been lost. Cheapened industrial production ensured that every mother could prudishly reprimand her children for not eating properly. In retaliation, Caresse and her guests followed Gide's invective: "Épater les bourgeois."

The Surrealists delighted in inspiring squeamish, gut-wrenching revulsion. Dalí's image of a swarming mass of insects feeding on an open wound never appears more gruesome than in the film *Un Chien andalou,* which he made with Luis Buñuel, with its scene of ants horribly buzzing and crawling in festering skin. However, as an expert on repugnance, Dalí stated, "The Jaw is our best tool to grasp philosophical knowledge. Disgust is the ever present watchman of my table, sternly overseeing my meals obliging me to choose my food with caution."

Though Caresse's guests reveled in the taste of a good snail, a delicacy gathered in the Moulin's garden by Monsieur Henri, they did not, as Vincent Holt, author of a bizarre Victorian text titled *Why Not Eat Insects?* (1885) earnestly suggests, dine on worms fried in butter, slug soup, or stag beetle larvae on toast. Nor did they feast upon the unsavory concoctions proposed by the Futurists, whose cookbook, published on the heels of an outrageous series of trans-European banquets, appeared in the same year as Caresse's picnic. Futurists categorically banned utensils from their table and subjected diners to "Totalrice" (rice, salad, wine, and beer), "Meal-in-the-Air" (tactile, with noises and aromas), and "Elasticake." Roasted chickens were stuffed with steel ball bearings and salami served in a marinade of strong, black coffee mixed with eau-de-cologne. Even the Futurists had to admit that dishes such as "Aerofood" (a slice of fennel, an olive, and a kumquat, next to a piece of cardboard glued with a strip of velvet, silk, and sandpaper, to be stroked with the right hand as the left brought food to the mouth) were not recommended for the hungry. Their ultimate goal was to "kill off the old, deeply-rooted habits of the palate; and prepare men for future chemical foodstuffs; we may even prepare mankind for the not too distant possibility of broadcasting nourishing waves over the radio." Futurist meals were conceptual events destined to make any foodie weep.

Surrealist food appeared in surprising guises. It could be worn: Caresse's close friend and favorite designer, Elsa Schiaparelli, created a mutton chop hat. It could even be the art on exhibition; when Dalí finally did come to New York for a solo exhibition at Julien's gallery, he wrote to request materials to create a ten-foot-tall hard-boiled egg, made from the separated yolks and whites of more than a thousand eggs molded into shape, which would be displayed with an enormous spoon, so that visitors might taste it. However, in whatever form it appeared, it was always supremely delicious. When Dalí painted his portrait of Gala with lamb chops on her shoulder, a playful analogy of the sacrificial lamb, he told the baffled reporters why he had done so: "I like chops and I like my wife. I don't see any reason not to paint them together."

The wealthy American expatriate in Paris, Bob Pitney, who liked to entertain the Surrealist circle, held the most lavish and surprising dinners of the group, at which, Julien recalled, "a typical menu might begin with oysters on the halfshell, baked and served on heated shards of glass, looking so well chilled that any unwary tongue would be burned. For dessert perhaps there would be coffee and vanilla ice cream pressed in molds, shaped like roast squab and crusted with brown sugar for a roasted effect, served with a sauce of maple syrup. Between the oysters and dessert there might be such a delicacy as *foie gras* sculptured into cutlets, with tiny mushroom-shaped truffled and mashed potatoes served in toast ice cream cones." Julien ranked the host as an uncompromising gourmand who could "out-trompe-le-goût" of any Frenchman; indeed, he eventually died from obesity.

The Surrealists augmented the gustatory, olfactory, visual, and tactile enjoyment of cuisine by dislocating it from its usual guises to expose its hidden meanings. The purpose of illogical whimsy was, in Breton's words, "to arrest the spread of this cancer of the mind which consists of thinking all too sadly that certain things 'are,' while others, which well might be, 'are not.' " By Julien's definition, their goal was "To remystify mythology, FETICHISM, parable, PROVERB, and METAPHOR. . . . To exploit the mechanisms of inspiration. To intensify experience." Nothing embodies the quixotic, paradoxical juxtapositions of Surrealism more than the Swiss artist Meret Oppenheim's *Object (Luncheon in Fur)* of 1936, now at the Museum of Modern Art, in New York, which consists of a fur-lined teacup, saucer, and spoon: startling, soft, luxurious, and sexual. Giuseppe Arcimboldo's bizarre sixteenth-century portraits, composed of fruits and vegetables, inspired their aesthetic. Beauty, for the Surrealists, lay in stimulating the sense of wonder. Breton found its ideal in Louis Aragon's line, "During a short break in the party, as the players were gathering around a bowl of flaming punch, I asked the tree if it still had its red ribbon." Often violent and always strange, the Surrealist feast never forfeited visceral, aesthetic, and sensual pleasure. Dalí declared "a woodcock *'flambée'* in strong alcohol, served in its own excrements, as is the custom in the best of Parisian restaurants, will always remain for me in that serious art that is gastronomy, the most delicate symbol of true civilization."

It was not their Futurist contemporaries with whom the Surrealists shared their gastronomic spirit, but rather Grimod de La Reynière, one of the greatest epicures of all time, author of the *Almanach des gourmands* and *Manuel des Amphitryons,* who, consumed with resentment for being born with strangely deformed webbed hands, took the same twisted pleasure in his meals that his contemporary, the Marquis de Sade, whom Breton claimed as an ancestor of the Surrealists, found in his violent sexual escapades. In 1783, Grimod bolted his hapless guests into his parents' house until the early hours of the morning, taunting and badgering them as he served up his culinary delights in a room draped entirely in black, with a catafalque as a centerpiece dramatically lit up with a blaze of candles, while a boys' choir sang appropriately funereal chants. In 1812, to outdo the macabre banquet of his youth, Grimod falsely announced his own death, invited Parisian society to attend his magnificent funeral collation, and personally welcomed his horrified guests to the succulent feast laid out in the dining room.

The soul of Caresse's picnic reached farther back into the past; Petronius (d. A.D. 66) had his fictional character Trimalchio deluge his guests in a death-inducing quantity of food, wine, and morbid wonder—dancing silver skeletons; a great platter of food arranged like the signs of the zodiac which disguised the real treasure of sows' udders, fowls, and fish hidden underneath; a wild boar carved to liberate living thrushes; cakes that vaporized into noxious smoke when touched—after which he finally implores his guests, "I want you to think you've been invited to my wake," and then "Pretend I'm dead and say something nice," upon which the cornet players perform a death march that summons the fire brigade.

Like a banquet offered to the dead in an ancient Egyptian tomb, the Surrealist meal was a mystical journey to the River Styx. While the old adage says, "To depart is to die a little," to dine, in Dalí's opinion, was, always "to die a lot. . . . The specter of death creates supreme delights, salivary expectations, and this is why the greatest of gastronomical refinements consists in eating 'cooked and living be-ings.' " In his view, the ultimate expression of this magical cuisine of purgatory was a sixteenth-century recipe by a Neapolitan of Catalan descent, Giambattista della Porta, from *The Treatise on Natural Magic,* in which a live goose, smeared with suet and lard, is placed in a fiery trench, where it is free to walk about and cool down with large drinks of water until it begins to stumble when its heart gives way. The reader is then instructed to "set him on the table to your Guests who will cry out as you pull off his parts and you shall eat him before he is dead."

Lobsters, however, steamed or boiled alive, were almost as good. Known as the scavenger of the ocean's floor, a crustacean whom many sailors disdain because it ruthlessly feeds on the rotting flesh of drowned seamen, the lobster offered a vicar-ious link to the darkest and most taboo of human abominations, cannibalism. Like the viscous, oozing form consuming itself in Dalí's *Autumnal Cannibalism* (color plate XIV), now in the Tate Gallery in London, ripping into its own flesh with fork and knife as it ingests apples, beans, and bread, the guests at Caresse's Moulin tore at shells and at each other, invoking death as they enjoyed the food that gave them life. They called up ghosts reaching farther and farther back in time, beyond even Trimalchio, summoning Rimbaud's Gallic ancestors of "Mau-vais sang."

In Harry's day, the Sunday lunches that began with free-flowing champagne in the Moulin garden typically ended with orgies and opium up in the tower attic. But for Harry, the call of the dead had been too alluring. Assembled in the garden in 1932, the revelers lacked his Pan-like presence to incite them to their most de-bauched escapades. Instead, "a gigantic stranger, a blond Apollo," suddenly ap-peared in their midst. Julien recalled, "Nobody seemed to know who he was or where he came from, but it was immediately apparent that he belonged to Caresse, that he was prodigiously drunk, and that Caresse belonged to him, was to be drowned in him, infatuated in a most self-destructive way." His booming voice even disrupted Breton's fishing. Bert Young, a planter from Virginia, later became Caresse's third husband, an abusive alcoholic who left her and came back over and over again. Nineteen years younger than she, he was, in her words, "handsome as

Hermes, militant as Mars." It was, however, neither his drinking nor his vitriolic temper that Caresse's guests objected to, but his doltish bragging. He told "outrageous, incredible stories of his prowess on safari in Africa, in badman feuds in Dakota." "We were not to be taken in," Julien recollected.

Despite its call for freedom of expression and behavior, no intellectual or artistic movement has ever been so cliquish in its need to define who was, and who was not, a real Surrealist. Breton lorded over them all, excommunicating substandard devotees of the movement, eventually eliminating nearly every one of the original members of his group and Dalí. He even dictated where and what the Surrealists could drink. By anyone's reckoning, however, Bert Young was not a member of the group. He was altogether too much of a cowboy, devoid of intellectual subtlety or morbid playfulness.

Max declared, "I don't like him. There will be a fight. I am driving Marie-Berthe home." Julien opted to stay and take the late train back to Paris. As the moon rose over the garden, the remaining guests walked through the forest to attend the local fair, where they stared at the villagers in picturesque costumes, who, finding them equally if not more exotic, stared right back at them. At the carnival games, Bert Young turned out to be quite the cowboy he had promised, "shooting behind his back, over his arms, between his fingers." His bragging claims had been entirely literal, after all—altogether disappointing for the Surrealists.

There would be no all-night antics, tarot cards, or trysts because Young could not follow along. The outsider had dampened the essential mix of wordplay and hidden meanings, casting the others back into mundane reality. Like any work of art, the beauty of a meal rests in the eye of the beholder, but the soul of dining lies in its ability to express our humanity. Bert Young was a man for whom a lobster would always be just a lobster; he did not dine, but merely ate.

295

Notes and Credits

INTRODUCTION

The term *Gesamtkunstwerk* first appeared in Wagner's 1849 essay "The Art-Work of the Future."

Marsilio Ficino's quote from *"De sufficientia, fine, forma, materia, modo, condimento, auctoritate convivii,"* a letter to Bernardo Bembo of Venice, in *Opera Omnia* (2 vols.; Basel, Officina Henricpetrina, 1576), volume 1, pp. 739–740, was translated into English by Jeremy Whiteley and Emma Hughes in Michel Jeanneret's *A Feast of Words: Banquets and Table Talk in the Renaissance* (Chicago: University of Chicago Press, 1991). I am also very grateful to Clement Salaman for sending me his translation of the complete text of the letter.

Thomas Walker is quoted from *The Art of Dining; or, Gastronomy and Gastronomers* (London: 1835, John Murray, 1853).

Montaigne is quoted from his *Essays,* Book 3, no. 13: "Of Experience," from the translation by J. M. Cohen (Harmondsmith, U.K.: Penguin, 1962) used in *A Feast of Words.* The translation by Donald Frame in *The Complete Works of Montaigne: Essays, Travel, Journals, Letters, Newly Translated by Donald Frame* (Stanford, Calif.: Stanford University Press, 1948) was also consulted.

Shakespeare is quoted from *A Midsummer Night's Dream,* act 5, scene 1, line 215, from the Cambridge Edition Text of *The Complete Works of William Shakespeare,* edited by William Aldis Wright (Garden City, N.J.: Garden City Books, 1936).

Goethe is quoted from "Joseph Bossi über Leonard da Vincis Abendmahl zu Mayland" in *Über Kunst und Alterthum am Rhein und Mayn* 3, pp. 113–188 (Weimar: 1817), translated by Georg Heinrich Noehden, 1821, reproduced in Lavinia Mazzucchetti, *Goethe e il Cenacolo di Leonardo* (Milan: Editore Ulrico Hoepli, 1939). An abridged version of Noehden's translation was also consulted in Ludwig H. Heylindeich's *Leonardo: The Last Supper* (New York: Viking Press, 1974). A fuller discussion of the subject can be found in my article, "Depictions of the Last Supper," in *Food in the Arts: Proceedings of the Oxford Symposium of Food and Cookery, 1998* (Totnes, Devon: Prospect Books, 1999), pp. 223–236.

CHAPTER ONE

Dining with God

Kirk Thomas Ambrose provided the valuable transcription and translation of the sign language compiled by the eleventh-century monks Ulrich and Bernard in the Cluniac Customaries, in the appendix of his Ph.D. dissertation, "Romanesque Vézelay: The Art of Monastic Contemplation" (University of Michigan, 1999). Other invaluable information provided by his thesis includes Peter the Venerable's sermon at Vézelay, and the importance of the Mystic Mill and the celebration of St. Martin's Feast Day. I am also very grateful to Dr. Ambrose for his comments on reading an early draft of the chapter. I am also indebted to Professor Christopher Brooke for reading my chapter.

For quotes from Saint Bernard and the analysis of Peter the Venerable's reforms I am indebted to Dom David Knowles, "Cistercians and Cluniacs: The Controversy Between St. Bernard and Peter the Venerable," originally delivered as the ninth lecture of the Friends of Dr. Williams's Library, London: 1955 and reprinted in Knowles, *The Historian and Character* (Cambridge: Cambridge University Press, 1963); and "The Reforming Decrees of Peter the Venerable," pp. 1–20, in Giles Constable and James Kritzeck, *Petrus Venerabilis, 1156–1956; Studies and Texts Commemorating the Eighth Centenary of His Death* (Rome: Orbis Catholicis, 1956), which also includes A. H. Bredero's "The Controversy Between Peter the Venerable and Saint Bernard of Clairvaux," pp. 53–71, as well as the archaeologist Kenneth J. Conant's helpful essay, "Cluniac Building During the Abbacy of Peter the Venerable." A photograph of Peter's lizard-crested crosier appears in the frontispiece of this text. Further background regarding Peter's abbacy is drawn from *Peter the Venerable: Selected Letters,* edited by Janet Martin in collaboration with Giles

Constable (Toronto: Medieval Latin Texts, 1974); on the rise of Cistercianism from Julie Roux, *Les Cisterciens* (Toulouse: MSM, 1999); on both the Cluniac and Cistercian Orders, *Moines et religieux au Moyen âge,* edited by Jacques Berlioz (Paris: Éditions du Seuil, 1994).

Further citations and background about the Customaries at Cluny, including the stories of the miraculous rescue of those who maintained silence and the transformation of Saint Odo's crumbs into pearls, from John of Salerno's *Vita Odonis,* are cited from Barbara H. Rosenwein, *Rhinoceros Bound: Cluny in the Tenth Century* (Philadelphia: University of Pennsylvania Press, 1982). Material on the weekly menu under Abbot Hugh is from Dominique Vingtain, *L'abbaye de Cluny* (Paris: CNRS Éditions, 1998). The schedule of the monks pertains to that during the abbacy of Odo (927–948) as cited in Emile Magnien, *Les deux grands siècles de Cluny (950–1150): Spiritualité, art et histoire* (Genelard, France: Le Caractère en Marche, 1994). Information regarding the growth of the abbey and food distribution to the *famuli* and Peter the Venerable comes from Giles Constable, editor, *Cluniac Studies* (London: Variorum Reprints, 1980); Marcel Pacaut, *L'Ordre de Cluny* (Paris: Fayard, 1998), which is the source for Bertrand du Colombier's installation of the *essui mains;* Sir G. F. Bart Duckett, *Record-Evidences, among the archives of the ancient abbey of Cluni, From 1077 to 1534: illustrative of the history of some of our early kings; and many of its English affiliated foundations* (Lewes, England: printed for the author, 1886); Noreen Hunt, *Cluny under Saint Hugh* (London: Edward Arnold, 1967); and a publication by the Musée Ochier, *Le Gouvernement d'Hugues de Semur à Cluny: Actes du Colloque scientifique international* (Cluny, France: September 1988), as well as visits to the ruins of Cluny and numerous Cluniac monasteries and churches in Burgundy.

Additional background information on food and wine of the period has been drawn from numerous sources including, for the history of wine making in Burgundy, *The Oxford Companion to Wine,* edited by Jancis Robinson (Oxford: Oxford University Press, 1999); for French monastic herb gardens, Laetitia Bourgeois-Cornu, *Les Bonnes herbes du Moyen âge* (Paris: Publisud, 1999) and Michel Cambornac, *Plantes et jardins du Moyen âge* (Paris: Edipso Edition, 1996); for French cooking and food preparation, Jean-Louis Flandrin and Carole Lambert, *Fêtes gourmandes au Moyen âge* (Paris: Imprimerie nationale, 1998); for the introduction of spices in Europe, C. Anne Wilson, "The Saracen Connection: Arab Cuisine and the Medieval West: Part 1" in *Petits*

Propos Culinaires 7 (March 1981), pp. 13–22. Caroline Walker Bynum's *Holy Feast and Holy Fast: The Religious Significance of Food to Medieval Women* (Berkeley: University of California Press, 1987) provided additional background on the history of food in Christianity, a subject discussed more broadly in Gillian Feeley-Harnik, *The Lord's Table: The Meaning of Food in Early Judaism and Christianity* (Washington, D.C.: Smithsonian Institution Press, 1981). Information on the use of fish as an Early Christian symbol is drawn from James Hall's *Dictionary of Subjects and Symbols in Art* (revised ed.; New York: Harper and Row, 1979).

Saint Benedict is quoted from his *Rule for Monasteries;* Saint Augustine, from his *Confessions,* translated by E. Pusey (London: J. M. Dent & Sons, 1907).

CHAPTER TWO
Friendship

Marsilio Ficino's *De amore,* published as a critical edition with a translation into French by Raymond Marcel, as *Commentaire sur le banquet de Platon* (Paris: Les Belles Lettres, 1978) serves as the primary source for this story. Translations from the French are my own. Quotes from Ficino regarding food are taken from his *Three Books on Life,* first published as *De vita libri tres,* published as a critical edition and translation with introduction and notes by Carol V. Kaske and John R. Clark (Tempe, Ariz.: Medieval and Renaissance Texts and Studies, 1998). Citations from Platina come from Mary Ella Milham's critical edition and translation of *De Honesta Voluptate et Valetudine,* published as *On Right Pleasure and Good Health* (Tempe, Ariz.: Medieval and Rennaissance Texts and Studies, 1998). Quotes from Giovanni Corsi are taken from his "Life of Marsilio Ficino" in vol. 3 of *The Letters of Marsilio Ficino,* translated from Latin by members of the Language Department of the School of Economics, London (London: Shepheard-Walwyn, 1975–1994). Letters by Ficino in this text provide Ficino's definition of friendship, 1:51, letter to Giovanni Cavalcanti; comments on dress, 3:19, letter to Francesco Bandini; enjoyment, 1:105, letter to Banco, 13 August 1458; music, 1:7, letter to Antonio Canigiani, and 1:92, letter to Peregrino Agli, 1 December 1457, also Campano's praise of Ficino's playing; peripatetic philosophers, 1:96, letter to Francesco Tebaldi; feeding the mind, 1:22, letter to Niccolo degli Albizzi; feeding the soul, 2:60, letter to mankind; Platonic banquet at Bandini's, 1:107, letter to Jacopo Bracciolini; and humanity, 1:55, letter to Tommaso Minerbetti. I am also indebted to Clement Salaman for sending me his translation of Ficino's *De sufficientia, fine, forma, materia, modo, condimento, auctoritate convivii,* letter to Bernardo Bembo, 2:42, which is the source for quotes on the number of guests and the salt of genius. Michel Jeanneret's *Feast of Words: Banquets and Table Talk in the Renaissance,* translated by Jeremy Whitely and Emma Hughes (Chicago: University of Chicago Press, 1991) provides the extract from this same letter at the chapter heading. Other background information about Ficino and his thinking came from his *Platonic Theology,* vol. 1, Books 1–4, translated by Michael J. B. Allen with John Warden (Latin text edited by James Hankins with William Bowen; Cambridge, Mass.: The I Tatti Renaissance Library, Harvard University Press, 2001).

The Medici Villa Careggi, now owned by the hospital of Florence, which graciously allowed me to tour and photograph the site, is currently undergoing restoration and will shortly be open to the public. Additional information about the villa was garnered from Guido Carocci, *La villa medicea di Careggi: memorie e ricordi* (Florence: privately published, 1888) and Daniela Mignani, *The Medicean Villas by Giusto Utens,* 2d ed. (Florence: Arnaud, 1995). Background on the decoration of the villa and the setting of the table at this period is drawn from extensive sources, especially Peter Thornton, *The Italian Renaissance Interior, 1400–1600* (London: Weidenfeld & Nicholson, 1991), which places Pollaiuolo's *Annunciation* in the *saletta* of Careggi. Thornton cites Eleonora della Rovere on maiolica (letter of 15 November 1524) and Lorenzo's incense burner at Poggio. Another background source is *Disegno: Italian Renaissance Designs for the Decorative Arts* (New York: Cooper-Hewitt National Design Museum, Smithsonian Institution, 1997), edited by Beth L. Holman, especially Susan H. Vicinelli's chapter, "Dining Etiquette and Renaissance Silverware," which cites the forks in Lorenzo's inventory. Maria Grazia Ciardi Duprè Dal Poggetto's *L'oreficeria nella Firenze del Quattrocento* (Florence: Studio per Edizioni Scelte, 1977) was also helpful.

The story of the Doge's wife was recorded by Saint Peter Damian, first cited in Norbert Elias, *The Civilizing Process: The History of Manners,* translated by Edmund Jephcott (originally published as *Über den Prozess der Zivilisation* [Basel: Haus zum Falken, 1939; New York: Urizen Books, 1978] in two volumes). The reference to forks in

Homer comes from *The Odyssey,* Book 3, lines 362–434. For forks in ancient Rome, see Michael Vickers, "Early Silver," in Charles Truman, editor, *Sotheby's Concise Encyclopedia of Silver* (London: Conran Octopus, 1993). Further information regarding the early use of the fork and Renaissance dining can be found in Phyllis Pray Bober, *Art, Culture, and Cuisine: Ancient and Medieval Gastronomy* (Chicago: University of Chicago Press, 1999); Alain Gruber, *Silverware,* originally published as *L'Argenterie de maison du XVIe au XIXe siècle* (New York: Rizzoli, 1982); Klaus Marquardt, *Eight Centuries of European Knives, Forks, and Spoons: An Art Collection* (Stuttgart: Arnoldsche, 1997); and Jochen Amme, *Bestecke: Die Egloffstein'sche Sammlung (15. – 18. Jahrhundert) auf der Wartburg* (Stuttgart: Arnoldsche, 1994).

The silver lyre commissioned by Lorenzo from Leonardo is cited by Mark Levy, director of the National Gallery, in "Music and Art in Renaissance Florence," the text for the CD to accompany the exhibition "Renaissance Florence: The Art of the 1470's," held from 20 Oct. 1999 to 16 Jan. 2000 at the National Gallery, London. I am also indebted to the Biblioteca Berenson, at the Villa I Tatti, for generously allowing me to use its extensive reference sources pertaining to the Italian Renaissance.

Further background on dining and cooking in Renaissance Italy comes from numerous sources. Especially important to this text are Terence Scully, *Cuoco Napoletano: The Neapolitan Recipe Collection (New York, Pierpont Morgan Library, MS Bühler, 19), A Critical Edition and English Translation, initially with the collaboration of Rudolf Grewe* (Ann Arbor: University of Michigan Press, 2000), which is the source of the eggplant recipe. Further information on its history as well as that of sugar and sandal comes from *The Oxford Companion to Food,* edited by Alan Davidson (Oxford: Oxford University Press: 1999); Giuseppe Maffioli, *Il ghiottone veneto* (Milan: Bramante Editrice, 1968); Claudio Benporat, *Storia della gastronomia italiana* (Milan: Mursia, 1990); and Françoise Sabban and Silvano Serventi, *La Gastronomie à la Renaissance: 100 recettes de France et d'Italie* (Baume-les-Dames, France: Stock, 1997). Allen J. Grieco's *The Meal* (London: Scala Books, 1992) is the source for information about Andrea del Sarto's cooking club. The reference to the Wednesday night Impressionist dinners is from Richard Shone's monograph *Alfred Sisley* (London: Phaidon, 1979).

Information on food in ancient China comes from K. C. Chang, editor, *Food in Chinese Culture: Anthropological and Historical Perspectives* (New Haven: Yale University Press, 1977), as well as Elaine Kris, "Yan and Ying Today" in *Petits Propos Culi-naires* 7 (March 1981, pp. 37–41).

Quotes from Giorgio Vasari come from his *Lives of the Artists, A selection translated by George Bull,* vol. 1 (London: Penguin Books, 1965).

The theory that Botticelli's *Primavera* visually illustrates Ficino's philosophy, put forth by E. H. Gombrich in "Botticelli's Mythologies; A Study in the Neoplatonic Circle," in the *Journal of the Warburg and Courtauld Institute* 7 (1945), is discussed at length in Erwin Panofsky's *Renaissance and Renascences in Western Art* (Stockholm: Almqvist and Wiksell/Gebers Förlag AB, 1960).

The quoted edition of Plato's *Symposium* was translated with introduction and notes by Alexander Nehemas and Paul Woodruff (Indianapolis, Ind.: Hackett Publishing, 1989).

I am also especially grateful to Ken Albala, *Eating Right in the Renaissance* (Berkeley: University of California Press, 2002), for his thoughtful comments of drafts of this chapter, as well as the two that follow.

CHAPTER THREE
Fête Champêtre

The story is based upon Francesco Priscianese's letter "al molto reverendo messer Lodovico Becci, et al suo M. Luigi del Riccio," published after *Della lingua romana,* bound in one volume with *De primi principi della lingua romana* (Venice: Bartolomeo Zanetti da Brescia, August 1540), a copy of which is at Harvard University's Houghton Library. The translation used is that in volume 2 of Joseph Archer Crowe and Giovanni Battista Cavalcaselle's *Titian: His Life and Times, With Some Account of His Family, Chiefly from New and Unpublished Records* (2 vols., London: John Murray, 1877). The last portion of the story is adapted by the author's reading of the original and the translation published in Edward Hutton's *The Pageant of Venice* (London: John Lane the Bodley Head, Ltd., 1927). Portions of this letter are also reprinted in English in James Cleugh, *The Divine Aretino* (New York: Stein and Day, 1966), and Juergen Schulz's chapter, "The Houses of Titian, Aretino and Sansovino," pp. 73–118 in *Titian: His World and His Legacy,* edited by David Rosand (New York: Columbia University

Press, 1982). This essay also provided detailed research on Titian's house and garden in Cannaregio (built before the Fondamente Nuove were added); Sansovino's apartment at 153A Calle, in the two bays nearest the clock towers; and Aretino's palazzo on the Grand Canal, No. 4168. I am also indebted to the owners of the Ristorante agli Omnibus, currently occupying No. 4168, who allowed me to tour and photograph the building. Hugh Honour's *Companion Guide to Venice* (London: Collins, 1990) provided the text of the anonymous song at the chapter heading, as well as many insightful leads for very enjoyable field research of my own.

Ariosto's nickname for Aretino appears in his famous *Orlando furioso,* canto 46 (first published in 3 volumes, 1516, 1521, and 1532; presented by Italo Calvino with introduction, notes, and bibliography by Lanfranco Caretti, 2 vols., Turin: Einaudi, 1966). General background on Aretino was drawn from Cleugh's *The Divine Aretino,* which contains the published letter from Marcolini to Aretino. In addition, Cleugh's biography was the source for the excerpts from *The Philosopher,* and for Aretino's remarks concerning gondolas, his servants, and following his sensual appetites, as well as the story of his palazzo being mistaken for an inn. Aretino's letter to Simon Bianco, 25 June 1528, on the solitary life; and his letter to Girolamo Sarra, 4 November 1537, on salad, appear in the Italian in Giuseppe Maffioli, *Il ghiottone veneto* (Milan: Bramante Editrice, 1968), and were kindly translated into English for this publication by Luigi Attardi. Edward Hutton's *The Pageant of Venice* provided quotes on Aretino's international guests, "Nature, Mistress of all Masters," and "I am a free man." All other quotations from Pietro Aretino, including the excerpt from *The Courtesan,* are taken from *The Works of Pietro Aretino,* 2 vols., translated into English from the original Italian, with a critical and biographical essay by Samuel Putnam (Chicago: Pascal Covici, 1926); on his gold chain, letter to the King of France, 10 Nov. 1533; on summer months and conversing under a beech tree, letter to Messer Agostino Ricci, 10 July 1537; on eating thrushes with Titian, letter to Count Monfredo di Coltalto, 10 Oct. 1532; on his preference for a simple diet and *antipasti,* letter to Friar Vitruvio dei Rossi, 6 Sept. 1537; on Titian's wild chickens, letter to the little Monsignor Pomponio (Titian's son), 26 Nov. 1537; demand for artichokes, letter to Francesco Marcolini, 3 June 1537; and on thrushes with lettuce and sausage, letter to Messer Matteo Durastante da San Giusto, 20 Oct. 1537. Further background on Aretino was provided by Christopher Cairns, *Pietro Aretino and the Republic of Venice: Researches on Aretino and his Circle in Venice,*

1527–1556 (Florence: Leo S. Olschki, 1985). Luba Freedman's *Titian's Portraits Through Aretino's Lens* (University Park: Pennsylvania State University Press, 1995) was useful for the relationship between Titian and Aretino.

John Ruskin is quoted from *The Stones of Venice* (1853; London: Penguin Books, 2001). Vasari is quoted from his *Lives of the Artists, A selection translated by George Bull,* vols. 1 and 2 (London: Penguin Books, 1965); Cellini, from his *Autobiography,* written 1558–1566, translated with an introduction by George Bull (London: Penguin Books, 1956).

Kenneth Clark's *Landscape into Art* (London: John Murray, 1949) provided the inspiration for this chapter, which extends his analogy to the art of dining, as well as an analysis of the development of the Arcadian idyll and the excerpt from Sannazaro. Among numerous sources on the development of landscape painting in Venice, the classic is Bernard Berenson's *Italian Painters of the Renaissance,* vol. 1, *Venetian and North Italian Schools,* first published 1894–1907 (London: Phaidon Paperback, 1968). Both writers are heavily steeped in Ruskin in their arguments.

The quote from Marie-Antoinette, from a letter written to her sister, is taken from Vincent Cronin, *Louis and Antoinette* (London: William Collins and Sons & Co., 1974). For further information on the development of pleasure dairies in France, see my article "Marie-Antoinette's Pleasure Dairy at Rambouillet," in *The Magazine Antiques,* vol. 158, no. 4 (October 2000), pp. 542–553.

Citations of Eustachio Celebrino da Udine's pamphlet *Opera nova che insegna appararechiar una mensa a uno convito: e etiam a tagliar in tavola de ogni sorte carne e dar li cibi secondo lordine che usano gli scalchi p[er] far honore a forestieri, inititulat[a] Refettorio* (Venice: 1526) and the background to this text come from Claudio Benporat, "A Discovery at the Vatican: The First Italian Treatise on the Art of the *Scalco* (Head Steward)," *Petits Propos Culinaires* 30, November 1988, pp. 41–45. I am also indebted to the Biblioteca Marciana in Venice for permitting me to handle original Venetian recipe treatises. Two anonymous tracts, *Opera nuova intitolata Dificio di Ricette, nella quale si contengono tre utilissimi ricettari* (Venice: Giovanniantonio e fratelli da Sabio, 1526) and *Opera nova intitolata dificio de ricette: nella quale si contengono tre utilissimi ricettarii* (Venice [Vinegia]: Francesco Bindoni & Mapheo Pasino, 1530), which provided the melon compote recipe, were particularly instructive.

The reference to Martin Luther and the fork comes from Jochen Amme, *Bestecke:*

Die Egloffstein'sche Sammlung (15. – 18. Jahrhundert) auf der Wartburg (Stuttgart: Arnoldsche, 1994).

Successive editions of Cristoforo di Messisbugo's *Banchetti, composizioni di vivande e apparecchio generale* (first published 1549) appeared in Venice from 1552 to 1626. The descriptions of banquets included here are from the facsimile of the 1557 edition, published with the longer title *Libro novo nel qual s'insegna a' far d'ogni sorte di vivande secondo la diversità de i tempi così di carne come di pesce* and prepared by Giuseppe Mantovano (Bologna: Arnaldo Forni Editore, 1982). Mantovano's introduction to this edition was instructive about Messisbugo's history. Baldassare Pisanelli, *Trattato della natura de' cibi et del bere* (Venice: Domenico Imberti, 1611; fascimile reprint, Bologna: Arnaldo Forni Editore, 1980) was also consulted.

Background concerning Venetian dining in this period was found in Castello Estense, *A Tavola con il Principe: Materiali per una mostra su alimentazione e cultura nella Ferrara degli Estense* (catalogue to the exhibition held 1 October 1988–27 March 1989, Ferrara, Italy: Amministrazione provinciale di Ferrara, ca. 1988); Claudio Benporat, *Storia della gastronomia italiana* (Milan: Mursia, 1990); Lynne Rosetto Kasper, *The Splendid Table: Recipes from Emilia-Romagna, the Heartland of Northern Italian Food* (New York: William Morrow and Company, 1992); and Françoise Sabban and Silvano Serventi, *La Gastronomie à la Renaissance: 100 recettes de France et d'Italie* (Baume-les-Dames, France: Stock, 1997).

The glass museum in Murano was particularly helpful with the history of glassmaking on the island; other sources include Reino Liefkes, *Glass* (London: Victoria and Albert Museum Publications, 1997).

For the history and symbolism of ancient Bacchanalian rites, James Hall's *Dictionary of Subjects and Symbols in Art,* rev. ed. (New York: Harper and Row, 1979) was very useful.

Edward E. Lowinsky's chapter, "Music in Titian's *Bacchanal of the Andrians:* Origin and History of the Canon per Tonos," pp. 191–282, in David Rosand's *Titian: His World and His Legacy,* provided an in-depth analysis of the music in the painting and at Alfonso d'Este's court, as well as the quote from Philostratus's *Imagines* (translated by Philip Fehl) that inspired the painting. Further information on the dating and background of Titian's bacchanals comes from Cecil Hilton Monk Gould's *The Studio of Alfonso d'Este and Titian's Bacchus and Ariadne: A Re-Examination of the Chronology of the Bacchanals and of the Evolution of One of Them* (London: The Trustees Publications Department, National Gallery, 1969).

Montaigne on courtesans is quoted from his *Travel Journal to Italy* from the translation in Edward Hutton's *The Pageant of Venice,* which appears in a different variation in *The Complete Works of Montaigne: Essays, Travel, Journal, Letters, Newly Translated by Donald M. Frame* (Stanford, Calif.: Stanford University Press, 1948).

Chapter Four
Cementing a Bond

The most invaluable resource for this chapter was Sara Mamone's *Firenze e Parigi: due capitali dello spettàcolo per una regina Maria de' Medici* (Milan: Amilcare Pizzi, 1987), an exhaustive, scholarly study of all the events surrounding Maria de' Medici's wedding. Her study of the State Archives of Florence unearthed a 292-box dossier, "Alcune lettere dei Deputati sopra le nozze della Regina Maria de' Medici. Note di personne addette ai servizi di Corte e di Gentiluomini. Appunti vari concernenti le spese e i preparativi per le nozze ed il viaggio della Regina da Livorno a Francia, e carte varie," which included Ferdinando's letter to Eleonora Gonzaga, 12 May 1600, concerning the date of the wedding; the letter from the Deputies to Ferdinando with their plans; the origin of allegorical symbols appropriate for the wedding; and the proclamations regarding the food, the organization of the servants, Cardinal Aldobrandini's procession (also in Pardoe), the wedding procession, and the wedding ceremony (also described by Denis Raisin-Dadre); and the decoration of the banquet, its menu, the subsequent parties, and the galley.

Also indispensable, was Julia Pardoe's *The Life of Marie de Medici, Queen of France, Consort of Henri IV, and Regent of the Kingdom under Louis XVIII,* 3 vols. (New York: Scribner and Welford, 1890). This includes excerpts from L'Etoile's *Journal de Henri IV,* with the account of d'Alincourt's arrival in Paris, as well as Sully's *Mémoires,* with the conversation between Sully and the King regarding his betrothal; the Duke de Bellegarde's entry into Paris and Maria's reply at the dinner, from Bernard de Montfauchon, *Les Monuments de la monarchie française;* a description of the serving of Maria's banquet and her journey from Florence to Lyon and then Paris. Descriptions of Maria's reception at Avignon come from Léon-Honoré Labande, *Fêtes et Réjouis-*

sances D'autrefois. Entrée de Marie de Médicis à Avignon (19 Novembre 1600) (Avignon: Seguin Frères, 1893).

References to the Medici glassworks are from Lisa Goldenberg Stoppato, Medici Archive Project, MdP 5031, fol. 348, May 1592, entry 4079 and MdP 283, fol. 126, 24 Aug. 1592, and *The Penguin Dictionary of Decorative Arts* edited by John Fleming and Hugh Honour (London: Viking, 1989). The history of the Medici porcelain factory was researched in Galeazzo Cora and Angiolo Fanfani, *La porcellana dei Medici* (Milan: Fabbri Editori, 1986), and Susan S. Hermanos, "Contemporary Influence on Medici Porcelain: 1575–87" (master's thesis, Cooper-Hewitt/Parsons School of Design, 1993). The flask for Philip II (inv. MNC 8372) and several plates (MNC 5355, MNC 8372) can be seen at the Musée National de Céramique, Sèvres; only sixty known examples of Medici porcelain survive.

Excerpts from Caranus's wedding feast come from Andrew Dalby's translation and article, "The Wedding Feast of Caranus the Macedonian by Hippolochus," in *Petits Propos Culinaires* 29 (July 1988), pp. 37–45. The banquet was described in a letter by Hippolochus, transcribed by Athenaeus in *The Deipnosophists.* Dalby gives an annotated translation of the original text in addition to discussing its contents.

Information on the Salone dei Cinquecento is courtesy of the Palazzo Vecchio, as well as George Bull's introduction to Vasari's *Lives of the Artists.* In addition to Mamone's description of the decorations for the banquet and entertainment, further information came from the exhibition *Teatro e spettacolo nella Firenze dei Medici: Modelli dei luoghi teatrali,* held at Palazzo Medici Riccardi, Florence, 1 April–9 September, 2001, and its corresponding catalogue by Elvira Garbero Zorzi and Mario Sperenzi (Florence: Leo S. Olschki, 2001). Additional background on Buontalenti was culled from two books by Amelio Fara, *Buontalenti. Architettura e teatro* (Florence: La Nuova Italia Editrice, 1979) and *Bernardo Buontalenti: l'architettura, la guerra e l'elemento geometrico* (Genova: Sagep Editrice, 1988). Allen Grieco's *The Meal* provided the reference to the bronze version of Tacca's sugar sculptures. Information regarding the spectacles of previous Medici weddings was also taken from Emma Micheletti, *Family Portrait: The Medici of Florence,* translated by Paul Blanchard (Florence: Giusti di S. Becocci & C., 1999).

Vincenzo Cervio is cited from his *Il trinciante* (1593; facsimile reproduction,

Bologna: Arnaldo Forni Editore, 1980); Bartolomeo Scappi, *Opera dell'arte del cucinare* (Venice, 1570; facsimile reproduction presented by Giancarlo Roversi, Bologna: Arnaldo Forni Editore, 1981); and Ottaviano Rabasco, *Il convito overo discorsi di quelle materie che al convito s'appartengono . . .* (Florence: Donato, e Bernardino Giunti & Compagni, 1615). Further background on Florentine banquets at this date was drawn from Stefano Francesco di Romolo Rosselli, *Mes secrets à Florence au temps des Médicis 1593: Pâtisserie, Parfumerie, Médecine,* introduced and translated into French by Rodrigo de Zayas (Paris: Jean-Michel Place, 1996).

Information regarding the music for Maria's wedding came from the Doulce Mémoire recording directed by Denis Raisin-Dadre, *Henri IV et Marie de Medicis: Messe de mariage* (Austria: Astrée naïve, 2000); and the Huelgas Ensemble recording, directed by Paul van Nevel, *La Pellegrina: Music for the Wedding of Ferdinando de' Medici and Christine of Lorraine, Princess of France, Florence 1589* (recorded at the Abbaye-aux-Dames, Saintes, France, 14–17 July 1997; Sony Music Entertainment, 1998), which also provided the English translation of Nicolas Rapin's song "To the Queen."

CHAPTER FIVE
Taking Office

The most crucial resource for this chapter was Church of England, *The Manner of the Coronation of Charles the First of England at Westminster, 2 February 1626,* edited by Charles Wordsworth (London: printed for the members of the Henry Bradshaw Liturgical Text Society, 1892). In addition to reprinting the Coronation Book used at the ceremony, Wordsworth compares all known copies of it for discrepancies and annotations; particularly useful were Laud's own margin notes. He found the copies believed to have been used by Charles and Laud at St. John's College, Cambridge. His text also re-creates the events leading up to the Coronation in detail, including information regarding the plague and Charles's substitution of Laud for the Dean of Westminster. Wordsworth includes a transcription of the "Order of the Procession to the Coronation" (from the State Papers Office, Dom. K. Charles I, vol. 20), which provided the source for the description of this event. John Bradshaw, Windsor Herald's, "The Form of the Coronation" (S.P.O., Dom. K. Charles I, vol. 20, art. 12), is also transcribed in full. His citation of Heylen's *Cyprianus Anglicus,* fol. (1671) is quoted for Charles's outfit.

Houghton Library at Harvard University kindly gave me access to an original copy of Charles I's "By the King: A Proclamation to Declare His Maiesties Pleasures touching His Royall Coronation . . ." (London: Bonham Norton & Iohn Bill, 1625, i.e., 1626), and allowed it to be reproduced in this book. Great Britain Exchequer, "Lists of Esquires and Gentlemen in Cheshire and Lancashire, Who Refused the Order of Knighthood at the Coronation of Charles I," drawn up in the years 1631 and 1632 and edited by J. P. Earwaker (London: Record Society, 1885), provided evidence of those who declined the honor.

Reference to edibles distributed at the time of Charles's accession comes from Eileen White, "Civic Banquets and Banqueting Stuff," *Petits Propos Culinaires* 66 (February 2001, pp. 55–61).

Francis Sanford is quoted from *The History of the Coronation of . . . James II.* (London: Thomas Newcombe, 1687). Further information on the history of the British Coronation ceremony is culled from John Ogilby, *The Entertainment of His Most Excellent Majestie Charles II. In His Passage through the City of London to His Coronation . . .* (London: Thomas Roycroft, 1662); and Richard Thompson, editor, *A Faithful Account of the Processions and Ceremonies of the Kings and Queens of England: Exemplified in that of their late Majesties King George The Third, and Queen Charlotte: With All the Other Interesting Proceedings Connected with that Magnificent Festival* (London: John Major, 1820). Lawrence E. Tanner's *The History of the Coronation* (London: Pitkin Pictorials, 1952) is the source for the Walpole quote; Elizabeth I's response to the Champion; and Queen Victoria. Allied Newspapers Limited, *Crowning the King: The History, Symbolism, and Meaning of the Coronation Ceremony* (London: Syndicate Publishing, Co., 1937) provides the wording for the perquisites accorded to the Dean of Westminster (although paid in cash since 1937, they still hold); the Challenge of the Champion of George IV and the Style for Elizabeth I, and drinking to the Health of the King. Robert Douglas, *The Form and Order of the Coronation of Charles the II. King of Scotland, together With the Sermon then Preached, by Mr. Robert Dowglas &c. and the Oath then taken, with several Speeches made. As it was done at Scoone, The first day of January, 1651* (Aberdene: Imprinted by Charles Brown, and reprinted in London, 1660) was useful for comparison.

Charles's youthful performances in court masques is cited from Thomas N. Corns, editor, *The Royal Image: Representations of Charles I,* (Cambridge: Cambridge University Press, 1999). Further information comes from William Brenchley Rye, editor, *England as Seen by Foreigners in the Days of Elizabeth and James the First* (London: John Russell Smith, 1865); and John Macleod, *Dynasty: The Stuarts, 1560–1807* (London: Hodder and Stoughton, 1999). Useful background about political events came from John P. Kenyon, *Stuart England,* 2nd ed. (London: Penguin Books, 1987).

Stephen Mennell, "Food at the Late Stuart and Hanoverian Courts," *Petits Propos Culinaires* 17 (June 1984), pp. 23–24, compares the menu at James II's Coronation Feast with Elizabethan cuisine. Mennell's *All Manners of Food: Eating and Taste in England and France from the Middle Ages to the Present,* 2d ed. (Urbana: University of Illinois Press, 1996) helped me understand the larger context of British culinary history, as did Barbara Ketcham Wheaton's December 1999 seminar "Reading British and American Historical Cookbooks in Context," given for members of the Culinary Historians of New York. Further information regarding the Coronation of James II and background on the history of dining in Britain come from Ivan Day, editor, *Eat, Drink, and Be Merry: The British at Table, 1600–2000* (London: Philip Wilson Publishers, 2000).

Background on the tradition of banqueting and banquet houses also comes from: for the Greenwich house, Alison Sim, *Food and Feast in Tudor England* (New York: St. Martin's Press, 1997); Peter Brears, *English Heritage Food and Cooking in Seventeenth-Century Britain: History and Recipes* (England: English Heritage, 1985); and Elizabeth David, "Banketting Stuffe," *Petits Propos Culinaires* 3 (November 1979), pp. 39–44.

In addition to information gleaned from visits to the Banqueting House, Whitehall, further insights into the tradition of the court masque come from Towner Art Gallery, *A Selection of the Festival Designs by Inigo Jones: Scenery and Costumes from the Court Masques of James I and Charles I from the Chatsworth Collection* (catalogue to the exhibition held at the Towner Art Gallery, Eastbourne, England, 23 February–4 April 1972) and D. R. Watson, *The Life and Times of Charles I* (London: Weidenfeld and Nicolson, 1972). The recording *Music at the Court of Charles I,* produced by Tim Smithies (England: Metronome, 1999) for the exhibition *Orazio Genteleschi at the Court of Charles I,* held at the National Gallery, London, 3 March–23 May 1999, was particularly helpful regarding the foundation of the King's Musick.

Instructions for creating the centerpiece come from Robert May, *The Accomplisht Cook, or the Art and Mystery of Cookery,* (facsimile of the 1685 edition, with foreword, introduction, and glossary by Alan Davidson, Marcus Bell, and Tom Jaine; Totnes, Devon: Prospect Books, 1994). Invaluable to understanding food at the court of Charles I was Louise A. Richardson and J. R. Isabell, "Joseph Cooper, Chief Cook to Charles I," *Petits Propos Culinaires* 18 (November 1984), pp. 40–53, which led me to the British Library to examine Joseph Cooper, *The Art of Cookery Refined and Augmented* . . . (London: J. G. for R. Lowndes, 1654). *The Compleat Cook and A Queens Delight,* by W. M., (facsimile reproduction of the 1671 edition of two of a trilogy titled *The Queens Closet Opened,* first published 1655; London: Prospect Books, 1984) was also useful.

Constance B. Hieatt and Sharon Butler, editors, *Curye on Inglysh: English Culinary Manuscripts of the Fourteenth Century (Including The Forme of Cury)* (London: Oxford University Press, 1985) provided information on the history of the "subtletie" and shows earlier use of sugar in England. The Archbishop of Canterbury's subtlety is cited in Sara Paston Williams, *The Art of Dining* (London: The National Trust, 1993).

The Sergeant at Arms at Westminster Palace graciously gave me access to visit and photograph the Hall, and was helpful in providing information regarding the history of the room.

I am very grateful to Ivan Day for reading and commenting on a draft of this chapter.

CHAPTER SIX
Showing Off

I am extremely indebted to Patrice de Vogüé, the current owner of Vaux-le-Vicomte, for his patient cooperation with my research and my numerous sessions photographing the château, as well as for leading me to Paul Micio and his scrupulous work on Fouquet's silver inventories. Micio's generosity in sharing his unpublished discoveries proving that Fouquet did not own the five hundred dozen gold plates, which appeared in "Les Inventaires inédits de l'argenterie du grand argentier Fouquet," in the *Bulletin de la société de l'histoire de l'art français* (Paris, 2001), and in meticulously reviewing my article on the dinner at Vaux-le-Vicomte for *Petits Propos Culinaires,* were invaluable.

The well-known story of the château was researched in Anatole France, *Vaux-le-Vicomte* (reprint of Calmann-Lévy, 1933; Étrépilly, France: Les Presses du Village, 1987), who provides the anonymous account of the menu; Jean-Marie Pérouse de Montclos, *Vaux-le-Vicomte* (Paris: Éditions Scala, 1997); and Maurice Fleurent, *Vaux-le-Vicomte: La clairière enchantée* (Paris: Éditions Sous Le Vent, 1989). Further background on Fouquet comes from Daniel Dessert, *Fouquet* (Montreuil, France: Librairie Arthème Fayard, 1987); Paul Morand, *Fouquet: ou Le Soleil offusqué* (Paris: Gallimard, 1961); and Jules Lair, *Nicolas Fouquet, Procureur Général, Surintendant des Finances, Ministre d'État de Louis XIV,* 2 vols. (Paris: Librarie Plon, 1890). Eugène Grésy, *Château de Vaux-le-Vicomte: Documents sur les artistes, peintres, sculpteurs, tapissiers et autres qui ont travaillé pour le Surintendant Fouquet* (Melun, France: H. Michelin, 1861) provided information on those employed in building Vaux.

La Fontaine's famous letter to Maucroix, 22 August 1661, recording the festivities of the evening, which is quoted in my text, is reprinted in full in Pérouse de Montclos. This letter, and the unfinished poem, "Le Songe de Vaux," were also consulted in the original French in Jean de la Fontaine, *Oeuvres complètes* (Paris: Éditions du Seuil, 1965). Quotes from M. L'abbé de Choisy, who attended the event, come from his *Mémoires pour servir à l'histoire de Louis XIV,* 5th ed. (Utrecht: Van-de-Water, 1727). By his account, the three ladies accompanying Louis were the Comtesse d'Armagnac, the Duchesse Valentinois, and the Comtesse de Guiche. (This was also recorded in the 18 August 1661 report of the party in *La Gazette*.) He is also the source for the estimate of six thousand attendees, which most agree is high; the warning slipped to Fouquet before the party, and the oft-repeated story of Louise de la Vallière. Jules Lair, *Louise de la Vallière and the Early Life of Louis XIV,* translated by Ethel Colburn Mayne (New York: G.P. Putnam's Sons, 1908) provided further background on her relationship with the King.

Background on Vatel comes from Dominique Michel, *Vatel et la naissance de la gastronomie* (Paris: Librairie Arthème Fayard, 1999). Michel proposes that the meal at Vaux was set up *en ambigu,* which seems extremely likely. Loret, *La Muse Historique,* letters of 27 May 1656 and 19 August 1656, in Michel is quoted for the food at Fouquet's prior parties.

Mlle. de Scudéry is quoted from *Clelia: An Excellent New Romane: The Whole Work in Five Parts,* English translation (London: H. Herriman, T. Cockerel, S. Heyrick, W. Cadman, S. Loundes, G. Mariot, W. Crook, and C. Smith, 1678); she is the source of the description of Le Brun's intended decoration of the ceiling of the *Grand Salon.* Le Brun's preparatory drawings survive at Vaux and at the Louvre.

Descriptions of the festivities at Versailles come from André Félibien, *Relation de la feste de Versailles. Du dix-huitième Juillet mil six cens soixante-huit* (Paris: Pierre le Petit, 1668), which provides the description of a collation; and his *Les plaisirs de l'isle enchantée.* (Paris: L'imprimerie royale, 1673), which is the source for the description of the rock grotto.

Molière, *Oeuvres complètes de Molière,* edited by René Bray, vol. 2, *Théâtre de 1661–1663* (Paris: Société de Belles Lettres, 1939), provided his own account of writing *Les Fâcheux,* whose subsequent performances were set into context in this edition.

Saint-Simon is quoted from his *Louis XIV et sa cour: portraits, jugements et anecdotes: extraits des mémoires authentiques* (Paris: L. Hachette et Cie, 1853). Louis XIV's views on the value of magnificent entertaining, was researched in Roger Weigert, *Louis XIV: Faste et décors,* catalogue to the exhibition, May–Oct. 1960 (Paris: Musée des Arts Décoratifs).

The reconstruction of the meal is taken from a compendium of period texts: *L'Escole parfaite des officiers de bouche, . . .* (Paris: Ve P. David, 1662; 3rd ed., Paris: Jean Ribou, 1666, as well as the 4th ed. of 1682); Nicolas de Bonnefons, *Les delices de la campagne, suite du Jardinier françois,* (1654; 6th ed., Paris: Nicolas Le Gras, 1684); and François Pierre de La Varenne, *Le Cuisinier francois, enseignant la maniere de bien apprester & assaisonner toutes sortes de viandes . . .* (1651; 5th ed., Paris: Chez Pierre David, 1654), as well as the revised edition of 1680 (Lyon: Jacques Canier, 1680). Gilles and Laurence Laurendon, editors, *L'Art de la cuisine française au XVIIe siècle* (Paris: Payot & Rivages, 1995) provided reprints of L. S. R., *L'Art de bien traiter* (1674); Pierre de Lune, *Le Cuisinier* (1656); and Audiger, *La maison reglée* (1692). A first edition of *L'Art de bien traiter* (Paris: Jean Du Puis, 1674) was also consulted.

Montaigne's reaction to iced wine, recorded in his journals, is cited by Elizabeth David, "The Harvest of Cold Months," *Petits Propos Culinaires* 3 (November 1979). Further background on French culinary history is owed to Barbara Ketcham Wheaton, for both *Savoring the Past: The French Kitchen and Table from 1300 to 1789* (New York: Touchstone Books, 1996), the source for the Feast of the Pheasant and the transition to "service à la française," and her tireless ideas and suggestions. Notable among other sources consulted are Ronald W. Tobin, *Tarte à la Crème: Comedy and Gastronomy in Molière's Theater* (Columbus: Ohio State University Press, 1990); Georges and Germaine Blond, *Histoire pittoresque de notre alimentation* (Paris: Librairie Arthème Fayard, 1960); and Jean-Yves Patte and Jacqueline Queneau, *Mémoire gourmande de Madame de Sévigné,* preface by Bernard Loiseau (Paris: Éditions du Chêne, 1996).

Etiquette was drawn from Antoine de Courtin, *Nouveau traité de la civilité qui se pratique en france parmi les honnêtes gens* (1671; reprinted with notes by Marie-Claire Grassi; Saint-Étienne, France: Publications de l'Université de Saint-Étienne, 1998) and Nicolas de Sainctot, *Le Cérémonial de France à la Cour de Louis XIV* (reprint, Paris: P. Lethielleux, 1936). The King's dining rituals were also studied in Béatrix Saule, "Tables royales à Versailles, 1682–1789," in Sylvie Messinger, editor, *Versailles et les tables royales en Europe,* catalogue to the exhibition held 3 Nov. 1993–27 Feb. 1994, Musée National des Châteaux de Versailles et Trianon (Paris: Éditions de Réunion des musées nationaux); as well as Jacques Levrin, *La cour de Versailles aux XVIIe et XVIIIe siècles* (2d ed., Paris: Hachette Littératures, 1999).

Further background on the decorative arts comes from Peter Thornton's excellent texts, *Authentic Décor: The Domestic Interior, 1620–1920* (New York: Viking, 1984) and *Form and Decoration: Innovation in the Decorative Arts, 1470–1870* (New York: Harry N. Abrams, 1998). Nicole Garnier-Pelle's *André Le Nôtre (1613–1700) et les jardins de Chantilly,* catalogue to the exhibition held 14 June to 9 October 2000, Musée Condé, château de Chantilly (Paris: Somogy Éditions d'Art, 2000) provided additional information on Le Nôtre and the development of French garden design.

General background on the period is also taken from W. H. Lewis, *The Splendid Century: Life in the France of Louis XIV* (New York: Anchor Books, 1953) and Richard S. Dunn, *The Age of Religious Wars: 1559–1715,* 2nd ed. (New York: W. W. Norton and Co., 1979).

CHAPTER SEVEN

Insatiable Gluttony

Ulrich Pietsch, editor, *Schwanenservice: Meissener Porzellan für Heinrich Graf von Brühl* (Berlin: Edition Leipzig, 2000), provided an invaluable scholarly study of the Swan Service and its context within Brühl's life. Walter Fellmann's biography of the Count, *Heinrich Graf Brühl, Ein Lebens- und Zeitbild* (Leipzig: Koehler & Amelang, 1989), provided further background, while Joseph Kraszewski's historical novel, *Count Brühl: A Romance of History*, translated by the Count de Soissons (London: Greening & Co., 1911) painted a colorful picture of the wider cast of characters.

Johann Christoph Adelung is quoted from his *The Life and Character, Rise and Conduct, of Count Brühl, Prime Minister to the King of Poland, Elector of Saxony; In a Series of Letters, by an Emminent Hand. Throwing a light on the real Origin of the Past and Present War in Germany, and the Intrigues of Several Powers,* translation from the German ascribed to H. G. von Justi and J. C. Adelung (London: M. Cooper and C. G. Seyffert, ca. 1765).

Amaranthes [Gottlieb Siegmund Corvinus] is cited from *Nutzbares, galantes und curiöses Frauenzimmer-Lexicon . . . ,* first published 1715 (Frankfurt and Leipzig: Joh. Friedrich Gleditsch und Sohn, 1739), revised and augmented 1768. Further background on German dining in the period comes from Uta Schumacher-Volker, "German Cookery Books, 1485–1800," *Petits Propos Culinaires* 6 (October 1980), pp. 34–46. Comparison with French cuisine of the period owes much to Barbara Ketcham Wheaton, *Savoring the Past: The French Kitchen and Table from 1300 to 1789* (New York: Touchstone, 1996), as well as to my own study of French culinary texts. Most relevant to this chapter were Vincent La Chapelle, *The Modern Cook* (London: Nicolas Prevost, 1733); Joseph de Gilliers, *Le Cannaméliste français. . . .* (1751; Nancy: Jean-Baptiste-Hiacinthe Leclerc, and Paris: Merlin, 1768); Menon, *Les Soupers de la Cour ou l'Art de travailler toutes sortes d'aliments* (reprint of the 1755 Paris edition; Paris: Librairie Soete, 1978); François Massialot, *The Court and Country Cook. . . . ,* translated from French into English by J. K. (London: W. Onley, for A. and J. Churchill. At the Black Swan in Pater-noster-row, and M. Gillyflower in Westminster-hall, 1702); François Massialot, *Le nouveau cuisinier royal et bourgeois, ou cuisinier moderne . . . ,* 3 vols. (Paris: Chez la Veuve Prudhomme, 1740, "Avec privilege du roi"), as well as the 1742 edition.

Vitellius is taken from Suetonius, *Life of Vitellius,* chapter 13. Lucullus is taken from Plutarch, *The Lives of the Noble Grecians and Romans* (translated by John Dryden and revised by Arthur Hugh Clough (1864; New York: The Modern Library, 1932). Archestratus is quoted from *The Life of Luxury,* translated with introduction and commentary by John Wilkins and Shaun Hill (Totnes, Devon: Prospect Books, 1994).

A.J.A. Symons is quoted from "The Epicure and the Epicurean," *The Epicure's Anthology; or Banqueting Delights,* collected by Nancy Quennell (London: Golden Cockerel Press, 1936).

For Chinese beliefs about gluttony, see K. C. Chang, editor, *Food in Chinese Culture: Anthropological and Historical Perspectives* (New Haven: Yale University Press, 1977). Background on medieval perceptions of gluttony is drawn from Caroline Walker Bynum, *Holy Feast and Holy Fast: The Religious Significance of Food to Medieval Women* (Berkeley: University of California Press, 1987).

CHAPTER EIGHT

Seduction

The primary text for this chapter is taken from Casanova's *History of My Life;* the episode of the meal with M. M. comes from vol. 4, chap. 3. Quotes are adapted from the Willard R. Trask translation of the unedited manuscript (New York: Harcourt, Brace and World, 1966), 12 vols. in 6, although my story is based upon a reading of Casanova's original, prepared by Robert Laffont (Paris: Bouquins, 1993), 3 vols. The classic translation of the French by Arthur Machen was also consulted, and, for its flowing language, has been used in instances where it corresponds to Casanova's authentic manuscript.

Further background on Casanova was consulted in Stefan Zweig, *Adepts in Self-Portraiture: Casanova, Stendhal, Tolstoy,* translated from the German by Eden and Cedar Paul (New York: The Viking Press, 1928); Luigi Ballerini, "Casanova, Man of Appetites," *The Magazine of La Cucina Italiana* 3, no. 5 (Sept.–Oct. 1998): pp. 80–82; James Rives Childs, *Casanova: A New Perspective* (New York: Paragon House Publishers, 1988); and the edition translated into French by Francis L. Mars, (Paris: Jean-Jacques Pauvert aux Éditions Garnier Frères, 1983); Casanova's *Plaisirs de bouche: Six épisodes extraits d'Histoire de ma vie,* edited by Ilona Kovács (Paris: Librio, 1998); Tom

Jaine, "Casanova: A Sensible Man," *Petits Propos Culinaires* 57 (Dec. 1997): pp. 45–50; Catherine Toesca, *Casanova: un Vénitien gourmand,* edited by Jean-Bernard Naudin (Paris: Éditions du Chêne, 1998); Hippolyte Romain, *Casanova: Les menus plaisirs* (Paris: Éditions Plume, 1998); and Giandomenico Romanelli, editor, *Il Mondo di Giacomo Casanova: Un Veneziano in Europa, 1725–1798,* catalogue to the exhibition held 12 Sept. 1998–10 June 1999, Museo del Settecento Veneziano, Ca' Rezzonico (Venice: Marsilio, 1998).

Lady Wortley Montagu, letter to Countess Pomfret, 1736, and Joseph Addison, *Remarks on Several Parts of Italy, 1701–1703,* are cited from H. C. Robbins Landon and John Julius Norwich, *Five Centuries of Music in Venice* (New York: Schirmer Books, 1991).

Information on Cardinal de Bernis is taken from *Mémoires du cardinal de Bernis,* preface by Jean-Marie Rouart, annotated by Philippe Bonnet (Mesnil-sur-l'Estrée, France: Mercure de France, 1986).

Culinary texts consulted for the meal include *Le Manuel des Officiers de Bouche* . . . (Paris: Le Clerc, 1759); Joseph Gilliers, *Le Cannameliste français* . . . (first published Nancy: Abel-Denis Cuisson, 1751; reprinted Nancy: Jean-Baptiste-Hiacinthe Leclerc, 1768); Vincent La Chapelle, *The Modern Cook* (London: Nicolas Prevost, 1733); François Marin, *Les dons de Comus, ou les Délices de la table* . . . (Paris: Prault, 1739); François Massialot, *Le nouveau cuisinier royal et bourgeois, ou cuisinier moderne* . . . , 3 vols. (Paris: Chez la Veuve Prudhomme, 1739, "Avec privilège du roi"); and revised edition, 1740, and edition augmented with recipes by Vincent de La Chapelle (Paris: Chez la Veuve Prudhomme, 1742); François Menon, *Les Soupers de la cour* . . . (reprint of the 1755 Paris edition; Paris: Librairie Soete, 1978) and *La Cuisinière bourgeoise* . . . (revised edition, Brussels: François Foppens, 1759) and reprint of the 1774 Brussels edition prepared by Alice Peeters (Paris: Messidor/Temps Actuel, 1981); and Père Polycarpe Poncelet, *Chimie du goût et de l'odorat* (reprint of 1755 edition; France: Klincksieck, 1993). *Le Cuisinier gascon* is reprinted in full in Beatrice Fink, *Les liaisons savoureuses: Réflections et pratiques culinaires au dix-huitième siècle* (Saint-Étienne, France: Publications de l'Université de Saint-Étienne, 1995).

For additional information on the history of French eighteenth-century cuisine, I am indebted to the researches of Barbara Ketcham Wheaton, *Savoring the Past: The French Kitchen and Table from 1300 to 1789* (New York: Touchstone Books, 1996) and

"Le Cuisinier Gascon," *Petits Propos Culinaires* 14 (June 1983): pp. 55–57; Philip and Mary Hyman, "La Chapelle and Massialot: An Eighteenth Century Feud," *Petits Propos Culinaires* 2 (Aug. 1979): pp. 44–54; and "Vincent La Chapelle," *Petits Propos Culinaires* 8 (June 1981): pp. 36–40; and Christian Guy, *Histoire de la gastronomie en France* (Paris: Éditions Fernand Nathan, 1985).

The history of aphrodisiacs is taken from a series of articles published in *Petits Propos Culinaires,* including Lesley Chamberlain, "On Aphrodisiacs" (no. 55, May 1997): pp. 8–11; Patience Gray, "More on Aphrodisiacs" (no. 56, Sept. 1997): pp. 44–46; and Andrew Dalby, "The Name of the Rose Again; or, What Happened to Theophrastus on Aphrodisiacs?" (no. 64, April 2000): pp. 9–15. Alan Davidson is cited from his article "Aphrodisiacs" (no. 57, Dec. 1997): pp. 8–10. See also *The Oxford Companion to Food* (Oxford: Oxford University Press, 1999). Further background on the subject comes from Peter V. Taberner, *Aphrodisiacs: The Science and the Myth* (Philadelphia: University of Pennsylvania Press, 1985); Curnonsky and André Saint-Georges, *La table et l'amour: Nouveau traité des excitants modernes* (Paris: La Clé d'Or, 1950); and Georges Duby, editor, *Amour et sexualité en Occident* (Paris: Éditions du Seuil, 1991).

For M.F.K. Fisher, see *Consider the Oyster* (New York: Duell, Sloan and Pearce, 1941). Further research on oysters comes from Eleanor Clark, *The Oysters of Locmariaquer* (New York: Pantheon Books, 1966); and Joan Reardon and Ruth Ebling, *Oysters: A Culinary Celebration* (Orleans, Mass.: Parnassus Imprints, 1984).

Elizabeth David's series of articles on the history of ice cream from *Petits Propos Culinaires* provided background on the subject: "Hunt the Ice Cream" (no. 1, Feb. 1979): pp. 8–13; "Fromage Glacés and Other Iced Creams" (no. 2, Aug. 1979): pp. 23–35; and "Savour of Ice and Roses," (no. 8, June 1981): pp. 7–17.

Eighteenth-century wine and champagne was researched in Jancis Robinson, editor, *The Oxford Companion to Wine,* 2nd ed. (Oxford: Oxford University Press, 1999), James M. Gabler, *Passions: The Wines and Travels of Thomas Jefferson* (Baltimore: Bacchus Press, 1995), and at the Burgundy Wine Museum, Beaune.

I am grateful to Tamara Préaud, director of the Archives of the Manufacture at Sèvres, for her insights on what cardinal de Bernis might have owned; no record for a purchase exists in the archive. A rare pair of cooking Sèvres pans can be seen at the Wallace Collection, London. Among sources on the history of the decorative arts are Marie-Noëlle Pinot de Villechenon, *Sèvres: Une collection de porcelaines, 1740–1992*

(Paris: Réunion des musées nationaux, 1993); Philippa Glanville, editor, *Silver* (London: Victoria and Albert Museum, 1996); Karen Hess, "The Chafing Dish," *Petits Propos Culinaires* 2 (Aug. 1979): pp. 58–60, from whom I quote Seneca; and G. Bernard Hughes, "The Evolution of the Orange Strainer," *Country Life* 143, no. 3714 (May 9, 1968): pp. 1240–1242. For Jefferson's dumbwaiters, see Susan R. Stein, *The Worlds of Thomas Jefferson at Monticello* (New York: Harry N. Abrams, 1993).

The definition of a musical caprice is quoted from *The Oxford Dictionary of Music*, edited by Michael Kennedy with Joyce Bourne (Oxford: Oxford University Press, 1994). Donald Grant Mitchell is cited from the "Second Reverie" of *Reveries of a Bachelor, or, A Book of the Heart,* published under the pseudonym Ik Marvel (New York: Scribner's, 1890).

Theodore Zeldin is cited from *An Intimate History of Humanity* (New York: Harper Perennial, 1996) and is the source of the quote on eroticism.

Jean-Anthelme Brillat-Savarin is quoted from *The Physiology of Taste,* translated by Anne Drayton (first published in Paris: 1825; London: Penguin Classics, 1970).

Further background on the period was researched in Philippe Ariès and Georges Duby, editors, *Histoire de la vie privée*, vol. 3, *De la Renaissance aux Lumières* (Paris: Éditions du Seuil, 1999); and Claudine Marenco, *Manières de table, modèles de mœurs, 17ème – 20ème siècle* (Clamecy: Laballery, 1992).

CHAPTER NINE
Diplomacy

Charles-Maurice de Talleyrand-Périgord, *Mémoires: L'époque napoléonienne,* edited with notes by Jean Tulard (Paris: Imprimerie nationale, 1996), as well as the English edition of the complete memoirs, *Memoirs of the Prince de Talleyrand,* edited with a preface and notes by the Duc de Broglie, translated by Raphaël Ledos de Beaufort, 5 vols. (New York: G.P. Putnam's Sons, 1895), from which I have quoted, provided a glimpse into the Foreign Minister's mind. My knowledge of Talleyrand's background is further indebted to biographies by Jean Orieux, *Talleyrand: The Art of Survival,* translated by Patricia Wolf (New York: Alfred A. Knopf, 1974), which provided the primary basis for the account of the 1798 ball; J. F. Bernard, *Talleyrand: A Biography* (New York: G.P. Putnam's Sons, 1973); Crane Brinton, *The Lives of Talleyrand* (New York: W.W.

Norton & Company, 1963); Frédéric Loliée, *Talleyrand et la société européenne* (Paris: Émile-Paul, 1911); Joseph McCabe, *Talleyrand: A Biographical Study* (London: Hutchinson & Co., 1906); and Duff Cooper, *Talleyrand* (New York: Grove Press, 1932).

Vincent Cronin, *Napoleon* (London: HarperCollins, 1971), provided background on the Emperor and his relationship with Talleyrand, as did Constant, *Mémoires intimes de Napoléon Ier par Constant, son valet de chambre,* edited and annotated by Maurice Dernelle (Mesnil-sur-l'Estrée, France: Mercure de France, 2000); Proctor Paterson Jones, *Napoleon: An Intimate Account of the Years of Supremacy, 1800–1814* (San Francisco: Proctor Jones Publishing Co., 1992); and Alan Schom, *Napoleon Bonaparte* (New York: HarperCollins, 1997).

Anne Louise Germaine Necker de Staël-Holstein is quoted from her *Ten Years of Exile,* translated by Doris Beik (New York: Saturday Review Press, 1972).

Antonin Carême is cited from *Le Cuisinier parisien, ou l'art de la cuisine française au dix-neuvième siècle . . .* (first published 1828: new edition, Paris: 1854); *L'art de la cuisine française au XIXe siècle* (reprint, France: Éditions Payot & Rivages, 1994); *Le Pâtissier royal parisien,* 2 vols. (new edition, Leipzig and Paris: Au dépôt de librairie, 1854); and *Le Pâtissier royal parisien . . .* (reprint of 3rd ed. of 1841, Marseille: Lafitte Reprints, 1980). Translations are my own. Additional information comes from his biography by Georges Bernier, *Antonin Carême, 1783–1833: La sensualité gourmande en Europe* (Paris: Bernard Grasset, 1989); Jean-Claude Bonnet, "Carême, or the Last Sparks of Decorative Cuisine," in Alan S. Weiss, ed., *Taste Nostalgia* (New York: Lusitania Press, 1997); and Délégation à l'action artistique de la ville de Paris, *L'art Culinaire au XIXe siècle: Antonin Carême,* catalogue to the exhibition held at the Orangerie de Bagatelle, Paris, 1984 (Paris: Imprimerie Alençonnaise, 1984).

Pierre Waleffe, ed., *Les Classiques de la table* (Lausanne: La porte d'or, 1967) contains Carême's "Mémoires" as well as Louis de Cussy's "L'art culinaire" and Alexandre-Balthazar-Laurent Grimod de La Reynière's "Calendrier gastronomique de l'Almanach des Gourmands." Grimod is also quoted from Grimod de La Reynière, *Écrits gastronomiques . . .* edited by Jean-Claude Bonnet (Paris: Éditions 10/18, 1997). For Brillat-Savarin, see *The Physiology of Taste,* translation and introduction by Anne Drayton, (London: Penguin Books, 1970); for Alexandre Dumas, *Dumas on Food: Recipes and Anecdotes from the Classic Grand Dictionnaire de Cuisine,* translated by Alan and Jane

Davidson (Oxford: Oxford University Press, 1978). See also Eugène Briffant, *Paris à table* (Paris: J. Hetzel, 1846). I am especially indebted to Julia Abramson, not only for her article, "Grimod's Debt to Mercier and the Emergence of Gastronomic Writing Reconsidered," in *EMI: Early Modern France* 7, no. 2 (2001), pp. 141–162, but also for her comments on a draft of this chapter.

My kind thanks go out to Tamara Préaud at the Archives de la Manufacture, Sèvres, who helped me locate Talleyrand's porcelain orders. Among other sources, her texts—one with Nicole Blondel, *La manufacture nationale de Sèvres: Parcours du blanc à l'or* (Paris: FLOHIC, 1996), and another with Marcelle Brunet, *Sèvres—Des origines à nos jours* (Switzerland: Office du livre, 1978)—provided background on the factory under Brongniart. Also of use were Marie-Noëlle Pinot de Villechenon, *Sèvres: Une collection de porcelaines, 1740–1992* (Paris: Réunion des musées nationaux, 1993); and Régine de Plinval de Guillebon, *Faïence et porcelaine de Paris, XVIIIe – XIXe siècles* (Dijon: Éditions Faton, 1995).

Pier Luigi Pizzi, general editor, *Versailles et les tables royales en Europe,* catalogue to the exhibition held at the Musée National des Châteaux de Versailles et de Trianon, 2 Nov. 1993–27 Feb. 1994 (Paris: Éditions de la Réunion des musées nationaux, 1993), provided background on the imperial nef (now at Malmaison). Other helpful sources about the decorative arts include Gertrud Benker, *Alte Bestecke* (Munich: Verlag Georg D. W. Callway, 1978); Faith Denis, *Three Centuries of French Domestic Silver: Its Makers and Its Marks* (New York: Metropolitan Museum of Art, 1960); Claude Frégnac, general editor, *French Master Goldsmiths and Silversmiths from the Seventeenth to the Nineteenth Century* (New York: French and European Publications, 1966); and Marie-Josée Linou, *À table! Les arts de la table dans les collections du Musée Mandet de Riom, XVIIe – XIXe siècles* (Riom, France: Réunion des musées nationaux, 1997).

I am also grateful to the Italian Cultural Institute of Paris, which kindly allowed me to tour and photograph the Hôtel Gallifet.

Further background on dining in the period was researched in Jean-Louis Flandrin and Massimo Montinari, *Food: A Culinary History from Antiquity to the Present Time,* translated by Albert Sonnenfeld (New York: Columbia University Press, 1999); Leo Moulin, *Les Liturgies de la table: Une histoire culturelle du manger et du boire* (Anvers: Fonds Mercator, 1988); Anne-Marie Nesbit and Victor-André Massena, *L'Empire à table* (Paris: Adam Biro, 1988); and *Sucre d'Art,* catalogue to the exhibition held 8 Feb.–17 April 1978 (Paris: Musée des arts décoratifs, 1978).

Chapter Ten
Family

I am profoundly grateful for the assistance of Norah C. Gillow, Keeper of the William Morris Gallery, Walthamstow, London, for her patient suggestions, and for providing photographs, as well as to the gallery's exhibitions for quotes regarding the Red House from Georgiana Burne-Jones.

The primary source for this story is George Bernard Shaw's essay "William Morris As I Knew Him" (New York: Dodd, Mead & Co., 1936), reproduced in May Morris, *William Morris: Artist Writer Socialist,* 2 vols. (Oxford: Basil Blackwell, 1936). Quotes from May Morris and William Morris, including excerpts from "The Lesser Arts," "The Beauty of Life," and *News from Nowhere* and the letter to Eirikr Magnússon are taken from the same volumes. Gillian Naylor, editor, *William Morris by Himself: Designs and Writings* (Boston: Little Brown and Company, 2000) provided useful quotes, including journal entries from 9 and 15 July 1871, regarding the trip to Iceland and the letter from Warrington Taylor to Rossetti regarding Morris's spending on wine. Further background on Morris comes from Peter Stansky, *William Morris* (Oxford: 1983) and Elbert Hubbard, *Little Journeys to the Homes of English Authors: William Morris* (East Auroria, N.Y.: Roycrofters, 1900), which is the source of the Whistler quote.

Discussion of Shaw's personality comes from Edith Nesbitt, letter to Ada Breakell, 19 August 1884; on vegetarianism, published in *The Vegetarian,* London, 15 January, 1898; William Archer's remarks; and Shaw on social avoidance are taken from Archibald Henderson's *George Bernard Shaw: Man of the Century* (New York: Appleton-Century-Crofts, Inc., 1956). Shaw's *Collected Letters: 1874–1897,* vol. 1, edited by Dan H. Laurence (New York: Viking Penguin, 1985), and *An Unsocial Socialist,* with introductions by R. F. Dietrich and Barbara Bellow Watson (New York: W.W. Norton & Co., 1972), were also helpful.

Jan Marsh's *Jane and May Morris: A Biographical Story, 1839–1938* (West Sussex, England: The Printed Word, 2000) provided useful background on Jane's upbringing and education as well as the domestic life of the Morrises. Helena Sickert is cited from this text, as well as Morris's grumblings about Bessie Burden. Debra N. Mancoff's *Jane Morris: The Pre-Raphaelite Model of Beauty* (San Francisco: Pomegranate, 2000) contains the stories of Rossetti's party behavior and further details of Jane's domestic life.

Mrs. Isabella Beeton is quoted from the first edition of *The Book of Household Management* (London: S. O. Beeton, 1861). Background on kitchens and etiquette in this period were researched in sources that include John Cordy Jeafferson, *A Book About the Table,* vol. 2 (London: Hurst & Blackett, 1875); Robert Roberts, *Roberts' Guide for Butlers & Other Household Staff* (Boston: 1827; Bedford, Mass.: Applewood Books, 1993).

Information regarding the Mackay silver service is drawn from Charles L. Venable, *Silver in America, 1840–1940: A Century of Splendor,* catalogue to the exhibition held at the Dallas Museum of Art, Dallas, Texas (New York: Harry N. Abrams, 1995); and Charles H. Carpenter, "The Mackay Service Made by Tiffany and Company," *The Magazine Antiques* 114, no. 10 (October 1978): pp. 794–800. I am indebted to the teaching of Edward Munves Jr. at James Robinson, Inc., for further background on the introduction of new flatware pieces in this period.

François Maximilien Misson is quoted from "Pudding," in Alan Davidson, editor, *The Oxford Companion to Food* (Oxford: Oxford University Press, 1999), which is also the source for information on vegetarianism in Victorian England. Early English pudding recipes are taken from A. W., *A Book of Cookyre: very necessary for all such as delight therein* (London: Edward Ailde, 1587), a facsimile of which was kindly provided to me by Barbara Ketcham Wheaton; and Joseph Cooper, *The Art of Cookery Refined and Augmented . . .* (London: J. G. for R. Lowndes, 1654). Early English cooking and kitchens were also researched in P. W. Hammond, *Food and Feast in Medieval England* (Thrup, Stroud, Gloucestershire: Sutton Publishing, 1993); Pamela A. Sambrook and Peter Brears, *The Country House Kitchen, 1650–1900: Skills and Equipment for Food Provisioning* (Thrup, Stroud, Gloucestershire: Sutton Publishing in association with the National Trust, 1996); and Alison Sim, *The Tudor Housewife* (Thrup, Stroud, Gloucestershire: Sutton Publishing, 1996).

Further background on the Victorian period is drawn from Philippe Ariès, *Centuries of Childhood: A Social History of Family Life,* translated from the French by Robert Baldick (New York: Vintage Books, 1962); Michelle Perrot, editor, *A History of Private Life,* vol. 4, *From the Fires of Revolution to the Great War* (Cambridge, Mass.:

The Belknap Press of Harvard University Press, 1990); and Norman Rich, *The Age of Nationalism and Reform, 1850–1890,* 2nd ed. (New York: W.W. Norton & Co., 1977).

Chapter Eleven
Eat, Drink, and Be Merry, for Tomorrow We Die

This chapter is based upon Alma Mahler-Werfel's diary entries for 18 and 19 January 1900, in *Diaries, 1898–1902,* selected and translated by Antony Beaumont, from the German edition transcribed and edited by Antony Beaumont and Susanne Rode Breymann (Ithaca, New York: Cornell University Press, 1999). This edition also contains reproductions of the invitation and menu cards. Further quotes from Alma are taken from her autobiography, *And the Bridge Is Love* (New York: Harcourt Brace and Co., 1958). Additional background on Alma was researched in Susanne Keegan, *Bride of the Wind* (New York: Viking, 1993); Karen Monson, *Alma Mahler: Muse to Genius* (Boston: Houghton Mifflin Co., 1983); and Susan Filler, *Gustav and Alma Mahler* (New York: Garland, 1989); and, pertaining to her relationship with Kokoschka, their love letters in Alfred Weidinger, *Kokoschka and Alma Mahler,* English translation by Fiona Elliott (Munich: Prestel, 1996); and Oskar Kokoschka, *Oskar Kokoschka Letters: 1905–1976,* selected by Olda Kokoschka and Alfred Marnau (New York: Thames and Hudson, 1992).

Quotes from *Ver Sacrum* and the Wiener Werkstätte are reprinted from the English translations appearing in Peter Vergo, *Art in Vienna, 1898–1918: Klimt, Kokoschka, Schiele, and Their Contemporaries,* 3rd ed. (London: Phaidon Press, 1993). Sources consulted for further background on the Secession include Edwin Becker and Sabine Grabner, general editors, *Wien 1900: Der Blick nach innen,* catalogue to the exhibition held 21 March–15 June 1997, Van Gogh Museum, Amsterdam, and 13 July–5 October 1997, Von der Heydt-Museum, Wuppertal (Amsterdam: Van Gogh Museum, 1997); Gabriele Fahr-Becker, *Wiener Werkstætte, 1903–1932,* English translation by Karen Williams and High Warden (Cologne, Germany: Taschen, 1995); Werner J. Schweiger, *Meisterwerke der Wiener Werkstætte Kunst und Handwerk* (Vienna: Verlag Christian Brandstätter, 1990); and Peter Noever, editor, *Josef Hoffmann Designs* (Munich: Prestel, for the MAK [Austrian Museum of Applied Arts], Vienna, 1992). Visits to the Secession Building, the MAK, and the Hohe Warte in Vienna provided additional insights.

I am also indebted to Helen Smith for sharing her unpublished paper and photographs of the Moll residence from "Josef Hoffmann's Artists' Colony in the Hohe Warte: A Reaction to Metropolis" (unpublished paper for Prof. Esther da Costa Meyer, Yale University, April 1993).

Moll's recollection of evenings with Moser is from Hans Dirchland, *Carl Moll, seine Freunde, sein Leben, sein Werk* (Salzburg: Verlag Galerie Welz Salzburg, 1985); further information on Moll is from G. Tobias Natter and Gerbert Frodl, *Carl Moll (1861–1945)*, catalogue to the exhibition held at the Belvedere, 10 Sept.–22 Nov. 1998 (Vienna: Österreichische Galerie; and Salzburg: Verlag Galerie Welz, 1998). Dr. Natter was also kind enough to assist me with photo research.

References to Katharina Schratt and her recipe collection are taken from Gertrud Graubart Champe, editor, *To Set Before the King: Katharina Schratt's Festive Recipes*, translated by Paula von Haimberger Arno in collaboration with Chef Louis Szathmáry, foreword by David E. Schoonover (Iowa City: University of Iowa Press, 1996), except for Alma's story about Burckhard, which appears in her autobiography.

Other particularly useful sources in illuminating Vienna of the day were Frederic Morton's *A Nervous Splendor: Vienna, 1888–1889* (London: Penguin Books, 1979); and Allan Janik and Stephen Toulmin, *Wittgenstein's Vienna* (New York: Simon & Schuster, 1973).

CHAPTER TWELVE
Shocking the World

The story of Caresse Crosby's picnic was kindly pointed out to me by Lisa Jacobs, who also generously shared her notes and insights from her article "Julien Levy's Surrealist Art Galaxy," published in *Surrealistas en el exilio y los inicios de la Escuela de Nueva York*, catalogue to the exhibition held at the Museo Nacional Centro de Arte Reina Sofía, Madrid, 12 Dec. 1999–27 Feb. 2000, pp. 396–399. Jacobs's book with Ingrid Schaffner, *Julien Levy: Portrait of an Art Gallery* (Cambridge: M.I.T. Press, 1998), provided additional background. I am also indebted to Ms. Jacobs for her video collage from the related exhibition, which includes the film shot by Levy and Ernst; as well as for putting me into contact with the Julien Levy Estate, who has kindly allowed me to publish stills from it. I am also grateful to Karole Vail, not only for sharing her insights on

Peggy Guggenheim and the Surrealist coterie but also for introducing me to Ms. Jacobs.

The primary source for this story is Julien Levy's *Memoir of an Art Gallery* (New York: G.P. Putnam's Sons, 1977). Levy is also quoted from his *Surrealism* (New York: Black Sun Press, 1936; New York: Arno Press, 1968), which is also the source for Harry Crosby's "On the Grounds of Indecency." Caresse Crosby's autobiography, *The Passionate Years* (New York: Dial Press, 1953; reprinted, New York: The Ecco Press, 1979), also discusses the event. I am also indebted to Desmond O'Grady for his recollections of Caresse and for pointing me to Anne Conover's *Caresse Crosby: From Black Sun to Roccasinibalda* (Santa Barbara: Capra Press, 1989), which contained the quote by Dalí on the Moulin; Harry's "*One*-ness" and diary extract; and Anaïs Nin on Caresse.

Dalí is quoted from *The Secret Life of Salvador Dalí,* translated by Haakon M. Chevalier (New York: Dial Press, 1942); Robert Descharnes, *The World of Salvador Dalí,* translated by Albert Field and Haakon Chevalier (New York: The Viking Press, 1962); *Les dîners de Gala,* translated by Captain J. Peter Moore (New York: Felicie, 1973) and *Pensées et anecdotes,* introduction by Robert Descharnes (Paris: Le Cherche Midi, 1995). Robert Irwin's "The Disgusting Dinners of Salvador Dalí," in *Food in the Arts: Proceedings of the Oxford Symposium on Food and Cookery, 1998* (Totnes, Devon: Prospect Books, 1999), pp. 103–111, offered further insight into Dalí's use of food, in addition to my own study of the artist's work. Quotes from Breton, and the poets he extolled are taken from his *Manifestoes of Surrealism,* translated from the French by Richard Seaver and Helen R. Lane (Ann Arbor: Ann Arbor Paperbacks, University of Michigan Press, 1990). Alfred Jarry's "Fable" is my own translation from the French, which appears in Jacques-Henry Levesque, *Alfred Jarry, une étude par Jacques-Henry Levesque* (Paris: Seghers, 1951).

René Crevel is quoted from *Mr. Knife, Miss Fork,* translated by Kay Boyle, illustrated by Max Ernst (Paris: Black Sun Press, 1931). Lautréamont is quoted from *Les Chants de Maldoror,* translated by Guy Wernham, together with a translation of Lautréamont's *Poésies* (New York: New Directions, 1946). Ruth Brandon's *Surreal Lives: The Surrealists, 1917–1945* (New York: Grove Press, 1999) provided further biographical background on the movement.

I am grateful to Andy Smith for pointing me toward Vincent M. Holt's *Why Not Eat Insects?* (1885), reprinted with an introduction by Laurence Mound, Keeper of Entomology, British Museum (Yorkletts, Whitstable, Kent: Pryor Publications, ca. 1992). Information regarding Futurist meals is taken from Filippo Tommaso Marinetti, *The Futurist Cookbook,* translated by Susanne Brill, edited with an introduction by Lesley Chamberlain, first published as *La cucina futurista,* 1932 (London: Trefoil Publications; and San Franscisco: Bedford Arts Publishers, 1989). Trimalchio's feast comes from Petronius, *The Satyricon,* published with Seneca's *The Apocolocyntosis,* rev. ed., translated with an introduction and notes by J. P. Sullivan (London: Penguin Books, 1986). A discussion of Grimod de La Reynière's funereal banquets is provided in Jean-Claude Bonnet's introduction to Grimod's *Écrits gastronomiques: Almanach des gourmands (Première année: 1803) suivi de Manuel des Amphitryons (1808)* (Paris: Éditions 10/18, 1997). Barbara Ketcham Wheaton's *Savoring the Past* (New York: Touchstone, 1996) also touches on these events. The story of the Natanson cocktail party is taken from Arthur Gold and Robert Fizdale, *Misia: The Life of Misia Sert* (New York: Vintage Books, 1992).

Select Bibliography

Abramson, Julia. "Grimod's Debt to Mercier and the Emergence of Gastronomic Writing Reconsidered." *EMI: Studies in Early France* 7, no. 2 (2001): pp. 141–162.

Adelung, Johann Christoph. *The Life and Character, Rise and Conduct, of Count Bruhl, Prime Minister to the King of Poland, Elector of Saxony; In a Series of Letters, by an Emminent Hand. Throwing a light on the real Origin of the Past and Present War in Germany, and the Intrigues of Several Powers.* Translation from the German ascribed to H. G. von Justi and J. C. Adelung. London: M. Cooper and C. G. Seyffert, ca. 1765.

Albala, Ken. *Eating Right in the Renaissance.* Berkeley: University of California Press, 2002.

Albertine, Susan, ed. *A Living of Words: American Women in Print Culture.* Knoxville: University of Tennessee Press, 1995.

Algar, Ayla. "Bushaq of Shiraz: Poet, Parasite, and Gastronome." *Petits Propos Culinaires* 31 (March 1989): pp. 9–20.

Allied Newspapers Limited. *Crowning the King: The History, Symbolism, and Meaning of the Coronation Ceremony.* London: Syndicate Publishing, Co., 1937.

Amaranthes [Gottlieb Siegmund Corvinus]. *Nutzbares, galantes und curiöses Frauenzimmer-Lexicon: Worinnen nicht nur Der Frauenzimmer geistlich und weltliche Orden, Aemter, Würden, Ehrenstellen, Professionen und Gewerbe, Privilegia und Rechtliche Wohlthaten, Hochzeiten und Trauer-Solemnitäten, Gerade und Erb-Stücken, Nahmen und Thaten der Göttinnen, Heroinen, gelehrter Weibes-Bilder, Künstlerinnen, und anderer merckwürdigen Personen weiblichen Geschlechts; Dererselben Trachten und Moden, und was zum Putz und Kleidung des Frauenzimmers, und Auszierung der*

Gemächer gehöret; ihre häusliche Verrichtungen, Ergötzlichkeiten, Redens-Arten, und was sonst einem Frauenzimmer zu wissen nöthig, ordentlich nach dem Alphabeth kurtz und deutlich erkläret zu finden, sondern auch ein vollkommenes und auf die allerneueste Art verfertigtes Koch-, Torten- und Gebackens-Buch, Samt denen darzu gehörigen Küchen-Zetteln und Rissen von Taffel-Aufsätzen, 1715. Frankfurt and Leipzig: Joh. Friedrich Gleditsch und Sohn, 1739.

Amaranthes [Gottlieb Siegmund Corvinus]. *Nutzbares, galantes und curiöses Frauen-zimmer-Lexicon.* . . . Frankfurt and Leipzig: Joh. Friedrich Gleditsch und Sohn, 1739, revised and augmented 1768.

Ambrose, Kirk Thomas. "Romanesque Vézelay: The Art of Monastic Contemplation." Ph.D. diss., University of Michigan, 1999.

Amme, Jochen. *Bestecke: Die Egloffstein'sche Sammlung (15. – 18. Jahrhundert) auf der Wartburg.* Stuttgart: Arnoldsche, 1994.

Archestratus. *The Life of Luxury: Europe's Oldest Cookery Book.* Translated with introduction and commentary by John Wilkins and Shaun Hill. Totnes, Devon: Prospect Books, 1994.

Aretino, Pietro. *The Works of Pietro Aretino.* 2 vols. Translated into English from the original Italian, with a critical and biographical essay by Samuel Putnam. Chicago: Pascal Covici, 1926.

Ariès, Philippe. *Centuries of Childhood: A Social History of Family Life.* Translated from the French by Robert Baldick. New York: Vintage Books, 1962.

Ariès, Philippe, and Georges Duby, eds. *Histoire de la vie privée.* Vol. 3, *De la Renais-sance aux Lumières.* Paris: Éditions du Seuil, 1999.

Ariosto, Lodovico. *Orlando furioso,* 2 vols. (First published in 3 volumes, 1516, 1521, and 1532.) Presented by Italo Calvino, with introduction, notes, and bibliography by Lanfranco Caretti, 2 vols. Turin: Einaudi, 1966.

Artusi, Pellegrino. *The Art of Eating Well.* Translated by Kyle M. Phillips III. Originally published as *La scienza in cucina e l'arte di mangiar bene;* Italy: 1891. New York: Random House, 1996.

Audoin-Rouzeau, Frédérique. *Ossements animaux du Moyen âge au monastère de La Charité-sur-Loire.* Paris: Publications de la Sorbonne, 1986.

Augustine, Saint. *Confessions.* Translated by E. Pusey. London: S. M. Dent & Sons, 1907.

Bailey, Charles Thomas Peach. *Knives and Forks.* London: The Medici Society, 1927.

Ballerini, Luigi. "Casanova, Man of Appetites," *The Magazine of La Cucina Italiana* 3, no. 5 (Sept.–Oct. 1998): pp. 80–82.

Barofsky, Paul. *Michelangelo's Nose.* University Park: Pennsylvania State University Press, 1990.

Becker, Edwin, and Sabine Grabner, eds. *Wien 1900: Der Blick nach innen.* Catalogue to the exhibition held 21 March–15 June 1997, Van Gogh Museum, Amsterdam, and 13 July–5 October 1997, Von der Heydt-Museum, Wuppertal. Amsterdam: Van Gogh Museum, 1997.

Beeton, Mrs. Isabella. *The Book of Household Management.* London: S. O. Beeton, 1861.

Bement, Lewis D. *The Cutlery Story.* Deerfield, Mass.: Associated Cutlers of America, 1950.

Benedict, Saint. *La Règle de Saint Benoît.* A.D. 534–547. New translation by a monk of Solesmes, 2nd ed. Sablé-sur-Sarthe, France: Abbaye Saint-Pierre de Solesmes, 1988.

Benker, Gertrud. *Alte Bestecke.* Munich: Verlag Georg D.W. Callway, 1978.

Benporat, Claudio. "A Discovery at the Vatican: The First Italian Treatise on the Art of the *Scalco* (Head Steward)." *Petits Propos Culinaires* 30 (November 1988): pp. 41–45.

———. *Storia della gastronomia italiana.* Milan: Mursia, 1990.

Berenson, Bernard. *Italian Painters of the Renaissance.* Vol. 1, *Venetian and North Italian Schools.* 1894–1907. London: Phaidon Paperback, 1968.

Berlioz, Jacques, ed. *Moines et religieux au Moyen âge.* Paris: Éditions du Seuil, 1994.

Bernard, Jack F. *Talleyrand: A Biography.* New York: G.P. Putnam's Sons, 1973.

Bernier, Georges. *Antonin Carême, 1783–1833: La sensualité gourmande en Europe.* Paris: Bernard Grasset, 1989.

Bernis, François-Joachim [de Pierre] de. *Mémoires du cardinal de Bernis.* Preface by Jean-Marie Rouart. Annotated by Philippe Bonnet. Mesnil-sur-l'Estrée, France: Mercure de France, 1986.

Bibliothèque nationale de France. *Livres en bouche: Cinq siècles d'art culinaire français.* Catalogue to the exhibition held 21 November–17 February, 2001, at the Bibliothèque de l'Arsenal, Paris. Paris: Hermann, 2001.

Blair, Claude, ed. *The History of Silver.* New York: Ballantine Books, 1987.

Blond, Georges and Germaine. *Histoire pittoresque de notre alimentation.* Paris: Librairie Arthème Fayard, 1960.

Blondel, Nicole, and Tamara Préaud. *La manufacture nationale de Sèvres: Parcours du blanc à l'or.* Paris: FLO HIC, 1996.

Bober, Phyllis Pray. *Art, Culture, and Cuisine: Ancient and Medieval Gastronomy.* Chicago: University of Chicago Press, 1999.

Bonnefons, Nicolas de. *Les délices de la campagne, suite du Jardinier françois.* 6th ed. First published 1654. Paris: Nicolas Le Gras, 1684.

Bonnet, Jean-Claude. "Carême, or the Last Sparks of Decorative Cuisine." In *Taste Nostalgia,* edited by Alan S. Weiss. New York: Lusitania Press, 1997.

Bourgeois-Cornu, Laetitia. *Les Bonnes herbes du Moyen âge.* Paris: Publisud, 1999.

Bourin, Jeanne, with Jeannine Thomassin. *Cuisine médiévale pour tables d'aujourd'hui.* Paris: Flammarion, 2000.

Brandon, Ruth. *Surreal Lives: The Surrealists, 1917–1945.* New York: Grove Press, 1999.

Brears, Peter. *English Heritage Food and Cooking in Seventeenth-Century Britain: History and Recipes.* England: English Heritage, 1985.

Breton, André. *Manifestoes of Surrealism.* Translated from the French by Richard Seaver and Helen R. Lane. Ann Arbor: Ann Arbor Paperbacks, University of Michigan Press, 1990.

Briffant, Eugène. *Paris à table.* Paris: J. Hetzel, 1846.

Brillat-Savarin, Jean-Anthelme. *The Physiology of Taste.* Translated by Anne Drayton. First published in Paris: 1825; London: Penguin Classics, 1970.

Brinton, Crane. *The Lives of Talleyrand.* New York: W.W. Norton & Company, 1963.

Brunet, Marcelle, and Tamara Préaud. *Sèvres—Des origines à nos jours.* Switzerland: Office du livre, 1978.

Buisine, Alain. *Cènes et banquets de Venise.* Cadeilhan, France: Zulma, 2000.

Bynum, Caroline Walker. *Holy Feast and Holy Fast: The Religious Significance of Food to Medieval Women.* Berkeley: University of California Press, 1987.

Cairns, Christopher. *Pietro Aretino and the Republic of Venice: Researches on Aretino and his Circle in Venice, 1527–1556.* Florence: Leo S. Olschki, 1985.

Callea, Olivia. *Régions gourmandes: La Bourgogne.* Paris: Hatier, 1995.

Cambornac, Michel. *Plantes et jardins du Moyen âge.* Paris: EDIPSO Édition, 1996.

Carême, Antonin. *Le pâtissier royal parisien, ou, Traité élémentaire et pratique de la pâtisserie ancienne et moderne, de l'entremets de sucre, des entrées froides et des socles; suivi d'observations utile au progrès de cet art, d'une série de plus de soixante menus, et d'une revue critique des grands bals de 1810 et 1811. Composé par M. A. Carême; Ouvrage orné de 70 planches dessinées par l'auteur, comprenant plus de 250 sujets. Paris: J. G. Dentu, 1815.

———. Le maître d'hôtel français. Paris: Firmin Didot, 1822.

———. Le Cuisinier parisien, ou l'art de la cuisine française au dix-neuvième siècle: traité élémentaire et pratique des entrées froides, des socles, et des entremets de sucre, suivi d'observations utiles aux progrès de ces deux parties de la cuisine moderne. Paris: Firmin Didot, 1828. New edition, Paris: 1854.

———. Le Pâtissier royal parisien, ou Traité élémentaire et pratique de la pâtisserie ancienne et moderne; suivi d'observations utiles aux progrès de cet art, et d'une revue critique des grands bals de 1810 et 1811. 2 vols. New edition, Leipzig and Paris: Dépôt de librairie, 1854.

———. Le Pâtissier royal parisien: ou Traité élémentaire et pratique de la pâtisserie ancienne et moderne. Reprint of 3rd ed. of 1841, Marseille: Lafitte Reprints, 1980.

———. L'art de la cuisine française au XIXe siècle. Reprint. France: Éditions Payot & Rivages, 1994.

Carocci, Guido. La villa medicea di Careggi: memorie e ricordi. Florence: 1888.

Carpenter, Charles H. "The Mackay Service Made by Tiffany and Company." The Magazine Antiques 114, no. 10 (October 1978): pp. 794–800.

Casanova, Giovanni Giacomo [de Seingalt]. The Life and Memoirs of Casanova. Translated from the French by Arthur Machen. First complete and unabridged translation in English. 1929; New York: G.P. Putnam's Sons, 1959.

———. History of My Life. 6 vols. Translated into English from the original French manuscript by Willard R. Trask. New York: Harcourt, Brace and World, 1966.

———. Histoire de ma vie. Selections edited by Jean-Michel Gardair. Paris: Gallimard, 1986.

———. Histoire de ma vie. 3 vols. Prepared by Robert Laffont. Paris: Bouquins, 1993.

———. Mémoires: Histoire de ma vie. Paris: Arléa, 1993.

———. History of My Life. Translated by Willard R. Trask. Reprint; 12 volumes in 6 books. Baltimore: Johns Hopkins University Press, 1997.

———. Plaisirs de Bouche: Six épisodes extraits d'Histoire de ma vie. Edited by Ilona Kovács. Paris: Librio, 1998.

Castello Estense. *A tavola con il Principe: materiali per una mostra su alimentazione e cultura nella Ferrara degli Estensi*. Catalogue to the exhibition held 1 October 1988–27 March 1989 at Castello Estense, Ferrara, Italy. Ferrara: Amministrazione provinciale di Ferrara, ca. 1988.

Castiglione, Baldassare. *The Book of the Courtier*. Translated with an introduction by George Bull. Harmondsworth: Penguin, 1967.

Cato, Marcius Porcius. *On Farming*. Commentary and translation by Andrew Dalby. Totnes, Devon: Prospect Books, 1998.

Cellini, Bevenuto. *Autobiography*. Written 1558–1566. Translated with an introduction by George Bull. London: Penguin Books, 1956.

Cervio, Vincenzo. *Il trinciante*. 1593, facsimile reproduction, Bologna: Arnaldo Forni Editore, 1980.

Chamberlain, Lesley. "On Aphrodisiacs." *Petits Propos Culinaires* 55 (May 1997): pp. 8–11.

Champe, Gertrud Graubart, ed. *To Set before the King: Katharina Schratt's Festive Recipes*. Translated by Paula von Haimberger Arno in collaboration with Chef Louis Szathmáry. Foreword by David E. Schoonover. Iowa City: University of Iowa Press, 1996.

Chang, K. C., ed. *Food in Chinese Culture: Anthropological and Historical Perspectives*. New Haven: Yale University Press, 1977.

Charles I, Sovereign, England and Wales. *By the King: A Proclamation to Declare His Maiesties Pleasures Touching His Royall Coronation*. London: Bonham Norton & Iohn Bill, 1625, i.e., 1626.

Childs, James Rives. *Casanova: A New Perspective*. New York: Paragon House Publishers, 1988.

———. *Casanova*. Translated into French by Francis L. Mars. First published in English in 1961. Paris: Jean-Jacques Pauvert aux Éditions Garnier Frères, 1983.

Choisy, abbé de. *Mémoires pour servir à l'histoire de Louis XIV, par sieur M. l'abbé de Choisy*. 5th ed. 2 vols. in 12. Utrecht: Van-de-Water, 1727.

Church of England. *The Manner of the Coronation of Charles the First of England at Westminster, 2 February, 1626*. Edited by Christopher Wordsworth. London: Henry Bradshaw Liturgical Text Society, 1892.

Ciardi Duprè Dal Poggetto, Maria Grazia, curator. *L'oreficeria nella Firenze del Quattrocento*. Florence: Studio per Edizioni Scelte, 1977.

Clark, Eleanor. *The Oysters of Locmariaquer.* New York: Pantheon Books, 1966.

Clark, Kenneth. *Landscape into Art.* London: John Murray, 1949.

Cleugh, James. *The Divine Aretino.* New York: Stein and Day, 1966.

Conover, Anne. *Caresse Crosby: From Black Sun to Roccasinibalda.* Santa Barbara: Capra Press, 1989.

Constable, Giles, ed. *Cluniac Studies.* London: Variorum Reprints, 1980.

Constable, Giles, and James Kritzeck. *Petrus Venerabilis, 1156–1956; Studies and Texts Commemorating the Eighth Centenary of His Death.* Rome: Orbis Catholicis, 1956.

Constant. *Mémoires intimes de Napoléon Ier par Constant, son valet de chambre.* Edited and annotated by Maurice Dernelle. Mesnil-sur-l'Estrée: Mercure de France, 2000.

Cooper, Duff. *Talleyrand.* New York: Grove Press, 1932.

Cooper, Joseph. *The Art of Cookery Refined and Augmented. Containing an Abstract of some rare and rich unpublished Receipts of Cookery: Collected from the practise of that incomparable Master of these Arts, Mr. Jos. Cooper, chiefe Cook to the Late King; With Severall other practises by the Author, with an addition of Preserves, Conserves, &c. offering an infallible delight to all Judicious Readers.* London: J. G. for R. Lowndes, 1654.

Cora, Galeazzo, and Angiolo Fanfani. *La porcellana dei Medici.* Milan: Fabbri Editori, 1986.

Corns, Thomas N., ed. *The Royal Image: Representations of Charles I.* Cambridge: Cambridge University Press, 1999.

Coryat[e], Thomas. *Coryats Crudities Hastily gobled up in five Moneths travells in France, Savoy, Italy, Rhetia commonly called the Grisons country, Helvetia aliàs Switzerland, some parts of high Germany, and the Netherlands; Newly digested in the hungry aire of ODCOMBE in the County of Somerset, & now dispersed to the nourishment of the travelling Members of this Kingdome.* London: W. S[tansby, for the author], 1611.

Courtin, Antoine de. *Nouveau traité de la civilité qui se pratique en France parmi les honnêtes gens.* 1671. Reprinted with notes by Marie-Claire Grassi, Saint-Étienne, France: Publications de l'Université de Saint-Étienne, 1998.

Crevel, René. *Mr. Knife, Miss Fork.* Translated by Kay Boyle. Illustrated by Max Ernst. Paris: Black Sun Press, 1931.

Cronin, Vincent. *Napoleon.* London: HarperCollins, 1971.

———. *Louis and Antoinette.* London: William Collins and Sons & Co., 1974.

Crosby, Caresse. *The Passionate Years.* New York: Dial Press, 1953; reprinted, New York: The Ecco Press, 1979.

Crowe, Joseph Archer, and Giovanni Battista Cavalcaselle. *Titian: His Life and Times, With Some Account of His Family, Chiefly from New and Unpublished Records.* 2 vols. London: John Murray, 1877.

Curnonsky and André Saint-Georges. *La table et l'amour: Nouveau traité des excitants modernes.* Paris: La Clé d'Or, 1950.

Dalby, Andrew. "The *Banquet* of Philoxenus: A New Translation with Culinary Notes," *Petits Propos Culinaires* 26 (July 1987): pp. 28–36.

———. "The Wedding Feast of Caranus the Macedonian by Hippolochus," *Petits Propos Culinaires* 29 (July 1988): pp. 37–45.

———. "The Name of the Rose Again; or, What Happened to Theophrastus on Aphrodisiacs?" *Petits Propos Culinaires* 64 (April 2000): pp. 9–15.

Dalí, Salvador. *The Secret Life of Salvador Dalí.* Translated by Haakon M. Chevalier. New York: Dial Press, 1942.

———. *Les dîners de Gala.* Translated by Captain J. Peter Moore. New York: Felicie, 1973.

———. *Pensées et anecdotes.* Introduction by Robert Descharnes. Paris: Le Cherche Midi, 1995.

David, Elizabeth. "Hunt the Ice Cream," *Petits Propos Culinaires* 1 (Feb. 1979): pp. 8–13.

———. "Fromages Glacés and Other Iced Creams," *Petits Propos Culinaires* 2 (Aug. 1979): pp. 23–35.

———. "The Harvest of Cold Months," *Petits Propos Culinaires* 3 (Nov. 1979): pp. 8–16.

———. "Banketting Stuffe," *Petits Propos Culinaires* 3 (Nov. 1979): pp. 39–44.

———. "Savour of Ice and Roses," *Petits Propos Culinaires* 8 (June 1981): pp. 7–17.

Davidson Alan. "Aphrodisiacs," *Petits Propos Culinaires* 57 (Dec. 1997): pp. 8–10.

———, ed. *The Oxford Companion to Food.* Oxford: Oxford University Press, 1999.

Day, Ivan, ed. *Eat, Drink, and Be Merry: The British at Table, 1600–2000.* London: Philip Wilson Publishers, 2000.

Descharnes, Robert. *The World of Salvador Dalí.* Translated by Albert Field and Haakon Chevalier. New York: The Viking Press, 1962.

Délégation à l'action artistique de la ville de Paris. *L'art Culinaire au XIXe siècle: Antonin Carême.* Catalogue to the exhibition held at the Orangerie de Bagatelle, Paris, 1984. Paris: Délégation à l'action artistique de la ville de Paris, 1984.

Denis, Faith, *Three Centuries of French Domestic Silver: Its Makers and Its Marks.* New York: Metropolitan Museum of Art, 1960.

Dessert, Daniel. *Fouquet.* Montreuil, France: Librairie Arthème Fayard, 1987.

Dirchland, Hans. *Carl Moll, seine Freunde, sein Leben, sein Werk.* Salzburg: Verlag Galerie Welz Salzburg, 1985.

Di Romolo Rosselli, Stefano Francesco. *Mes secrets à Florence au temps des Médecis 1593; Pâtisserie, parfumerie, médecine.* Introduced and translated into French by Rodrigo de Zayas. Paris: Jean-Michel Place, 1996.

Douglas, Robert. *The Form and Order of the Coronation of Charles the II. King of Scotland, together With the Sermon then Preached, by Mr. Robert Dowglas &c. and the Oath then taken, with several Speeches made. As it was done at Scoone, The first day of January, 1651.* Aberdene: Imprinted by Charles Brown, and reprinted in London, 1660.

Dube, Wolf-Dieter. *The Expressionists.* English translation by Mary Whittall. London: Thames and Hudson, 1972.

Duby, Georges, ed. *Amour et sexualité en Occident.* Paris: Éditions du Seuil, 1991.

Duckett, Sir George Floyd. *Record-Evidences, among the archives of the ancient abbey of Cluni, From 1077 to 1534; illustrative of the history of some of our early kings; and many of its English affiliated foundations.* Lewes, England: printed for the author, 1886.

Dumas, Alexandre. *Dumas on Food: Recipes and Anecdotes from the Classic Grand Dictionnaire de Cuisine.* Translated by Alan and Jane Davidson. Oxford: Oxford University Press, 1978.

Dunn, Richard S. *The Age of Religious Wars: 1559–1715,* 2nd ed. New York: W. W. Norton and Co., 1979.

Elias, Norbert. *The Civilizing Process: The History of Manners.* 2 vols. Translated from the German by Edmund Jephcott. New York: Urizen Books, 1978.

Ennès, Pierre, Gérard Mabille, and Philippe Thiébaut. *Histoire de la table: les arts de la table des origines à nos jours.* Paris: Flammarion, 1994.

L'Escole parfaite des officiers de bouche: contenant le vray maistre-d'hostel. Le grand escuyer-tranchant. Le sommelier royal, le confiturier royal, le cuisinier royal. Et le pastissier royal. First published 1662. 3rd ed., Paris: Jean Ribou, 1666. 4th ed., Paris: Jean Ribou, 1682.

Fara, Amelio. *Buontalenti. Architettura e teatro.* Florence: La Nuova Italia, 1979.

———. *Bernardo Buontalenti: L'architettura, la guerra e l'elemento geometrico.* Genoa: Sagep Editrice, 1988.

Fahr-Becker, Gabriele. *Wiener Werkstätte, 1903–1932.* English translation by Karen Williams and High Warden. Cologne, Germany: Taschen, 1995.

Faucheux, Michel. *Fêtes de table.* Paris: Philippe Lebaud, 1999.

Feeley-Harnik, Gillian. *The Lord's table: The Meaning of Food in Early Judaism and Christianity.* Washington, D.C.: Smithsonian Institution Press, 1981.

Félibien, André. *Les Fêtes de Versailles: Chroniques de 1668 & 1674.* Presented by Martin Meade. Maisonneuve et Larose, France: Éditions Dédale, 1994.

———. *Relation de la feste de Versailles. Du dix-huitième Juillet mil six cens soixante-huit.* Paris: Pierre le Petit, 1668.

———. *Les plaisirs de l'isle enchantée. Course de bague; collation ornée de machines, comedie, meslée de danse et de musique; ballet du Palais d'Alcine; feu d'artifice: et autres festes galantes et magnifiques faites par le roy à Versailles, le VII May, 1664 et continuées plusieurs autres jours.* Paris: L'imprimerie royale, 1673.

Fellmann, Walter. *Heinrich Graf Brühl, Ein Lebens- und Zeitbild.* Leipzig: Koehler & Amelang, 1989.

Ficino, Marsilio. *Commentaire sur le banquet de Platon.* French translation by Raymond Marcel from the original Latin manuscript *De amore.* Paris: Les Belles Lettres, 1978.

———. *The Letters of Marsilio Ficino.* 5 vols. London: Shepheard-Walwyn, 1975–1994.

———. *Meditations on the Soul: Selected Letters of Marsilio Ficino.* Selected from *The Letters of Marsilio Ficino.* London: Shepheard-Walwyn, 1975–1994. Rochester, Vt.: Inner Traditions, 1996.

———. *Platonic Theology.* Vol. 1, Books 1–4. English translation by Michael J. B. Allen with John Warden. Latin text edited by James Hankins with William Bowen. Cambridge, Mass.: The I Tatti Renaissance Library, Harvard University Press, 2001.

———. *Three Books on Life.* First published as *De vita libri tres,* Florence: 1489. Introduction, translation, and notes by Carol V. Kaske and John R. Clark. Tempe, Ariz.: Medieval and Renaissance Texts and Studies, 1998.

Filler, Susan. *Gustav and Alma Mahler.* New York: Garland, 1989.

Fink, Beatrice. *Les liaisons savoureuses: réflections et pratiques culinaires au dix-huitième siècle.* Saint-Étienne, France: Publications de l'Université de Saint-Étienne, 1995.

Fisher, M.F.K. *Consider the Oyster.* New York: Duell, Sloan and Pearce, 1941.

Flandrin, Jean-Louis, and Carole Lambert. *Fêtes gourmandes au Moyen âge.* Paris: Imprimerie nationale, 1998.

Flandrin, Jean-Louis, and Massimo Montinari. *Food: A Culinary History from Antiquity to the Present Time.* Translated by Albert Sonnenfeld. New York: Columbia University Press, 1999.

Fleming, John, and Hugh Honour. *The Penguin Dictionary of Decorative Arts.* Revised edition. New York: Viking, 1989.

Fleurent, Maurice. *Vaux-le-Vicomte: La clairière enchantée.* Paris: Éditions Sous Le Vent, 1989.

France, Anatole. *Vaux-le-Vicomte.* Reprint of Calmann-Lévy, 1933. Étrépilly, France: Les Presses du Village, 1987.

Franklin, Peter. *The Life of Mahler.* Cambridge: Cambridge University Press, 1997.

Freedman, Luba. *Titian's Portraits Through Aretino's Lens.* University Park: Pennsylvania State University Press, 1995.

Frégnac, Claude, ed. *French Master Goldsmiths and Silversmiths from the Seventeenth to the Nineteenth Century.* New York: French and European Publications, 1966.

Gabler, James M. *Passions: The Wines and Travels of Thomas Jefferson.* Baltimore: Bacchus Press, 1995.

Garnier-Pelle, Nicole. *André Le Nôtre (1613–1700) et les jardins de Chantilly.* Preface by Alain Decaux of the Académie française. Catalogue to the exhibition held 14 June–9 October 2000 at the Musée Condé, château de Chantilly. Paris: Somogy Éditions d'Art, 2000.

Gendler, Paul F., ed. *Encyclopedia of the Renaissance.* 6 vols. New York: Scribner, 1999.

Giblin, James Cross. *From Hand to Mouth: Or How We Invented Knives, Forks, Spoons, and Chopsticks and the Table Manners to Go with Them.* New York: Thomas E. Crowell, 1987.

Gilliers, Joseph, Sieur de. *Le Cannameliste français, ou Nouvelle instruction pour ceux qui désirent d'apprendre l'office, rédigé en forme de dictionnaire, contenant les noms, les descriptions, les usages, les choix & les principes de tout ce qui se pratique dans l'office, l'explication de tous les termes dont on se sert; avec la manière de dessiner & de former toutes sortes de contours de Tables & de Dormants.* First published, Nancy: Abel-Denis Cusson, 1751; Nancy: Jean-Baptiste-Hiacinthe Leclerc, 1768.

Glanville, Philippa, ed. *Silver.* London: Victoria and Albert Museum, 1996.

Gleeson, Janet. *The Arcanum: The Extraordinary True Story of the Invention of European Porcelain.* London: Bantam Press, 1998.

Goethe, Johann Wolfgang von. "Joseph Bossi über Leonard da Vincis Abendmahl zu Mayland." First published in *Über Kunst und Alterthum am Rhein und Mayn.* Weimar: 1817. Translated by G. H. Noelden, 1821. Reprinted in Lavinia Mazzucchetti, *Goethe e il Cenacolo di Leonardo.* Milan: Editore Ulrico Hoepli, 1939.

Gold, Arthur, and Robert Fizdale. *Misia: The Life of Misia Sert.* New York: Vintage Books, 1992.

Gould, Cecil Hilton Monk. *The Studio of Alfonso d'Este and Titian's Bacchus and Ariadne: A Re-Examination of the Chronology of the Bacchanals and of the Evolution of One of Them.* London: The Trustees Publications Department, National Gallery, 1969.

Gourarier, Zeev. *Arts et manières de la table en Occident, des origines à nos jours.* Thionville, France: Gérard Klopp, 1994.

Gray, Patience. "More on Aphrodisiacs," *Petits Propos Culinaires* 56 (Sept. 1997): pp. 44–46.

Grandchamp, Pierre Garrigou, Michael Jones, Gwen Meirion-Jones, and Jean-Denis Salvèque. *La ville de Cluny et ses maisons, XIe – XVe siècles.* Paris: Picard, 1997.

Great Britain Exchequer. "Lists of Esquires and Gentlemen in Cheshire and Lancashire, Who Refused the Order of Knighthood at the Coronation of Charles I." Drawn up in the years 1631 and 1632. Edited by J. P. Earwaker. London: Record Society, 1885.

Gregorietti, Guido. *Argenti italiani dal XVI al XVIII secolo.* Milan: Museo Poldi Pezzoli, 1959.

Grésy, Eugène. *Château de Vaux-le-Vicomte: Documents sur les artistes, peintres, sculpteurs, tapissiers et autres qui ont travaillé pour le Surintendant Fouquet.* Melun, France: H. Michelin, 1861.

Grieco, Allen J. *The Meal.* London: Scala Books, 1992.

Grimod de La Reynière, Alexandre-Balthazar [Laurent]. *Écrits gastronomiques: Almanach des gourmands (Première année: 1803) suivi de Manuel des Amphitryons (1808)*. Edited and presented by Jean-Claude Bonnet. Paris: Éditions 10/18, edition first published 1978, reprinted 1997.

Gruber, Alain. *Silverware*. Originally published as *L'Argenterie de Maison du XVIe au XIXe siècle*. New York: Rizzoli, 1982.

Guy, Christian. *Histoire de la gastronomie en France*. Paris: Éditions Fernand Nathan, 1985.

Hale, John. *The Civilization of Europe in the Renaissance*. New York: Atheneum, 1994.

Hall, James. *Dictionary of Subjects and Symbols in Art*. Rev. ed. New York: Harper and Row, 1979.

Hammond, P. W. *Food and Feast in Medieval England*. Thrup, Stroud, Gloucestershire: Sutton Publishing, 1993.

Hayward, Helena, ed. *World Furniture: An Illustrated History*. New York: Crescent Books, 1990.

Henderson, Archibald. *George Bernard Shaw: Man of the Century*. New York: Appleton-Century-Crofts, 1956.

Hermanos, Susan S. "Contemporary Influence on Medici Porcelain: 1575–87." Master's thesis, Cooper Hewitt/Parsons School of Design, 1993.

Hess, Karen. "The Chafing Dish," *Petits Propos Culinaires* 2 (Aug. 1979): pp. 58–60.

Heylindeich, Ludwig H. *Leonardo: The Last Supper*. New York: Viking, 1974.

Hieatt, Constance B., and Sharon Butler, eds. *Curye on Inglysh: English Culinary Manuscripts of the Fourteenth Century (Including The Forme of Cury)*. London: Oxford University Press, 1985.

Himsworth, Joseph Beeston. *The Story of Cutlery: From Flint to Stainless Steel*. London: Ernest Benn, 1953.

Holman, Beth L., ed. *Disegno: Italian Renaissance Designs for the Decorative Arts*. New York: Cooper-Hewitt, National Design Museum, Smithsonian Institution, 1997.

Holt, Vincent M. *Why Not Eat Insects?* 1885. Reprinted with an introduction by Laurence Mound, Keeper of Entomology, British Museum. Yorkletts, Whitstable, Kent: Pryor Publications, ca. 1992.

Homer. *The Odyssey*. Translated by Robert Fitzgerald. New York: Doubleday, 1961.

Honour, Hugh. *Companion Guide to Venice*. London: Collins, 1990.

Hubbard, Elbert. *Little Journeys to the Homes of English Authors: William Morris.* East Auroria, N.Y.: Roycrofters, 1900.

Hughes, G. Bernard. "Old English Wedding Knives," *Country Life* 105 (no. 2723, March 25, 1949): pp. 666–667.

———. "Old English Table Knives and Forks," *Country Life* 107 (no. 2770, February 17, 1950): pp. 450–452.

———. "Silver Sugar Tongs," *Country Life* 112 (no. 2910, October 24, 1952): pp. 1329–1331.

———. "The Evolution of the Silver Table Fork," *Country Life* 126 (no. 3264, September 24, 1959): pp. 364–365.

———. "The Evolution of the Orange Strainer," *Country Life* 143, (no. 3714, May 9, 1968): pp. 1240–1242.

Hunt, Noreen. *Cluny Under Saint Hugh.* London: Edward Arnold, 1967.

Hutton, Edward. *The Pageant of Venice.* London: John Lane the Bodley Head, 1927.

Hyman, Philip and Mary, "La Chapelle and Massialot: An Eighteenth Century Feud," *Petits Propos Culinaires* 2 (Aug. 1979): pp. 44–54.

———. "Vincent La Chapelle,"*Petits Propos Culinaires* 8 (June 1981): pp. 36–40.

Irwin, Robert. "The Disgusting Dinners of Salvador Dalí." In *Food in the Arts: Proceedings of the Oxford Symposium on Food and Cookery, 1998.* Totnes, Devon: Prospect Books, 1999, pp. 103–111.

Jacobs, Lisa. "Julien Levy's Surrealist Art Galaxy." In *Surrealistas en el exilio y los inicios de la Escuela de Nueva York.* Catalogue to the exhibition held at the Museo Nacional Centro de Arte Reina Sofia, Madrid, 12 December 1999–27 February 2000, pp. 396–399.

Jaine, Tom. "Casanova: A Sensible Man," *Petits Propos Culinaires* 57 (Dec. 1997): pp. 45–50.

Janik, Allan, and Stephen Toulmin. *Wittgenstein's Vienna.* New York: Simon & Schuster, 1973.

Jeafferson, John Cordy. *A Book About the Table.* Vol. 2, London: Hurst & Blackett, 1875.

Jeanneret, Michel. *A Feast of Words: Banquets and Table Talk in the Renaissance.* Translated by Jeremy Whiteley and Emma Hughes. Chicago: University of Chicago Press, 1991.

Joelson, Annette. *Courtesan Princess: Catherine Grand, Princesse de Talleyrand.* Philadelphia: Chilton Books, 1965.

Jones, Proctor Paterson. *Napoleon: An Intimate Account of the Years of Supremacy, 1800–1814.* San Francisco: Proctor Jones Publishing Co., 1992.

Jungk, Peter Stephan. *Franz Werfel: A Life in Prague, Vienna, and Hollywood.* New York: Grove Weidenfeld, 1993.

Kasper, Lynne Rosetto. *The Splendid Table: Recipes from Emilia-Romagna, the Heartland of Northern Italian Food.* New York: William Morrow and Company, 1992.

Keegan, Susanne. *Bride of the Wind.* New York: Viking, 1993.

Kennedy, Michael, ed., and Joyce Bourne, assoc. ed. *The Oxford Dictionary of Music.* Oxford: Oxford University Press, 1994.

Kenyon, John P. *Stuart England.* 2nd ed. London: Penguin Books, 1987.

Knowles, Dom David. *The Historian and Character.* Edited by Giles Constable and Christopher Brooke. Cambridge: Cambridge University Press, 1963.

Kokoschka, Oskar. *Oskar Kokoschka Letters: 1905–1976.* Selected by Olda Kokoschka and Alfred Marnau. New York: Thames and Hudson, 1992.

Kraszewski, Joseph. *Count Bruhl: A Romance of History.* Translated by the Count de Soissons. London: Greening & Co., 1911.

Kris, Elaine. "Yin and Yang Today," *Petits Propos Culinaires* 7 (March 1981): pp. 37–41.

Labande, Léon-Honoré. *Fêtes et Réjouissances D'autrefois. Entrée de Marie de Médicis à Avignon (19 Novembre 1600).* Avignon: Seguin frères, 1893.

La Chapelle, Vincent. *The Modern Cook.* London: Nicolas Prevost, 1733.

La Fontaine, Jean de. *Œuvres completes.* Paris: Éditions du Seuil, 1965.

Lair, Jules. *Nicolas Fouquet: Procureur Général, Surintendant des Finances, Ministre d'État de Louis XIV.* 2 vols. Paris: Librairie Plon, 1890.

———. *Louise de la Vallière and the Early Life of Louis XIV.* Translated by Ethel Colburn Mayne. New York: G.P. Putnam's Sons, 1908.

Landon, H. C. Robbins, and John Julius Norwich. *Five Centuries of Music in Venice.* New York: Schirmer Books, 1991.

Laurendon, Gilles and Laurence, eds. *L'Art de la cuisine française au XVIIe siècle.* Includes reprints of L. S. R., *L'Art de bien traiter,* 1674; Pierre de Lune, *Le Cuisinier,* 1656; Audiger, *La Maison reglée,* 1692. Paris: Payot & Rivages, 1995.

Lautréamont, Comte de [Isidore Lucien Ducasse]. *Les Chants de Maldoror.* First published 1868–9. Translated by Guy Wernham. Together with a translation of Lautréamont's *Poésies.* New York: New Directions, 1946.

La Varenne, François Pierre de. *Le Cuisinier francois, ou est enseigne la menière d'apprêter toute sorte de viandes, de faire toute sorte de patisseries et de confitures. Revue, & augmenté d'un Traité de confitures seiches & liquide, & pour apprêter les festins aux quatre saisons de l'année.* Revised from first edition 1651. Lyon: Jacques Canier, 1680.

Levesque, Jacques-Henry. *Alfred Jarry, une étude par Jacques-Henry Levesque.* Paris: Seghers, 1951.

Levrin, Jacques. *La cour de Versailles aux XVIIe et XVIIIe siècles.* 2d ed. Paris: Hachette Littératures, 1999.

Levy, Julien. *Surrealism.* New York: Black Sun Press, 1936; New York: Arno Press, 1968.
———. *Memoir of an Art Gallery.* New York: G.P. Putnam's Sons, 1977.

Lewis, W. H. *The Splendid Century: Life in the France of Louis XIV.* New York: Anchor Books, 1953.

Liefkes, Reino, ed. *Glass.* London: Victoria and Albert Museum Publications, 1997.

Linou, Marie-Josée. *À table! Les arts de la table dans les collections du Musée Mandet de Riom, XVIIe – XIXe siècles.* Riom, France: Réunion des musées nationaux, 1997.

Livingston, Charles H. *History and Etymology of English Pie.* Brunswick, Maine: Brunswick Publishing Co., 1959.

Loliée, Frédéric. *Talleyrand et la societé européenne.* Paris: Émile-Paul, 1911.

M., W. *The Compleat Cook and A Queens Delight.* Facsimile reproduction of the 1671 edition of two of a trilogy titled *The Queens Closet Opened,* first published 1655. London: Prospect Books, 1984.

Macleod, John. *Dynasty: The Stuarts, 1560–1807.* London: Hodder and Stoughton, 1999.

Maffioli, Giuseppe. *Il ghiottone veneto.* Milan: Bramante Editrice, 1968.

Magna Charta, The Bill of Rights; with the Petition of Right, Presented to Charles I. London: J. Bailey, 1823.

Magnien, Émile. *Les deux grands siècles de Cluny (950–1150): Spiritualité, art et histoire.* Genelard, France: Le Caractère en Marche, 1994.

Mahler-Werfel, Alma. *And the Bridge Is Love.* In collaboration with E. B. Ashton. New York: Harcourt Brace and Co., 1958.

Mahler-Werfel, Alma. *Diaries, 1898–1902.* Selected and translated by Antony Beaumont, from the German edition transcribed and edited by Antony Beaumont and Susanne Rode Breymann. Ithaca: Cornell University Press, 1999.

Mamone, Sara. *Firenze e Parigi: due capitali dello spettàcolo per una regina Maria de' Medici.* Milan: Amilcare Pizzi, 1987.

Mancoff, Debra N. *Jane Morris: The Pre-Raphaelite Model of Beauty.* San Francisco: Pomegranate, 2000.

Le Manuel des Officiers de Bouche, ou le precis de tous les Apprêts que l'on peut faire des Alimens pour servir toutes les Tables, depuis celles des grands Seigneurs jusqu'à celles des Bourgeois, suivant l'ordre des Saisons & des Services: Ouvrages très-utile aux Maîtres pour ordonner des Repas, & aux Artistes pour les exécuter. Paris: Le Clerc, 1759.

Marenco, Claudine. *Manières de table, modèles de mœurs, 17ème – 20ème siècle.* Clamecy: Laballery, 1992.

Marin, François. *Les Dons de Comus, ou les Délices de la table. Ouvrage non-seulement utile aux officiers de bouche pour ce qui concerne leur art, mais principalement à l'usage des personnes.* Paris: Prault fils, 1739.

Marinetti, Filippo Tommaso. *The Futurist Cookbook.* Translated by Susanne Brill. Edited with an introduction by Lesley Chamberlain. First published as *La cucina futurista,* 1932. Lonfon: Trefoil Publications; and San Francisco: Bedford Arts, Publishers, 1989.

Marquardt, Klaus. *Eight Centuries of European Knives, Forks, and Spoons: An Art Collection.* Stuttgart: Arnoldsche, 1997.

Marsh, Jan. *Jane and May Morris: A Biographical Story, 1839–1938.* West Sussex, England: The Printed Word, 2000.

Massialot, François. *Nouvelle instruction pour les confitures, les liqueurs et les fruits, avec la manière de bien ordonner un Dessert & tout le reste qui est le Devoir des Maîtres d'Hôtels, Sommeliers, Confiseurs, & autres Officiers de bouche. Suite du Cuisinier Roïal & Bourgeois.* 2nd. ed., revised, corrected, and augmented; first published 1692. Paris: Charles de Sercy, 1698.

———. *The Court and Country Cook: Giving New and Plain Directions How to Order all manner of Entertainments, and the best sort of the Most exquisite a-la-mode Ragoo's. Together with Instructions for Confectioners: Shewing How to preserve all sorts of Fruits, as well dry as liquid: Also, How to make divers Sugar-Works, and other fine*

Pieces of Curiosity; How to set out a Dessert, or Banquet of Sweet-Meats to best advantage; And How to Prepare Several Sorts of Liquors, that are proper for every season of the year. Translated from French into English by J. K. London: W. Onley, for A. and J. Churchill. At the Black Swan in Pater-noster-row, and M. Gillyflower in Westminster-hall, 1702.

———. *Le Nouveau Cuisinier Royal et Bourgeois, ou Cuisinier Moderne. Qui apprend a ordonner toute sorte de Repas en gras & en maigre, & la meilleure manière des Ragoûts les plus délicats & les plus à la mode; & toutes sortes de Pâtisseries: avec des nouveaux desseins de Tables. Augmenté de nouveaux Ragoûts par le Sieur Vincent de La Chapelle, Chef de Cuisine de S.A.S. Monseigneur le Prince d'Orange & de Nassau &c.* Paris: Chez la Veuve Prudhomme, 1739.

———. *Le nouveau cuisinier royal et bourgeois, ou cuisinier moderne. Qui Apprend à ordonner toute sorte de Repas en gras & en maigre, & la meilleure manière des Ragoûts les plus délicats & les plus à la mode; & toutes sortes de Pâtisseries: avec des nouveaux desseins de Tables. Augmenté de nouveaux Ragoûts par le Sieur Vincent La Chapelle, Chef de Cuisine de S.A.S. Monseigneur le Prince d'Orange & Nassau, &c.* 3 vols. Paris: Chez la Veuve Prudhomme, 1740, "Avec privilege du roi."

———. *Le Nouveau cuisinier royal et bourgeois ou cuisinier moderne qui apprend à ordonner toute sorte de Repas en gras & en maigre, & la meilleure manière des Ragoûts les plus délicats & les plus à la mode; & toutes sortes de Pâtisseries avec des nouveaux desseins de table. Augmenté de nouveaux Ragoûts par le sieur Vincent de la Chapelle.* Vol. 1. Paris: Chez la Veuve Prudhomme, 1742.

May, Robert. *The Accomplisht Cook, or the Art and Mystery of Cookery.* Facsimile of the 1685 edition, with foreword, introduction, and glossary by Alan Davidson, Marcus Bell, and Tom Jaine. Totnes, Devon: Prospect Books, 1994.

McCabe, Joseph. *Talleyrand: A Biographical Study.* London: Hutchinson & Co., 1906.

Mennell, Stephen, "Food at the Late Stuart and Hanoverian Courts." *Petits Propos Culinaires* 17 (June 1984): pp. 23–24.

———. *All Manners of Food: Eating and Taste in England and France from the Middle Ages to the Present.* 2nd. ed. Urbana: University of Illinois Press, 1996.

Menon. *Nouveau traité de la cuisine, avec de nouveaux dessins de tables et vingt-quatre menus.* 2 vols. Paris: Michel-Etienne David, 1739.

———. *La Cuisiniere bourgeoise, suivie de l'office: A l'usage de tous ceux qui se mêlent de la dépense des Maisons: Contenant la manière de disséquer, connoître & servir toutes sortes de Viandes. Nouvelle édition. Augmenté de plusieurs Ragoûts des plus nouveaux & de différentes Recettes pour les Liqueurs.* Brussels: François Foppens, 1759.

———. *Les Soupers de la Cour ou l'Art de travailler toutes sortes d'aliments.* Reprint of the 1755 Paris edition. Paris: Librairie Soete, 1978.

———. *La Cuisinière bourgeoise, suivie de l'office, à l'usage de tous ceux qui se mêlent de dépenses des Maisons, Contenant la manière de disséquer, connoître & servir toutes sortes de Viandes.* Reprint of the 1774 Brussels edition prepared by Alice Peeters. Paris: Messidor/Temps Actuel, 1981.

Menzhausen, Ingelore. *Early Meissen Porcelain in Dresden.* New York: Thames and Hudson, 1990.

Messinger, Sylvie, ed. *Versailles et les tables royales en Europe.* Paris: Réunion des Musées Nationaux. Catalogue to the exhibition held 3 November 1993–27 February 1994, Musée National des Châteaux de Versailles et Trianon. Paris: Éditions de Réunion des musées nationaux, 1993.

Messisbugo, Cristoforo di. *Libro novo nel qual s'insegna a' far d'ogni sorte di vivande secondo la diversità de' i tempi così di carne come di pesce.* Venice, 1557. Fascimile reprint with an introduction by Giuseppe Mantovano, Bologna: Arnaldo Forni, 1982.

Michel, Dominique. *Vatel et la naissance de la gastronomie.* Paris: Librairie Arthème Fayard, 1999.

Micheletti, Emma. *Family Portrait: The Medici of Florence.* Translated by Paul Blanchard. Florence: Giusti di S. Becocci & C., 1999.

Micio, Paul. "The Silver Inventories of Le Surintendant Fouquet." English-language text of "Les Inventaires inédits de l'argenterie du grand argentier Fouquet," *Bulletin de la société de l'histoire de l'art français* (Paris: 2001).

Mignani, Daniela. *The Medicean Villas by Giusto Utens.* 2nd ed. Florence: Arnaud, 1995.

Minkoff, George Robert. *A Bibliography of the Black Sun Press.* With an introduction by Caresse Crosby. Great Neck, N.Y.: G. R. Minkoff, 1970.

Mitchell, Donald Grant. *Reveries of a Bachelor, or, A Book of the Heart.* Published under the pseudonym Ik Marvel. New York: Scribner's, 1890.

Molière, Jean-Baptiste Poquelin. *Œuvres complètes de Molière.* Edited by René Bray. Vol. 2, *Théâtre de 1661–1663.* Paris: Société de Belles Lettres, 1939.

Monson, Karen. *Alma Mahler: Muse to Genius.* Boston: Houghton Mifflin Co., 1983.

Montaigne, Michel Eyquem de. *The Complete Works of Montaigne: Essays, Travel, Journal, Letters, Newly Translated by Donald M. Frame.* Stanford, Calif.: Stanford University Press, 1948.

Morand, Paul. *Fouquet, ou Le Soleil offusqué.* Paris: Gallimard, 1961.

Morris, May. *William Morris: Artist Writer Socialist.* 2 vols. Includes "William Morris As I Knew Him" by Bernard Shaw. Oxford: Basil Blackwell, 1936.

———. *The Introductions to the Collected Works of William Morris.* 2 vols. New York: Oriole Editions, 1973.

Morton, Frederic. *A Nervous Splendor: Vienna, 1888–1889.* London: Penguin Books, 1979.

Moulin, Leo. *Les Liturgies de la table: une histoire culturelle du manger et boire.* Anvers: Fonds Mercator, 1988.

Musée des arts décoratifs. *Sucre d'art.* Catalogue to the exhibition held 8 February–17 April 1978. Paris: Union centrale des arts décoratifs, 1978.

Musée Mandet. *À table! Les arts de la table dans les collections du Musée Mandet de Riom, XVIIe–XIXe siècles.* Riom, France: Réunion des Musées Nationaux, 1997.

Musée Ochier. *Le Gouvernement d'Hugues de Semur à Cluny: Actes du Colloque scientifique international.* Cluny, France: September 1988.

Natter, G. Tobias, and Gerbert Frodl. *Carl Moll (1861–1945).* Catalogue to the exhibition held at the Belvedere, 10 September–22 November 1998. Vienna: Österreichische Galerie; and Salzburg, Verlag Galerie Welz, 1998.

Naudin, Jean-Bernard, ed., and Catherine Toesca, text. *Casanova: un Vénitien gourmand.* Paris: Éditions du Chêne, 1998.

Naylor, Gillian, ed. *William Morris by Himself: Designs and Writings.* Boston: Little Brown and Company, 2000.

Nesbit, Anne-Marie, and Victor-André Massena. *L'Empire à table.* Paris: Adam Biro, 1988.

Newman, Harold. *An Illustrated Dictionary of Silverware.* London: Thames and Hudson, 1987.

Noever, Peter, ed. *Josef Hoffmann Designs.* Munich: Prestel, for the Austrian Museum of Applied Arts, Vienna, 1992.

Norman, Barbara. *Tales of the Table: A History of Western Cuisine.* Englewood Cliffs, N.J.: Prentice-Hall, 1972.

Ogilby, John. *The Entertainment of His Most Excellent Majestie Charles II. In His Passage through the City of London to His Coronation, Containing an exact account of the whole of the Solemnity; the Triumphal Arches, and Cavalcade, delineated in Sculpture, the Speeches and Impresses illustrated from Antiquity. To These is Added, A Brief Narrative of His Majestie's Solemn Coronation: With His Magnificent Proceeding, and Royal Feast in Westminster Hall.* London: Thomas Roycroft, 1662.

Opera nuova intitolata Dificio di ricette, nella quale si contengono tre utilissimi ricettari. Venice: Giovanniantonio e fratelli da Sabio, 1526.

Opera nova intitolata Dificio de ricette: nella quale si contengono tre utilissimi ricettarii. Venice [Vinegia]: Francesco Bindoni & Mapheo Pasino, 1530.

Orieux, Jean. *Talleyrand: The Art of Survival.* Translated by Patricia Wolf. New York: Alfred A. Knopf, 1974.

Pacaut, Marcel. *L'Ordre de Cluny.* Paris: Fayard, 1998.

Panofsky, Erwin. *Renaissance and Renascences in Western Art.* Stockholm: Almqvist and Wiksell/Gebers Förlag AB, 1960.

Pardoe, Julia. *The Life of Marie de Medici, Queen of France, Consort of Henri IV, and Regent of the Kingdom under Louis XVIII.* 3 vols. New York: Scribner and Welford, 1890.

Paston-Williams, Sara. *The Art of Dining: A History of Cooking and Eating.* London: The National Trust, 1993.

Paterno, Salvatore. *The Liturgical Content of Early European Drama.* Potomac, Md.: Scripta Humanistica, 1989.

Patte, Jean-Yves, and Jacqueline Queneau. *Mémoire gourmande de Madame de Sévigné.* Preface by Bernard Loiseau. Paris: Éditions du Chêne, 1996.

Pedrocco, Filippo. *Titien.* Translated into French by Laura Meijir. Florence: Scala, 1993.

Pérouse de Montclos, Jean-Marie. *Vaux-le-Vicomte.* Paris: Éditions Scala, 1997.

Perrot, Michelle, ed. *A History of Private Life.* Vol. 4, *From the Fires of Revolution to the Great War.* Cambridge, Mass.: The Belknap Press of Harvard University Press, 1990.

Peter the Venerable. *Peter the Venerable: Selected Letters.* Edited by Janet Martin in collaboration with Giles Constable. Toronto: Medieval Latin Texts, 1974.

Petronius, *The Satyricon,* and Seneca, *The Apocolocyntosis.* Rev. ed. Translated with an introduction and notes by J. P. Sullivan. London: Penguin Books, 1986.

Pietsch, Ulrich, ed. *Schwanenservice: Meissener Porzellan für Heinrich Graf von Brühl.* Berlin: Edition Leipzig, 2000.

Pinot de Villechenon, Marie-Noëlle. *Sèvres: Une collection de porcelaines, 1740–1992.* Paris: Réunion des musées nationaux, 1993.

Pisanelli, Baldassare. *Trattato della natura de' cibi et del bere.* Venice: Domenico Imberti, 1611. Fascimile reprint, Bologna: Arnaldo Forni Editore, 1980.

Pizzi, Pier Luigi, ed. *Versailles et les tables royales en Europe XIIème – XIXème siècles.* Catalogue to the exhibition held at the Musée National des Châteaux de Versailles et de Trianon, 2 November 1993–27 February 1994. Paris: Éditions de la Réunion des musées nationaux, 1993.

Platina. *On Right Pleasure and Good Health.* Critical edition and translation of *De honesta voluptate et valetudine,* by Mary Ella Milham. Tempe, Ariz.: Medieval and Rennaissance Texts and Studies, 1998.

Plato. *Symposium.* Translated with introduction and notes by Alexander Nehemas and Paul Woodruff. Indianapolis, Ind.: Hackett Publishing Co., 1989.

Plinval de Guillebon, Régine de. *Faïence et porcelaine de Paris, XVIIIe – XIXe siècles.* Dijon: Éditions Faton, 1995.

Plutarch. *The Lives of the Noble Grecians and Romans.* Translated by John Dryden and revised by Arthur Hugh Clough. First published 1864. New York: The Modern Library, 1932.

Poncelet, Père Polycarpe. *Chimie du goût et de l'odorat.* Reprint of 1755 edition. France: Klincksieck, 1993.

Priscianese, Francesco. *De primi principi della lingua romana* and *Della lingua romana,* bound in one volume with a letter to Lodovico Becci and Luigi del Riccio. Venice: Bartolomeo Zanetti da Brescia, 1540.

R., L. S. *L'Art de bien traiter. Divisé en trois parties. Ouvrage nouveau, curieux, et fort gallant, utile à toutes personnes, et conditions.* Paris: Jean Du Puis, 1674.

Rabasco, Ottaviano. *Il convito overo discorsi di quelle materie che al convito s'appartengono . . .* Florence: Donato, e Bernardino Giunti & Compagni, 1615.

Reardon, Joan, and Ruth Ebling. *Oysters: A Culinary Celebration.* Orleans, Mass.: Parnassus Imprints, 1984.

Reed, Sue Welsh. *French Prints from the Age of the Musketeers.* Catalogue to the exhibition 21 Oct. 1998–10 Jan. 1999. Boston: Museum of Fine Arts, 1998.

Rich, Norman. *The Age of Nationalism and Reform, 1850–1890.* 2nd ed., New York: W.W. Norton & Co., 1977.

Richardson, Louise A., and J. R. Isabell. "Joseph Cooper, Chief Cook to Charles I," *Petits Propos Culinaires* 18 (November 1984): pp. 40–53.

Roberts, Robert. *Roberts' Guide for Butlers & Other Household Staff.* Boston: 1827; Bedford, Mass.: Applewood Books, 1993.

Robinson, Jancis, ed. *The Oxford Companion to Wine.* 2nd ed. Oxford: Oxford University Press, 1999.

Romain, Hippolyte. *Casanova: Les menus plaisirs.* Paris: Éditions Plume, 1998.

Romanelli, Giandomenico, ed. *Il mondo di Giacomo Casanova: un veneziano in Europa, 1725–1798.* Catalogue to the exhibition held 12 Sept. 1998–10 June 1999, Museo del Settecento Veneziano, Ca' Rezzonico. Venice: Marsilio, 1998.

Rosand, David, ed. *Titian: His World and His Legacy.* New York: Columbia University Press, 1982.

Rosenwein, Barbara H. *Rhinoceros Bound: Cluny in the Tenth Century.* Philadelphia: University of Pennsylvania Press, 1982.

Roux, Julie. *Les Cisterciens.* Toulouse: MSM, 1999.

Rowley, Anthony. *Les Français à table: Atlas historique de la gastronomie française.* Paris: Hachette, 1997.

Ruskin, John. *The Stones of Venice.* 1853. London: Penguin Books, 2001.

Rye, William Brenchley, ed. *England as Seen by Foreigners in the Days of Elizabeth and James the First.* London: John Russell Smith, 1865.

Sabban, Françoise, and Silvano Serventi. *La Gastronomie à la Renaissance: 100 recettes de France et d'Italie.* Baume-les-Dames, France: Stock, 1997.

Sainctot, Nicolas de. *Le Cérémonial de France à la Cour de Louis XIV.* Reprint, Paris: P. Lethielleux, 1936.

Saint-Simon [Louis de Rouvroy], Duc de. *Louis XIV et sa cour: portraits, jugements et anecdotes; extraits des mémoires authentiques.* Paris: L. Hachette et Cie, 1853.

Sambrook, Pamela A., and Peter Brears, eds. *The Country House Kitchen, 1650–1900:*

Skills and Equipment for Food Provisioning. Stroud, Gloucestershire: Sutton Publishing in association with the National Trust, 1996.

Sanford, Francis. *The History of the Coronation of the Most High, Most Mighty and Most Excellent Monarch James II. By the Grace of God, King of England, Scotland, France and Ireland, Defender of the Faith, &c. And His Royal Consort Queen Mary: Solemnized in the Collegiate Church of Saint Peter in the City of Westminster, on Thursday the 23 of April, being the Festival of Saint George, in the Year of Our Lord 1685.* London: Thomas Newcombe, 1687.

Scappi, Bartolomeo. *Opera di M. Bartolomeo Scappi, cuoco segreto di Papa Pio Quinto. Divisa in sei libri, nel primo si cõtiene il ragionamento que fa l'autore con Gio. Suo discepolo. Nel secondo si tratta di diverse vivande di carne, sì di quadrupedi, come di volatili. Nel terzo si parla della statura e stagione de' pesci. Nel quarto si mostrano le liste del presentar le vivande in tavola, così di grasso come di magro . . . Con il discorso funerale che fu fatto nalle esequie di papa Paolo III. . . . .* Venice: F. e M. Tramezino, 1570.

———. *Opera dell'arte del cucinare.* Venice, 1570. Facsimile reproduction presented by Giancarlo Roversi, Bologna: Arnaldo Forni Editore, 1981.

Schaffner, Ingrid, and Lisa Jacobs, eds. *Julien Levy: Portrait of an Art Gallery.* Cambridge, Mass.: M.I.T. Press, 1998.

Schiller, Gertrude. *Iconography of Christian Art.* Vol. 2, *The Passion of Christ.* Translated by Janet Seligman. Greenwich, Conn.: NY Graphic Society, 1972.

Schom, Alan. *Napoleon Bonaparte.* New York: HarperCollins, 1997.

Schroder, Timothy. *The National Trust Book of English Domestic Silver, 1500–1900.* London: Penguin Books, 1988.

Schumacher-Volker, Uta. "German Cookery Books, 1485–1800," *Petits Propos Culinaires* 6 (Oct. 1980): pp. 34–46.

Schweiger, Werner J. *Meisterwerke der Wiener Werkstætte: Kunst und Handwerk.* Vienna: Verlag Christian Brandstätter, 1990.

Scudéry, Mlle. [Madeleine] de. *Clelia: An Excellent New Romane: The Whole Work in Five Parts.* English translation. London: H. Herriman, T. Cockerel, S. Heyrick, W. Cadman, S. Loundes, G. Mariot, W. Crook and C. Smith, 1678.

Scully, Terence. "The Medieval French *Entremets.*" *Petits Propos Culinaires* 17 (June 1984): pp. 44–56.

———. *Cuoco Napoletano: The Neapolitan Recipe Collection (New York, Pierpont Morgan Library, MS Bühler, 19), A Critical Edition and English Translation. Initially with the collaboration of Rudolf Grewe.* Ann Arbor: University of Michigan Press, 2000.

Seranne, Ann, and John Tebbel, eds. *The Epicure's Companion.* New York: David McKay Company, 1962.

Shakespeare, William. *The Complete Works of William Shakespeare.* The Cambridge Edition Text. Edited by William Aldis Wright. Preface by Christopher Morley. Garden City, N.J.: Garden City Books, 1936.

Shaw, George Bernard. *William Morris As I Knew Him.* New York: Dodd, Mead and Co., 1936.

———. *An Unsocial Socialist.* With Introductions by R. F. Dietrich and Barbara Bellow Watson. New York: W. W. Norton, 1972.

———. *Collected Letters 1874–1897.* Vol. 1. Edited by Dan H. Laurence. New York: Viking Penguin, 1985.

Shone, Richard. *Alfred Sisley.* London: Phaidon, 1979.

Sim, Alison. *The Tudor Housewife.* Stroud, Gloucestershire: Sutton Publishing, 1996.

———. *Food and Feast in Tudor England.* New York: St. Martin's Press, 1997.

Singleton, H. Raymond. *A Chronology of Cutlery.* Sheffield: Sheffield City Museum, 1966.

Smith, Helen. "Josef Hoffmann's Artists' Colony in the Hohe Warte: A Reaction to Metropolis." Unpublished paper for Prof. Esther da Costa Meyer, Yale University, April 1993.

Staël-Holstein, Anne Louise Germaine Necker de. *Ten Years of Exile.* Translated by Doris Beik. New York: Saturday Review Press, 1972.

Stansky, Peter. *William Morris.* Oxford: Oxford University Press, 1983.

Stein, Susan R. *The Worlds of Thomas Jefferson at Monticello.* New York: Harry N. Abrams, 1993.

Symons, A.J.A. "The Epicure and the Epicurean" in *The Epicure's Anthology; or Banqueting Delights.* Collected by Nancy Quennell. London: Golden Cockerel Press, 1936.

Taberner, Peter V. *Aphrodisiacs: The Science and the Myth.* Philadelphia: University of Pennsylvania Press, 1985.

Talleyrand-Périgord, Charles-Maurice de. *Memoirs of the Prince de Talleyrand.* Edited with a preface and notes by the Duc de Broglie, translated by Raphaël Ledos de Beaufort, with an introduction by The Honorable Whitelaw Reid. 5 vols. New York: G. P. Putnam's Sons, 1895.

———. *Mémoires: L'époque napoléonienne.* Edited with notes by Jean Tulard. Paris: Imprimerie nationale, 1996.

Tanner, Lawrence E. *The History of the Coronation.* London, Pitkin Pictorials, 1952.

Thompson, Richard, ed. *A Faithful Account of the Processions and Ceremonies of the Kings and Queens of England: Exemplified in that of their late Majesties King George The Third, and Queen Charlotte: With All the Other Interesting Proceedings Connected with that Magnificent Festival.* London: John Major, 1820.

Thornton, Peter. *Seventeenth-century Interior Decoration in England, France, and Holland.* New Haven: Yale University Press, 1978.

———. *Authentic Décor: The Domestic Interior, 1620–1920.* New York: Viking, 1984.

———. *The Italian Renaissance Interior, 1400–1600.* London: Weidenfeld & Nicolson, 1991.

———. *Form and Decoration: Innovation in the Decorative Arts, 1470–1870.* New York: Harry N. Abrams, 1998.

Tobin, Ronald W. *Tarte à la Crème: Comedy and Gastronomy in Molière's Theater.* Columbus: Ohio State University Press, 1990.

Towner Art Gallery. *A Selection of the Festival Designs by Inigo Jones: Scenery and Costumes from the Court Masques of James I and Charles I from the Chatsworth Collection.* Catalogue to the exhibition held at the Towner Art Gallery, Eastbourne, England, 23 February–4 April 1972.

Train, Arthur, Jr. *The Story of Everyday Things.* New York: Harper Brothers, 1941.

Truman, Charles, ed. *Sotheby's Concise Encyclopedia of Silver.* London: Conran Octopus, 1993.

Vasari, Giorgio. *Lives of the Artists.* A selection translated by George Bull. 2 vols. London: Penguin Books, 1965 and 1987.

Venable, Charles, L. *Silver in America, 1840–1940: A Century of Splendor.* Catalogue to the exhibition at the Dallas Museum of Art, Dallas, Texas. New York: Harry N. Abrams, 1995.

Vergo, Peter. *Art in Vienna, 1898–1918: Klimt, Kokoschka, Schiele, and Their Contemporaries.* 3rd ed. London: Phaidon Press, 1993.

Victoria and Albert Museum. *Masterpieces of Cutlery and the Art of Eating.* Catalogue to the exhibition held 11 July–26 August 1979 at the Victoria and Albert Museum in conjunction with the Worshipful Company of Cutlers of London. London, 1979.

Vié, Gérard, with Marie-France Noël. *À la table des Rois.* Versailles: Art Lys, 1993.

Vingtain, Dominique. *L'abbaye de Cluny.* Paris: CNRS Éditions, 1998.

Visser, Margaret. *The Rituals of Dinner: The Origins, Evolution, Eccentricities, and Meaning of Table Manners.* New York, Grove Weidenfeld, 1991.

W., A. *A Book of Cookyre: very necessary for all such as delight therein.* London: Edward Ailde, 1587.

Waleffe, Pierre, ed. *Les Classiques de la table.* Lausanne: La porte d'or, 1967.

Walker, Thomas. *The Art of Dining; or, Gastronomy and Gastronomers,* 2nd ed. London: John Murray, 1853.

Watson, D. R. *The Life and Times of Charles I.* London: Weidenfeld and Nicolson, 1972.

Weidinger, Alfred. *Kokoschka and Alma Mahler.* English translation by Fiona Elliott. Munich: Prestel, 1996.

Weigert, Roger. *Louis XIV: Faste et décors.* Catalogue to the exhibition held May–Oct. 1960 at the Musée des arts décoratifs, Paris.

Wheaton, Barbara Ketcham. "Le Cuisinier Gascon." *Petits Propos Culinaires* 14 (June 1983): pp. 55–57.

———. *Savoring the Past: The French Kitchen and Table from 1300 to 1789.* New York: Touchstone Books, 1996.

White, Eileen. "Civic Banquets and Banqueting Stuff." *Petits Propos Culinaires* 66 (February 2001): pp. 55–61.

Williams, Sara Paston. *The Art of Dining.* London: The National Trust, 1993.

Wilson, C. Anne. "The Saracen Connection: Arab Cuisine and the Medievel West: Part 1," *Petits Propos Culinaires* 7 (March 1981): pp. 13–22.

Young, Carolin C. "Depictions of the Last Supper." *Food in the Arts: Proceedings of the Oxford Symposium on Food and Cookery 1998.* Harlan Walker, ed. Totnes, Devon: Prospect Books, 1999, pp. 223–236.

————. "Marie Antoinette's Dairy at Rambouillet." *The Magazine Antiques* 158, no. 4 (October 2000): pp. 542–553.

————. "Le Songe de Vaux." *Petits Propos Culinaires* 67 (June 2001): pp. 37–57.

Zaluska, Yolanta. *L'enluminure et le scriptorium de Cîteaux au XIIe siècle.* Published with the cooperation of the Centre national de la recherche scientifique and the Centre national des lettres, Cîteaux, Nuits-Saints-Georges, 1989.

————. *Manuscrits enluminés de Dijon.* Paris: Éditions du Centre national de la recherche scientifique, 1991.

Zeldin, Theodore. *An Intimate History of Humanity.* New York: Harper Perennial, 1996.

Zorzi, Elvira Garbero, and Mario Sperenzi. *Teatro e spettacolo nella Firenze dei Medici: modelli dei luoghi teatrali.* Catalogue to the exhibition held at the Palazzo Medici Riccardi, 1 April–9 Sept. 2001. Florence: Leo S. Olschki, 2001.

Zweig, Stefan. *Adepts in Self-Portraiture: Casanova, Stendhal, Tolstoy.* Translated from the German by Eden and Cedar Paul. New York: The Viking Press, 1928.

Select Discography

Albinoni, Tomaso, Alessandro Marcello, Francesco Geminiani, Alessandro Scarlatti, Pietro Locatelli, and Antonio Vivaldi. *Baroque in Italy.* CD recording by Jean-Claude Malgoire, oboe, Le Florilegium Musicum de Paris, I Solisti Veneti, and Claudio Scimone. New York: Sony Classical, 1975.

Cavalieri, Emilio de', Giovanni de' Bardi, Cristofano Malvezzi, Ottavio Rinuccini, Luca Marenzio, Giulio Caccini, Giovambattisto Strozzi, and Jacopo Peri. *La Pellegrina: Music for the Wedding of Ferdinando de' Medici and Christine de Lorraine, Princess of France, Florence 1589.* CD recording by the Huelgas Ensemble under the direction of Paul Van Nevel. Introductory text by Paul Van Nevel and English translation of the libretto by Cecile Stratta. New York: Sony Classical, 1998.

Henri IV et Marie de Médicis: Messe de mariage. CD recording of Doulce Mémoire under the direction of Denis Raisin-Dadre. France: Naïve Astrée, 2000.

Lully, Jean-Baptiste. *Grands Motets, vol. 1: Te Deum, Miserere, Plaude lætare Gallia.* CD recording by Le Concert Spirituel under the direction of Hervé Niquet. Canada: Naxos, 1994.

———. *Grands Motets, vol. 2: Quare fremuerunt, O Lachrymae, Dies irae, De profundis.* CD recording by Le Concert Spirituel under the direction of Hervé Niquet. Canada: Naxos, 1994.

———. *L'Orchestre du Roi Soleil: Symphonies, Ouvertures et Airs à jouer.* CD recording by Le Concert des Nations under the direction of Jordi Savall, with commentary by Philippe Beaussant. Bellaterra: Alia Vox, 1999.

Mahler, Alma, Arnold Schönberg, and Richard Strauss. *Alma Mahler: Ausgewählte Lieder; Arnold Schönberg: Brettl-Lieder; Richard Strauss: Krämerspiegel.* CD record-

357

ing with Heinz Zednik, tenor, and Konrad Leitner, piano. Austria: Preiser Records, 1991.

Music and Art in Renaissance Florence. CD compilation to complement the exhibition *Renaissance Florence: The Art of the 1470s,* held 20 October 1999–16 January 2000 at the National Gallery, London. Directed by Mark Levy. Cornwall, England: Metronome Recordings, 1999.

Music and Art: Lanier & Lawes at the Court of Charles I. CD compilation to complement the exhibition *Orazio Gentileschi at the Court of Charles I,* held 3 March 1999–23 May 1999 at the National Gallery, London. Text by executive producer Tim Smithies. Cornwall, England: Metronome Recordings, 1999.

Peter the Venerable. *Cluny: La transfiguration, Chants de Pierre le Vénérable.* CD recording by Ensemble Venance Fortunat under the direction of Anne-Marie Deschamps. Cluny, France: Office Municipal de la Culture de Cluny and the city of Cluny, 1998.

Rameau, Jean-Philippe. *Pièces de Clavecin en Concerts (Complete).* CD recording of Alan Cuckston on harpsichord; Elisabeth Parry, flute; Kenneth Mitchell, violin; and Alison Crum, viola da gamba; recorded at St. Wilfred's Church, Harrogate, in North Yorkshire on 6 and 7 November 1990. Munich: Naxos, 1990.

Strauss, Johann, II. *Famous Strauss Waltzes.* CD recording by the Johann Strauss Orchestra of Vienna under the direction of Willi Boskovsky. Hollywood, Calif.: Angel, 1982.

Wagner, Richard. *Tristan und Isolde.* CD recording of the Orchestra and Chorus of the Vienna State Opera, under the direction of Carlos Kleiber, recorded live in Vienna 7 October 1973. Vienna: Exclusive, 1992.

Photography Credits

My profound thanks go out to all of the individuals and institutions that have generously allowed me to reproduce works from their collection, and helped me obtain photographs.

COLOR PLATES

I. From Dijon 141, no. 19, f. 75., Bibliothèque municipale de Dijon. Photo: F. Perrodin.

II. Chiesa di Ognissanti, Florence. Photo: © Scala/Art Resource, New York.

III. National Gallery of Art, Washington, D.C., Widener Collection. © 2002 Board of Trustees, National Gallery of Art, Washington, D.C. Photo: Richard Carafelli.

IV. Museo Nacional del Prado, Madrid.

V. Louvre, Paris. Photo: © Réunion des musées nationaux, Paris/Art Resource, New York.

VI. The Royal Collection, Great Britain. © 2002 Her Majesty Queen Elizabeth II.

VII. Courtesy of Patrice de Vogüé/Vaux-le-Vicomte. Photo: Carolin C. Young.

VIII. Courtesy of Patrice de Vogüé/Vaux-le-Vicomte. Photo: Jérôme Letellier.

IX. Private collection. Photo: courtesy of Sotheby's, New York.

X. Musée Nissim de Camondo, Paris. © Union centrale des arts décoratifs. Photo: Laurent-Sully Jaulmes.

XI. Palace of Fontainebleau, France. Photo: © Réunion des musées nationaux, Paris/Art Resource, New York.

XII. William Morris Gallery, Walthamstow, London.

XIII. Private collection. Photo: Natter/Frodl. Courtesy of Verlag Galerie Welz, Salzburg.

XIV. Tate Gallery, London. © 2002 Gala-Salvador Dalí Foundation/Artists Rights Society (ARS), New York. Photo: © Tate Gallery/Art Resource, NY.

BLACK-AND-WHITE PHOTOGRAPHS

FRONTISPIECE

Santa Maria delle Grazie, Milan. Photo: © Scala/Art Resource, New York.

CHAPTER ONE

1.1. Ornamental letter "P," Latin bible, late eleventh to early twelfth century, France. Ms. 0004, f. 317, Bibliothèque Mazarine, Paris. Photo: Suzanne Nagy.

1.2. Musée Cluny, Cluny, France. Photo: Giraudon/Art Resource, New York.

1.3. Musée Cluny, Cluny, France. Photo: © Foto Marburg/Art Resource, New York.

1.4. Dijon 170, no. 3, fol. 75v, Bibliothèque municipale de Dijon, France. Photo: F. Perrodin.

1.5. Photo: © James Austin—Fine Art Photography.

1.6. Musée Cluny, Cluny, France. Photo: © Foto Marburg/Art Resource, New York.

1.7. Photo: © James Austin—Fine Art Photography.

CHAPTER TWO

2.1. Sant'Apollonia, Florence. Photo: © Alinari/Art Resource, New York.

2.2. Ms. Ricc. 492, fol. 75r, Biblioteca Riccardiana, Florence. Photo: © Microfoto srl.

2.3. Accademia, Venice. Foto: © Scala/Art Resource, New York.

2.4. Bibliothèque nationale de France, Paris.

CHAPTER THREE

3.1. Bibliothèque nationale de France, Paris.

3.2. Cooper-Hewitt National Design Museum, Smithsonian Institution, New York. Museum Purchase through gift of various donors and from Eleanor G. Hewitt, 1938-88-7848. Photo: © Cooper-Hewitt National Design Museum, Smithsonian Institution, New York.

3.3. Robert Lehman Collection, inv. 1975.1.1216, Metropolitan Museum of Art, New York.

CHAPTER FOUR

4.1. N. 433 ORN, Gabinetto Disegni e Stampe, Uffizi, Florence. Courtesy of the Ministero dei Beni e le Attività Culturali.

4.2. Bibliothèque nationale de France, Paris.

4.3. Bibliothèque nationale de France, Paris.

4.4. Bibliothèque nationale de France, Paris.

4.5. Bibliothèque nationale de France, Paris.

4.6. Bibliothèque nationale de France, Paris.

4.7. N. 97178, Gabinetto Disegni e Stampe, Uffizi, Florence. Courtesy of the Ministero dei Beni e le Attività Culturali.

4.8. Musée national de céramique, Sèvres, France. © Réunion des musées nationaux/Art Resource, New York. Photo: M. Beck-Coppola.

4.9. (a) & (b) Typ 525.70.773, Department of Printing and Graphic Arts, Houghton Library, Harvard College Library.

4.10. Bibliothèque nationale de France, Paris.

CHAPTER FIVE

5.1. pSTC 8820, Department of Rare Books, Houghton Library, Harvard University.

5.2. Bibliothèque nationale de France, Paris.

5.3. (a) & (b) Guildhall Library, Corporation of London. Photo: Geremy Butler.

5.4. Bibliothèque nationale de France, Paris.

5.5. Guildhall Library, Corporation of London. Photo: Geremy Butler.

CHAPTER SIX

6.1. Musée Carnavalet, Paris. © Photothèque des Musées de la ville de Paris. Photo: Degraces.

6.2. Musée Carnavalet, Paris. © Photothèque des Musées de la ville de Paris. Photo: Lifermann.

6.3. Courtesy of Patrice de Vogüé/Vaux-le-Vicomte. Photo: Jérôme Letellier.

6.4. Bibliothèque nationale de France, Paris.

6.5. Bibliothèque nationale de France, Paris.

6.6. Bibliothèque nationale de France, Paris.

6.7. Bibliothèque nationale de France, Paris.

6.8. Bibliothèque nationale de France, Paris.

CHAPTER SEVEN

7.1. Private collection. Photo: courtesy of Sotheby's, New York.

7.2. Staatliche Kunstsammlungen Dresden, Porzellansammlung im Zwinger, Dresden. Photo: Karpinski.

7.3. Bibliothèque nationale de France, Paris.

7.4. Bibliothèque nationale de France, Paris.

7.5. Bibliothèque nationale de France, Paris.

CHAPTER EIGHT

8.1. Musée Carnavalet, Paris. © Photothèque des musées de la ville de Paris. Photo: Lifermann.

8.2. Musée Carnavalet, Paris. © Photothèque des musées de la ville de Paris. Photo: Lifermann.

8.3. Gift of J. Pierpont Morgan. Wadsworth Atheneum, Hartford, Connecticut.

8.4. Bibliothèque nationale de France, Paris.

8.5. Bibliothèque nationale de France, Paris.

8.6. Bibliothèque nationale de France, Paris.

Chapter Nine

9.1. From the Paris, Au dépôt de librairie, 1854 ed. New York Public Library.

9.2. Louvre, Paris. © Réunion des musées nationaux/Art Resource, New York. Photo: Arnaudet.

9.3. Musée Carnavalet, Paris. © Photothèque des musées de la ville de Paris. Photo: Joffre.

9.4. Wrightsman Fund 2002.31, Metropolitan Museum of Art, New York.

9.5. Bibliothèque nationale de France, Paris.

9.6. Bibliothèque nationale de France, Paris.

9.7. From the Paris, Au dépôt de librairie, 1854 ed. New York Public Library.

9.8. From the Paris, Au dépôt de librairie, 1854 ed. New York Public Library.

9.9. From the Paris, Au dépôt de librairie, 1854 ed. New York Public Library.

9.10. From the Paris, Au dépôt de librairie, 1854 ed. New York Public Library.

9.11. Courtesy of Cathy Kaufman. Photo: Carolin C. Young.

Chapter Ten

10.1. Victoria and Albert Museum, London. Photo: © V&A, London/Art Resource, New York.

10.2. Tate Gallery, London. Photo: © Tate Gallery, London/Art Resource, New York.

10.3. National Portrait Gallery, London. Photo: Emery Walker.

10.4. The William Morris Gallery, Walthamstow, London.

10.5. The William Morris Gallery, Walthamstow, London.

10.6. The William Morris Gallery, Walthamstow, London.

Chapter Eleven

11.1. The Alma Mahler-Werfel Archive, Annenberg Rare Book & Manuscript Library, Van Pelt–Dietrich Library Center, University of Pennsylvania Library, Philadelphia, Pennsylvania.

11.2. Staatliche Kunstsammlungen Dresden—Gemäldegalerie Neue Meister, Dresden.

11.3. MAK—Austrian Museum for Applied Arts/Contemporary Art, Vienna.

11.4. MAK—Austrian Museum for Applied Arts/Contemporary Art, Vienna.

11.5. The Alma Mahler-Werfel Archive, Annenberg Rare Book & Manuscript Library, Van Pelt–Dietrich Library Center, University of Pennsylvania Library, Philadelphia, Pennsylvania.

11.6. The Alma Mahler-Werfel Archive, Annenberg Rare Book & Manuscript Library, Van Pelt–Dietrich Library Center, University of Pennsylvania Library, Philadelphia, Pennsylvania.

11.7. The Alma Mahler-Werfel Archive, Annenberg Rare Book & Manuscript Library, Van Pelt–Dietrich Library Center, University of Pennsylvania Library, Philadelphia, Pennsylvania.

11.8. The Alma Mahler-Werfel Archive, Annenberg Rare Book & Manuscript Library, Van Pelt–Dietrich Library Center, University of Pennsylvania Library, Philadelphia, Pennsylvania.

CHAPTER TWELVE

12.1. The Estate of Julien Levy. Still: Vincent Lacava, POP NYC.

12.2. The Estate of Julien Levy. Still: Vincent Lacava, POP NYC.

12.3. The Estate of Julien Levy. Still: Vincent Lacava, POP NYC.

12.4. The Estate of Julien Levy. Still: Vincent Lacava, POP NYC.

12.5. The Estate of Julien Levy. Still: Vincent Lacava, POP NYC.

12.6. The Estate of Julien Levy. Still: Vincent Lacava, POP NYC.

12.7. The Estate of Julien Levy. Still: Vincent Lacava, POP NYC.

12.8. The Estate of Julien Levy. Still: Vincent Lacava, POP NYC.

12.9. The Estate of Julien Levy. Still: Vincent Lacava, POP NYC.

12.10. © 2002 Gala-Salvador Dalí Foundation/Artists Rights Society (ARS), New York. Photo: New York Public Library, New York.

12.11. Tate Gallery, London. © 2002 Gala-Salvador Dalí Foundation/Artists Rights Society (ARS), New York. Photo: © Tate Gallery, London/Art Resource, New York.

ABOUT THE AUTHOR

Carolin C. Young earned her B.A. in European history from Oberlin College and was awarded a Royal Society of Arts Diploma from Christie's Education in London. She has done public relations for Christie's, New York, and has researched antique porcelain, silver, and glass for James Robinson, Inc. She lives in New York City, where she lectures on dining history at Sotheby's Institute of Art.